D1282909

The Eastern Association in the
English civil war

The Eastern Association
in the
English civil war

CLIVE HOLMES

Assistant Professor of History, Cornell University

CAMBRIDGE UNIVERSITY PRESS

Published by the Syndics of the Cambridge University Press
Bentley House, 200 Euston Road, London NW1 2DB
American Branch: 32 East 57th Street, New York, N.Y. 10022

© Cambridge University Press 1974

Library of Congress Catalogue Card Number: 73-91616

ISBN 0 521 20400 3

First published 1974

Printed in Great Britain by
Western Printing Services Ltd
Bristol

Contents

Preface

I wish to thank all those who have contributed in a multitude of ways to the production of this work.

My research was funded for two years by a grant from the Department of Education and Science and by a Teichmann Research Studentship from Gonville and Caius College, Cambridge, until in 1967 I was elected to a Research Fellowship by the Master and Fellows of Christ's College, who then became the patrons of the project. Since my appointment at Cornell the work has been subsidized by the Department of History and by the University's Humanities Research Grants Committee. The generosity of these institutions has been matched by the assistance and advice which I have invariably received from librarians and archivists. I should like to express my debt to the staffs of those depositories, both national and local, that have provided materials for this study: the British Museum, the Public Record Office, the Bodleian Library and the Cambridge University Library; the county record offices of Cambridgeshire, Essex, Hertfordshire, Huntingdonshire, Kent, Lincolnshire, Norfolk, Northamptonshire, East Suffolk and West Suffolk; also the borough archivist of Great Yarmouth, the curator of the Cromwell Museum at Huntingdon, and the Librarian of Worcester College, Oxford. In the United States I have been helped by the librarians of the Regenstein Library at the University of Chicago, who have kindly allowed me to cite documents from the Bacon collection, of the Beinecke Library at Yale, and of Cornell University. I am also indebted to Lord Sackville, the dowager Lady Hastings, the late Richard de Grey of Merton, the secretary of the Essex Archaeological Society, the bursar of Gonville and Caius College, the town clerks of Colchester, Grantham and King's Lynn, the incumbents of Gissing and of Croft, and Mrs E. Farmery of that parish, for providing facilities for me to examine documents in their custody or possession. The book has benefited from the clerical assistance I have received from Marjorie Rath, Nanette Eichell and Margaret Hobbie, and from the expertise of the editorial staff of the Cambridge University Press.

Since the inception of the work I have received considerable assistance from those who have suggested further sources for investigation, shared their own ideas, and commented on the themes that I was developing: I am particularly grateful in this respect to D. W. Boorman, Professor Alan Everitt, Dr Derek Hirst, the late R. W. Ketton-Cremer, Dr Alan Macfarlane, Arthur Searle and

Christopher Thompson, and to Dr A. Hassell Smith and the other participants in the seminars of the Centre for East Anglian Studies at Norwich. At various stages in its production the manuscript has been read by Professor G. E. Aylmer, Professor J. R. Jones, Dr Valerie Pearl, Dr Brian Quintrell, Dr Kenneth Shipps, Professor Lawrence Stone, Dr Blair Worden, and my colleagues at Cornell, D. A. Baugh and F. J. Marcham: the criticism and suggestions of these scholars have been invaluable, and the beneficial influence of their comments will be apparent in many sections of the book. The overall interpretation presented is my own, as are those errors which may remain in the work.

In this litany of thanks two names deserve especial mention. Professor J. H. Plumb supervised my work as a graduate student, and then and since has been a generous source of criticism, advice and friendship, and has, with admirable patience, provided continuous encouragement to a congenital pessimist. My wife has done all this, and more, and it is to her that I dedicate this book.

Cornell   C.H.
November 1973

The Publisher wishes to thank the Committee of the Hull Memorial Publication Fund of Cornell University for help in the publication of this book.

Abbreviations

A.P.C.	*Acts of the Privy Council of England*
Abbott	W. C. Abbott (ed.), *The Writings and Speeches of Oliver Cromwell*
Add.	Additional Manuscripts in the British Museum
Ash and Goode	Newsletters from Manchester's army written by Simeon Ash and William Goode (for a complete list of titles, see p. 305)
B.L.	Bodleian Library
Baillie	David Laing (ed.), *The letters and journals of Robert Baillie*
C.C.C.	*Calendar of the Committee for Compounding*
C.J.	*Journal of the House of Commons*
C.S.P.D.	*Calendar of State Papers, Domestic Series*
C.S.P. Ven.	*Calendar of State Papers and Manuscripts relating to English Affairs existing in the Archives of Venice*
C.U.L.	Cambridge University Library
D.N.B.	*Dictionary of National Biography*
E.	Exchequer records in the Public Record Office
E.H.R.	*English Historical Review*
E.R.O.	Essex Record Office
E.S.R.O.	Ipswich and East Suffolk Record Office
Ec.H.R.	*Economic History Review*
Egerton	Egerton Manuscripts in the British Museum
Firth and Rait	C. H. Firth and R. S. Rait (eds.), *Acts and Ordinances of the Interregnum*
G.Y.C.	Records of the Corporation of Great Yarmouth, now deposited in the Norwich and Norfolk Record Office
Gardiner	S. R. Gardiner, *The History of the Great Civil War*
H.M.C.	*Royal Commission on Historical Manuscripts, Reports*
H.R.O.	Hertfordshire Record Office
H. of L.M.P.	House of Lords Record Office: Main Papers collection
Harleian	Harleian Manuscripts in the British Museum
Hu. R.O.	Huntingdonshire Record Office
The Knyvett Letters	Bertram Schofield (ed.), *The Knyvett Letters 1620–1644*

L.A.C.	Lincolnshire Archives Committee
L.J.	*Journal of the House of Lords*
Luke Letter Book	H. G. Tibbutt (ed.), *The letter books of Sir Samuel Luke 1644–1645*
Morant	Morant Manuscripts at the Library of the Essex Archaeological Society
N.R.O.	Norwich and Norfolk Record Office
Nalson	Nalson Manuscripts in the Bodleian Library (see note on p. 299)
P.C.	Records of the Privy Council, in the Public Record Office
P.C.C.	Wills proved in the Prerogative Court of Canterbury, now in the Public Record Office
P.R.O.	Public Record Office
Quarrel	David Masson and John Bruce (eds.), *The Quarrel Between the Earl of Manchester and Oliver Cromwell*
R.O.	Record Office
Rushworth	John Rushworth (ed.), *Historical Collections*
S.P.	State Papers in the Public Record Office
Stowe	Stowe Manuscripts in the British Museum
T.E.A.S.	*Transactions of the Essex Archaeological Society*
T.R.H.S.	*Transactions of the Royal Historical Society*
Tanner	Tanner Manuscripts in the Bodleian Library
V.C.H.	*Victoria County History*
W.O.	Records of the War Office in the Public Record Office
W.S.R.O.	Bury St Edmunds and West Suffolk Record Office

Map 1   The eastern counties

Introduction

East Anglia and the Fens have an assured place in the mythology of the English Revolution. In that area, wrote Alfred Kingston the first historian of its civil war experience, 'was to be found in a pre-eminent degree that "depository of the sacred fire of liberty" which history has justly credited to the old Puritan stock'. There Cromwell, 'the one man whose acts were destined to colour all our subsequent history', rose to prominence. There he raised his Ironsides, the military and intellectual shock troops of the Revolution, who were to shatter both the Royal army and the ideological foundations upon which Stuart despotism had been raised.

But, while it is easy to ridicule the platitudes of nineteenth-century liberal historiography, at one point Kingston's judgment stands. East Anglia was 'the one great historic unity' of the civil war.[1] Banded together in the Eastern Association, the counties of the region maintained their territorial integrity against internal Royalist uprisings and the assaults of Oxford cavaliers and Newcastle's 'popish army'. In 1644, under the Earl of Manchester, they organized the largest and most effective Parliamentary army then in service, which was to conquer Lincolnshire, play the major part in the crushing victory over Prince Rupert at Marston Moor, and was ultimately, in 1645, to form the backbone of the reorganized New Model Army.

These achievements appear the more considerable when contrasted with the dismal record of the failures of the other local Associations established by Parliament in 1642 and 1643. None of them were able to achieve any comparable degree of effective unification, or to develop a centralized army and military administration. The Association of eight midland counties, constituted by the Ordinance of 15 December 1642, was stillborn: Lord Grey of Groby, who had been appointed supreme commander of the conjoint forces of the area, exercised only the most nominal control and the Parliamentary authorities in the individual counties organized the defense of their localities independently.[2] In the adjacent Association of Warwickshire, Staffordshire and Shropshire the Earl of Denbigh strove to secure some measure of central control, but his efforts were undermined by the opposition of the county committees and local commanders, who neglected the Earl's orders, feuded with his aides and, without any regard for the principle of Association, worked covertly at Westminster to have their *de facto* power legitimized. Denbigh was unable to tap the financial resources of the area ostensibly subject to his command, and the pay of his forces fell months in arrear.[3]

Only the South-Eastern Association approaches the achievement of the eastern counties under Manchester. Its formation had initially been resisted by the local committees in the area, but, in the winter of 1643–4, under pressure from Hopton's Royalists, the counties had combined for mutual defense and their forces constituted a major element in the army of Sir William Waller at Cheriton and Cropredy Bridge. However, Waller was notoriously unable to capitalize upon his victories, and he himself ascribed this to a fatal flaw in the structure of the South-Eastern Association. Control of the local levies was retained by the counties and it proved impossible to develop a centralized military administration of the sort which Manchester had established at Cambridge. Worse, Waller's relations with the county authorities were uniformly unhappy. Hampshire refused to permit him to take command of one of its cavalry regiments; Kent demanded the right to commission the officers of its troops, and later encouraged certain mutinous regiments raised in the county in their defiance of the general; Sir William wrote that he had 'received nothing but constant incivilities' from the Sussex committee. The decentralized system of military organization and Waller's squabbles with the local authorities dissipated the potential strength of the South-Eastern Association. As Waller later wrote, his 'borrowed forces, having no dependence upon me, but upon them that sent them, would not follow me further then pleased themselves, but would be ready to march home when they should have pursued their point, as if they had don enough when they had don any thing'.[4]

Each of these three attempts by Parliament to group a number of contiguous counties under a commander for the purpose of military co-operation, as with similar Royalist experiments,[5] was ultimately a failure. Lord Grey was a cypher; Denbigh and Waller were forced to waste their energies in futile efforts to secure the collaboration of the county authorities, who controlled the raising and disposal of men and money, and for whom local needs invariably took precedence over the demands of the regional association. Centrifugal forces triumphed – except in the Eastern Association.

In this respect the counties grouped in the Eastern Association were 'the one great historic unity' of the war, and in this study I hope to provide an explanation of their singular record of success, given the failures and frustrations which marked the other, superficially similar, combinations of counties established by Parliament and the Royalists for this purpose of military co-operation.

The search for an explanation is certainly not an original undertaking. Writing in the 1890s Kingston addressed himself to the same problem, and concluded that the unrivaled military achievement of the Association was a product of the general commitment to Puritanism in East Anglia: a more recent commentator, Professor Everitt, has argued that the success stemmed from the unique socio-economic structure of the region which differentiated it from the rest of England.[6] But while the difference between the two analyses is considerable, a mark, perhaps, of changing fashions of historical interpretation in the seventy years which separates them, both take a similar form. Both scholars seek to account for the success of the Eastern Association in terms of factors, whether social or ideological, unifying the constituent counties prior to the outbreak of hostilities. At the beginning of this study I will evaluate explanations of this order by an examination of the political, religious and social environment in East Anglia in the 1620s and 1630s. It is my conclusion that the civil war Association cannot be seen as a necessary product of the pre-existent socio-economic or ideological unity of East Anglia, as the homogeneity of the constituent counties and the peculiarity of the region with respect to the rest of the Kingdom have been seriously exaggerated.

But even had this investigation of the pre-civil war environment substantiated the conclusions of Kingston or Everitt it would still be incumbent upon the historian to demonstrate how the immanent became manifest: how the universal religious zeal or the common social structure which are thought to explain the successful conjunction of the eastern counties, were geared down through the political process into the institutional form which the Association eventually took. Having argued in the opening section that East Anglia was not a unique organic entity prior to the outbreak of the war, my explanation of the Association's comparative success will necessarily emphasize these more immediate considerations. In the course of the study I will examine the composition of the army victorious at Marston Moor, and detail the centralized administration which the Earl of Manchester developed at Cambridge to supervise the payment and supply of his forces in early 1644. But the successful establishment of this military organization was dependent upon Parliamentary legislation; the passage of the critical Ordinance of 20 January, like the initial conjunction of the counties in December 1642 and the eventual supersession of the army of the Eastern Association by the New Model in 1645, can only be understood by reference to political developments at Westminster, which must be examined. Finally the study will detail and analyze the attitudes of the local authorities, whose own conception of the purpose and proper function of the Association was frequently at odds with that of the Parliamentary legislators.

In conclusion it will be argued that the history of the Eastern

Association can only be explained adequately, not by the invocation of the region's unique homogeneity however defined, but by the close analysis of the complex and tension-ridden dialogue of the three principals: the legislators at Westminster, the Association's authorities and administrators at Cambridge, and the county committees in the localities.

PART I

The eastern counties: society, religion and politics in the reign of Charles I

The central purpose of this section will be to evaluate those explanations of the unique success of the Eastern Association which emphasize the prior homogeneity of the counties of East Anglia, and argue that their civil war military alliance was in some sense prefigured in the socio-economic or ideological uniformity of the region. It will be necessary first to study the economic development and the elite structure of the eastern counties; then the strength of Puritanism within East Anglia and the political temper of the shires, as it emerges from their reactions to the ship-money levy, to the summoning of Parliament in 1640, and to events at Westminster in 1642, will be examined. These analyses, far from demonstrating uniformity or homogeneity, will suggest that there were wide divergences of environment and experience among those counties which were to be incorporated in the Association.

Social organization in East Anglia

Economic development

It has been argued that the division of England into the Royalist and Parliamentary camps in the civil war is largely explicable in terms of the patterns of socio-economic development within the country: economically backward regions remained loyal to King Charles, while the advanced areas followed King Pym and his allies at Westminster.[1] In general such political geography is unsatisfactory. In the absence of detailed comparative studies of the economic structure of the regions, the criteria which determine whether an area is to be categorized as economically advanced or backward are impressionistic, and, in consequence, elastic; nor is it shown why the relative speed of modernization should, in itself, result in support for, or opposition to, the Parliamentary cause. But, relative to East Anglian society, the suggestion is illuminating. In the early seventeenth century much of the industry and agriculture within the region was becoming increasingly specialized and oriented towards market production, and it can be shown that the concomitant mercantile contacts resulted in the dissemination of radical political and religious ideas within the region.

In the early Stuart period the City of London dominated the distribution of the cloth manufactured in the industrial towns of the Stour valley region of Essex and Suffolk. In 1633 Colchester sent bays and says to the value of £3000 weekly to the City, while in 1619 and again in 1637 the bankruptcy of London merchants ruined many Stour valley clothiers; not surprisingly in 1642 the Essex and Suffolk cloth manufacturers described the city merchants as those 'in whom the breath of our trade and livelihood consisteth'.[2] The Norwich industry was equally dependent upon London. In 1636 the local Puritans petitioned Charles against Bishop Wren, claiming that his religious persecution had driven some leading merchants and manufacturers to seek asylum in the Netherlands, and was thus responsible for the slump in the cloth industry and the consequent unemployment. One of the Bishop's supporters retorted that this was 'an impudent lie', the real reason for the depression of local industry was the dislocation caused by the plague in London, 'for the city trade doth consist all most wholly in commerce with Londoners'.[3]

East Anglian agriculture, too, was drawn within the orbit of

London as 'the city's feeders crept steadily northward'.[4] Hertford-shire, with good channels of communication with the metropolis by way of the Colne and Lea rivers and the Great North Road, supplied London with fattened livestock, malt and corn, a trade dominated by citizens who had driven out the local middlemen. Essex also produced foodstuffs for the London market. The coastal marsh provided valuable pasture which was utilized for fattening beasts brought by drovers from the midlands, Wales and the north for the London market; corn was supplied from the eastern hundreds of the shire, while the plague which ravaged the city in 1625 dislocated the Essex hop-masters' trade.[5] Suffolk, adjoining 'the quickest and readiest markets of best trade', was noted for its dairy produce so coveted by the London cheesemakers; even in the sixteenth century the trade of Ipswich, increasingly dominated by Londoners, con-sisted of countless routine trips to the capital with shipments of agricultural produce. Specialization was equally well developed in Norfolk, although its production was less dominated by London than that of the other East Anglian shires. Grain from the county was shipped through King's Lynn and Yarmouth to the north of England, but the city only imported supplies from Norfolk in times of extreme dearth.[6]

An effect of the development of commercial communications between London and East Anglia was the penetration of the region by radical religious and political ideas emanating from the city. In 1634 Laud was informed of the activities of an Essex gentleman, 'a great depraver of government', who received weekly newsletters from London containing slanted accounts of current events which he then read publicly at Colchester market, 'about whom the zealots throng as people use where ballads are sung'. Two years later the Archdeacon of Colchester's insistence that communicants receive the Sacrament kneeling at the chancel rail was bitterly opposed, 'espe-cially in great clothing townes, because they see no such thing, as they say, in the churches in London'. It was a Blackwall Hall cloth merchant who distributed pro-Scottish propaganda to the Essex levies at Braintree as they set out for the Bishops' war, a London glassmaker who led the conventicle of separatists near Yarmouth, and a citizen who preached a seditious sermon at Maldon in 1638.[7]

The eastern counties were also closely tied to another area produc-tive of religious radicalism. Large quantities of East Anglian cloth and grain were exported to the Netherlands, particularly from Lynn and Yarmouth; indeed, during the civil war Manchester's treasurers had to calculate rates of exchange for the Dutch coin in which many Norfolk men paid their assessments.[8] By the seventeenth century a wide-ranging cultural relationship had developed between the two regions, involving more than commerce. In Elizabeth's reign Dutch and Walloon clothworkers, fleeing from Spanish persecution, had taken refuge in eastern England, and were still organized in semi-independent communities in Norwich and Colchester. Conversely the Yarmouth boat carried East Anglian craftsmen going abroad to study Dutch techniques, those who proposed to serve in the army of 'the States', trippers wishing to visit friends or merely 'to see the country' and, particularly in the 1630s slump, clothworkers seeking short-term employment and higher wages in the Low Countries.[9]

The ecclesiastical authorities regarded the 'vicinitie and continuall entercourse of trade' between East Anglia and the Netherlands with a jaundiced eye, fearing that the imports included, besides new crops and improved agricultural and industrial techniques, non-conformity. A minister who had 'spent some time in the Low Countries' yet who was 'conceived to be very right to the Church governement', was the occasion of surprised comment in Orthodox circles.[10] Archbishop Laud was particularly concerned to check the malign religious influence emanating from the Netherlands, and sought to regulate travel, to prevent Englishmen from attending the Dutch refugee churches in Norwich and Colchester and to bring the liturgical forms of the latter into line with those of the Anglican church, and to control the English congregations abroad.[11] In this last respect Laud's success was limited, and the Netherlands remained a haven for East Anglian laymen and ministers dissatisfied with the Arminian innovations, who used the mercantile contacts between the two regions to distribute propaganda against the religious regime. In November 1637 a 'sylly weaver' landed at Yarmouth carrying copies of the seditious tract *Dr Bastwick's Litany* for delivery to two Norwich merchants, the Toft brothers, 'principal refractories' in the city; the books had been dispatched by 'some of their holy frendes from Delph'. Aboard the same ship, in disguise, were William Greenhill and Jeremiah Burroughes, two well-connected Puritan ministers who had taken refuge in the Low Countries, having been silenced by Bishop Wren in the autumn; they were entertained at the house of Miles Corbett, the reorder of Yarmouth and future regicide, where they left books and letters.[12] The religious dimension of the commercial and cultural relationship between the Low Countries and the eastern counties, exemplified in the 1637 incident, was well expressed in the image used by Sir William Denny when petitioning for the governorship of Yarmouth after the Restoration: 'that towne has served as a port to let in much schisme and faction which to this day doth extreamelie infect and infest the whole country round about'.[13]

But, while it may be argued that some aspects of the East Anglian economy were relatively advanced, the development of industry, agriculture and trade within the region was not uniform. The

Thames-side parishes of south-western Essex, the Hertfordshire 'thoroughfare townes' on the Great North Road, the cloth-producing centers of the Stour valley, the dairying region of Suffolk and the Norfolk ports were involved in substantial mercantile communication with London or the Low Countries, and so exposed to new influences, but it is illegitimate to argue from these areas to East Anglia as a whole. Other parts of the region were still isolated, largely engaged in subsistence farming, untouched by agricultural specialization or industrialization. The Cambridgeshire men who, in 1648, got hopelessly lost in 'strange country' when only a few miles from their homes, their Suffolk counterparts described by Celia Fiennes, and the Fenmen, hating the 'Upland men' and the drainers who threatened their traditional way of life, demonstrate that the economic development of the eastern counties was uneven.[14] Areas of intense commercial specialization and areas of traditional agrarian practice existed side by side within the region.

This conclusion, besides suggesting that those who interpret the geographical split of 1642 in terms of broad socio-economic characteristics fall into the ecological fallacy,[15] also undermines one explanation of the successful combination of the eastern counties in the Association: that it was a product of the sense of regional community which developed from the counties' 'incipient economic unity'.[16] The economies of the individual counties were not structurally homogeneous, nor can it be argued that they were interdependent from the few examples of contact between them – that the Norwich worsted weavers used yarn from Essex and Suffolk; that the dairy farmers of 'high Suffolk' were dependent upon Norfolk for their grain; that King's Lynn was the entrepôt for the agricultural produce of the counties intersected by the Ouse and its tributaries.[17] Such limited interdependence can scarcely be said to create an 'economic unity', nor was it necessarily productive of a sense of community. The corporations of Lynn and Cambridge were on the most unfriendly terms throughout the sixteenth century, each accusing the other of restrictive practices designed to secure a monopoly of the Ouse river traffic; in 1623 the Norfolk combers and spinners protested the dumping of inferior quality yarn on the Norwich market by 'forraine' producers – those of Essex and Suffolk.[18]

This survey of the economic structure of East Anglia suggests that certain parts of the region were relatively advanced, engaging in specialized market production, and that their mercantile contacts resulted in the dissemination of new ideas. But economic development, and thus the permeation of radical influences within the eastern counties, was uneven; large areas of the region were still engaged in traditional subsistence agriculture, effectively isolated.

In consequence it is impossible to argue that East Anglia possessed a sense of regional community, the product of 'incipient economic unity'. The economic patterns apparent in the separate counties were not uniform, nor were the shires interdependent. The argument that the Eastern Association was the necessary product of the economic substructure of East Anglia can only be maintained by isolating and emphasizing evidence which relates only to a geographical or social segment.

But it may be thought that a detailed examination of one segment of the socio-economic structure of the region is a very necessary procedure. Most of the effective decisions in the 1640s were made, not by the inhabitants of East Anglia generally, but by a minority, the political elite. The study of the economy or the structure of society as a whole may result in a neglect of those aspects of the experience of the East Anglian gentry which underlay their adherence to Westminster and their subsequent readiness to work together in the Association. Indeed, it has been suggested that the unique success of the latter owed much to the atypical social experience of the gentry of the region, a claim which will now be examined.

Elite structures within the eastern counties

Recent studies of the provincial gentry have emphasized their insularity; distinct and self-contained local communities, rather than the 'community of the realm', were the cynosures of their loyalties.[19] Deeply rooted on estates painstakingly built up by generations of their ancestors, inter-marrying with neighboring families of similar status to form local clans, the gentry attached most significance to the community of their county, which, significantly, they invariably called 'my country'. Most of them spent much of their time in its service as Deputy-Lieutenants, Justices of the Peace, special commissioners or high constables, while those with intellectual interests wrote of its antiquities and topography, or researched local genealogy. So in the early seventeenth century the county was more than a useful administrative sub-division; its borders circumscribed the social, political and cultural horizons of the gentry. Each shire formed a distinct and insular community, and national political consciousness was limited. 'The England of 1640', writes Professor Everitt, 'resembled a union of partially independent county-states . . . each with its own ethos and loyalty.'

The insights provided by the new emphasis on the importance of the county community as a focus of a gentry loyalty which might outweigh any sense of responsibility to a wider entity have proved valuable in explaining aspects of the civil war previously neglected or misunderstood by historians who concerned themselves primarily with events at Westminster or Oxford.[20] In particular, the failure of

most of the programs developed by both the belligerents for inter-
county military co-operation is explicable in terms of local particularism stemming from devotion to the traditional ideal of the
priority of the interests of the county community. Local authorities
were reluctant to abandon their autonomy or to sacrifice policies
which they considered to be to the immediate advantage of their
particular community to regional or national strategic considerations.

But if the efforts of Denbigh or Waller to exercise more than a
nominal control within their regional commands were frustrated by
the deeply imbedded attachment of the Stuart gentry to their county
communities, how are we to explain the achievement of the Earl of
Manchester? Professor Everitt, who has glanced at this problem, has
suggested that the comparative success of the Eastern Association
was a product of the atypical circumstances which prevailed among
the gentry of eastern England, whereby particularist sentiments
centering on the county community were muted. The social experience
of the East Anglian gentry encouraged the development of a cohesive
sense of regional community; a significant proportion of the political
elite of the region were 'capable of thinking in terms, not only of
their native village and county, but of East Anglia as a whole'.[21]

It has been suggested that the loyalty which the county community could command among the gentry in the civil war period was
a product of certain social circumstances, in particular the antiquity
of the gentry families' settlement in the shire, and their patterns of
landholding and of marriage. An investigation of East Anglian
society within these categories certainly discloses differences between
the shires of that region and the paradigm county community, that
of Kent. While in the latter the estates of the greater part of the
gentry were not merely confined to that county, but to a few parishes
within it, landholding within the eastern counties was more diversi-
fied. In no county in East Anglia could more than half the gentry
trace their family's occupation of their estates into the pre-Tudor
period, as could nearly three-quarters of the Kentish gentry. And,
finally, while in Kent 82% of the untitled gentry married into local
families, only 55% of their East Anglian counterparts matched with
girls from their own county.[22]

So it is clear that the East Anglian gentry were neither so deeply
rooted in their counties, nor so inbred as were those of Kent, and it
may be suggested that this encouraged the growth of a broader outlook among the gentry, and made them less politically introverted
and thus less obsessed with the maintenance of the integrity of the
county community. But this in itself did not guarantee the success
of the Association: other areas of England were structurally similar
to East Anglia, in that the gentry were largely newcomers to the

county, or married or held land outside its borders,[23] but no success-ful politico-military organization was established with neighboring shires. And further examination of gentry landholding and marriage in East Anglia, far from revealing behavioral patterns which might be considered the social underpinnings of the Association, demon-strates the diversity of experience within the area. The gentry of the eastern counties cannot be said to form a cohesive community, nor were the constituent counties of the Association structurally homo-geneous.

There was a good deal of inter-county marriage and landholding in East Anglia between the gentry of neighboring shires. So 5.7% of the manors in Norfolk were held by inhabitants of Suffolk and 6.0% of the manors in the latter county by Norfolk men, while in both just over a tenth of the untitled gentry found brides in the other county. The figures also suggest, if less emphatically, that similar contacts existed between the gentry of Suffolk and Essex, and those of Essex and Hertfordshire. But such relationships between neigh-boring shires, which were particularly close in the adjacent border areas, cannot be said to demonstrate the existence of a cohesive East Anglian community. The latter would surely require significant levels of social intercourse between those non-contiguous counties which were subsequently grouped in the Association, and there is little evidence that this was the case. In 1640 only three men from Norfolk and Suffolk owned Hertfordshire and Huntingdonshire manors, and only five had married within those two counties. The inverse relation-ship was scarcely more significant; nine Hertfordshire gentlemen had married into Norfolk and Suffolk families, and Hertfordshire residents owned ten manors in the area, about 0.6% of the total – and six of these ten were owned by one man, Arthur Capel. The contacts between the gentry of Norfolk and Essex were equally limited. So an examination of the patterns of marriage and land-holding among the gentry of the eastern counties does not prove the existence of a pan-East Anglian community, only that contiguous counties were laced together: the success of the civil war Association cannot be said to be based on such tenuous relationships.

It has been argued that while the East Anglian gentry's lack of deep roots in their counties, and their readiness to marry outside their immediate neighborhoods may have made them less politically introverted than their Kentish counterparts, attempts to explain the success of the Association by reference merely to the social experience of the ruling class of the region are less persuasive. Indeed, the survey of the familial and tenurial patterns of the East Anglian gentry reveals one factor which might be thought to militate against the formation and successful operation of the Association: structural diversity among the constituent counties.

Marriage patterns in Norfolk and Suffolk are not dissimilar: approximately seven-tenths of the gentry in both counties married endogamously, a fifth married into families from other counties in East Anglia, and one-tenth found wives beyond the borders of the Association. But in Essex only 43.3%, and in Hertfordshire 37.1% of the gentry married in their home counties, while over a third of the former and half of those from Hertfordshire married into non-East Anglian families. This spectrum is virtually repeated with respect to the antiquity of settlement in the shire. At one extreme is Norfolk, with about four-tenths of its gentlemen able to trace their families' tenure of their estates into the pre-Tudor period, and one-tenth who had settled in the shire since 1603; in Suffolk, Essex and Hertfordshire the proportion of deeply-rooted gentry families progressively decreases until in the latter the Norfolk proportions are reversed: only one-tenth of the Hertfordshire gentry families had held their estates in the medieval period, and four-tenths were parvenus.

The patterns of marriage and of antiquity of settlement displayed in Hertfordshire, in both respects the county which least resembles Kent, is largely a reflection of its proximity to the capital. The shire was invaded by those Londoners whose wealth enabled them to invest in land: of the fifteen gentlemen appointed to execute the Commission of Array or to serve on the Parliamentary committee before March 1643, who had recently settled in the shire and whose origins can be determined, the fortunes of thirteen derived from Court or city. This contact with London was reinforced by marriage: 30% of the Hertfordshire gentry in 1640 had married into city families. Similar influences were also strong in Essex, where many gentry families had purchased their estates with the profits of trade or office,[24] and a fifth of whom were allied by marriage to London, but were far less apparent in Suffolk or Norfolk.

Two shires subsequently incorporated in the Association have been disregarded in this comparative survey of the marriage alliances and antiquity of settlement of the gentry of the eastern counties. In Cambridgeshire investigation of these patterns was not possible owing to the regrettable lack of reliable sources which would provide information in the categories obtained for the other counties.[25] Huntingdonshire was excluded because its social structure was so different from that in the other four counties as to make comparison almost meaningless. Two families, those of Montagu and Cromwell, owned nearly a quarter of the manors in the shire, and beneath these giants, as the Lord Lieutenant complained in 1625, there were few resident 'persons of quality'. Indeed, by 1640, 22% of the manors in the county were in the hands of outsiders. The few resident gentry were for the most part newcomers to the shire who tended to marry outside its borders; less than a quarter of those who recorded their pedigrees in the 1613 visitation had matched with local families.[26]

This investigation of the social patterns of the East Anglian gentry suggests conclusions which parallel those from the analysis of the general economic development and structure of the region. As specialization and market production potentially opened some areas within the eastern counties to new ideological influences, so the gentry of the region, who were less inbred and less deeply rooted on their estates than were their contemporaries from Kent, might be expected to be more extrovert, less dominated by the ideal of the county community. But neither analysis demonstrates that economic or social factors in the eastern counties could have created a sense of regional community guaranteeing the success of the Association. Indeed, the lack of homogeneity among the individual constituent counties – no uniform economic structures, divergent rates of development, very different patterns of social experience among the elite – suggests that the Association was formed in spite of, rather than because of, the socio-economic substructure of the region.

2

Religion and politics in the eastern counties

Having examined the contention that the peculiar success of the Eastern Association was the product of the homogeneous socio-economic structure of the region, and found it less than convincing, we must now evaluate the older general explanation of the Association's achievements: that the eastern counties were united by ideology; that the strength of their Puritan conviction and of their hostility to the pretensions of the Stuart monarchs united the counties of the area prior to the outbreak of war in 1642, and distinguished East Anglia from other parts of the realm.

Religion

The argument that East Anglia as a region was the stronghold of seventeenth-century English Puritanism is not without some warrant in contemporary opinion. In 1629 an Essex vicar, complaining to the authorities of the diocese of London of the extraordinary local influence wielded by the great Puritan minister Thomas Hooker, wrote bitterly, 'such is the disposition of our people as I know not any county where he is like so much to prevail as here, unless it be in the diocese of Norwich'.[1] But such impressionistic accounts, modern or contemporary, cannot sustain the proposition that the success of the Eastern Association was a product of the universal Puritan zeal of the region, for they fail to provide satisfactory answers to certain critical questions: was Puritanism in the eastern counties stronger than in, say, Buckingham or Northampton, shires which did not become members of an effective Association? was it equally powerful a force within all the constituent counties? Unfortunately any attempt to push beyond conclusions based on the partial and impressionistic use of evidence is fraught with difficulty. A comparative examination of even the most obvious elements potentially susceptible to statistical analysis – the number of ministers prosecuted in a county for non-conformity, for instance – may, given the wide variations in the availability and quality of the necessary diocesan records, be a better indicator of the enthusiasm of the local bishop and the efficiency of his administration, than of the strength of Puritanism.

However, even recognizing the insuperable problems presented by the nature of the sources, which, in the context of East Anglia, make it impossible to present such detailed information for Cambridge-shire, Huntingdonshire, and Hertfordshire as is available for Norfolk, Suffolk and Essex, it can be shown that Puritanism was not uniformly influential throughout the eastern counties.

The Puritanism of Norfolk, Huntingdonshire and Cambridge-shire was predominantly an urban phenomenon. The Puritan influence apparent in some of the colleges and parishes of Cambridge in the 1630s was scarcely felt in the villages of the county, and in Huntingdonshire had little purchase outside the borough of Hunting-don and the market-town of St Ives.[2] In Norfolk, too, Puritanism was strongest in the larger boroughs.[3] Yarmouth was a hot-bed of dissent. In the 1620s the corporation engaged in an extended feud with the Dean and Chapter of Norwich over the right to appoint the town's vicar, a right which the borough had arrogated to itself and had used to patronize 'unconformable ministers'. Having lost this dispute, the corporation proceeded to make life as unpleasant as possible for the Dean and Chapter's nominee, who was harassed with lawsuits, imprisoned on trumped-up charges, and reviled, even assaulted, in public. The leaders of the town's opposition refused to attend services or to send their children to be catechized, but supported a radical Puritan lecturer who denounced the vicar from his pulpit. A small group of separatists flourished in the town, apparently with the connivance of the authorities, and conventicles were held in the borough and the surrounding parishes.[4]

Norwich was the scene of another major confrontation between the Anglican establishment and the Puritans in the 1630s, although, unlike Yarmouth, the city's rulers were divided in their allegiance. In 1630 a group modeled on the London-based feoffees for impropriations, the 'trustees for the religion in Norwich and Norfolk', was established in the city with the intention of soliciting donations with which to buy advowsons and impropriations. In 1631 the trustees purchased the living of St Peter's Hungate, to which they presented William Bridge who quickly became the spiritual leader of the Puritans in the city and organized a combination lectureship to which eminent Puritan divines from Norfolk and Suffolk were invited to preach. In 1636 Wren, the new Bishop of Norwich, determined to crush the clerical Puritans in the city and ultimately eight ministers, including Bridge, were deprived. Bridge's supporters in the city government responded by organizing a petition to the King blaming Wren's persecution for many of the economic ills afflicting Norwich, which they presented under the common seal of the city despite the efforts of a group of aldermen who supported the Bishop to suppress it. The petition was unavailing, and for the next four years the Norwich Puritans could do little more than skirmish with the authorities over the implementation of the Laudian ceremonial innovations, although they were careful to enhance their strength on the governing body of the city.[5]

But, outside Yarmouth, Norwich and Lynn, which, although it enjoyed a quieter relationship with the ecclesiastical authorities, did maintain a Puritan lecturer, Puritanism was a far less dynamic force. There were locally influential non-conformist ministers in the county, like Robert Peck of Hingham, whose parishioners were 'so adicted to hym' that after his deprivation they refused to attend services at which his replacement officiated, continued to pay their tithes to his wife, and ultimately emigrated to Massachusetts Bay with him,[6] but in general Norfolk gave Wren little trouble. Only fifteen county ministers seriously offended against Laudian practice and were prosecuted by the Bishop, there were only seven lectures not associated with the three major urban communities, and few of the gentry patronized dissident clerics.[7]

At the end of his first year as Bishop of Norwich Wren informed Laud that the implementation of the Arminian program would present more difficulties in Suffolk than in Norfolk. Ipswich proved to be the 'most refractory and styf place' in the diocese.[8] The Bishop sought to break the Puritan corporation's hold over the appointment and funding of ministers in the town: the urban authorities replied by petitioning the King against Wren's policies and ceremonial innovations, by opposing their implementation in local churches, and, in 1636, by tacitly encouraging popular rioting when first the Bishop's commissaries and then Wren himself visited the borough. But in Suffolk Puritanism was not limited to the larger towns. Forty county ministers were prosecuted by Wren for non-conformity, there were nineteen lectures in the shire besides those at Ipswich and Bury, and a substantial proportion of the gentry were active champions of the Puritan cause.

The patronage of the gentry took many forms in the shire. Those gentlemen with advowsons in their gift presented Puritan ministers to their livings, and, if their protégés were troubled by the ecclesiastical authorities, sought to protect them from persecution; others employed non-conformists as their private chaplains or schoolmasters. The Suffolk gentry were also active in promoting 'the ratsbayne of lecturing'; as Laud noted, there were many lectures in the county 'sett upp by private gentlemen, even without soe much as the knowledge of the Ordinary, and without any due observation of the Canons'. Some gentlemen openly refused to comply with the obnoxious ceremonial innovations, or even publicly protested against them.[9]

The paucity of source materials makes it impossible to establish the degree to which the gentry patronized Puritan clerics in Hertfordshire, but it is clear that, as in Suffolk, Puritanism was widely dispersed. It was particularly strong in the boroughs of St Albans and Hertford, and in the small market-towns of the shire, like Ware, Bishop's Stortford and Watford, but it was also an influential force in a number of the villages.[10]

In Suffolk forty county ministers were censured by the ecclesiastical authorities for non-conformity in the 1630s; more than double that number were prosecuted in Essex.[11] Not only were Puritan ministers more numerous in the latter, but Puritanism appears to have been better organized and more determined in its opposition to the Laudian program. Twice grand-juries in the county brought in indictments against Arminian clergymen for refusing to give the sacraments to their parishioners except at the altar-rail: a similar effort was made without success in Suffolk.[12] The qualitative difference in the strength of the Puritan movements in the two counties was largely a function of the nature of their lay support. In Essex not only were the Puritan ministers enthusiastically patronized by a substantial proportion of the gentry, but by the leading magnate of the shire, its Lord Lieutenant the Earl of Warwick, 'whose countenance of good ministers procured more prayers to God for him than most noble men in England'.[13]

The twenty-two benefices in the county to which Warwick possessed the right of presentation provided livings for a solid nucleus of Puritan ministers of whom the hierarchy was justifiably suspicious – men like Hugh Peter, who was given a curacy at Rayleigh, or Edmund Calamy, presented to the living of Rochford. The Earl also nominated the masters of Felsted school, where in the 1630s posts were held by Seton, 'a bold boy and unlicensed', and Holbech, 'whoe scarce bred any man that was loyall to his prince'.[14] The Earl displayed his zeal not only in the presentation of Puritans to his livings, but in the protection of those persecuted by the hierarchy. When the influential Thomas Hooker was prosecuted at Chelmsford in 1630 and bound over to appear before the High Commission one of the Earl's tenants stood bail for him, and forfeited his bond when Warwick provided a hiding place for the minister prior to his flight to the Low Countries. John Wilson, the lecturer at Sudbury, and Hugh Peter were similarly protected from prosecution or punishment by Warwick. In 1638 Jeremiah Burroughes, who had been deprived of his living in Norfolk by Wren, was given a chaplaincy at Warwick's house, until his support for the Scottish Covenanters and justification of popular sovereignty enforced his flight to Rotterdam.[15]

The conclusion of this survey must be that Puritanism did not affect the eastern counties with equal force. In Norfolk, Huntingdonshire and Cambridgeshire Puritanism was predominantly an urban phenomenon; in Hertfordshire and Suffolk it was widely dispersed throughout the county, and, at least in the latter, 'godly' ministers were actively supported by an influential group among the gentry. Non-conforming clerics were most numerous in Essex, and their defiance of the hierarchy was encouraged by the enthusiastic patronage of the leading magnate in the shire, the Earl of Warwick, the 'great patron and Mecaenas to the pious and religious ministry . . . one of the greatest friends that the godly and painful ministers had in England'.[16]

Political opposition

The differences in the degree to which Puritanism flourished within the counties of the future Eastern Association demonstrate that the supposed religious homogeneity of the region has been over-emphasized. Equally apparent, from a study of the responses of the shires to the pressures of the personal rule and to the policies of the Long Parliament prior to the outbreak of the civil war, is the wide divergence in their political tempers. For the purposes of analysis the counties' reactions to only three events will be examined: to the collection of ship-money in the 1630s, to the summoning of Parliament in 1640, and to the developments at Westminster in early 1642.

Ship-money

Generally the opposition to ship-money in the eastern counties followed a pattern similar to that discernible throughout the rest of England. Initially there was little resistance to the levy, but a growing reluctance of those assessed to pay culminated in 1639–40, when the sheriffs had the utmost difficulty in collecting a minimal proportion of the tax. However, there were divergences in detail among the counties from the general pattern, and the percentages of the sum assessed that was collected in 1640, while in part a function of the degree of enthusiasm displayed by the individual sheriffs, provides some indication of their respective reactions to the levy.[17] The Sheriff of Hertfordshire collected no money at all in 1640, while his colleagues in Suffolk and Huntingdonshire received approximately a tenth of the sum due from their counties; all three shires had substantial sums outstanding from the previous year. The authorities in Cambridgeshire and Norfolk were more successful: arrears for 1638–9 were negligible, while 35% of the sum assessed in 1639 was collected in the former, 22% in the latter.

In Essex, however, the development of resistance to the levy follows an eccentric course. Initially the most recalcitrant county in England, it became more compliant after 1637 when opposition was growing elsewhere. The local defiance of the sheriffs in 1635 and 1636 was certainly encouraged by the Earl of Warwick. The Earl himself denied payment, as did a number of gentlemen associated with him as patrons of Puritan ministers, like Sir William Masham and Sir

Richard Saltonstall. The minor county officials appointed by Warwick refused to assist the Sheriff, and, at the village level, resistance was fiercest in those parishes where the Earl and his friends were influential. Warwick's opposition culminated in a direct appeal to Charles in January 1637, when he 'made no bones of telling the King frankly that his tenants . . . were old and accustomed to the mild rule of Queen Elizabeth and King James and could not bring themselves to consent to such notable prejudices as ship-money', and pressed the King to summon Parliament. Faced with a coherent opposition in Essex organized by Warwick, the Court took unprecedentedly strict measures to bring the county to heel: the Privy Council gave all assistance to the new Sheriff, sixty refusers were arraigned in the Exchequer, deprivation from office was threatened against those gentlemen who would not pay and *quo warranto* proceedings were begun to test Warwick's right to appoint those minor officials who had hindered the collection. Under this barrage the Earl gave way, and resistance was negligible thereafter until 1639.[18]

The 1640 elections

The response to the collection of ship-money in Essex emphasizes Warwick's influence in the shire; this is equally apparent in the 1640 elections, both to the Short and the Long Parliaments. In March the defeated candidate at the county election, Henry Smyth Neville of Cressing Temple, a 'forward and entire' supporter of Archbishop Laud's program, sent an analysis of the reasons for his defeat at the polls to Secretary Nicholas.[19] His successful rivals were Sir Harbottle Grimston, a forced loan refuser in 1626 who had been in trouble with the High Commission ten years later, and Sir Thomas Barrington, an opponent of the Court over the saltpetremen, the forest law and ship-money, who had patronized Puritans as his family chaplains and as lecturers at his parish of Hatfield Broadoak.[20] Both men were wealthy and influential, but Neville was under no delusions as to the identity of his real opponent: Barrington's and Grimston's voters were those 'who gave their voyces for my Lord of Warwick'. The administrative and the clerical bases of the Earl's power were put to effective use in securing the return of his nominees. Warwick used his authority to instruct the trained-band captains to threaten those who failed to vote for Barrington and Grimston that their assessments for the militia would be increased, while Puritan ministers like the very influential Stephen Marshall of Finchingfield preached 'often out of theire own parishes before the election'.[21] On the day of the poll, where there was a large popular turnout including contingents from the boroughs, Daniel Rogers the suspended lecturer of Wethersfield was given a place of honor at the Chelmsford

sessions house by Warwick's command, while a man arrested by
Lord Maynard for threatening those gentlemen who opposed
Barrington and Grimston, was immediately released by Warwick
upon bail being offered by two militia captains.

In the October election there was a mass change round of seats.
Lord Rich, Warwick's heir, and Sir William Masham 'a very factious
Puritan',[22] were elected without contest for the shire, while Barrington took Masham's seat at Colchester and Grimston retired to
Harwich, the borough adjacent to his home. This exchange, presumably undertaken to ensure that Lord Rich would take the premier
county seat, emphasizes Warwick's influence. Announcing the
candidates to the Recorder of Colchester, Masham wrote 'I presume
you are well acquainted with my Lord of Warwick's proposition for
the Knights of this shire, and that my Lord hath propounded Sir
Thomas Barrington to Colchester for one of theyr burgesses.'[23] This
incident, and the other returns for the Long Parliament, demonstrates the Earl's influence in the Essex boroughs. Sir Henry
Mildmay's election for Maldon, where the Earl's authority as Lord
Lieutenant and Admiral of Essex gave him considerable power, was
certainly secured by Warwick, while Mildmay's fellow member was
Sir John Clotworthy, an Irish carpet-bagger, whose election Claren-
don ascribes to 'the connivance and recommendation of some
powerful persons' to head the attack on Strafford's Irish policies.[24]
The members for Harwich were the Earl's brother-in-law, Sir Thomas
Cheek, and Sir Harbottle Grimston.

The Essex elections were a triumph for the Puritan organization
in the shire headed by Warwick. His territorial magnificence, control
of the administrative organs of the shire and opposition opinions
were an irresistible combination at the polls. The Suffolk Puritans
also enjoyed considerable success in 1640, although their triumph
was less smooth than that engineered by Warwick.

Although there was no contest for the county seats in the Short
Parliament elections, the pre-poll maneuvering included an attempt
by certain lesser county officials, covertly supported by 'divers great
men', to adjourn the shire court at which the elections would be
held from Ipswich to Beccles.[25] The choice of that town is significant.
As the outraged Sheriff noted on the discovery of the plot, Beccles
was a 'remote place . . . whereabouts one man's power and revenues'
were 'so great as he shall be sure to carry it from the whole countie'.
The one man in question was Sir William Playters, an active Deputy-
Lieutenant during the Bishops' war whose brother was an enthusiastic
Laudian clergyman.[26] However, when the attempt was discovered
Playters, who may not have been a party to the conspiracy, withdrew
from the contest, and Sir Philip Parker and Sir Nathaniel Barnardiston were returned without opposition. Both men were Puritan

sympathizers. Parker had appointed the non-conformist Robert Wickes to his living, and had refused to have his child baptized with the ceremonial enjoined by the church.[27] Barnardiston had been imprisoned as a forced loan refuser in 1628 and was the patron of Christopher Burrell, one of the first to protest publicly against Wren's innovations, and Samuel Fairclough, the minister of his home village of Kedington, which became, through the co-operation of the minister and his patron, a paradigm of seigneurial Puritan godliness. Upon his election Barnardiston wrote to Governor Winthrop in New England to announce that God had called him despite his unworthiness 'to serve for my countrey' and desiring all assistance in 'this great work'.[28]

The violent autumn election, in which Parker and Barnardiston were opposed by Henry North, is well known from Carlyle's edition of the Sheriff's narrative.[29] Ideological issues were certainly to the forefront of this struggle, which was preceded by 'great preparation of subsidiarie forces and voices'. North's candidacy was supported by a vocal group of clergymen who were prosecuted by the local committees for Scandalous Ministers in 1644 for anti-Parliamentary activities or for their previous support for the Laudian program,[30] and by a number of gentlemen who, while not active Royalists during the war, did not participate in the Parliamentary administration of the county.[31] On the other side Parker and Barnardiston made no secret of their sympathies. Their clerks at the poll were three Ipswich men, Peter Fisher, Edward Bedwall and the constable, Samuel Duncon, not the poor Dogberry of Carlyle's account, but, like the others, a prominent Puritan: all three had been excommunicated by Wren, and Fisher and Duncon were to present the Ipswich petition to Parliament against the Bishop.[32]

Parker and Barnardiston ultimately triumphed over North by 700 votes, but their hotly contested return contrasts with the smooth efficiency of the contemporary Essex election. Nor were the Suffolk Puritans as successful in the jungle of borough franchises as was the Earl of Warwick in his shire. Ipswich predictably returned two enthusiastic Puritans, and little Aldeburgh rejected the courtier nominee of its traditional patron the Earl of Arundel, preferring local men 'acquainted with maratine affaires and our grievances therein'.[33] Sudbury elected one candidate supported by Sir Nathaniel Barnardiston, but rejected the Puritan Brampton Gurdon, who, upon the dissolution of the Short Parliament, had informed Winthrop how 'it comforteth the hartes of honest men . . . that they yelded not to geve a pene to help the King in his intended ware agenst the Skottes', in favor of the moderate Sir Robert Crane.[34] The other four boroughs in the shire returned either courtiers or moderates.

In Essex the Puritan group had swept the elections; in Suffolk their successes had been limited to the county and to the larger boroughs with open franchises. This, too, was the pattern in Hertfordshire, where the county and St Albans returned men openly opposed to Royal ecclesiastical and fiscal policies, but Hertford was unable to shake off the control traditionally exercised by its patrons, the Cecil and Fanshaw families. In Huntingdonshire the all-powerful Montagu family monopolized the borough and took one of the county seats, but the freeholders rejected the nominee of Sir Henry Cromwell the other great landowner in the shire, preferring Valentine Walton, whose popularity was a product of his resistance to ship-money.[35]

In Cambridgeshire and Norfolk the urban Puritan groups were largely successful in the autumn election. Cambridge rejected two Court nominees in favor of Oliver Cromwell and a townsman; Yarmouth returned Corbett and Owner, both leaders of the town's opposition to royal and ecclesiastical interference in the 1630s; Toll and Percivall, the Lynn representatives, were supporters of the town's Puritan lecturer.[36] However, in Norwich the Puritans suffered a reverse. In the spring the city had returned two aldermen attached to the group which had opposed Wren with such vigor in 1636, but in October two moderates were returned. Evidence is scanty, but it appears that the aldermen who had supported the Bishop in 1636 were active in opposing the radical candidate and securing the return of one of the moderates, the outsider Richard Catelyn, whose election was subsequently challenged in the Commons.[37]

The strong Puritan influence which is apparent in the borough returns from Norfolk and Cambridgeshire was not so important a feature in the election of knights of the shire in the two counties. In the October election in Cambridgeshire the great issues of the 1630s might as well not have existed. When Sir John Cutts, the Short Parliament representative whose re-election was thought to be a certainty, refused to stand, the county returned the future Straffordian, Thomas Chicheley, who secured his election by 'bestowing a dinner on the gentlemen and wine on the country'.[38] In the Short Parliament election in Norfolk[39] certain ideological issues were raised, but in the context of a struggle which was essentially personal and familial. The conflict between the three candidates, Sir John Holland, Sir Edmund Moundeford and John Potts, was bitter: 'sydings and faction' developed among the gentry, and tenants were dragooned into voting for their landlords' choices by threats that 'if they revolt we will turne them all out of their farmes'. The ideological element was introduced by the one obvious weakness of Holland as a candidate, which his opponents sought to exploit – his wife was a Catholic. During the campaign it was said that Holland had patronized a chaplain of his wife's, and that he kept an orthodox minister in his house only 'out of policy'. His detractors, noted one of Sir John's supporters, 'witisly say ther ar too many religons in Holland'. Despite these calumnies Holland was elected with Moundeford to the Short Parliament, but in the October election he retired to the Howard pocket-borough of Castle Rising. It appears that Holland, who had been profoundly disturbed by the polarization of the county in April, was unwilling to engage in another embittered campaign, and Potts and Moundeford were returned without a contest.

The summoning of the two Parliaments in 1640 elicited a variety of responses in the eastern counties. In Essex the Puritan political machine headed by Warwick swung smoothly into action to sweep the polls in both shire and boroughs; in Suffolk the Puritans were strong enough to win the county election and that for Ipswich, but lacked the organization and influence to capture the smaller boroughs. The electorates in Cambridgeshire and Norfolk were least influenced by ideological issues, and the contests in those shires, with their 'treating' of the voters and gentry feuds, bear a close resemblance to those of the Tudor period described by Sir John Neale – struggles for social prestige among the local elites.

The counties and Parliament, January–March 1642

Finally, the responses of the eastern counties to a third political stimulus, the King's abortive attempt to seize the Five Members in January 1642, will be examined. This analysis, as do the studies of reactions in East Anglia to the collection of ship-money and to the summoning of Parliament in 1640, demonstrates the wide divergence between the respective political attitudes of the counties, which, barely a year later, were to unite in the Eastern Association.

On 11 January 1642, a week after Charles's attempted coup had failed so miserably, 'a numerous multitude', perhaps four or five thousand strong, rode up to Westminster from Buckinghamshire bearing a petition in which they expressed their readiness to live and die in the defense of the privileges of Parliament. The petitioners also demanded that justice be done on the King's evil counsellors and that Bishops and Catholic Lords, who were thought to be retarding the work of reformation in the upper House, should be deprived of their votes. Their petition was the prototype for a wave of similar statements which surged into the two Houses in the following months, in which county after county expressed their confidence in Parliament and their hopes of a 'speedie refining and reforming of persons and things amisse among us'.[40] The language, with its echoes of the Grand Remonstrance and subsequent official Parliamentary declarations, and the demands of these petitions are largely stereo-typed, but the timing and even the content of those from the eastern counties shows that not all the East Anglian shires responded with equal alacrity to this opportunity to demonstrate their pro-Parliamentary zeal.

Essex was the second English shire, after Buckingham, to respond to the situation at Westminster. On 20 January petitions from the county to the Lords and to the Commons, each with a huge roll of signatures attached, and a petition from Colchester to the lower House, were presented. In all three the petitioners thanked Parliament for their previous endeavors 'for the settling of Church and State', and went on to press for the implementation of those policies supported by Pym and his allies in the Commons: that Roman Catholic peers and Bishops be excluded from the Lords, that the Kingdom be put in a 'posture of defense', and that immediate assistance be sent to the Irish Protestants. The swift collection of the huge numbers of signatures to these petitions, which appears to have been undertaken at the village level by Puritan ministers, is a further tribute to Warwick's local party organization, which had already demonstrated its worth in 1636 and 1640.[41]

Five days after the presentation of the Essex petition, similar documents arrived at Westminster from Hertfordshire.[42] Besides assuring the Houses of their readiness to uphold the privileges of Parliament 'to the utmost peril of their lives and estates', and making demands similar to those embodied in the Essex petition, the Hertfordshire petitioners adopted a very high tone in their statement to the upper House, denouncing those peers who had voted against bills passed by the Commons, 'that House for the common good', as 'enemies to this Kingdom'. However offensive these 'broade and plaine termes' might be to the small Royalist clique in the Lords, who formally protested against the petition, they were the language which Pym chose when he presented the Hertfordshire and Essex petitions, together with those received contemporaneously from the City of London and Middlesex to the Lords on 26 January. Arguing that in the four petitions could be heard 'the voice, or rather the cry of all England', Pym stressed the dangers which threatened the realm should the Lords continue to veto necessary legislation and hinted, none too subtly, that if the peers refused to work with the Commons the latter would be forced to ditch the upper House and 'save the Kingdom alone'.[43]

The petitions from Suffolk corresponding to those from Essex and Hertfordshire arrived a little too late for use by Pym at the conference with the Lords: the first, to the Commons, was received on 31 January, another, to the upper House, on 9 February.[44] The interval between the presentation of the two petitions may have been occasioned by the need to modify the substance of that delivered to the Lords. Pym's hectoring speech had made a considerable impression upon the upper House and on 1 February they had agreed to the Militia Ordinance, and on the 5th had finally passed the long-delayed Bishops' exclusion bill. Accordingly the Suffolk petition of the 9th, while making a number of requests concerning further reformation in the church, the punishment of delinquents and Catholics, and aid for Ireland, was essentially one of thanks and congratulation to the Lords. However, the ominous tone of the Hertfordshire petition recurs in a lower key; the petitioners' readiness to 'secure and serve' the House of Lords was dependent upon 'their continued concurrence with the . . . Commons in their just desires'. Despite the fact that in September 1641 the majority of the gentry and freeholders had apparently been prepared to sign a petition favoring the retention of episcopacy,[45] it was said that 16,000 people were prepared to accompany the 9 February petition backing Pym's policies up to Westminster.

While Essex, Hertfordshire and Suffolk responded with considerable alacrity to events at Westminster during the first months of 1642, the other counties of the future Association were far less forward. Some of the townsmen of the Norfolk ports joined in a pro-Parliamentary petition with the other east coast seamen on 12 February, and the City of Norwich added its voice ten days later,[46] but it was not until 4 March that the county presented a petition to the Commons: Cambridgeshire followed with petitions to both Houses on the 16th, and Huntingdonshire with one to the Commons on the 25th.[47] The Cambridgeshire petition to the Lords, in form very similar to that presented from Suffolk a month before, and that from Huntingdonshire are remarkable only for the late date upon which they were delivered, but the Norfolk petition includes an extraordinary feature. The Norfolk petitioners insist upon the abrogation of the votes of the Bishops and Roman Catholic peers in the upper House, yet the King had consented to the Bishops' exclusion bill on 13 February, three weeks prior to the presentation of their demand: as Speaker Lenthall noted in his reply to the delegation from that county, 'removing the Bishops . . . is already provided for'.[48] The superfluous clause suggests that the petition had been introduced in the county, perhaps sent down from Westminster, at least a month prior to its presentation, and that the collection of signatures had been extraordinarily slow, particularly when compared with the speed with which thousands of signatures had been obtained for the Essex petition of 20 January. Apparently many of the Norfolk gentry, while agreeing with Thomas Knyvett of Ashwellthorpe that it was 'a state necessity . . . to make them [the Bishops] altogether spirituall', also shared his fears of the radical direction of Pym's policies, and were not prepared to actively organize a petition, despite broad hints from their M.P.s in early February, who 'do much wonder thay have not heard of this county by petition'.[49] Similar doubts among those with local influence, and the consequent difficulties of organization, may explain the tardy presentation of the Huntingdonshire petition; in December 1641 the county gentry had implicitly criticized Parliament for the religious anarchy which was developing in the country in a petition favoring the retention of the episcopal hierarchy.[50]

The wide divergence in the reactions of those counties which were to be united in the Eastern Association to common political stimuli in the period 1635–42 reinforces the conclusion reached in the analysis of Puritanism within the region: the eastern counties were not ideologically homogeneous. In Essex the immediate resistance to ship-money, the complete success which recognizably Puritan candidates enjoyed at the polls in 1640, and the speed with which popular support for the January 1642 petition was mobilized, are all indicative of the influence and organization of the opposition group of 'godly' ministers and their gentry patrons, a group given added prestige and coherence by the dynamic leadership of the Earl of Warwick. Calamy's comment on the Earl's moral influence might equally well apply to his political authority in the shire; 'great men are like looking glasses according to which all the country dresse themselves, and if they be good they do a world of good'.[51] In Hertfordshire and Suffolk the Puritan opposition was a vital force, and both resistance to the Court's policies in the 1630s and support for Pym in 1642 was widespread, but in neither county was there a leader of Warwick's stature about whom the opposition could coalesce and thus be given focus. Norfolk, Huntingdonshire and Cambridgeshire present a marked contrast to Essex. Resistance to ship-money was far less fierce than in the latter, the elections were not much concerned with ideological considerations, and the counties' expressions of confidence in the policies of the majority at Westminster in early 1642 were tardy and half-hearted.

One final consideration must be discussed in this survey of those general environmental factors which might explain the establishment and success of the Eastern Association. Although the influence of the Puritan opposition varied considerably from county to county, could it be argued that the contacts and co-operation between these groups in East Anglia prior to the civil war were a precursor of the Association? At first sight the idea is attractive. The Puritans of the region had worked together, both in direct opposition to the Arminian program,[52] and in such ventures as the Providence Island and Massachusetts Bay companies. Moreover, the godly were intertwined in kinship groups based on religious compatibility, as 'the good beginnings of grace' became of greater importance in a prospective spouse than estate or ancestry.[53] The delineation of the resultant politico-genealogical connection is a prosopographer's dream. To give a single example, Sir William Lytton of Knebworth, the leader of the Hertfordshire opposition to ship-money, was related to Sir John Wentworth of Somerleyton in the extreme north-east of Suffolk, who 'brought good preachers into that Island of Lothingland, and ther was the chief patron of religion and honestye in his time',[54] through a chain of marriages crossing East Anglia. Every link-family in that chain – the Barringtons of Hatfield Broadoak, the Edens of Sudbury, the Harlackendens of Earl's Colne, the Mildmays of Graces, the Gurdons of Assington, the Parkers of Erwarton, the Barnardistons of Kedington and the Soames of Little Thirlow – was either involved in the Providence Island Company, or was interested in the New England settlement of Governor Winthrop and his associates, or was a patron of non-conformist ministers.[55]

However, to halt the investigation at this point and assert that the Association was prefigured in the East Anglian Puritan 'connection' of the 1620s and 1630s would involve a partial reading of the evidence. For the Puritan gentry of the eastern counties were linked by similar ties of kinship and interest to men who shared their opinions throughout England. In the Providence Island Company Barrington and his East Anglian colleagues worked with the opposition magnates Lord Brooke and Lord Saye and Seale, and with Pym, the Knightleys, Sir Gilbert Gerard and Oliver St John. Sir William Lytton was allied by marriage not only to Sir John Wentworth of Suffolk, but with such Puritan families as the Wallops of Hampshire, the Lukes of Bedfordshire, the Fleetwoods and Knightleys of Northampton. The experience and contacts of the Puritan gentry certainly extended beyond the boundaries of their own shires, but neither were their horizons constricted by the borders of the East Anglian region.

Conclusion

This survey, by examining the structure of society within the East Anglian counties and the religious and political disposition of the latter, has sought to demonstrate the insufficiency of explanations which seek to relate the unrivalled success of the Eastern Association to the supposed pre-existent homogeneity of the region, whether social or ideological. Far from there being a cohesive and discrete East Anglican community, close analysis suggests that there were considerable differences among the counties later to be incorporated within the Association. While parts of the region were relatively advanced economically, with wide-ranging commercial contacts which had become the vehicle for the dissemination of radical ideas, modernization had not proceeded with equal speed throughout East Anglia. This is partly reflected in the variant structures of the counties' ruling elites: at the extremes were Hertfordshire, where the bulk of the gentry were relative newcomers, their wealth derived from the City, and Norfolk, where they were both more deeply rooted in the county and more inbred. Similar differences emerge from an analysis of the degree to which Puritanism was influential within the counties, and of their reactions to Royal policies in the 1630s and to Pym's program in early 1642. In every case the counties exhibit a spectrum of responses to the common stimulus, not homogeneity.

As the diversity of environment and experience among the constituent counties undermines those broad causal leaps which endeavored to link the achievements of the Association to a sense of community apparent in the region prior to the outbreak of the civil war, what alternative explanatory framework can be offered? It will be a more prosaic approach, detailing the build-up of the army of the Association and analyzing both party conflict at Westminster and the dialogue between the central authorities and the localities, which underlay the development of that military organization. But first the origins of the Association in the confused response within East Anglia to the outbreak of war in the last six months of 1642 must be examined: this period, too, illustrates the wide divergences of temper among the eastern counties.

PART II

The creation of the Eastern Association: from the outbreak of war to the Ordinance of 22 January 1644

The outbreak of the civil war in East Anglia, and the formation of the Eastern Association, June 1642 – March 1643

In May 1642 as Thomas Knyvett of Ashwellthorpe was sauntering through Westminster he was accosted by a local M.P., Sir John Potts, who presented him with a commission signed by the Earl of Warwick, the Lord Lieutenant of Norfolk appointed by Parliament, instructing him to take command of a trained-band company in the county. A few hours later he read a Royal Declaration denouncing the Militia Ordinance. 'Oh! sweete hart,' he wrote to his wife, 'I am nowe in a greate strayght what to doe.'[1]

Recent studies of the local dimension of the civil war have shown that Knyvett's hesitancy when faced with the intractable problem of allegiance, as the leaders of the Houses and the Court moved inexorably towards armed conflict, was not peculiar. In a number of English counties many were as reluctant as was he to gallop to York or to throw in their lots with Pym and the Earl of Essex. In some areas the desire to stave off the fatal choice posed by the conflicting claims of the Militia Ordinance and the Commission of Array, designed to gear a county into the war-effort of Parliament or the King respectively, was institutionalized in a local pacification or declaration of neutrality. Elsewhere, as in Kent and Cornwall, small cliques of the committed struggled for control of the shire, while the bulk of the inhabitants 'sat still as neuters assisting neither'.[2] In June Lincolnshire accepted the Militia Ordinance 'with all readiness and alacrity', but in July the King was given a tumultuous popular reception, and horse were subscribed for his army: this apparent reversal of loyalty stemmed from a reluctance to disobey the positive commands of either party, and a desire to follow a course of action which would be approved by all 'that are not . . . malignants either against King or Parliament'.[3]

That many were reluctant to rush headlong into either camp is scarcely surprising. The horrors of civil war had been incessantly urged by official propagandists throughout the previous century, and contemporary conflicts, both the 'German desolation' and the bloody struggle in Ireland,[4] were ghastly warnings of the probable accuracy of those dire predictions. Men feared not only the physical devastations of civil war – though bloodshed, rapine, high taxation and the dislocation of commerce were terrifying enough – but the disruption of the traditional local and national communities: hostilities among friends, neighbors and countrymen made domestic conflagration, in a phrase repeated endlessly by the pamphleteers, 'unnatural war'. And such a breach in the unity of the political nation could provide an opportunity for foreign enemies, and posed the threat of the subversion of the social hierarchy by the 'many-headed monster'.[5]

And so, although all England was ultimately divided into two armed camps, the process whereby the individual counties were geared into the Royal or Parliamentary war-effort was seldom smooth and never uniform. Consideration of the differing degrees of en-thusiasm, of the hesitation and uncertainty, of the formal pacifi-cations, and of the apparent tergiversations has led one authority to write of the 'confused, mercurial, and at first sight incomprehensible' reactions to the civil war in the localities.[6] This is as true for East Anglia as for other regions of England, despite the *idée reçue* that the eastern counties were 'wholeheartedly for Parliament'.[7] A detailed analysis of events in 1642 will show that the counties of East Anglia were not politically homogeneous, and that in none of them was enthusiasm for the Parliamentary cause universal. It will also appear that the initial pressure for the formation of the Eastern Association came from those counties which were least enthusiastic in their support for the Parliamentary cause.

Essex

The county of Essex appears to provide convincing evidence for the argument that eastern England was zealously dedicated to the policies of the leaders at Westminster: a 'place of most life of religion in the land', wrote Hampden; a county 'whose universall and unanimous affections are set to defend the . . . Parliament', enthused a pamphleteer.[8] The county was one of the first to put the Militia Ordinance into effect, despite some bureaucratic difficulties occasioned by the absence of the Parliamentary Lord Lieutenant, the Earl of Warwick, with the Fleet.[9] On 1 June the Essex M.P.s requested that Warwick, then at sea, should be permitted to leave his charge to attend the first muster of the trained-bands at Brentwood on the 7th for the execution of the Militia Ordinance. A Norfolk M.P., commenting on this request, wrote 'Essex deputy lieutenants, doubt-ing their own strength, procured a letter from the Lords to the Erle of Warwick . . . to cum to animat his countrymen'. The writer also correctly estimated the probable effect of Warwick's appearance; 'doubt not but all will be of one peece in Essex'. Apparently part of the process of 'animation' was the dissemination of a rumor that the Queen had landed with a force of 13,000 papists, but, however achieved, the effect was one of unanimous enthusiasm.[10]

At the Brentwood muster on 7 June Warwick and the local M.P.s reviewed five militia companies, one of double its official strength, and an additional force of 500 volunteers. When Warwick read his commission and the Parliamentary declarations the assembled militiamen resolved to dedicate themselves to the cause, and their officers presented a petition to the Earl, expressing their gratitude for Parliament's legislation, in particular the Militia Ordinance, designed to thwart 'the hellish designs and actings of a malignant party', who, having seduced the King, intended to 'deprive us both of religion and laws and . . . reduce us to a condition no less miserable than slavish'. The officers concluded with a resolution to defend to the death the 'high court of Parliament . . . and therein his Majesty's person and authority'. At the next muster, held at Dunmow on 10 June for the north-west of the county, the assembled soldiers signed a petition dedicating themselves to the service of Parliament – 'with our hands on our swords we stand ready at your command', which was circulated through the county in the next few days and presented to Parliament on 17 June with 10,000 signatures.[11]

After its swift and enthusiastic execution of the Militia Ordinance, the county was further geared into the Parliamentary war effort during the summer of 1642. A local organization was established for the collection of money to be loaned upon the Propositions for the maintenance of the army, and the commissioners appointed began successfully soliciting subscriptions.[12] Those few 'debausht and disordered persons' who spoke against Parliamentary policy or its supporters were disarmed and arrested,[13] and particular care was taken to suppress the expression of opposition from the pulpit. While pro-Parliamentarian ministers roused their parishioners to support the cause,[14] those who preached upon such texts, as did Edward Symmons of Rayne, 'that, if David's heart smote him for cutting Saul's garment, what would it have done if he had kept away his castles, towns and ships', were summoned to Westminster to answer for their temerity.[15] The one manifestation of militant Royalism in the shire was easily checked.

This incident itself deserves some analysis as it demonstrates that pro-Parliamentary sentiment was not the prerogative of the leaders of Essex society, or the agricultural and urban middle-class who subscribed money on the Propositions, and were financially responsible for the provision of arms and men for the trained-band. In August 1642 Sir John Lucas of Colchester, a courtier who had been the most active of the Essex sheriffs in the collection of ship-money in the 1630s, decided to join the King, gathered a few horses and arms, and arranged his departure for the night of the 21st. But his plans were betrayed by a servant, and the mayor of Colchester, having warned the neighboring villages to be prepared to intercept

Lucas's party should he break out, surrounded the house with a detachment of the trained-band; when Lucas and his ten companions endeavored to leave, they were halted by the guard. But while the mayor was acting so circumspectly, garbled rumors of events at Lucas's house, said to be filled with hundreds of armed men, had spread like wildfire through Colchester. 'The town got into an uproar', and soon the militia, originally deployed to prevent Lucas's departure, were defending his house from a large and unruly mob. At dawn the 'rude sort of people' succeeded in breaking in, and the mayor had the greatest difficulty in protecting Lucas from lynching. Having rifled the house, the Colchester mob moved on to Beerechurch and St Osyth to raid the homes of two 'papists', Sir Thomas Audley and Lady Rivers, while similar riots broke out in the clothing towns on both sides of the Stour valley, and the property of supposed Catholics and unpopular Laudian ministers was plundered.[16]

Not only did the populace demonstrate its 'zeale to the Parliament' in the suppression of Lucas's attempt to join the King, but in the volunteers the county provided for the Parliamentary field-army. Throughout the summer men for Lord Saye's and the Lord General's own regiment were raised in the north-east of the county, while the Liberty of Havering raised a troop for Nathaniel Fiennes.[17] In October and November a further effort was made to raise soldiers in Essex, and the incident again suggests Parliament's reliance on the loyalty of the county, and on Warwick's influence within it.

As the armies of the Earl of Essex and the King maneuvered in the midlands, the Parliamentary leaders, suddenly aware that Charles commanded a formidable force, thought it prudent to embody a substantial reserve for the defense of London. They immediately turned to Warwick. The Earl was summoned from the fleet, and, on 22 October, was appointed captain-general of a force to be raised in the city and parts adjacent.[18] But although Warwick's 'second army' contained contingents of seamen and godly apprentices from London, and some volunteers and trained-bands from the home counties, it was generally recognized that the bulk of his force was raised in Essex, and some journalists wrote as though his commission was limited to that county.[19] Certainly Warwick made his greatest effort to raise men in his home county; on 24 October he held a general meeting at Chelmsford, at which the gentry and freeholders agreed to raise a substantial force of volunteers.[20]

Warwick's reserve remained on foot until 22 November, when the Earl, stressing the great expense of his force, its superfluity given the strength of the main Parliamentary army under the Lord General which had moved into a position to defend London, and the need for his return to the fleet, resigned his commission.[21] In the course of its short career Warwick's corps twice took on added significance in view of the military situation, and on both occasions Parliament turned to Essex for additional assistance. The first crisis occurred immediately after Edgehill, when the Lord General's withdrawal to Warwick left the road to London open to the King, an opportunity he failed to exploit; the second was on 12 November when the cavaliers assaulted the unprepared Parliamentary outpost at Brentford, threatening an attack on London, a move which led to the confrontation at Turnham Green and the withdrawal of the Royal army. On both occasions Parliament instructed the Essex trainedbands to reinforce Warwick's army,[22] and, during the post-Edgehill scare, Westminster appealed to the county authorities to raise 1000 dragoon-horse with all speed 'for god's sake'. Essex responded with alacrity; Suffolk, which had received a similar appeal, took a week longer to dispatch only one-third of the required number.[23]

By October 1642 the Militia Ordinance had been executed, money was being collected upon the Propositions, and troops and horses raised for the Lord General or the defense of London; those ministers who preached against these developments had been silenced, and militant royalism suppressed. The success of Westminster's policies in the county is apparent: how can it best be explained? Not, I think, by invoking a universal enthusiasm for the Parliamentary cause for, as will be shown, a substantial group in the county never identified with the direction of events, and, as a collectivity, the county's devotion to central policies had serious limitations. Rather we should examine the leadership of the county in 1642.

As has been shown, in 1640 the Essex elections were swept by a tight-knit faction led by the Earl of Warwick. Its members were all men of substance in the county, but their horizons were wider than its borders and they were bound by ties of kinship, business interest and ideology to those who were to dictate the tone and direction of the opening session of the Long Parliament – Bedford, the Fiennes family, Pym, Hampden, St John. The Essex group had worked in conjunction with Pym throughout 1641, and, at the outbreak of hostilities, they remained a coherent, active political force dedicated to the successful prosecution of the war. The dynamic attitude of the Earl of Warwick, the central figure in this group in terms of local influence, appears in his letter to his son-in-law, Lord Mandeville, written in September as the Parliamentary army was preparing for action; 'I am glad to hear the army is to march, I pray stand well upon your garde both military and politicke, for you will never gett the like oportunity if you slip this which god hath put into your hands. And loose not the busines with cyvilities and compliment . . . doe the worke thourowly and looke to your selves.'[24] 'Doe the worke thourowly': Warwick had already given practical expression of his zeal in his July seizure of the fleet for Parliament, and, assisted by all the local M.P.s, in his execution of the Militia Ordinance in Essex in the previous month.

While Warwick and the Essex M.P.s were firmly committed to the Parliamentary cause, and, in consequence, acted with alacrity and determination, the supposed focus of Royalist sentiment in the shire, the Earl of Carlisle, nominated as Lord Lieutenant of the shire by the King, dithered. Appointed in mid-June, Carlisle had still made no move by August, when it was rumored that he intended to execute the Commission of Array, an idea he quickly abandoned; in September he finally summoned up the courage to endeavor to seize control of the Cambridgeshire militia for the King, but, when arrested and examined before Parliament, he denied any such intention and subserviently acknowledged the illegality of the Commission.[25] There were some dedicated Royalists in the shire, notably Sir John Lucas and Henry Neville of Cressing Temple,[26] but they were not members of leading county families, and were compromised as active agents of the King's government in the 1630s. In this respect, too, the Parliamentarian group had the advantage: the M.P.s were men of considerable local prestige, in particular Sir Thomas Barrington, upon whom the effective leadership of the county was to devolve in 1643–4 during Warwick's periodic absences at sea.[27] But the Earl's was the really decisive influence in Essex, as the M.P.s recognized when, in May, 'doubting their own strenth', they sent for him to execute the Militia Ordinance, and when, during the August riots in the Stour valley, they again summoned him to help restore order.[28] In October, when a large proportion of the Parliamentary 'second army' was raised by Warwick's exercise of his influence in the county, a journalist noted that the Earl was 'so highly beloved' in Essex 'that he can rayse more men for the defence of the King and Parliament then any other nobleman in the whole Kingdom', and another wrote that the county raised volunteers 'to show their zeale to Parliament and love to the Earle of Warwick'.[29]

But this last comment provokes a further, and fundamental, question. Did the inhabitants of the county observe the Militia Ordinance, contribute upon the Propositions, and march to the defense of the city because of their 'zeale to the Parliament' – their ideological commitment to the cause? Or were their actions more a function of their 'love to the Earle of Warwick', whose dynamic leadership they followed with minimal consideration of the substantive issues involved, because his local prestige was great, and his authority familiar? To pose the complex question of individual motivation in terms of a bare dichotomy, either ideological conviction or personal and local loyalty, obviously over-simplifies the issue, but it does provide a suggestive analytical approach to the sentiment displayed in the county. While we may document the personal religious or political convictions of some individuals as the critical determinant of their enthusiasm for the cause,[30] the behavior of some of the Essex men suggests that, as in Nottinghamshire, the influential leadership provided by a great peer was the dominant consideration informing their actions in 1642.

That loyalty to Warwick predominated over affection to the Parliamentary cause for many of the Essex men is demonstrated most clearly in the circumstances surrounding the disbanding of the Earl's 'second army' in November. The substantial Essex contingent in this force had been raised by the county with the express desire that Warwick should be its commander:[31] that this was understood literally appeared upon the Earl's resignation on 22 November. Westminster hoped to retain the services of the Earl's corps, either as part of a newly conceived 'running army', a highly mobile force designed as a counter-weight to the King's cavalry superiority, or as reinforcements to fill the gaps in the Lord General's regiments. But the response of the Essex men was thoroughly unsatisfactory; few were prepared to remain in service after the Earl's resignation, and the bulk of the contingent returned to their homes.[32]

Indeed, many of the Essex soldiers had deserted long before 22 November. On the 14th, Parliament, endeavoring to encourage the 'worthy gentlemen and honest freeholders' of the county to serve in person, denounced those volunteers, 'being people merely mercenary', who had 'withdrawn themselves' without permission, thus severely weakening the Earl's force. The letters of John Langley, captain of the Colchester volunteer company, who consoled himself in his difficulties by reminding himself that 'my lord suffered more for me', certainly bear out the official complaint of indiscipline and desertion.[33] Why were the Essex men so eager to return home? In part, desertion was a response to the lack of pay and supplies, and generally chaotic administration of an army hastily conceived in response to an emergency situation.[34] But contemporary commentators also suggested two factors, both of which provoke further consideration of Warwick's local power. First, it was argued that many of the soldiers wished to return to Essex because they were concerned for the safety of their homes and families. While Warwick was guarding the city rumors of a sea-borne invasion of Essex by foreign mercenaries, to be supported by the 'most unspeakable cruell' cavaliers, abounded, even in official circles, and, in consequence, many of the soldiers saw local defense as their first priority.[35] The second factor is related to the localism apparent in the first. At the Chelmsford meeting of 24 October, it was agreed that the volunteers to be raised in the county should be commanded by local officers, elected by the shire. But Warwick, arguing that 'the present occasion doth require men bred in warre', endeavored to replace the local cadre with more experienced commanders, chiefly Scots professionals. This move elicited an angry response from the disappointed Essex officers; their spokesman, Henry Farr of Gt Burstead, attacked the 'high indignity' and slur on their ability and courage involved in their enforced resignations. He also claimed, correctly, as the subsequent desertion proves, that the transfer of command would discourage the soldiers and lead to 'mutinous repining'. The troops had confidence in the local men appointed by the county to lead them, and, with the change of officers, 'you have withdrawne from you the hearts of the Essex soldiers'.[36]

Farr's final phrase deserves emphasis: these were 'Essex soldiers', not a national army. Many served not because of ideological enthusiasm for the Parliamentary cause, but from their 'love to the Earle of Warwick'. His combination of personal enthusiasm and local prestige was the motivating force which brought the Essex men to the defense of London, as it had to execute the Militia Ordinance and to contribute upon the Propositions. But there were limits to the Earl's power in Essex. He was respected and obeyed as the focus and the symbol of the county's opposition to the King's policies in the 1630s. When, in November 1642, his demands seemed to run counter to the best interests of the county, which he had always previously been thought to represent, the Essex men were put in a quandary, a conflict of interest. Some of the local soldiers deserted Warwick's command when their presence around London left their homes open to expected invasion, and when, with excellent military justification, their local officers were replaced by 'outsiders'. Most remained loyal to the Earl, but upon his return to the fleet they marched home despite Parliament's endeavors to retain their services: their 'zeale to the Parliament' terminated with the Earl's commission.

If much of the enthusiasm for the Parliamentary cause, traditionally believed to be general in the county, proves, on examination, to be a product more of 'love to the Earle of Warwick', there is also evidence of the existence of a previously neglected group who lacked even the qualified enthusiasm of those who executed Parliamentary legislation with little consideration of the ideological issues from devotion to the accepted and prestigious leader of the county. The neglect is understandable, for the group made little positive attempt to resist those activities to which they objected, and even their two collective protests were muted and ineffective.

Their first intervention occurred in the early summer when Warwick and his aides were organizing the Militia and the raising of money upon the Propositions, and, apparently, were meeting negligible resistance. The anomaly occurred at the county assizes in mid-July, when the presiding judge, Sir Thomas Malet, read a letter from the King at York. In the missive Charles stressed his determination to uphold the Church 'in its purity', suppressing both Popery and Anabaptism, to govern by the law of the land, and to maintain the 'just' privileges of Parliament, whilst rejecting its 'unwarrented power . . . lately usurped'. The King also played on fears of popular unrest by instructing his judges to punish such 'loose and ungoverned' persons who might be encouraged by the 'distemper of these times' to 'make a prey of our good subjects'.[37] In response to the letter, 25 of the J.P.s and 6 of the grand-jury subscribed a petition which was presented to the King at York by a deputation, thanking Charles for his 'zealous resolution' and promising 'that for the safety of your Majestie's royall person and posterity, defence of your rights and just prerogatives we will be ready . . . to assist your Majestie with our persons, lives and fortunes whensoever you shall be pleased to command us'.[38]

So, while Warwick and the county M.P.s were seizing absolute control of the shire, a royal letter of grace could command an enthusiastic response from a substantial number of the leading gentlemen of Essex. How can we explain the paradox of the assizes petition? In the absence of the diaries or personal correspondence of the signatories we cannot determine individual motivation, but analysis of the subsequent careers of the 25 J.P.s who signed provides some clues. Despite the positive, even belligerent Royalism of the petition, only eight of the signatories were subsequently sequestered for malignancy, of whom only one, Sir John Lucas, endeavored to fight for the King. Eleven men remained inactive during the first civil war, avoiding charges of Royalism, yet not participating in the Parliamentary county administration; the remaining six J.P.s were to be appointed to the local committee by the authorities at Westminster.[39] While the signatories' combination of pro-monarchical rhetoric in the July petition and practical passivity, even collaboration with Westminster, might suggest that for some the petition was little more than a cynical insurance policy, designed to secure royal favor, while subserviently following the lead of Warwick and his allies in the county,[40] comparison with events in Lincolnshire suggests a different interpretation. If the signatories' actions belie their words, they were not conscious hypocrites when affirming their devotion to the King; rather they were hesitant and uncommitted men, caught in the dilemma of allegiance. Like the Lincolnshire gentry, hoping to avoid appearing 'malignants against either King or Parliament', they temporized, unwilling to commit themselves to one side to the exclusion of the other. So they conformed with the actions taken by Warwick and his group, yet, prompted by Malet in July, endeavored to persuade themselves of their continued loyalty to Charles.

In the late summer and autumn of 1642 this group who could

neither fully approve of the direction of Parliamentary legislation, nor nerve themselves to resist its progress, were quiescent, but in the winter they prepared another public statement. In early January two petitions favoring peace were presented to the King and to Parliament, each signed by 20 baronets and knights, 63 esquires, over 80 ministers, 118 gentlemen and approximately 6000 others. The petitions, stressing the signatories' horrified sense of the 'present distractions and bloody miseries wherein this nation is most unhappily involved, whereby the ruine of our religion, estates, lives and liberties is inevitably threatened, in a most unnaturall and unchristian manner, the nearest and dearest relations plotting and acting destruction each to other', begged both King and Parliament to consider an accommodation on terms designed to guarantee 'the true Protestant Religion, his Majestie's safety and honour, the peace and prosperity of all his subjects'.[41]

The deputation bearing the petition to the King were made very welcome at Oxford, where the courtiers were pleasantly surprised by the existence of such sentiments in a county 'so subject to the power of some of the great incendiaries of the Commonwealth, and from whence the authors of the present distractions have promised themselves such ayd and assistance to continue the same'. Understandably, Westminster's reaction to the petition was less enthusiastic. The Lords took offense at its 'prescribing what way the House should proceed in'; the deputation who brought the petition were jeered and robbed by the city guard, and the signatories were denounced in a letter to the upper House from the Earl of Warwick as 'the slightest part of the country, and men of no religion or credit'.[42]

The list of 6000 signatures, for the most part organized by parishes, survives, but, rather than providing an inclusive statement of the location of anti-war sentiment in the county, it reflects the hasty organization of the petitioners, who canvassed support in a period of little over a week.[43] The bulk of the signatures came from six blocks of virtually contiguous parishes, and four of these center on the estates of men of the greater gentry class who themselves were signatories of the petition and who probably undertook the mobilization of support in their areas.[44] Within individual parishes in these blocks the petition was often circulated and propagandized by enthusiastic clergymen, like John Mow, curate of Bardfield, who preached a sermon supporting its principles, or Robert Fisher of Belchamp St Paul, who 'was very active to promote the . . . petition, and was angry with those that opposed it'.[45]

What provoked the substantial group of gentlemen and clergymen, previously quiescent, with the exception of the 15 who had signed the 'loyal' petition in July, to organize a public demonstration of their disquiet with the progress of the war? Perhaps the most immediate cause was the example provided by the City of London. Throughout December a chorus of demands for peace had risen in volume from the capital, and the pressure thus exerted had eventually persuaded Parliament to re-open negotiations with the King. The Essex men, like similar groups in other counties, encouraged by the success of the Londoners, sought to further the progress of the negotiations for a settlement by adding their voices to the city's clamor for peace.[46]

But, while contemporary events in the city triggered the public statement by the Essex pacifists, disillusionment with the war had been growing throughout the autumn of 1642.[47] One factor creating or enhancing pacific sentiment was almost certainly the Lucas affair in August and its aftermath. The riots looked ominously like that 'inundation of the vulgar', that rising of the 'many-headed monster', against the propertied classes which Cassandras like Sir Simonds D'Ewes had prophesied would be the immediate and inevitable effect of civil war. The element of class conflict in the August riots was partly concealed by the political and religious motivation claimed by some of the participants: the rioters, many 'the better sort', argued that their actions had been inspired by a document which purported to be a Parliamentary Declaration; when informed that it was spurious by the Essex M.P.s they returned some of the goods taken. Understandably Parliament chose to view the riots as a manifestation of genuine, if over-zealous, enthusiasm for the cause, and published a manifesto thanking the 'honest inhabitants' for their 'very acceptable service . . . one as doth express a great zeal to their religion and liberties', and only requesting them to disperse for fear that their 'peaceable intentions' might be subject to malicious misconstruction.[48] But those present during the riots, even Parliamentary supporters, had no illusions about 'honest inhabitants' with 'peaceable intentions'. The mayor of Colchester was scared out of his wits by the violence of the 'rude people'; 'we know not how to quiet them . . . we could not repress them if we had five trained bands'. The Earl of Warwick's steward, the historian Arthur Wilson, who traveled through the Stour valley on his master's instructions during the riots, hoping to rescue the recusant Lady Rivers from the fury of the mob, was equally certain that he was witnessing the actions of the 'unruly multitude . . . the rabble', not those of 'honest inhabitants'. The rioters' pretense was religious fervor, but 'spoile and plunder was their ayme', and they acted as if 'theire had been a desolution of all government'; Wilson concluded the account of his adventures 'so monstrous is the beast when it holds the bridell in its teeth'.[49]

But if the activities of the August rioters could be rationalized, at least by those distant from events, as a product of 'zeal to their

religion and liberties', the general undercurrent of violence throughout the autumn of 1642 was less obviously a product of popular
support for the Parliamentary cause. In the Stour valley, the major
center of unrest, in September the mob, having initially confined
itself to attacking the local Catholic community, became less
discriminating and plundered 'as well Protestants as Papists';
similar unpolitical incidents involving the 'lewde and disorderly
people' were reported in the area in the last three months of the
year.[50]

A number of the rioters must have felt like the anti-enclosure mob
at Newport who said 'they would take advantage of these tymes
least they have not the like againe'.[51] The opportunity for the riots
was provided by the confusion among the local governors occasioned
by the events at the center – for example, the uncertainty of the
sheriffs as to whether they might employ the local trained-bands to
suppress the mob on their own initiative.[52] But the effect of the central
upheaval was probably as much psychological as practical: all
authority was called in question. In May 1642, when a group of
Essex poachers were threatened by the keepers with legal penalties,
one replied, 'that there was noe lawe setled at this tyme that hee
knewe'.[53] But if the opportunity for the riots was provided by the
confusion and uncertainty attendant upon the political crisis, the
motive, at least in the Stour valley, was an economic crisis of serious
dimensions.

During the 1628–9 depression the Essex J.P.s estimated that there
were some 50,000 persons grouped in twelve towns in the Stour
valley who were entirely dependent upon the clothing industry for
their livelihood, 'few or none . . . can subsist unlesse they bee paied
theire wages once a week, and many of them that cannot live unlesse
they bee paied every night, many hundreds of them havinge noe
bedds to lye in nor foode, but from hand to mouth'. During the
slump the clothiers laid off their laborers and, in consequence,
'multitudes of the poorer sort must starve or use unlawfull meanes
to support themselves'. The industry recovered from the 1629 nadir,
but stagnated throughout the 1630s, and was again plunged into a
depression with the crisis of confidence and desire for liquidity
attendant upon the worsening political situation in 1641–2.[54] In
January 1642 Grimston and Pym, in speeches made upon the
presentation of the Essex petition against the participation in
Parliament of 'Popish Lords and Bishops', dwelt upon the decay of
the cloth trade and the concomitant social dislocation, which, they
suggested, were products of political uncertainty which the removal
of the Catholic peers and the episcopate from the upper House
would alleviate. Pym in particular stressed the danger of 'tumults and
insurrections of the meaner sort of people, by reason of their ill vent

of cloth . . . whereby great multitudes are set on work, who live for the most upon their daily gettings, and will in a short time be brought to great extremitie, if not employed. Nothing is more sharp . . . then necessitie . . . : what they cannot buy they will take.'[55] That this was more than rhetoric designed to frighten the Lords into compliance with Pym's legislative program appears from a petition addressed to the King from the Stour valley clothiers in the next month, praying for economic assistance: eighteen months' stock lay on their lands as the merchants would not export, and 'the cryes . . . of many thousands of poore, who depend on this trade, doe continually presse us, not without threats and some beginnings of mutinies'. The economic situation did not improve in the course of the year,[56] and in August the long-threatened riots finally broke out. During the Lucas affair one journalist saw through the smoke screen of religious and political rhetoric to the hard reality of subsistence crisis; the rioters, 'their wives and children were brought in to great want and extremity, by the decay of trading'. In December the continuing incidents of popular violence were entirely ascribed to the economic crisis.[57]

Unlike the contemporary pro-peace petition from Hertfordshire, which stressed that a number of people 'breaking the bonds of law, submit not themselves to government, but threaten and commit outrages . . . to the terror of your petitioners',[58] the Essex pacifists did not mention a fear of popular insurrection as a factor informing their desire for peace. But the riots must have added force to those who stressed that a civil war would inevitably lead to social revolution which only a re-unification of the divided ruling class by a compromise settlement of political differences could prevent, not least as some of the petitioners had been attacked or threatened by the populace.[59]

Besides the fear of popular unrest an additional motive for the production of the petition was the growing demands of Parliament upon the inhabitants of the area under its control. Demands on the pocket book, and, for some, on the conscience. In December the first Ordinance instituting compulsory universal taxation had been passed, but even before this pressure had been increasingly applied to secure military service and financial contributions which were theoretically voluntary. In October the Essex M.P.s had begun a campaign of scarcely-veiled threats against those who refused to contribute upon the Propositions, instructing the Deputy-Lieutenants to approach the recalcitrant individually and to forward lists of those who still refused to make a loan up to Parliament. John Wenlock of Langham was similarly threatened when he refused to contribute towards the equipping of Warwick's second army, and was subsequently subjected to petty harassment.[60]

Many had believed at the beginning of the war that its duration would be short; by December a drawn battle had been fought, military advantage lay with neither side, and no immediate termination of hostilities could be expected except through a treaty. The growing costs of an extended war may have persuaded a number of men to sign the petition for peace: the decay of trade and the exhaustion of men's estates by an extension of the conflict was stressed by the Hertfordshire petitioners. But for others the enhanced Parliamentary demands were a conscientious rather than an economic burden. It has been argued that many of the signatories of the 'loyal' July petition were endeavoring to persuade themselves that their passive acceptance of Warwick's authority could be reconciled with continued devotion to the King. But this comfortable fiction became increasingly unrealistic as Parliament screwed up its demands for assistance: could a man maintain the pretense of loyalty while contributing to the Parliamentary war-effort? In this respect the oath of Association, imposed in Essex in early January, the signatories of which pledged to 'aid and assist one another, under the command . . . of such persons as now hath . . . by the authority of . . . Parliament, the command in chief' and to provide 'horses and arms' for that purpose, was probably the last straw; Warwick reported that a number of the leaders of the peace movement had opposed the Association.[61]

The peace movement ultimately achieved nothing in the face of the intransigence of the belligerents, so clearly displayed in the abortive negotiations in February.[62] But in Essex the petitioners had been silenced even before the end of the Oxford treaty, when Parliament had taken action against some of their leaders, who, after the presentation of the petitions, had become increasingly vocal in their hostility to the authorities at Westminster. On his return from Oxford, Sir Thomas Bendish distributed copies of some Proclamations which the King had given the deputation which had brought the petition, including a general pardon to the inhabitants of the county conditional upon their giving no further assistance to Parliament, while Sir Benjamin Ayloffe was sworn in as Sheriff of the county by two other organizers of the peace petition, and published Royal Proclamations against contribution to the 'rebels'. Parliament moved quickly to smash this development. Ayloffe was seized by a troop of horse, and he, Bendish and Sir Francis Cooke, another peace petition organizer, accused of inciting his neighbors to violently resist Parliamentary agents, were all imprisoned.[63] Ayloffe's case is the most interesting of the three, for it epitomizes the uncertainty and hesitation of the group of moderates whose collective behavior we have been examining. Sir Benjamin had signed the 'loyal' declaration of July, but when the King appointed him Sheriff of

Essex in the following November he traveled to Westminster to surrender his commission to the Commons, whose permission he then unsuccessfully sought to go to Oxford to explain his action to the King. In December he was a leading organizer of the petition for peace, and, in January, on receipt of a message from the King confirming his appointment as Sheriff, he accepted the office and published the Proclamations. This symbolic act – for, given Parliament's military control of the county, it could be little more – was suicidal, but it may have given Ayloffe peace of mind: he had finally declared himself, the conflict of allegiance was over.[64]

The petition for peace was the last collective demonstration of opposition to the policies of Pym's group in the course of the first civil war; by March 1643 the gentry who had organized it and signed the earlier 'loyal' declaration either were imprisoned, or had fled to the King's quarters, or had compromised their consciences and passively accepted the government of the county committee. Despite occasional scares, when it was rumored that a substantial fifth column of malignants were waiting only for external military assistance to rise on the King's behalf,[65] the only vocal opposition to the Parliamentary administration was provided by the sermons of a number of disaffected ministers, most of whom were silenced by 1645, and the verbal abuse of a few village hotheads, their tongues often loosened by drink: the alehouse at Roxwell was denounced both as a center for 'singing prophane songs' and a place where 'the proceedings of Parliament have beene reviled, ministers of the Gospell scandalized and termes of disgrace fastened upon those that are well affected'.[66]

So Essex became, as Sir Edmund Moundeford had predicted in June, 'all of one peece'; active opposition to Parliament in the county was negligible. But enthusiasm for the policies of the leaders at Westminster was not universal. The existence of the two groups whose behavior in 1642 has been studied, the signatories of the petition for peace, and those who, during the raising of Warwick's second army, demonstrated that their ideological zeal was qualified by their prior concern for their local interests, meant that the tasks of the Parliamentary administration would not be easy. Warwick, Barrington and the M.P.s, fervently committed to the cause, would have to bully or cajole a substantial proportion of their countrymen to pay increasingly heavy taxes, raise men and generally pursue the strategy and policies dictated by Westminster.

In Essex the illusion of universal enthusiasm for the cause is in part a product of the rapidity with which the major Parliamentary enactments were put into effect in the shire. The myth of the zeal of the other eastern counties receives little support from similar evidence, for in none was the Militia Ordinance executed until September and in all of them, with the exception of Suffolk, Parliament's dominance was only finally assured by external military intervention.

Suffolk

In the two months of June and July, when the Essex M.P.s were organizing the county on behalf of Parliament, executing the Militia Ordinance and raising money upon the Propositions, there was virtually no official activity in Suffolk. The only reports in the Journals and the press concern isolated and individual incidents: in late July Parliament licensed the establishment of a company of local volunteers for the defense of Bury St Edmunds, some recruits for the Lord General's army were raised in Ipswich, and the vicar of Hartest was hauled before Parliament upon the information of one of his parishioners for publishing the Royal Declaration against the levy of troops and money.[67] Some indication of a more general political discussion in the county is provided by the petitions produced at the July assizes, but the evidence is incomplete and, in consequence, difficult to interpret. As at the Essex assizes, when the judge had read the King's letter an attempt was made to secure subscriptions to a loyal response, phrased in similar terms to that from Essex, but omitting the final clauses in which the petitioners promised to assist the King 'with our persons, lives, and fortunes'. This provoked Parliamentary sympathizers to draw up a counter-petition, purportedly from the 'freeholders' to the J.P.s on the bench, in which they asked the latter to represent to the King their fear of his military preparations and the 'boldness' of the papists, and their desire that he should return to Westminster and accept certain items of legislation passed by the Houses.[68] But in neither case does a subscription list survive with the petition, and it is impossible to determine the relative degree of support commanded by the two groups at the assizes.

At the end of July and in August Parliament began to display more interest in Suffolk: a committee of local gentlemen was appointed to raise money upon the Propositions, the local Deputy-Lieutenants were ordered to execute the Militia Ordinance, and to secure control of the county magazine at Bury St Edmunds.[69] But only in the last order is there any evidence that Parliament's instructions were acted upon; the execution of the Militia Ordinance and of the Propositions was not undertaken until late September, when the county was finally organized behind the Parliamentary war-effort.

The long delay may in part be attributed to the pusillanimity of the Lord Lieutenant of the county appointed by Parliament, the Earl of Suffolk. During the summer Suffolk stayed away from Westminster and in late August, in response to a letter from the

Commons demanding his 'speedy resolution' concerning his readiness to take control of the trained-bands for Parliament, the Earl obsequiously assured the House of his willingness 'to observe theire directions' but claimed, speciously, that he knew nothing of their intention to execute the Ordinance.[70] This was eleven weeks after Warwick had mobilized the Essex trained-bands.

But while the Earl hesitated, the county M.P.s, unlike their colleagues from Northamptonshire who had executed the Militia Ordinance in June, displayed no great enthusiasm to act as his surrogates.[71] Their reluctance may have stemmed from their lack of political unity at this time. Two of the fourteen[72] M.P.s from the county, the courtiers Thomas Jermyn and Sir Frederick Cornwallis, had already thrown in their lots with the King, while four representatives, Henry Coke, Sir Charles le Gros, Sir Thomas Jermyn and Sir Robert Crane, expressed their disquiet at the direction of Parliament's proceedings by absenting themselves from the Commons.[73] The House was particularly suspicious of Jermyn, probably because of his sons' Royalism. In August Sir Thomas was summoned to attend at Westminster, and the Deputy-Lieutenants of Suffolk were ordered to secure the county magazine at Bury, probably for fear of Jermyn's influence in the town. In October his house was searched for arms, and in mid-November he was again summoned to Westminster, accused by the radical M.P. from Ipswich, John Gurdon, of sending money to the King and discouraging the townsmen of Bury from contributing upon the Propositions. He was eventually allowed to return home, after a close vote in the Commons, upon offering 100 marks upon the Propositions.[74] Crane's career is perhaps the most interesting of the four. He had begun absenting himself from the House early in 1642, and in March was excluded from the list of Parliamentary Deputy-Lieutenants because of his failure to attend. In early June, when the members of the House each declared his contribution for the defense of Parliament, Crane was present and donated four horses, but, significantly, 'for the defence of King and Parliament not divided'. After this he again retired to Suffolk, from where, in early August in a letter to his friend the Norfolk M.P., Sir John Holland, he quoted with apparent approval the King's Declaration against the 'bold and bloudye minded men' who were dictating policy at Westminster, and expressed the hope that Norfolk would be able to 'escape the Militia and the Commission of Array . . . where either of them meet there is no securitye': probably a similar neutrality was also his ideal for Suffolk.[75]

Of the eight Suffolk M.P.s who remained at Westminster, one at least, Sir Simonds D'Ewes, was bitterly opposed to the activities of the majority, and deeply regretted the drift to war which, he felt, could only result in the overthrow of the social and political order.

He spoke frequently against war measures in the House, and, on 9 September, when the Earl of Essex took leave of the Houses to take command of the army, he entered a long jeremiad in his diary which epitomizes his attitude throughout 1642. Although acknowledging the necessity of opposing the prelatical 'designe . . . to have extirpated all the power and puritie of Religion and to have overwhelmed [it] in ignorance, superstition and idolatrie', D'Ewes could see nothing but a catalogue of woes as a product of war: 'plunder and pillage . . . of the gentrie' by 'the rude multitude'; 'a stopp to all trading . . . and the paiement of rents'; 'miseries and calamities . . . as great . . . as those of Germany it selfe'.[76]

The political convictions of the other seven Suffolk M.P.s cannot be documented as fully as those of Sir Simonds D'Ewes, but it seems probable that four were fully in sympathy with the policies of the majority at Westminster, while three were more moderate. Of the latter both Sir William Playters and Sir Roger North, deeply involved in the administration of the shire in the 1630s, had opposed the Puritan candidates in the 1640 election, and, although they contributed to the Propositions in June 1642, they give little indication of great enthusiasm for the Parliamentary cause; North may have absented himself from Parliament in the summer of 1642, and in early 1643 Playters was viewed with extreme suspicion by his more radical colleagues: the sons of both men fought for the King. Evidence of the convictions of Sir Philip Parker is equally scanty, but that which is available does not suggest zeal for the cause: there is no indication that he contributed to the defense of Parliament in June, while in March 1643 he was unwilling to involve himself in the execution of the assessment Ordinance in Suffolk; in the following November he temporarily refused to subscribe to the Covenant.[77]

Three of the four M.P.s who supported Pym in the Commons, the merchants Bence and Cage, and John Gurdon,[78] were not from the ranks of the traditional leaders of the shire, but the last member of this group, Sir Nathaniel Barnardiston, was probably the most prestigious and influential figure in Suffolk. He had been the leading opponent of Royal religious and fiscal policies in the 1630s, was a fervent Puritan, and, as such, had been chosen knight of the shire in 1640. In June 1642 he demonstrated his complete identification with the policies of the majority in the Commons by the very substantial gift of two horses and £500 upon the Propositions.[79] Yet, despite this gesture of commitment, Barnardiston did not insist upon the execution of the Militia Ordinance in Suffolk in the summer of 1642. In the absence of correspondence, and given his silence in debate, Sir Nathaniel's motives are hidden. But we may speculate that, aware of the obvious hesitance and doubts of other influential men in the county, Barnardiston preferred to maintain peace in Suffolk by following a moderate course, rather than risk dividing the county into conflicting factions by pressing the performance of Parliament's enactments. The equally Puritan gentleman, Robert Reyce, noted that the Suffolk gentry held unity as their highest ideal.[80]

With the Lord Lieutenant supine, and the county M.P.s divided politically and unwilling to take action to execute Parliamentary legislation, Suffolk remained a backwater until mid-September, when a committee of M.P.s and local gentlemen, headed by Barnardiston, organized the militia on Parliament's behalf, and raised money upon the Propositions. They met virtually no opposition.[81]

What caused this development, whereby Barnardiston finally determined to bring Suffolk formally into the Parliamentary camp and was not resisted by those M.P.s and local gentlemen who had previously demonstrated no enthusiasm for the imposition of the major Parliamentary enactments in the shire? The critical event was the violence in the Stour valley in late August. Faced with the fury of the rioters against 'his Majesties subjects as well protestants as papists' the local J.P.s of all persuasions, the moderate Sir Robert Crane and the Puritan activist Brampton Gurdon, agreed on the necessity to mobilize the trained-bands to suppress the marauders.[82] Yet there was considerable debate as to the legality of the J.P.'s summons both locally and in the Commons, where it was feared that the raising of troops might be a cover for an attempt to implement the Royal Commission of Array; in consequence, the Sheriff was advised by the House that no action should be taken against the rioters 'untill the kingdom be setled . . . least it make the cure the more dangerous'. Yet the local J.P.s at a county meeting on 6 September, with the poor of the Stour valley still mutinous and threatening to release their friends imprisoned for involvement in the insurrection and to plunder those gentlemen who had arrested them, insisted on their need for the authority and power to suppress any further riots.[83]

For both Parliament and the local governors the execution of the Militia Ordinance was the only mutually acceptable solution: Suffolk was brought into the Parliamentary camp and the local gentry were given the requisite authority to raise forces. At a county meeting at Stowmarket on 14 September Barnardiston both executed the Parliamentary legislation concerning the militia and the Propositions, some of the money from which was, significantly, used to provide relief for the poor of Sudbury,[84] and promulgated the House's order against riotous assemblies.[85] Those who assisted Barnardiston in the execution of the legislation were not solely enthusiastic devotees of the Parliamentary cause.[86] Sir Robert Crane's disquiet with the policies of the leaders at Westminster has already been examined; two other local gentlemen, Sir William Playters and Sir John Wentworth, were questioned by the Commons in early 1643, the former for riding by night to secret meetings in the county and warning his delinquent son of a summons to attend the Commons, enabling him to escape to Oxford; Wentworth for involvement in the abortive Royalist coup at Lowestoft.[87]

So in Suffolk, after three months in which the county was a backwater, officially neglected, in September the Parliamentary military legislation was executed in the shire. But this was not undertaken in a spirit of universal enthusiasm by gentlemen united on national political issues, but as a necessity in response to the late August incidents in the Stour valley. The gentry, none of whom had demonstrated any apparent zeal to act positively until September when faced with the specter of lower-class revolt, recognized the need to be able to mobilize a military force legitimately and rallied to Sir Nathaniel Barnardiston. They maintained their class unity at the expense of their previous conscientious scruples concerning the wisdom or legality of Parliament's enactments. Throughout the remainder of 1642 their implementation of orders from Westminster was informed by their fear of social unrest. So, when in November the central Committee of Safety ordered the Suffolk authorities to raise horsemen for the defense of London, the local committee of M.P.s and gentlemen encouraged service and subscription by announcing that part of the force would be retained in the county, 'forasmuch as at this present there are disorders and distempers . . . and evill affected persons who hunger after rapines and spoyleings and plunder of mens houses'.[88]

Hertfordshire and Cambridgeshire

In both Hertfordshire and Cambridgeshire, as in Suffolk, the official organization of the county as part of the Parliamentary war-machine, by the implementation of the Militia Ordinance and the county-wide raising of money upon the Propositions,[89] was not undertaken until the late summer through the reluctance of the Lord Lieutenants nominated by the Houses to act upon their Commissions. Lord North, appointed in Cambridgeshire, was stricken with that mysterious indisposition of health which afflicted a number of his fellow peers, and although in mid-August the Commons instructed the local Deputy-Lieutenants to act in his absence the Militia Ordinance was not executed for another month.[90] The position in Hertfordshire was complicated by the flight of the Parliamentary Lord Lieutenant, the Earl of Salisbury, to the Court in May, only to slink back to Westminster a month later having thought better of his temerity. The Earl lost his Lieutenancy to his son, Lord Cranborne, as a penalty for his vacillation, but the latter procrastinated and, despite the urgings of the Commons, the Ordinance was not executed until 30 August.[91] But, unlike Suffolk, both the counties had been the scenes of vigorous, if inchoate, conflict in the early summer, and in both the finalization of effective Parliamentary control pre-dated the implementation of the Militia Ordinance, through the intervention, as in Kent, of an external military force.

In Hertfordshire a great deal of individual pro-Parliamentary activity went on throughout the summer: volunteer companies trained at St Albans and Hertford; some individuals journeyed to London to make financial contributions to the Parliamentary war-chest, while a number of towns independently organized collections upon the Propositions, notably Watford, where by 1 July the inhabitants, spurred on by their influential minister, Cornelius Burgess, had raised £1250 and 50 horses towards a cavalry troop for the service of Parliament.[92]

But the county also contained an active group of Royalists. In June the townsmen of Hertford, who had formed a company of volunteers, were insulted and prosecuted at the quarter sessions by a group of local J.P.s, including the recorder and mayor of the town: the latter, with the mayor of St Albans, published the King's Declaration against Parliamentary levies of troops and money in the following month.[93] In August the Royalists' activities took a more dangerous turn. Early in the month Sir John Boteler of Watton-at-Stone, one of the J.P.s who had persecuted the Hertford volunteers, received a copy of the Royal Commission of Array and summoned a group of local gentlemen to meet at Hertford on the 18th to execute the Commission. The plan was scotched by external inter-ference. Warned of the danger, the Earl of Bedford's troop of horse marched from London and occupied Hertford; when the Royalist gentry came to the Bell Inn the next day, Bedford's troop drew up outside, and the potential Array men slipped away quietly without executing their Commission. Later in the same month Bedford's troop, reinforced by some Londoners, searched the houses of sus-pected malignants and disarmed them.[94]

The action of these cavalry units from the Parliamentary army crushed the military potential of the Royalists in the shire, and the Militia Ordinance was subsequently implemented without incident. But at the end of the year there was a resurgence of anti-Parliamentary feeling. In Hertfordshire, as in Essex, a petition directed to both King and Parliament stressing the signatories' fears of the 'great distractions and distempers of the Kingdom', in particular the threat of anarchic popular revolt, and favoring a compromise peace was circulated.[95] The group who presented the petition to the King, led by the irrepressible Sir John Boteler, returned from Oxford with a Royal pardon conditional upon the county's providing no further assistance to his enemies and a number of Proclamations against Parliamentary levies, which were published by the Sheriff at St Albans market on 14 January. The Sheriff, Thomas Coningsby, then intended to raise a force to arrest those in the county who were in arms for Parliament, but again the threatened danger was dissipated by the intervention of an external force. Cromwell's troop, on their march from London to Cambridge, arrested the Sheriff and his adherents, and then fought off 'a large multitude' who endeavored to rescue them.[96]

In Cambridgeshire Parliamentary control was finally established in September by the intervention of a force raised outside the shire. In the early summer, as relations between town and gown steadily deteriorated, Cambridge was the scene of a number of clashes between university Royalists and pro-Parliamentarian townsmen. The urban volunteers, training with arms bought for them by Cromwell, displayed their zeal by firing into college windows, while, on the other side, a number of prominent academics conveyed money to the King and arms from London to the colleges' vaults.[97]

A major incident erupted in August. On 25 July Charles wrote to the Vice-Chancellor inviting the colleges to deposit their plate with him for its safe-keeping, and many heads of houses prepared to comply with the request. In early August Valentine Walton, who had been unsuccessfully endeavoring to secure loans upon the Propositions in Huntingdonshire, issued warrants in that county to raise men to halt the expected convoy, but his orders were scorned or neglected and a large body of countrymen gathered, ready to assist in the transportation of the plate.[98] However, the University authorities failed to take advantage of this opportunity and on the 10th, when the bulk of the plate was ready to be sent, Cromwell, who had hurried up from London when warned of the danger and raised a force in western Cambridgeshire, with the assistance of two local gentlemen, intercepted some of the plate on the road and occupied Cambridge castle. In response the Sheriff, Sir John Cotton, with the support of a number of gentlemen, sent a detachment of the county trained-band into town, which marched with drums beating and colors flying into King's College Yard, where the greater part of the plate had been stored preparatory to its being sent to the King. How this impasse, with Cromwell holding the castle, and thus blocking the Huntingdon road, and the Sheriff's force occupying King's, was finally resolved is uncertain, but it does appear that no further attempt was made to transport the plate in bulk.[99]

The Royalist sentiment displayed in the shire during the plate affair was as apparent in the Isle of Ely in the same period. Bishop Wren had stockpiled arms at the episcopal palace, and in late August the 'chiefe officers' of the Isle, his appointees, were involved

in the publication of the Royal Proclamation against the Earl of
Essex at the assizes. When William Dodson of March vigorously
protested against this action he had to be quickly hustled away for
fear of the power of 'the Bishop and his friends'; Dodson later had
little success in trying to raise men for the Parliamentary army on
the Isle.[100]

However, despite the strength of Royalist sentiment in the county,
Cambridgeshire was secured for Parliament in early September.
Cromwell, recognizing that his indigenous force was too weak to
control the area, sought further assistance, and on 30 August
Cambridge was occupied by a force of 500 'London Dragooners'. In
addition to arresting the masters of those colleges which had sent
their plate to the King, they arrived in time to prevent an attempt
by the Earl of Carlisle and Sir John Russell to execute the Commission of Array in the town. From Cambridge the force rode to the
Bishop of Ely's palace and seized both Wren and the arms stored
there. With this coup Parliament gained effective control of the
shire, and in September the Militia Ordinance and the Propositions
were put in execution.[101] However, the control obtained was not
absolute. The University remained a center of disaffection until
Manchester's purge in the winter of 1643–4, and the malignants of
the Isle of Ely, involved in a series of insurrections in May, June and
July 1643, were a danger to the Parliamentarians until the Isle was
permanently garrisoned later in that year. Nor was the adjacent
county of Huntingdon, which had demonstrated its Royalist sympathies during the plate affair, effectively secured for Parliament
from 'the mighty boldnesse and impudencye of the adverse party',
until its occupation by Cromwell in April 1643.[102]

Norfolk

Like Huntingdonshire, Norfolk[103] was not finally secured for
Parliament until early 1643 when Cromwell and Lord Grey scotched
Royalist risings at Norwich, Lowestoft and Lynn. Before August 1642
the county was a political backwater like neighboring Suffolk. The
Parliamentary Lord Lieutenant, the Earl of Warwick, had little
personal influence in the shire, and his involvement in naval affairs
left the county without official leadership; the legislation of Westminster remained in abeyance.

Most of what little unofficial political activity there was centered
on the towns. Yarmouth, like its M.P.s Owner and Corbett, identified
with the majority in Parliament: suspicious cargoes of arms from the
Low Countries were seized, and the authorities agreed not to publish
Royal Declarations in accordance with a Parliamentary order as the
'most fitt way to preserve the publick peace both for kinge and
kingdome'. Lynn and Norwich were more ambivalent. A volunteer

company trained at the former, but some members of the corporation opposed Parliamentary orders. At Norwich while some citizens organized a volunteer company and a pro-Parliamentary petition in July, a vocal group of their fellow townsmen, tavern-based, drank the King's health, sang derisory verses against the leaders at Westminster and insulted their more godly neighbors. The civic authorities seem to have pursued a compromise policy, reading both Parliamentary and Royal missives.[104]

It was an incident in one of the Corporations that finally focused Westminster's attention on the county. In late July Captain Treswell, with a commission from the King's General, Lindsey, sought to raise recruits in the shire for the Royal army. At Lynn the corporation contented themselves with making a copy of the captain's commission which they forwarded to Parliament, but at Norwich the aldermen denied Treswell's request to beat his drums for volunteers; when the captain scorned their order, they arrested him and sent him prisoner to London. With typical circumspection the city fathers then sent letters to Lindsey and to the King explaining their action.[105]

When this incident was reported in the Commons Sir John Potts, knight of the shire for Norfolk, informed the House that the Treswell incident was a probable harbinger of further, more dangerous Royalist activity in the county. Not only had many gentlemen refused to accept Parliamentary commissions to command militia detachments, but others had visited the Royal Court, and then returned to the county 'and that it was likely that they would bee ready to assist my Lord Matravers who was shortly expected in that county with the Commission of Array'. In response Parliament ordered that a deputation of Norfolk M.P.s should go to the county, instructing them to suppress any attempt to implement the Commission of Array, to execute the Militia Ordinance and Propositions, and to justify Parliament's policies to their countrymen. Four days later similar instructions were voted for the City of Norwich.[106]

The M.P.s entrusted with the execution of these instructions displayed limited enthusiasm for their task. Of the Norwich M.P.s Catelyn utterly refused to act, and was eventually sequestered for his intransigence, while Harman initially pleaded poor health as grounds for his remaining in London.[107] Of the six M.P.s nominated to secure control of the shire, four failed to observe the order for their going down to Norfolk immediately.[108] Sir John Holland, whose diplomatic illnesses were to become proverbial in the Commons, informed the House that sickness prevented him from undertaking the service, but he had already demonstrated a lack of sympathy with the war policy of the Parliamentary majority with his carefully worded offer of a contribution upon the Propositions 'for maintenance of the true Protestant religion, the defence of the King's person, his royal authoritie and dignitie, our lawes, liberties, and privileges conjunctively'.[109] However, though reluctant to go to Norfolk himself, Holland wrote to his colleague, Sir John Potts, who had made the journey, to persuade him to adhere to the program that they had discussed and agreed upon, and which had been accepted by 'the most eager-bent off our country-men remeyning heere'. Its essential point was 'not to have the Ordinance put in execution, but in case'. Holland had already written to his friends in the county whom he suspected might be involved with the Royal Commission of Array to suspend its execution, and had argued in the Commons that 'in respect of the present constitution off our country . . . the House would take order that upon noe Commissions or directions whatsoever the noyse of a drum might for present bee heard in Norfolk'. Holland's ideal, apparently shared by other local M.P.s, was a situation in which both groups would agree to suspend operations in the shire – an effective neutralization. He feared that otherwise Norfolk would be rent asunder by the strife of the contending factions, and his ultimate goal was the 'peace of my country'. This phrase was to become the rallying-cry of the Norfolk gentry in the autumn of 1642.[110]

Of the two M.P.s who did journey into Norfolk in early August, Sir John Potts was attracted by Holland's ideal. Sir Edmund Moundeford, more closely identified with Pym's group in the Commons, was suspicious of the Norfolk neutrals, but determined to follow Potts's policy. However, Moundeford was to play only a very limited role in events in the shire in the autumn, being taken seriously ill on his journey.[111] In his absence Parliament was represented in the county by Potts, who, though involved in the issue of Parliamentary commissions to the Militia Officers in May and June, was supporting 'an accomodation' with the King in July,[112] and by Holland, who eventually joined him in Norfolk in mid-August. The policy the two M.P.s initially pursued was that outlined in Holland's letter: no attempt was made to implement the Militia Ordinance or the Propositions, while contact was made with potential Royalists and they were persuaded to forbear acting upon the Commission of Array. Holland wrote to the Royal Lord Lieutenant, Lord Mowbray and Maltravers, who had entered the shire in early August and was trying to rally support for the King among the gentry, in an endeavor to persuade him to abandon the attempt. When some of the Royalists approached Potts to secure a formal, negotiated pacification of the shire, he replied that he 'was not authorized in way of bargaine to answer, but bad them judg of my actions which should rather hazard the censure of slacknesse then my countrye's quiet'. The aim of both Holland and Potts is well expressed in a note from the latter to a friend at Westminster: 'I labour to preserve peace.'[113]

Potts believed that the weight of popular sentiment in the shire favored Parliament,[114] but he had no desire to appeal for mass support; 'whensoever necesssity shall enforce us to make use of the multitude, I doe not promise my self safety', he wrote. 'Ungovernable numbers' could only result in 'remidiless dangers'.[115] It may have been consideration of the possible effects of an appeal to the masses by the Parliamentary deputation should the Royalists take militant action, given the contemporary enclosure riots and the depressed condition of the Norwich clothing industry which had resulted in 'such poverty as we can scarce keep the poor from mutiny',[116] which decided some of those who had attended the meetings organized by Lord Mowbray that it would be unwise to attempt to execute the Commission of Array. Others 'did really endeavour the surcease' of the latter fearing that its implementation 'would bring the warre into the country'. For whatever reason, Holland's ideal of the 'peace of the country' proved attractive to the potential Royalists, and in late August Mowbray left the county without acting upon his Royal Commission as 'the gentlemen of that side held it not service-able'.[117]

With the removal of the Royalist Lord Lieutenant, the Parlia-mentary deputation, now joined by Wodehouse and Gawdy, were in a position to take effective control of Norfolk. But this opportunity presented a real dilemma. Potts and Holland had pacified the county in August by emphasizing their own moderation and devotion to the ideal of the 'peace of my country', and yet they were increasingly under pressure from the central authorities at Westminster to implement the major provisions of the Instructions of 1 August, the Militia Ordinance and the Propositions. In late August Potts learned that the fabian policies he and Holland had pursued in the shire were being questioned in Parliament, and his loyalty to the cause challenged; it was being said 'that I decline the service of the hous and encourage the Commission of Array'.[118] The deputation had to implement the major items of Parliamentary legislation, yet without compromising its own ideals, or forcing the potential Royalists into revolt with the consequent dissolution of the shire into warring factions.

On 6 September a meeting of the Deputy-Lieutenants was held in which the first moves were made towards realizing Parliamentary control of the shire. The four M.P.s and five country gentlemen present agreed that the major provisions of 1 August instructions would be observed – they would take charge of the militia, money would be solicited upon the Propositions, and measures would be taken against those who spoke or acted against Parliament.[119] Yet the subsequent implementation of these decisions was undertaken so tentatively and with such circumspection, and in a tone so low-key that it is apparent that the August ideal of the 'peace of the country' had not been abandoned.

Indeed, the phrase occurs in the Deputy-Lieutenant's deliberations on 5 September: the first step in securing control of the militia was to be a meeting ten days later in Norwich with the captains of the trained-bands, 'for the peace of the county'. It was also agreed on the 5th that should any tumult break out, or external force disturb the peace, then the trained-band nearest the danger would endeavor to suppress the insurgents or invading force. At Norwich on the 15th both themes recur: twenty-four of the assembled captains, including eight who were later to be sequestered or questioned for anti-Parliamentary activities, agreed to serve under the Earl of Warwick 'for his Majesty, and both Houses of Parliament, and for the peace of this county'. A larger group of local gentlemen, not militia officers, agreed to join with the Deputy-Lieutenants to defend Norfolk from 'all kyndes of plunderers'. In October the Deputy-Lieutenants busied themselves with a number of practical tasks – musters were held, arms checked, the local magazines inventoried: it seems that the Militia Ordinance itself was finally executed formally at the end of the month. Yet throughout this period, as the Parliamentary deputation secured and exercised control over the militia, there is no mention of national issues or the military situation. The emphasis is entirely upon the trained-bands' function of local defense, defense not against the 'Cavaliers without . . . fear either of God or man' but the ambiguous 'all kyndes of plunderers'.[120] The Norfolk leaders continued to avoid studiously the rhetoric of factional strife into December 1642. A force of volunteer dragoons was established to 'keep the county from plundering', arms were bought 'for the defence of the county', and when the Deputy-Lieutenants wished to hold a general meeting of the county gentry to advise on military affairs it was the 'imminent danger' presented by 'diverse forreigne forces nowe upon the coasts of Norfolk' that was used to justify the urgent request for attendance. No mention was made of the hostilities of the Royal and Parliamentary armies within England.[121]

In the collection of money upon the Propositions the Parliamentary deputation endeavored to present a similar low-key, a-political image. At the local meetings of the gentry the fiercely denunciatory prose of the preamble to the Parliamentary Ordinance establishing the loan was omitted, and the contributors were asked only to give money 'for maintenance of the Protestant Religion, the King's authoritye, his person in his Royal dignity, the free cours of justice, the lawes of the lande, the peace of the Kingdome and the priviledges of Parliament'. Nor was the 'peace of the country' ideal forgotten in this contribution to the national war-effort. Potts himself subscribed £100 to be sent to Westminster and in addition 2 horsemen and 10 foot soldiers 'for defence of this county not to be sent out'; his example was followed by several other gentlemen, including the Deputy-Lieutenants Palgrave and Paston.[122]

Finally the Parliamentary deputation at 5 September meeting had agreed to punish those who opposed or spoke against Parliament. But again their actions were marked by a spirit of moderation and a readiness to 'bee favourable to converts'. Sir William Denny was summoned to Westminster for 'spreading . . . a scandalous pamphlet', but when he 'applyed himselfe' to the deputation and 'sought our favours', declaring his 'dutyfule affection to King and Parliament', Sir John Holland sought to obtain the remission of the penalty. Dr Coleby, the rector of Cawston, also benefited from the leniency of the Deputy-Lieutenants.[123] Further, the deputation gave those officers of the trained-bands who were reluctant to acknowledge Warwick's Lieutenancy considerable time to consider their decision before replacing them, and do not seem to have acted upon their own vote to disarm those who failed to subscribe on the Propositions. This appears in the case of the L'Estrange family of Hunstanton. From the first they had refused to recognize the authority of the deputation, and not only declined to assist in the collection of money upon the Propositions or to contribute, but insulted the committee and probably encouraged their neighbors in the 'more than remote three hundreds' of the north-west of the county not to subscribe. Yet Nicholas L'Estrange was not replaced as a Colonel in the militia until the end of October, and although the deputation were empowered to disarm the family in mid-October, and ordered that to be done in December, no action was in fact taken until March 1643. Throughout late 1642 the committee's hope was that 'quiet and connivance will keep these wasps from stinging'.[124]

In the autumn of 1642 the committee of local M.P.s and Deputy-Lieutenants in Norfolk, whilst nominally securing Parliamentary control of the shire, consistently pursued moderate policies designed to avoid pushing those whose sympathies were not behind Westminster into revolt. But this compromise settlement could not survive the strains imposed upon it by the national development of the war. Increasingly the potential Royalist group felt betrayed. In August they had been persuaded to abandon any attempt to organize the county in support of the King by Potts's and Holland's arguments emphasizing the 'peace of the country', yet in the autumn the Parliamentary committee were forwarding money to the central treasury, threatening those who would not subscribe, and making military preparations.[125] Under the cover of the slogan 'the peace of the country', Norfolk was being geared into the Parliamentary war-effort. The point was made in a moving letter to Sir John Potts by Sir John Spelman, the son of the famous antiquary, who was to die at Oxford in July. Spelman reminded Potts how, when Lord Mowbray had attempted to implement the Commission of Array, he 'did really endeavour the surcease of it, as persuaded that the raising force, by either the one side or the other, would bring the war into the county, which (God is my witness) I have to my understanding and power faithfully sought and still shall seek to divert; and were that endeavour as well pursued on the one side as I persuade myself it has been and yet is on the other I am confident our county . . . would have enjoyed . . . immunity from the common calamity . . . Sir it was and (I am persuaded) yet is your own judgement also. But to deal faithfully with you, Sir, how much soever your intention is the contrary, it is too much feared that the courses that are set on foot will inevitably bring the war upon us'.[126] While Spelman was writing his powerful appeal, other disillusioned members of the Royalist group were contemplating active resistance to Parliament: meetings were held 'under pretence of hunting' where efforts were made to send supplies to the King and there was talk of a rising.[127]

The response of the members of the Parliamentary committee to this burgeoning Royalist activism was not uniform. Sir John Potts could not appreciate that every new demand upon the county, however laxly enforced, could only further alienate the Royalists. Reflecting on the risks that he had taken to accommodate Royalist sensibilities, even risking Parliamentary censure for acting with insufficient zeal, he could see in the new militancy only the malice and ingratitude of the malignants, who 'care not to fire their own houses, soe as they may borne their neighbours'. But Sir John Holland was more in tune with the sentiments of Spelman and his friends, and recognized that only a national pacification could prevent an explosion in the county. On 17 January Holland presented a petition to the Commons from Norfolk, appealing for the immediate commencement of negotiations for a settlement; a similar document was presented to the King. The signatories stressed the 'universall desolution' which would be the product of conflict, and pleaded 'oh lett the miserable spectacle of a German devestation perswade you to decline those perilous casualties which may result from a civill warre'. On 10 February, during debate on the Oxford negotiations, Holland 'shewed that unlesse wee did procede with this treaty, it would bee occassion of much discontent in . . . [Norfolk] . . . which had long and earnestly desired for peace'.[128]

Other members of the Norfolk committee were even more sympathetic to the Royalists' predicament than was Holland, and objected to the Parliamentary military preparations in the shire. By February Sir Thomas Richardson, Sir Robert de Grey and Sir

William Paston, three of the eleven members of the committee who had served in the autumn, had withdrawn. In the next month Richardson was involved in the insurrection at Heigham, and de Grey's arrest was ordered; in June the latter was sequestered for reading an anti-Parliamentary manifesto to a trained-band company, causing it to mutiny. In the spring Sir William Paston, who in May 1642 had 'left Norfolk to avoid imployment' and sought the advice of the best lawyers in London on the legal issues raised by the conflict, but had served on the committee from September to December, fled to Rotterdam where he was accused of 'doing ill offices against the Parliament'.[129]

The Formation of the Association

The event which finally shattered the uneasy peace in Norfolk, which both the Parliamentary committee and Royalists like Spelman had sought to maintain with such tenacity, was the local implementation of the Ordinance establishing the Eastern Association in March. This legislation, viewed by Kingston as the product and symbol of 'the one great historic unity'[130] of the civil war, in fact owed more to the ideals of politicians at Westminster than to the initiative of Parliament's representatives in the eastern counties. The latter certainly contemplated some formalized inter-county co-operation, but the Ordinance passed on 20 December embodied a number of contentious provisions which were not altogether welcome to the Parliamentary committees in East Anglia. This can best be illustrated by consideration of the two disparate notions of the purpose of association co-existing in the autumn of 1642.

In one sense an association was simply a military alliance between a block of counties. As early as July 1642 Parliament had recognized that co-operation between the Deputy-Lieutenants of adjacent counties was desirable, and voted that any county might appeal to its neighbors for aid in the event of Royalist attack.[131] In late August, perhaps inspired by the Royalist association of the northern counties,[132] the Houses began to include a clause in the formal instructions issued to their committees in the counties empowering them, if they wished, 'to join in Association with the adjacent counties, for the mutual defence each of other county'.[133] As military activity stepped-up, Parliament sought to encourage the formation of associations among counties threatened by the King's army, and, in late October, abandoned their previous reliance upon co-operation undertaken by voluntary local effort; specified counties were combined for military purposes by Parliamentary fiat. This growth of central interference and increased formalization culminated in the passage of the Ordinance of 15 December for the association of eight midland counties; the legislation established a central com-

mittee of representatives from the shires empowered to levy forces
to be commanded by Lord Grey of Groby.[134]

But in the autumn of 1642 there was another idea of the form and
purpose of association co-existing in the Commons with the more
prosaic notion of a military alliance of certain counties. For Pym and
his allies the ideal association would parallel the Scottish National
Covenant. In late October Pym, 'with very great vehemence and
passion', moved that Parliament establish a national 'covenant or
association which all might enter into' with the intention of 'linking
ourselves together in a more firme bond and union'. The Houses
were persuaded to issue a declaration of their intention to publish
for general subscription an oath of association whose signatories
would 'covenant with God' to defend 'his truth . . . with the hazard
of our lives against the King's army'. However, thereafter enthusiasm
waned, and the oath was never forthcoming. But the national
Association, Protestation or Covenant remained a favored project
with Pym, and also received powerful backing from the radicals in
the City of London, who wanted an agreement among men zealous
for the cause to defend to the death their religion and liberty. Such
an association would also be a shibboleth, weeding out the malignant
goats from the pro-Parliamentary sheep; the 'sifting, distinguishing'
oath should be drawn in terms 'not subject to equivocation', forcing
men to declare themselves 'who are for us and who are against
us'.[135]

Of these two ideas of the function of an association, it was the
former, that of a defensive alliance, which had local support in East
Anglia. The first indication that some of the Parliamentary authorities
in the region were contemplating the establishment of military co-
operation on their own initiative occurs in late October, when the
Norfolk committee agreed that the county 'shall associate themselves with the countyes of Suffolk and Cambridgeshire for mutual
defence of one another, in such manner as shall be thought fittest
for the common safety'. The Deputy-Lieutenants of these three
counties had already been instructed to act in common for a number
of limited military purposes, such as the guarding of passages over
the Ouse, and they probably sought to extend such co-operation.[136]
A week after the Norfolk committee's vote to establish an Association, they and the Suffolk authorities consulted to establish common
policy for the security of Flegg, Lothingland and Great Yarmouth;
their agreement was described by the town as a product of the
'Association . . . for mutuall defence each to other'.[137] 'Mutuall
defence': the local authorities involved upon their own initiative in
the establishment of an Association certainly viewed its essential
function as a defensive alliance. It is highly unlikely that the Norfolk
committee, whose policy was one of moderation and conciliation,

contemplated the deliberately divisive Covenant-Shibboleth proposed by the radicals in Parliament and city. After the agreement for the defense of Yarmouth the proposed local Association lay dormant until the end of November, when the committees received a report from Cambridge of a plot whereby the cavaliers would raid the eastern counties, and would be supported by a rising of the indigenous papists. This revived interest in the proposed Association, and the county committees, after mutual discussion, approached Parliament for legislative assistance in the formation of the alliance. Every indication suggests that the counties hoped to establish a defensively-oriented military union. The report of the deliberations of the Suffolk committee was sent to the Houses by the arch-moderate, Sir Robert Crane, and even the radical Puritan, Samuel Duncon, who wrote from Ipswich to 'those who God have caused their spirits to be for him' at Colchester suggesting an Association, visualized it only as a military alliance.[138]

But Parliament had taken the initiative before the receipt of the letters from the local committees. Upon receiving the report of the threatened danger from Cambridge the Commons set up a committee to 'consider an Association' of Norfolk, Suffolk and Essex. Two days later, on 28 November, the committee reported to the House with a draft Ordinance for the conjunction of the three counties, and Cambridge and Hertfordshire, which had previously contemplated a military union with some south midland counties.[139] The Earl of Warwick was appointed to command the united forces of the five counties. No action was taken on this proposal for a fortnight, perhaps because of the difficulties into which the Ordinance for the Midland Association had run in the upper House concerning the respective jurisdictions of the Lords Lieutenant of the shires and the commander of the Association.[140] However, on 10 December the Ordinance was re-introduced, and, with some additions made in the following week, finally passed the Lords on the 20th. In the final version Lord Grey of Warke replaced Warwick as commander-in-chief, as the latter's involvement with the navy disenabled him from undertaking the office.[141]

When the committee first reported to the Commons on 28 November, the moderate Sir Simonds D'Ewes was horrified. Their proposals, 'full of dangerous consequences', could only result in 'the whole kingdome' being 'sett in combustion'. His fears were almost certainly based upon the section in the legislation which insisted upon individual subscription to an oath of Association:[142] the 'fierie spirits' who dominated the drafting committee had produced a strange hybrid, combining the counties' request for a defensive military alliance with a watered-down version of Pym's projected Covenant. In its final form the Ordinance empowered the local committees to summon all the inhabitants of their county, and to require them to take an 'oath of Association' in which they bound themselves to 'maintain and defend, with our lives, powers and estates, the peace of the said counties under the command of such person as . . . hath . . . by the authority of both houses . . . the command in chief', and to subscribe what arms or money they would contribute to the defense of the Association. The authorities were also instructed to raise money for the purchase of munitions and the building of fortifications by a compulsory rate. Finally it was ordered that those who had previously refused to contribute upon the Propositions, or to accept the Militia Ordinance, or who now refused to pay the tax were to be disarmed and their weapons and horses employed for the defense of the Association.[143]

That this legislation was not that which had been requested by some of the local committees in late November is apparent from their reluctance to execute it. Only the Essex M.P.s and Deputy-Lieutenants began soliciting subscriptions to the oath of Association at divisional meetings shortly after the passage of the legislation, meeting some resistance from those who had organized the petition for peace.[144] At the end of January the Hertfordshire committee, who had used their formal conjunction with the eastern counties as an excuse to avoid sending previously agreed assistance to the Buckinghamshire Parliamentarians who were suffering heavily from the raids of Royalist forces based on Oxford,[145] called a meeting of the local gentry to discuss the implementation of the Association. However, after a powerful speech questioning the legality of the Ordinance by the recorder of Hertford, they suspended further action until late February.[146] Although the Norfolk committee, prompted by the central authorities, agreed in principle on 11 January to execute the Ordinance, and their Suffolk counterparts expressed their readiness to act if the local M.P.s would come into the county to assist them,[147] in both shires and in Cambridge, those which had originally contemplated military co-operation in October, nothing was done until after the Bury conference of 9 February, when representatives of the counties agreed to the general implementation of the Ordinance throughout East Anglia.

The initiative for the crucial meeting at Bury came from two sources simultaneously. As has been shown, in Norfolk the Royalist group chafed under the Parliamentary yoke as further demands were made on their consciences with the development of the war. Sir John Potts, disturbed by their assemblies and by rumors of their preparations for an armed rising, increasingly felt that there were 'noe meanes of safety unless the countryes can be united'. On 26 January, on behalf of the Norfolk committee, he wrote to the Deputy-Lieutenants of Suffolk and Cambridgeshire, expressing his anxieties and inquiring 'what you doe in the business of Ascotiacion or what other cours you take for your own safety . . . that wee may proceed joinetly'. On the same day Cromwell, who had recently arrived in Cambridge with a small force raised in London, and the local committee wrote to Norfolk and Suffolk proposing a meeting at Mildenhall to discuss common action. Their request was backed by 'certain intelligence' confirming Potts's worst fears: the Norfolk papists were about to rise, and would be supported by Prince Rupert, perhaps by the King himself.[148]

The product of this flurry of correspondence was the Bury meeting of 9 February, attended by eleven representatives from Suffolk and seven each from Cambridge and Norfolk: no Hertfordshire deputation attended, and Essex was only represented because Lord Grey of Warke sent two Deputy-Lieutenants from that county to inform the others 'how far that businesse is advanced in Essex, and to receyve your resolutions therein'.[149] Those present agreed to 'doe our utmost indeavours, by assemblinge the inhabitants of our severall countyes respectively and by our own example and best persuasions, to further the effectuall association for the peace of the . . . countyes'. Significantly the signatories of this declaration of intent deliberately did not bind themselves to observe the House's instructions, or to employ its formal oath of Association: draft declarations to that effect were rejected.[150] And, typically, it was the Norfolk committee who used this loophole to mitigate some of the more rigorous features of the legislation. At a county meeting on 16 February for discussion of the Bury conference the committee gave the gentry the option of how forces should be raised, and at least one of the hundreds, that of North Erpingham, chose to 'afford their assistance by way of a rate' rather than by seeking personal subscriptions to the oath and donations of arms or money. An impersonal general levy seemed preferable to the individual commitment required by the Parliamentary oath and instructions.[151]

But with the acceptance, however qualified, of the Ordinance of Association by the Norfolk committee the uneasy peace in the county could not survive. At the end of February Lord Grey of Warke came to Norwich armed with his commission of Major-General of the Eastern Association from the Lord General, which extended the powers given him by the Parliamentary Ordinance, in particular instructing him to use the troops to be raised by the Association outside its borders.[152] Grey had no time for the Norfolk committee's habits of compromise and moderation. He demanded that forces be raised immediately, and ordered the arrest and seizure of the arms of all who had refused to contribute upon the Propositions, observe the Militia Ordinance or enter the Association. And, on 2 March when he left Norwich, Grey seized the mayor, whose anti-Parliamentary sympathies had already come to the attention of the Commons.[153] The next day Sir John Potts sadly prepared to leave Norfolk, 'seing I canot doe the service heer which was my aime, to preserve the country in peace'.[154]

Potts's forebodings were soon proved correct. Within a couple of days a group of citizens and country gentry, including Sir Thomas Richardson, a member of the local committee from its inception until February, 'stood upon their defence' at Heigham Hall, and sought assistance from other local gentlemen until flushed out by the Norwich volunteers. Perhaps because of this indication of the militancy of the Royalist element Cromwell and his troops were sent to Norwich, where on 13 March they were warned of a gathering of Norfolk and Suffolk Royalists at Lowestoft: on the 14th they seized the port and arrested the gentry involved. From Lowestoft Cromwell rode to Lynn on receipt of intelligence of unrest in the town; the presence of his troops temporarily overawed the Royalists, but the town was to remain a center of disaffection until August, when it finally declared for the King.[155]

So East Anglia, too, exhibits Professor Everitt's 'confused, mercurial' reactions to the civil war. In no county was the outbreak of hostilities greeted by the total and unqualified adherence to the Parliamentary cause of previous historiography. In some there was a substantial Royalist group, and the threat which they posed to Parliament's control had to be suppressed by the intervention of forces raised outside the county – the London-based troops that secured Hertford-shire and Cambridgeshire, Cromwell's men who pacified Norfolk. In other counties such Royalist activity was virtually non-existent, but in all there was a large group of 'moderates'. Men who found it impossible to identify openly with either of the belligerents, and who sought to avoid the choice of allegiance forced upon them; men who feared the possible consequences of the development of the war – social upheaval, religious and political revolution, or, more mundane, the dislocation of the economy and the growing charge on their own estates – and worked to secure a compromise peace. Some eventually found that their consciences would not allow them to submit to ever-increasing Parliamentary demands, and, like Sir Benjamin Ayloffe, they engaged in futile gestures of protest, or, like many Norfolk gentlemen,[156] fled to the continent. But most tem-porized, reluctantly submitting to Parliament's authority.

For some inhabitants of the region, who thoroughly approved of Parliament's policies, the war was welcome. Puritan ministers like William Bridge, who adjured the Norwich and Yarmouth volunteers 'what great matter is it to dye for your God, a little before your time; who would live when Religion is dead?'; townsmen like those who organized the Hertford volunteers, risking the scorn and petty harassment of the local J.P.s, or William Welbore the Cambridge draper, who prayed that no peace would be concluded until 'prelacy [is] rooted out . . . and those wholsesome lawes the which the Lord hath invested this Kingdome with may bee putt in execution'; village Hampdens like Goodman Collins of Bradwell who came into conflict with both parson and squire in his zealous adherence to the cause.[157] But in Essex alone did such enthusiasts predominate among the group of local gentlemen chosen by Parliament to enforce their policies in the shires. In Cambridgeshire, Hertfordshire and Suffolk the hesitancy of the bulk of the gentry appears in their procrastination in the establishment of a Parliamentary administration. In the first two this post-dated the military seizure of the county, and in Suffolk was undertaken *faute de mieux*, when, after the Stour valley riots, the gentry recognized the need for the establishment of some authority armed with military force to control the mob. In Norfolk a nominally Parliamentarian administration was only established in September, and then its major concern was not the implementation of central legislation, but the maintenance of the 'peace of the country'.

Wide divergences of experience among the counties in 1642 re-inforce the argument of the first chapter that the Association did not owe its subsequent military successes to the social, political or religious homogeneity of the region. Indeed, as has been shown, the Association Ordinance of 20 December owed more to the ideals of politicians in London than to the authorities in East Anglia, some of whom certainly envisioned a much more limited, defensively-oriented co-operation.

This introduces a major theme of the next chapters. In 1643 and 1644 the war-party at Westminster were to pile an ever-increasing fiscal burden and widening military responsibilities upon the Association, yet Parliament's local agencies were in many cases not wholly in sympathy with those measures and viewed the Association as essentially a defensive union. Even in Essex, where the committee was a more enthusiastic vehicle of Parliamentary policy, many of the inhabitants, those who had signed the petition for peace and those who had been reluctant to serve other than in the immediate defense of their country in November, had demonstrated their reluctance to support measures designed to promote an aggressive war. How was Parliament able to insist upon the execution of its policies by its local agents, and how could they implement those measures in the face of popular resentment?

Local autonomy and military weakness: the Association under Lord Grey of Warke, January–July 1643

On 9 February 1643 the local rulers of the five counties had finally agreed to implement the Parliamentary legislation, passed two months earlier, establishing the Eastern Association. Their previous reluctance to commit themselves, stemming from the fear that the compulsory Oath of Association would provoke the quiescent Royalists of the region to revolt, had been overcome by the threat of Royalist invasion and the need to organize local defense. But the Association, as conceived by its formulators at Westminster, was designed to do more than merely secure the territorial integrity of East Anglia. In drafting the Ordinance Corbett and his fellow 'fierie spirits' had not specifically stated whether the troops raised by virtue of the legislation could be employed outside the borders of the constituent counties. The ambiguity was resolved in the commission and instructions issued to Lord Grey of Warke, the Major-General of the Association, in February: Grey was ordered to 'drawe downe what strength volluntiers or other forces can be raised in the Association to . . . Cambridge', and then to march those troops to reinforce the main Parliamentary field army in the Thames valley. Accordingly, after the suppression of the Norfolk insurgents, Grey instructed all the available military units in the eastern counties to rendezvous at the university town, and the bulk of this force, commanded by Grey himself, prepared to join the Earl of Essex. Only a small detachment under Cromwell was retained to defend the northern and north-western flanks of the Associated counties.[1]

In the following chapter the largely undistinguished performance of both these brigades in the following four months will be described and analyzed. It will be shown that, while many of the military weaknesses were common to all the Parliamentary armies in the early stages of the war, others were peculiar to the Associated counties, and were a product of the tension between the localist, defensive ideals of the governors of the constituent counties and the nationally oriented policies of the majority at Westminster apparent at the inception of the Association.

Grey's detachment, some 5000 horse and foot, left Cambridge on 7 April and joined Essex at the siege of Reading twelve days later.

On their march they were reinforced by some infantry from the county of Essex, a body contemptuously dismissed by the Royalists as 'all raw inexperienced men, and very few of them armed'. The first part of the comment was borne out by the initial combat experience of Grey's division; a night sally by the besieged sent the Association's 'freshwater soldiers' scuttling from their positions, and they had to be reinforced by some of the Lord General's veterans.[2]

Thereafter, with the exception of a Hertfordshire regiment which garrisoned Aylesbury,[3] Lord Grey's force served as a brigade in Essex's army until July and, in conjunction with that army, registered not a single success in this period with the exception of the capture of Reading. And, like the other units in Essex's army, the military effectiveness of Grey's brigade sank rapidly. The officers had little authority or reputation among the men, and while the senior commanders were lax or refused to obey Grey's orders, their juniors squabbled with one another, connived at false musters and insulted the paymasters. The infantry were mutinous, and sickness and an extremely high incidence of desertion thinned the ranks dramatically.[4] As early as 16 June one foot company, supposedly 100 strong, could muster only 38 men; a month later Sir Thomas Barrington's Essex regiment, which should have contained over 1000 men, was only 200 strong, and Barrington wrote to the Lord General requesting that the three infantry regiments from the county be combined into one. This cannibalization would 'disburden us of that great disbursement which wee are compelled to make unto those many . . . officers that are in pay, in comparison of that number of common men now growen so small'.[5] The cavalry in Grey's brigade, normally composed of men of higher social status than the foot and more amenable to discipline, was in little better condition than the infantry. Accusations of plundering the countryside were leveled against both the Norfolk cavalrymen and Sir Thomas Martyn's Cambridgeshire troop, while deserters from the latter constantly trickled back into their home county, a process which culminated in the mass exodus of twenty-nine troopers.[6]

The force which remained in Cambridge under Cromwell after the April division of the Association's army was to be far more productively employed than that marched to Reading by Lord Grey. Yet Cromwell's achievement in this period cannot be regarded as an unqualified success. The historian's perspective of Oliver's early military career is too frequently warped by hindsight, and the genesis of future greatness seen in every incident.[7] In consequence disproportionate emphasis has been placed on individual victories, but the limited strategic achievement neglected. However, one major success was recorded: the defense of the territorial integrity of the Association.

In early February Cromwell had recognized the need for the

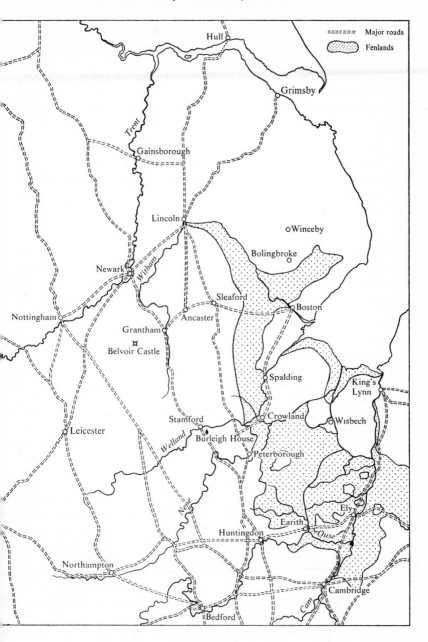

Map 2   The 1643 campaigns

defense of certain 'passages' into the Association, and with the removal of Grey's force from Cambridge the securing of these strong points became a task of critical importance, given the meteoric success of the Newark Royalists in late March and early April. Capitalizing on the growing disillusionment of the Lincolnshire Parliamentarians, the Newarkers undertook a series of successful raids into that county; on 11 April they emphasized their superiority at the battle of Ancaster Heath, and in consequence of their victory were able to occupy Grantham, Stamford and Peterborough, and plunder the adjacent parts of Northamptonshire.[8] In response to this threat Cromwell determined to hold the strong natural frontier to the Association formed by the Ouse. He sought subscriptions from the constituent counties for the fortification of a number of bridges over the river on 7 April, and within a few days moved his own troops to Huntingdon and endeavored to co-operate with the Parliamentary leaders in Bedfordshire.[9] In addition, Cromwell ordered a company of dragoons to occupy Wisbech, where they were soon joined by a Norfolk infantry regiment under Sir Miles Hobart. The occupation of Wisbech secured the key to the Association's strong natural frontier to the north, the maze of rivers, fen and marsh along the coasts of the Wash, and Hobart's forces were also instructed to 'maintaine guard' over the fenland town of Crowland whose inhabitants, inspired by their martial minister, had declared for the King and were raiding the surrounding countryside from their fastness in the marshes.[10]

For two weeks after the occupation of the strong points on the Ouse frontier the Association's forces stood on the defensive; Cromwell used his stay in Huntingdon to suppress local Royalists, gather money and men, and drill and discipline his troops.[11] But when events in the west midlands forced the Newarkers to withdraw from their advanced positions in Lincolnshire, Cromwell moved out to fill the vacuum. About 22 April he occupied Peterborough, then, joining up with Hobart's Wisbech detachment, attacked Crowland on the 25th. The immense natural strength of the town's position enabled its defenders to repel the initial assault, but it succumbed three days later after a prolonged bombardment.[12] The occupation of Crowland and Peterborough enabled the Association to use the River Nene as its northern boundary; Cromwell believed that this frontier was virtually impregnable – 'two or three hundred men in those parts are enough' – and his opinion was verified by the ease with which Colonel Palgrave was able to repulse an attack on Peterborough in July.[13]

Whilst Cromwell's advance to the Nene gave the Association a greater measure of security from an assault by the Newark Royalists, it was still endangered by threats of internal revolts. At Cambridge the garrison and newly built fortifications represented both a second line of defense against a Royalist invasion, and a means to overawe the 'multitude of malignants', chiefly scholars, in the town.[14] But the most vulnerable area was the Isle of Ely. Its naturally strong defensive position meant that if it were lost to the enemy it would become 'a stronghold like Dunkirk to plunder all our Countys'. The strength of pro-Royalist sentiment in the Isle had been very apparent in 1642, and an uprising, which had been threatening for some months, broke out in May 1643. Troops from Cambridge eventually suppressed the insurgents, and the scare resulted in permanent garrisons being established at Wisbech, Ely and Earith.[15] There were further minor disturbances on the Isle in the summer, and the loyalty of the majority of the local gentry and trained bands was considered doubtful, but the presence of the garrisons prevented the outbreak of any serious insurrection.[16]

Cromwell's success in securing the Nene frontier was not matched by his achievement in the next three months. Following the capture of Crowland the Lincolnshire Parliamentarians sought his assistance, and their appeals were soon reinforced by instructions from the Lord General that the commanders in the east midlands should join forces and intercept the convoy of ammunition which the Queen had dispatched from the north to Oxford.[17] But the localism of the respective commanders militated against co-operation. While Cromwell blamed Lord Grey of Groby's refusal to withdraw his troops from Leicester for the failure of the proposed combined action, the Lincolnshire committee thought him as remiss. On 5 May they wrote, 'There hath not at any time this three weeks passed one day that we have not writt to Colonel Cromwell, the Norfolk gentlemen and my Lord Grey to appoint a place of meeting, and we would march to them wheresoever it were; their answer alwayes was they would meet, but somthing of importance was first to be done in those countries they were then in.' In Cromwell's case the 'somthing of importance' appears to have been the raising of money and suppression of potential Royalists in Huntingdonshire and Northamptonshire.[18] Eventually Cromwell and the Lincolnshire forces rendezvoused at Sleaford on 9 May, but this was too late to prevent the munitions convoy getting through to Oxford or the plundering of Leicestershire and Northamptonshire by its covering force. This was a major failure, for which the partial success of the conjoint force at the skirmish near Grantham on 13 May was a poor substitute. The Parliamentarians were unable to pursue their advantage, and retired to Lincoln.[19]

On 24 May another attempt at combined action was begun. Cromwell and forces from Lincoln, Leicester and Derby rendezvoused at Nottingham with the intention of marching into Yorkshire to assist Lord Fairfax follow up his victory at Wakefield.[20] Again the operation was abortive. On 2 June the commanders of the united force wrote that they had learned that Newcastle's army was so weak that their assistance in Yorkshire was no longer required. The letter infuriated Fairfax, whose weakness had prevented him from consolidating his victory; he demanded that the forces at Nottingham join him, or else Newcastle would quickly overwhelm his small army. Moreover, a general rendezvous in Yorkshire was essential if the Queen, who was preparing to march to Oxford with a further convoy of munitions, was to be halted. But localism triumphed. The commanders at Nottingham refused to assist Fairfax, fearing that their marching north would enable the garrison of Newark, which, in conjunction with the Royalists of Gainsborough, had launched a series of raids into Lincolnshire, to gain complete control of the east midlands.[21]

In June the combined forces remained based on Nottingham, instructed to intercept the Queen's new convoy, and to prepare to launch a diversionary raid on Oxford should the Lord General's army move south. Again they failed, their efforts weakened by the dissensions which rent the high command.[22] The indiscipline of the Lincolnshire troops, and a growing suspicion that their commander, John Hotham, was in communication with the enemy, led to violent quarrels between the commanders; Hotham and Cromwell were 'ready to cut each other's throats' and their respective forces nearly came to blows. Eventually the Lord General, persuaded of the gravity of the situation by Cromwell and Lord Grey, sent the Scottish professional soldier, Sir John Meldrum, with orders to arrest Hotham and to take command of the forces at Nottingham. Hotham was imprisoned, but escaped to Lincoln protesting his innocence; he was eventually re-arrested at Hull as he tried to arrange the surrender of that town, and of Lincoln, to the Royalists.[23]

This incident smashed the combined force at Nottingham. The Lincolnshire troops had ridden off with Hotham upon his escape, and other contingents also returned to their bases. Meldrum could do no more than shadow the Queen's convoy into Warwickshire when it left Newark, and the munitions reached Oxford safely.[24] Essex then ordered Meldrum and the remaining forces at Nottingham to link up with him in an assault on Oxford to prevent the King capitalizing on the defeat of Waller at Roundway Down. But this plan was equally abortive. Lord Willoughby's seizure of Gainsborough, and the need for his immediate reinforcement if the strongpoint was to be held, and the contemporary capture of Stamford and assault on Peterborough by the cavaliers from Newark and Belvoir, forced Meldrum and Cromwell to pull back into Lincolnshire.[25]

Cromwell's major success in this period was the defense of the territorial integrity of the Association, and the consolidation of its naturally strong northern frontier. But his attempts to participate in a wider strategy failed: both of the Queen's convoys of munitions reached Oxford without interruption, Fairfax received no assistance, the combined forces at Nottingham did not reinforce Essex. In part these disappointments were caused by personal failings – the pusillanimity or sheer treachery of other local commanders. But equally material were weaknesses in the organization of Cromwell's forces.

The symptoms of this weakness, so apparent in Grey's brigade stagnating with the Lord General's army in the Thames valley, were less obvious in Cromwell's command. Morale in his own cavalry regiment, constantly active and zealously disciplined,[26] appears to have been high; his men were already 'a lovely company', although desertion was not unknown and some troops were 'very weake' at the skirmish near Grantham.[27] But the behavior of the foot and dragoon companies at Cambridge and of the Norfolk infantry regiments was less impressive. Desertion was rife in April, and in late May the foot operating with Cromwell were mutinous; two months later they were 'in a disorder . . . and ready to . . . disband'. At this time Captain Pell of Hobart's infantry cheerfully informed his father that the behavior of his company was no worse than that of the rest of the regiment – 'very much disorderly'. The Lieutenant Colonel of Palgrave's Norfolk infantry, in garrison at Wisbech, wrote of his soldiers' 'doinge what they list, haveing the power in theyre owne handes', while the Governor of the Isle of Ely complained that the well-affected inhabitants of Wisbech 'doe thinke them selves in lesse danger without them, then with them'.[28]

It was apparent to both Grey and Cromwell that the fundamental cause of the poor discipline and the rapidly thinning ranks of their forces was financial. The Treasurers operating with the Essex regiments in Grey's brigade wrote desperately to the county committee for money, while the soldiers became increasingly unsympathetic with their inability to pay them. One of the Treasurers wrote, 'they presse me intollerable for money and my Lord Grey is at me every daye': some infuriated officers wrote of him, 'wee have waited friday, saturday, moone-day, tuesday, wednesday upon Mr Treasurer Tailor to conveigh monies to the Army . . . wee wonder at his delays considering the necessity of the Regiment. This day wee advanced towards the Army, being tyred with waiting upon an inconstant man to no purpose'.[29] The senior officers were forced to borrow from the Earl of Essex, while a regimental minister raised money for the soldiers upon the security of his property and came close to having the latter seized in default of repayment. The troops, their pay substantially in arrear, threatened to pawn their weapons.[30] In the north-west the financial situation was little better – indeed, one of the first orders of the Cambridge Committee was designed to prevent the sale of powder and arms by the soldiers. In March Cromwell, informing the committee of Suffolk that their troop commander 'hath not wherewith to pay a troop one day', apologized that 'I should so often trouble you about the business of money: it's no pleasant subject to be too frequent upon'. But for the next five months his correspondence is filled with similar pleas for the pay of the units serving with him. In June one of the Cambridge Committee wrote that Cromwell was 'not past halfe for money, and importuning us dayly for supplies both of men and mony'. In the next month the Committee were unable to meet either the pay of Cromwell's troops, or the bills for the accommodation in Cambridge of recruits they were sending him; at Nottingham Cromwell could only quell a threatened mutiny by promising the immediate provision of pay, and then had to raise the money by borrowing from the leading merchants of the town. In the same period Sir John Palgrave was forced to subsidize his indisciplined Norfolk foot regiment from his own pocket, while, from March 1643, when they were embodied, until the end of July, Whalley's troop received approximately sixty-six days' pay for one hundred fifty-three days' service.[31]

To understand this history of endemic financial crisis, it is necessary to examine the process whereby the forces that served with Grey and Cromwell were raised, and the provision made for their payment.

The initial material base for the army of the Eastern Association was provided by the Parliamentary Declaration and Instructions of 20 December. The M.P.s, Deputy-Lieutenants and commissioners for the Propositions were to organize meetings of the 'gentlemen, freeholders and other inhabitants' in their counties, and, having apprised them of the 'imminent danger' which overshadowed the realm 'by the wicked advise and attempts and conspiracies of Papists and other persons now about his Majestie', were to invite them to join in the Oath of Association, and to declare what horse or foot soldiers they would equip and maintain for the defense of the constituent counties.[32]

At the Bury conference of 9 February the assembled representatives of the eastern counties agreed that these Instructions should be put in execution throughout the region. In both Essex, where the Oath of Association had been promulgated before the Bury conference, and Suffolk, the local M.P.s came down from Westminster and joined the Deputy-Lieutenants and committees at a series of exhortatory meetings.[33] Some subscriptions were taken at these general assemblies, but most at subsequent village meetings, where the wealthy well-affected would agree to provide the equipment for a volunteer soldier and his pay for a specified period, while their poorer or less enthusiastic neighbors might club together to buy equipment, or contribute smaller sums to make up the pay. There were some local variations upon this scheme: in Norfolk the representatives of some Hundreds chose to impose a rate on all property owners, rather than seek individual subscriptions.[34]

To secure subscriptions was one thing, the transmutation of those promissory notes into troops and companies quite another. Some subscribers deliberately endeavored to avoid fulfilling the commitments they had undertaken, but even the most well-affected might find that providing arms and persuading men to serve in them could present time-consuming difficulties. In the four Suffolk villages for which subscription lists survive, those who agreed to contribute managed to find an adequate number of their poor neighbors or servants willing to volunteer, but the corporation of Yarmouth were less fortunate; on being informed by Lord Grey that eighty dragoons would be an appropriate contribution they sent a deputation to inform him that they would be unable to raise a sufficient number of men as the bulk of the town's inhabitants were fishermen, and at sea.[35] When Grey ordered all available units to rendezvous at Cambridge in late March, a large proportion of the subscribed 'associated' forces had not been mobilized.

But Grey had other sources of manpower to meet this deficiency. First, he could call upon the services of a number of companies which had been embodied prior to the execution of the Declaration and Instructions for the Association. For example, Suffolk had raised a cavalry troop in November 1642 which they intended to employ 'for the safety of the Countye', meeting the cost of its equipment and pay from the proportion of the receipts upon the Propositions allocated for local defense by the Commons. This troop, and other units which had been raised in similar circumstances, joined Grey, who ordered that they were to be maintained in future from money subscribed 'according to the Association'.[36] Secondly, Grey, as he was empowered by his commission from the Lord General, summoned some contingents from the trained bands of the constituent counties to the rendezvous. This employment of local militia units was regarded as a temporary expedient; they were to be replaced as 'associated' forces became available. Indeed, those men from the Essex trained-band who had not already deserted, were withdrawn from front-line duty in mid-May, before the 'associated' companies which were to replace them were fully mobilized. Their early return was probably related to a financial difficulty that their employment had caused: trained-band soldiers were given a shilling a day during their peace-time drills and maneuvers, but daily pay in Parliament's army was only 8d; when the Essex militiamen learned that they were to be paid at the lower rate, they became 'mutinous' and threatened 'to stay no longer'.[37]

In addition to the 'associated' forces, themselves an amalgam of previously embodied troops and men raised in accordance with the terms of the Declaration and Instructions of 20 December and the temporarily employed trained-band detachments, the army of the Eastern Association in the spring of 1643 also contained the five troops of Cromwell's regiment.[38] Cromwell's own troop was embodied in London in the autumn of 1642, the cost being met by the central Parliamentary treasury, but the other four were raised between February and April 1643 – Whalley's in Suffolk, those of Disborough, Oliver Cromwell junior and the younger Walton in Cambridgeshire and Huntingdon. The treasuries of these two counties bore some of the cost of raising and equipping these troops, while additional horses and money were subscribed in those areas where Cromwell was operating, either by the well-affected, or those hoping to buy favor and protection – men like Sir John Wentworth, who had been involved in the Lowestoft rising and donated £1000 to have his offense overlooked.[39]

The pay of the 'associated' forces, with the exception of those from Hertfordshire,[40] was to be raised by voluntary subscriptions from those who had met the initial cost of equipping the men. Parliament's reliance on voluntary contribution for the raising and maintenance of its armies in the early months of the war, was a product of the sanguine belief that the conflict could be concluded swiftly.[41] It threw the burden of paying for the war largely on to the shoulders of the well-affected, and became increasingly unrealistic as the fighting dragged on. It was the insufficiency of this system which occasioned the difficulties faced by the Association's forces in the spring of 1643.

In March, when subscriptions were being solicited in the localities, Lord Grey had endeavored to introduce an element of compulsion into the voluntary scheme established by the Parliamentary Declaration and Instructions. He informed certain communities of the number of men he thought would be appropriate for them to raise, while the deputies whom he employed to disarm and arrest those who refused to 'enter into the Association', were instructed to interpret this clause to include those who had not made a contribution commensurate with their wealth.[42] But a comparison of the surviving Association subscription lists with tax data suggests that many of the wealthiest members of the communities were not making the largest contributions, and in Essex many who, in the first flush of enthusiasm or intimidated by Grey's warrants, had agreed to equip a volunteer or provide money, avoided fulfilling their commitments; a number of Essex soldiers left the front and returned to their villages hoping to persuade the recalcitrant to produce the promised pay.[43] The obvious inequities of the system led to the disillusionment of the well-affected; one of Sir Thomas Barrington's correspondents wrote to the Essex M.P. bewailing that the 'honest men . . . on whom the burden hath for the most part lyen', were ruining themselves while 'others, men of malignant dispositions . . . doing in noe measure answereable to their estates . . . laugh at their forwardnes'. The 'well-affected' had become 'wearie still to contribute . . . when the ill affected look with derision upon them'.[44]

In May 1643 the county of Essex faced a fiscal crisis which reveals the extent to which deliberate evasion by the malignant and the consequent disillusionment of the well-affected had undermined the system of voluntary subscription. On 19 May some Essex M.P.s and committeemen in London, to prevent the disbanding of their mutinous forces under Lord Grey, issued warrants for the 'Associators' to provide a third month's pay, of which they promised eventual repayment. But their colleague, Sir Thomas Barrington, who had been sent into the county to persuade the well-affected to forward a second month's pay to the troops three weeks previously, immediately protested; 'expect not that I should soe suddenly importune the Country for that which I have soe lately prevailed in soe much beyond my expectation'. They should remember how reluctant the subscribers had been to provide a second month's pay. He was unwilling to put the warrant into execution, unless some other M.P.s would come into the county 'with a new supply of reasons to winne the well-affected unto it', and would much prefer to borrow the money on his own credit than squeeze Parliament's friends any further. His London correspondents bowed to his knowledge of local sentiment, agreeing that it would be imprudent 'when a free horse hath gone as far as he is able at last to spurr out his gutts', and £1000 was borrowed in London to pay the forces.[45] Similar difficulties attended the collection of the third month's pay for the Cambridgeshire cavalry, and the Lord General had to pay the men from his own Treasury, although in this case the subscribers' revolt was enhanced by their suspicion that the troop captain was embezzling the money.[46]

Until May the provision made for the pay of Cromwell's regiment was even more tenuous than that of the forces raised and supported by the subscribers to the Association. Cromwell was dependent for the maintenance of his troops upon the gifts which could be entreated or extorted from the inhabitants of the areas where his force was operating, by the infrequent and often delayed donations of the well-affected in the constituent counties of the Association, and by money raised by the sale of the goods of maligants.[47]

The breakdown of the original voluntary system of finance in May forced Parliament to establish new machinery for the provision of money for the regiments of the Eastern Association. On 7 May, the Houses had passed an Ordinance whereby those persons 'as have not at all contributed or lent, or not according to their estates and abilities' should be assessed by the local committees; the latter, having determined the value of the defaulter's estate, were empowered to demand a sum not exceeding a fifth of his annual income, or a twentieth of the total value of his personal property. The sums so levied were originally intended to be paid into the central Parliamentary Treasury in London, but a further Ordinance of 18 May instructed the committees of the constituent counties to utilize the money for the payment of their forces.[48]

This was a welcome development, but the Ordinance of the Fifth and Twentieth was not the ideal legislation to assuage the very immediate needs of the constituent counties. The process of assessment, whereby the parish constables were instructed to provide estimates of a man's annual revenue, and the value of his personal estate in cash, stock, goods and debts for the local committee, who then imposed the individual assessments, not only provided the maximum opportunity for the exercise of corrupt influence,[49] but was necessarily slow. In Norfolk the constables' estimates were not forwarded to the committee until 5 June; the assessments were issued a week later, with instructions that the sums demanded should be paid by the 23rd of the month.[50] Even this was not the end of the process. The Ordinance established machinery for those assessed to appeal against the demands, and many availed themselves of this right; time had to be allowed for the payment of the larger sums assessed, and the goods of the recalcitrant distrained.[51] Ultimately large sums were raised upon the Ordinance in the eastern counties,[52] but a substantial part was not collected until the late summer and autumn of 1643.[53]

One measure of the grim financial situation in the Association, even after the passage of the Fifth and Twentieth legislation, is the degree to which local committees and commanders were forced to supplement their officially designated revenue by the appropriation of money originally intended for other services. The subscription raised for the relief of Ireland was taken 'by force' from its official collector on the Isle of Ely by the Governor of Wisbech, and money from the weekly assessment established for the maintenance of the Parliamentary field army under the Earl of Essex by the Ordinance of 24 February was syphoned off and employed locally in Norfolk and Huntingdonshire.[54] Perhaps the greatest inroads were made into the Propositions, originally designed to fill the Parliamentary war chests at the Guildhall. From the first the local committees had been empowered by Parliamentary orders, or warrants of the Committee of Safety, to employ specified amounts for local defense, but it is clear that substantial amounts were appropriated to local use without official sanction,[55] in particular those sums raised after March 1643.[56] The order of the House of Commons of 30 May by which any further sums raised on the Propositions in the Association were no longer to be sent up to the Guildhall but might be employed locally, appears merely to have regularized a *de facto* practice.[57]

The deficiencies in the financial provision for the Association's army also ensured that its supply system would be inadequate. By the Declaration and Instructions of 20 December 1642 the constituent counties were empowered to levy a sum not exceeding the fourth part of their assessment to the £400,000 provided to pay off the armies in the north, for the purchase of regimental supplies and munitions. But the money came in slowly,[58] and a substantial proportion was used for local defense or diverted to provide pay for the Association's forces.[59] Accordingly, ammunition, wagons and medical supplies were often in short supply, and some munitions had to be 'borrowed' from the local trained-band magazines. The supply of horses appears to have been adequate, but only because large numbers could be seized from 'papists and malignants' by virtue of Grey's warrants. The system had obvious drawbacks. The captains engaged in the work were not genuinely interested in investigating a man's guilt, and many were tarred with the brush of malignancy on the flimsiest evidence: one of the keepers in Waltham Forest had two horses seized by soldiers who had been informed of his 'royalist sympathies' by a couple of poachers whom he was prosecuting. Cromwell's regiment was not guiltless in this respect. In March Whalley was in trouble with the Lords for seizing horses of the Earl of Carlisle at Newmarket; his justification was that the local constable had told him that the Earl was a malignant. In the next three months Cromwell's agents requisitioned horses in Huntingdonshire, often 'from verie honest men', and in the summer Captain Margery's activities in Suffolk created similar difficulties.[60]

Further, the system invited corruption. Sir Thomas Martyn, one of the Cambridgeshire committee, seized the horse of a local papist, which he subsequently employed on his own farm. In Essex the activities of Joseph Mann, who was empowered by Lord Grey to seize delinquents' horses, occasioned a good deal of complaint, in that, without any warrant, he appointed deputies who allowed 'malignants' to redeem their horses for cash. Captain Poe was equally notorious in Suffolk, where 'extreame complaints of . . . miscarriages and oppressions' were leveled against him.[61]

The difficulties which beset Cromwell and Grey at the outset of their commands – military inefficiency, depleted ranks, endemic financial shortage and a ramshackle logistic structure – were not peculiar to the Eastern Association: the Earl of Essex's army, or other regional forces, were little better paid, disciplined or supplied. These common deficiencies of the Parliamentary war-effort resulted from the fumbling attempts of inexperienced legislators, county administrators and parish officers to mobilize resources to an unprecedented degree in a completely novel situation. But the Association's difficulties cannot be explained solely in these terms: the problems were compounded by the consistent refusal of the Parliamentary legislators to pass the Ordinances which the representatives of the constituent counties and the military authorities considered necessary if their financial position was to be improved.

In February a proposal from Cambridge that a monthly assessment should be levied on papists and malignants was rejected by the Commons, as was the suggestion of some East Anglian M.P.s in April that they might be allowed to use money and plate collected on the Propositions for the use of their forces. In early May one of the Essex M.P.s apologized to the local committee for the delay in the passage of legislation to secure the regular payment of their troops.[62] Two weeks later, although the Houses granted the Association its receipts upon the Ordinance of the Fifth and Twentieth part, they rejected a clause whereby the county committees would have been enabled to levy a weekly assessment for 'the payment of souldyers . . . for fortifications, bringing in of armes and amunition and discharging all other necessaryes'.[63] Later in May the Cambridge Committee again pressed for the passage of an Ordinance 'for the more due payment of the forces sent down from them into the Army', but this was turned down, and only the order allowing the constituent counties any further sums which could be raised on the Propositions passed. In June the Cambridge Committee was still endeavoring to extract new fiscal legislation from Westminster.[64]

The reasoning behind Parliament's consistent reluctance to grant the Association the financial supply which the latter considered essential, is exemplified in a speech made in April by William Cage. As burgess for Ipswich Cage was well aware of the pressing financial necessities of the Suffolk forces marching to join Lord Grey, yet he opposed the motion of some of his East Anglian colleagues that the Association should be allowed to pay their army from the Propositions, for 'hee feared that it should consume the monie to be raised in those counties for the maintenance of the Armie in generall upon particular forces'.[65] Parliament thought of the 'Armie in generall', that of the Earl of Essex, as their prime weapon, alone capable of delivering a knock-out blow against the Royalists; it must not be stinted by the diversion of resources to the maintenance of local brigades.

This subordination of the Association's conception of their optimum interests to the needs of Essex's army by Parliament can be seen in a number of other incidents, besides the question of financial priorities: for example, the support Westminster accorded the Lord General in his disputes with the county committees. In his dealings with the local administrators Essex displayed a notable lack of tact. Particularly offensive were his commissions empowering individuals to seize the goods and horses of malignants in certain localities without reference to the committees, and the bitterness of the subsequent jurisdictional conflicts were frequently enhanced by the over-zealous or blatantly corrupt behavior of his nominees. Yet in these disputes Parliament invariably backed Essex's agents, and upheld the legitimacy of his commissions. In May, upon the receipt of a letter from the Lord General, the Commons had released Captain Andrewes and allowed him to take the one hundred and twenty horses which he had requisitioned to the Army, although his operations in Hertfordshire had been marked by such grave irregularities that the local committee, headed by an M.P., had arrested him and proposed to return his booty to the victims of his strong-arm methods. For over two months the Commons refused to listen to bitter protests from the Essex committee against the activities of Colonel Long; D'Ewes thought that the House's attitude was determined by 'their tender regard to the Earle of Essex' by whose commission Long was seizing the horses and goods of malignants in the county. Only after a prolonged Parliamentary campaign, in which they stressed that the county was on the verge of insurrection against Long's extortions and the indiscipline of his troops, and the passage of the Ordinance of 18 May for the local collection of the Fifth and Twentieth which rendered the Colonel's position completely anomalous, could the Essex committee rid themselves of 'that domineeringe and insulting man'.[66]

Another aspect of Parliament's readiness to subordinate the Association to the needs of the Lord General's army is apparent in the abortive scheme for a *levée en masse* dreamed up by the Earl in June. Arguing that the war was dragging on because of the poor quality and low morale of the rank and file of the Parliamentary army, Essex felt that victory could be won swiftly only if 'such may appear in this cause as have most interest in it . . . men of religious lifes and affections fittest to bear Arms for the truth of religion; men of estates to defend those estates'. The well-affected gentry and yeomanry were to rise in arms and join his force, whereupon an irresistible assault on the Royalists would be launched. This appeal, backed personally by Hampden and by the Commons in general, was directed to the county of Essex – that 'place of most life of religion in the land' – alone. None of the other counties of the Association were involved, and the county of Essex's commitment to them was completely ignored. The Eastern Association might as well not have existed as far as the Lord General's scheme, applauded by the Commons, was concerned.[67]

The priority which Parliament attached to the needs of Essex's army in the first half of 1643, and their reluctance to divert funds from it to 'particular forces', reflects not only their initial belief that the Lord General alone could obtain the decisive victory which could bring the war to a successful conclusion, but also a distrust of the localism of the county authorities: a fear that funds provided for the local treasuries were unlikely to be employed in the vigorous prosecution of the war.

This general consideration applied with equal validity to the particular case of the Eastern Association. As has been shown, the local governors who had pressed for an Association in the autumn of 1642 had intended it to perform a primarily defensive role; they had not desired the radical Declaration and Instructions drawn up by Corbett and the 'fierie spirits', and they only implemented it after a delay of two months when threatened by internal insurrection and the invasion of Rupert's cavaliers. This localist, defensive mentality still flourished in 1643. The committees were lax in the execution of Ordinances for the financing of the national war-effort,[68] yet enthusiastic in their efforts to secure large sums for local defenses. Old Sir Harbottle Grimston, inspired by memories of 'eighty eight', and Richard Harman, respectively burgesses for Harwich and Norwich, constantly pressed Parliament for funds for the fortification of those communities. Nor was it only major centers of population, but small inland towns, like Hadleigh and Braintree, which erected defensive works.[69] Such monuments to localism were not popular with the radicals in Parliament, who probably considered that the substantial outlay could have been invested more profitably in the vigorous prosecution of the war.[70]

The prevalence of localism and a defensive mentality in this period is also apparent in the frequent criticisms from the constituent counties of 'their' forces serving beyond the borders of the Association. The relevant passage in the December Instructions was ambiguous on this critical point, but both Parliament and the Cambridge Committee argued that the establishment of the responsibility of mutual assistance among the constituent counties at the inception of the Association did not abrogate or take priority over 'that great duty wee owe unto the Kingdome in generall', and that, in consequence, their forces must serve wherever the Lord General commanded them.[71] But despite these categorical pronouncements, the contrary view, that the forces raised by the Associated counties were to be used solely for local defense, continued to be held by common soldiers, commanders, and some of the local governors in East Anglia. In April a Norfolk troop mutinied and had to be disarmed by loyal forces when ordered to march to Reading, and the men of an Essex regiment refused to leave their quarters in Hertfordshire without 'some speciall and authentick command' from Parliament.[72] The desertion from forces serving with Cromwell was ascribed by the Cambridge Committee to the 'eronious opinion . . . of our unexperienced country soldiers that they ought not to be drawne or ledd . . . beyond the bounds of the fyve counties', while in June and July Cromwell had the greatest difficulty in persuading Sir John Palgrave to join him in the midlands with his regiment of Norfolk infantry, despite the issue of a positive order to that effect by the Earl of Essex. Although Sir John put up a barrage of excuses his real fear was that if he left Wisbech, where his men were in garrison, the enemy might 'soone . . . brake into Norfolk'.[73]

The localism of the constituent counties was not only manifested in the belief that their forces should perform a primarily defensive role, but in their neglect of the Association, as represented by the Cambridge Committee, when its demands crossed their own estimate of their individual optimum interests.

Although not officially constituted until the issue of Lord Grey's commission of 22 April, later ratified by the Lord General, the Committee began meeting a week earlier, when instructions were issued for the regulation of the Cambridge garrison and a sub-committee of townsmen appointed to deal with routine administrative matters. As established by Grey's commission, the Committee was to consist of eleven members, two from each of the five counties and one from the City of Norwich; each representative was to stay for at least two days, and on his departure, the Committee were to summon another member for his county from a pool of commissioners nominated by Grey.[74] The Committee was a development of the conferences held during the period of the Association's inception; a meeting of the accredited agents of the constituent counties, with both consultative and executive functions. Its prime function was to supervise the defense of the Association in Grey's absence on campaign: the commanders of the trained-bands in the constituent counties were instructed to take their orders direct from Cambridge, and the keepers of the local magazines to issue supplies on the Committee's warrants.

But despite the issue of Lord Grey's commission, the Cambridge Committee was consistently neglected by the constituent counties. As the Committee recognized, their theoretical powers would remain a dead letter whilst the reality of fiscal control remained located in 'the particular committees in the severall counties', who alone could raise money by the Ordinances establishing the Association.[75] The Committee endeavored to remedy this situation by seeking legislation establishing a central treasury under their control, but without success: in early May a measure whereby money raised on the Ordinance for the Fifth and Twentieth part would be 'drawne out into our Generall Treasury' was rejected in Parliament, as were two other attempts later in the month and in June to obtain some measure of central financial control.[66]

The failure to win any measure of central control over the finances of the constituent counties led to the emasculation of the Cambridge Committee. The Committee had no sanctions with which to enforce its commands, and the counties, holding the purse strings, utilized their contingents with reference solely to their own best interests and neglected the Committee's endeavors to oversee the defense of the Association. On 16 May Cambridge issued a desperate appeal for reinforcements for their depleted garrison, threatened by a party of cavaliers at Wellingborough: the Essex committee spent three days checking the information before moving any troops.[77] In June only one of the three foot companies which the county of Essex was supposed to provide for garrison duty at Cambridge had been sent.[78] Aware of their impotence the Committee increasingly phrased their appeals for military assistance in a tone of hysterical self-righteousness,[79] and this, in addition to their gullible timidity, further weakened their credibility with the constituent counties and Westminster: in July the M.P. for Ipswich calmed his constituents' fears of an impending assault and complained of 'the Cambridge informations, which by their causeless alarmes hath severall tymes drawne our forces to Cambridge'.[80]

Not only did the Committee's appeals for men fall on deaf ears, their requests for money went unanswered too. As financial control was located in the individual counties the payment of 'common charges', those expenses incurred by Lord Grey or the Cambridge Committee which were not the responsibility of any one county, created considerable difficulty. For several months the senior officers of Grey's brigade and the men of his artillery corps went unpaid, and it was not until mid-July that the Committee of East Anglian M.P.s at Westminster agreed to apportion the cost upon the constituent counties. The order did not benefit Grey to any notable extent as the counties were lax in paying the money, while the officer appointed to collect it eventually absconded with the proceeds.[81] It was not until June that the East Anglian M.P.s agreed that the expenses of the Cambridge Committee should be apportioned equitably among the constituent counties. By this date the Committee had expended £1855-18-11d on 'common charges' – scouts, messengers, artillery, munitions and fortifications; two-thirds of this amount had been commandeered from the Cambridgeshire treasury, while Norwich, Essex and the Isle of Ely had provided nothing, and Suffolk only the desultory sum of £76-13-4d. For the future, the East Anglian M.P.s decided, Essex, Norfolk and Suffolk were each to provide a quarter of all sums disbursed by the Committee on 'common charges', Hertfordshire and Cambridgeshire a twelfth each, and Norwich and the Isle of Ely each a twenty-fourth. This order relieved the Cambridgeshire treasury to some extent, but the Committee could never extract the full proportion from Essex, Norfolk or Suffolk.[82]

Not only did the proportion established by the Committee of East Anglian M.P.s at Westminster not prove completely successful in meeting the financial needs of Cambridge, it also engendered a constitutional crisis within the Association which further weakened the Committee. Norwich had a long-standing feud with Norfolk concerning the proportion it should bear of any taxation levied upon the shire, and in the 1630s the city had fought both the Norfolk J.P.s and the Privy Council when it had been ordered to pay one-tenth of the sum set upon the county. In March 1643 the authorities of the shire and the city had reached an amicable agreement whereby the citizens were to pay one-twenty-fifth of any sum taxed on Norfolk. So when in June the Committee of East Anglian M.P.s assessed them at one-sixth of the sum rated on the county, the city protested volubly and their agent at Cambridge, Samuel Smyth, persuaded the Committee there to ratify the local agreement of March. However, on Smyth's being sent to Huntingdon on military business, the Committee reversed its decision and voted to abide by the objectionable rule of proportion. When Smyth returned and learned of this *volte face*, he threatened to go to London immediately to protest there, and again the Cambridge Committee stood down – 'Norwitch should be connived at for theare proportion rather than at this tyme to dispute it.' But a few days later they again voted to maintain the proportion originally established by the East Anglian M.P.s, and both parties tried to drum up support for their respective cases at Westminster. But this blatant log-rolling by factions on the Cambridge Committee brought that body into considerable disrepute; some M.P.s 'marvile the Committy there should take so much upon them', and others asserted that its power was inferior to that of the Deputy-Lieutenants of the individual counties.[83]

Criticized in the Commons, and its demands for men and money neglected by the counties, the Cambridge Committee was further weakened when in mid-July Lord Grey of Warke, from whose commission they derived the little power they had, was relieved of his command over the Association and imprisoned for his refusal to go to Scotland as part of an embassy to negotiate an alliance.[84] The Committee's impotence by the end of July is apparent in its membership. From its inception the Committee had found it difficult to persuade the counties to provide the number of commissioners required by Grey's instructions, but by the end of July the supposedly representative body of the Eastern Association consisted almost entirely of Cambridgeshire men, whose horizons, one observer suggested, were little wider than the interests of their own county.[85]

The limited achievements of the Association's forces in the period to the end of July 1643 were in part occasioned by the difficulties which also frustrated the Lord General's efforts: volunteer recruits became harder to find, and pay fell in arrears as the generosity of the well-affected flagged, and the central and local administrations grappled with the novel problems presented by the raising of large-scale war taxation. However, there were weaknesses peculiar to the Association which Parliament recognized but neglected, in particular the need for further, regular, reliable sources of financial supply. Westminster's reluctance to improve this situation was a function of a distrust of the Association. Parliament was unwilling to divert funds from the army of the Earl of Essex to an organization regarded by many of its members as having been instituted for defensive purposes; unwilling to give money to men who showed a greater interest in their local security than in the active prosecution of the war, and who neglected the financial and military demands of their own representative institution, the Cambridge Committee, when they conflicted with their individual assessments of the measures most conducive to their own defense.

Yet the Association could not play a more active role until Parliament would accord it more power. As the Cambridge Committee pointed out, the counties could not be expected to enthusiastically raise forces for service beyond the borders of the Association when Ordinances granting them funds to pay their men were rejected.[86] Want of confidence in the Association at Westminster and the consequent reluctance to pass legislation on its behalf fed the weaknesses which bred the initial mistrust. This vicious circle – in their case more of a vicious spiral – is most apparent in the history of the Cambridge Committee. 'Command, you, and be obeyed!' Cromwell exhorted the Association's representatives.[87] But in the absence of legislation institutionalizing their powers, and, in particular, establishing central direction of the finances of the constituent counties, their power to command was negligible. And Parliament was unwilling to grant them the requisite authority, seeing them only as the weak, hysterical and timid body, representing nothing more than the conflicting interests of the constituent counties – ultimately only the interests of Cambridgeshire – to which the absence of legislative backing for their authority had reduced them.

It was to require the conjunction of two crises, in the defense of the Association and in central politics, to break the vicious circle.

Central politics and the seven counties: the legislative establishment of the Earl of Manchester's command, August 1643 – January 1644

For months the Cambridge authorities and the East Anglian M.P.s had endeavored to elicit enhanced powers from Parliament: in the three weeks before 16 August the Association was transformed by legislative enactment. A series of orders and Ordinances passed the Houses strengthening the Cambridge Committee and building up a powerful army to replace the hotch-potch of ill-paid, poorly supplied and depleted troops and companies which had previously defended the eastern counties or served with Lord Grey. This transformation in the bureaucratic and military structure of the Association occurred as the men at Westminster were forced to re-think their overall military strategy in the light of the performance of the Earl of Essex's force and because of the specific threat posed by the advance of Newcastle's 'popish' army.

During the early months of the war it was believed that in the field army of the Earl of Essex lay the best hope of Parliament's attaining a decisive victory; accordingly, the bulk of Parliament's resources were directed toward its maintenance, to which the needs of local forces, such as those of the Eastern Association, were subordinated. But Essex's military performance produced little other than the disillusionment of some of his erstwhile adherents. After the fall of Reading in late April the Lord General stuck fast in the Thames valley, skirmishing desultorily with the Royalist army at Oxford. Not only were Rupert's cavalry able to ride circles around the ponderous Parliamentary force, but Essex did nothing to stop the inexorable advance of the western and northern Royalists under Hopton and Newcastle.[1] The quality of Essex's generalship had been questioned in the months before the fall of Reading,[2] but from May onwards his critics in Parliament, pulpit, and press, conveniently forgetting the desertion and disease, the shortages of money and supplies which racked his army, became more vehement in their attacks. The most active of Essex's detractors were those radical M.P.s who suspected that the Lord General's immobility was a function not merely of his incompetence, but of his political moderation; that his preference for a negotiated, compromise peace created in him a positive disinclination to pursue the absolute victory the radicals demanded.

On 9 July Essex confirmed the worst suspicions of his radical critics. In a letter to the Commons he announced that his ill-supplied army, inferior in cavalry to the Royalists, was unable to defend the countryside from their forays, and concluded that negotiations should be re-opened with the King. This 'confession of weakness and plea for peace' infuriated the radicals in Parliament. With the active support of powerful elements in the City of London they temporarily won control of the Commons from Pym and prepared to implement schemes involving either the complete supersession of the Lord General by Sir William Waller, a commander, in their opinion, of more ability and greater enthusiasm for the cause, or the establishment of another army under Waller which would operate independently of Essex's control.[3]

But for Pym the radicals' proposal to create an independent army was thoroughly unattractive. Not only would the new force owe its allegiance to such dangerous 'fierie spirits' as Henry Martin, but it was probable that their treatment of the Earl of Essex, a combination of insult and material neglect, would drive the Lord General, whose prestige was still considerable, into the arms of the peace party in Parliament. So, while Martin and his allies sought to replace Essex or to relegate his army to a minor role in the Parliamentary strategy, Pym's priorities were the rehabilitation of the Lord General, and the reorganization of his army. And, after momentary hesitation in the face of the radicals' onslaught, the sure hand of the master political manager reasserted itself. While the schemes of Essex's opponents ran into unexpected difficulties, and then spluttered out in the mutual bickering of the radical leaders, Pym regrouped his allies in the House and worked successfully to strengthen the Lord General's army: its worst deficiencies received immediate attention, increased financial provisions were made for its maintenance, and finally, on 10 August, the Ordinance for Impressment was passed which ended Essex's dependence on the virtually moribund volunteer system for the recruiting of his depleted ranks.[4]

But, while the Commons, guided by Pym, ultimately shelved the radicals' extreme schemes and renovated Essex's army, the crisis had a considerable effect. There was no reversion to the old military priorities and strategic concerns, and aspects of the radical program, rejected *in toto*, were incorporated into a new synthesis. The 'fierie spirits' had endeavored to raise a new army to supersede that commanded by the Lord General; Pym and the 'middle group' had no intention of sacrificing Essex, but they did recognize that given the existing military situation, the establishment of new forces would strengthen the Parliamentary war-machine. So the Commons refused Essex's demand for an investigation into the loss of the West, which the Lord General hoped would demonstrate the incapacity of the radicals' nominee for his replacement, Sir William Waller, while Pym and his allies eventually extracted a commission from the resentful Essex, for Waller to command a new army for the defense of the City of London.[5] In the words of the *Parliament Scout*, which frequently voiced the opinion of the middle group in Parliament, it was 'good discretion to give life to both the Armies, as well that of Sir William as my Lord General'.[6]

But while the July crisis predisposed the Parliamentary leaders to think in terms of a plurality of military forces, it was a specific threat which brought the powerful new army of the Eastern Association into being by mid-August.

The military crisis which precipitated Parliament's August legislation began auspiciously for the Association. In late July, as Cromwell and Meldrum prepared to join the Earl of Essex at a general rendezvous appointed by the latter at Stony Stratford, two contemporaneous events in Lincolnshire forced them to seek the Lord General's permission to move into that county. In the south a strong force from Newark and Belvoir had occupied Stamford, and was threatening Peterborough and the Association's fenland frontier; in the north the town of Gainsborough, a vital link in the Royalist lines of communication between Newark and the Earl of Newcastle's headquarters in Yorkshire, had been surprised by Lord Willoughby of Parham, who, realizing the certainty of a counter-attack, appealed for reinforcements and supplies.[7] While Meldrum marched north towards Gainsborough, Cromwell's cavalry moved through Northamptonshire against the cavaliers at Stamford, who had begun to fortify the town. On his approach the enemy took up a strong defensive position in the Earl of Exeter's great mansion near Stamford, Burleigh House, but with the arrival of two infantry regiments with artillery Cromwell was able to bombard and storm the house, which fell on 24 July.[8] From Stamford Cromwell's cavalry rode north to rendezvous with Meldrum again, and on 28 July the combined force relieved Gainsborough with necessary supplies after a sharp skirmish with the Royalist cavalry which was blockading the town. Cromwell and Meldrum's success was short-lived. Within hours of their victory Newcastle's entire army – 'about fifty colours of foot, with a great body of horse' – appeared before the town, and forced them to retreat precipitately, leaving Willoughby again besieged. The Parliamentarian commanders, believing that Newcastle would return to the siege of Hull, endeavored to organize a second relief force, but for once the Earl's elephantine army moved faster than its opponents. On 1 August Willoughby was forced to surrender Gainsborough, when Newcastle's mortars fired the town, and the population rioted; he retired to Lincoln, and then, as the Royalists advanced and his demoralized men slipped away, to

Boston, abandoning his artillery in his haste. Cromwell, too, fell back, withdrawing his infantry to Peterborough and Spalding as the Royalists pushed deep into Kesteven and Holland. By mid-August Newcastle controlled almost all Lincolnshire: his forces had executed the Commission of Array at Bourne, captured Tattershall Castle, and were raiding up to the walls of Boston.[9]

As the scope of the military disaster became apparent, the constituent counties of the Association were bombarded with anguished appeals for immediate assistance from Cromwell and the Cambridge Committee. After the fall of Gainsborough the latter wrote to the Essex Deputy-Lieutenants that 'the whole assotiacion will be exposed [to] the fury and cruelty of the popish Armie' unless all available forces were sent to Cambridge. Two days later the request was repeated with the darkly threatening peroration, 'if you desert us, give us leave to tell you, wee feare wee shall not sett heere, nor in these parts any longer to trouble you with letters any more'. Cromwell's letters of 6 August, reporting Willoughby's withdrawal to Boston, vibrate with urgency: 'it's no longer disputing, but out all you can. Raise all your bands; send men to Huntingdon; get up what volunteers you can; hasten your horses'.[10]

But the response from the counties was disappointing. Although there was much insistence on the desirability of 'unitinge all the neighbour counties', and the Norfolk and Suffolk committees proposed a new Bury conference for discussion of the best means to repel the 'soe formidable yet Popish enemy', the rhetoric was not supported by material provisions. Volunteers were a scarce commodity, particularly in harvest time, and consequently reinforcements came in slowly to Cambridge, where many of the men deserted on arrival.[11] Nor were adequate amounts of money provided. Manifestations of localism multiplied. The immediate reaction to the crisis of the citizens of Norwich was to strengthen their fortifications, while Cromwell was again plagued by the reluctance of some troops to serve beyond the confines of the Association and the Commons were obliged to reiterate their opinion that 'nothing is more repugnant to the . . . sence of this house, and dangerous to the kingdome than the unwillingness of their forces to march out of their severall countys'. Was this, Cromwell expostulated, 'any way to save a kingdom'?.[12]

But the appeals of Cromwell and the Cambridge Committee, if unheeded in East Anglia, were not neglected at Westminster. The Parliamentarians, already disposed toward the creation of a pluralist military machine, were compelled by the specter of Newcastle's army advancing into the eastern counties, and upon London, to re-evaluate the Association's role in their total strategy, and, in consequence, to initiate sweeping changes in its structure. In the three weeks before 16 August a series of orders and Ordinances strengthening the Cambridge Committee, and rebuilding the Association's army were passed.

The genesis of this process began on 18 July in a piece of legislation typical of Parliament's previous evaluation of the limited strategic role to be played by the Association. In his letter of 9 July Essex had complained of his inability to protect the countryside from Rupert's forays; in response some newspapers resurrected an old suggestion for the establishment of a 'flying army', a mobile force which could match the Royalists' cavalry, and prevent their plundering incursions.[13] On 18 July the city petitioned for the establishment of such an army, and Parliament agreed to raise 6500 men in London and 16 southern, eastern, and midland counties; it was originally intended that this force should operate in four bodies, and the horse to be raised by the Association was divided among these separate units.[14] Four days later the House first demonstrated its new awareness of the financial and military needs of the Association when, in response to the threat posed by the Royalist seizure of Stamford, it was voted that the Association should raise 2000 infantry with a month's pay, to be levied upon the individual counties according to the rules of proportion established by the Committee of East Anglian M.P.s. It was also decided that the contingent of the 'flying army' which was to rendezvous at Cambridge should be used in conjunction with the newly raised infantry for the defense of that area. On receipt of the news of the capture of Gainsborough on the 24th, Parliament instructed the Cambridge Committee to give Lord Willoughby all assistance, and the county committees to hasten the raising of reinforcements and money.[15] But at this juncture Parliament was still not contemplating any fundamental change in the Association's role, certainly not the creation of a powerful army for service on that front, for on 28 July the Essex committee were instructed to raise 1000 dragoons, which, with the cavalry they were raising as a result of the order of 18 July, were to serve with forces of the City of London under Sir William Waller.[16] This plan, like the June 'general rising', took no account of the Association, or of the county of Essex's commitment and responsibility to it.

But the deteriorating military situation soon enforced further Parliamentary consideration of the Association. On receipt of the intelligence of Newcastle's arrival before Gainsborough, the Commons sent a deputation of M.P.s to consult with the Cambridge Committee, and further missives to the localities to speed the raising of the troops voted on the 22nd. The House also discussed a petition from Norfolk pressing that an army of 8000 infantry and 2000 horse should be raised, to be maintained by a weekly assessment, suggestions which were ultimately referred to the Committee of East Anglian

M.P.s for further consideration, with the interesting *caveat*, defending the Lord General's financial resources, that any fiscal proposals should be 'without prejudice to the weekly assessments designed for the maintenance of the Publique'. On 4 August the House was informed of the fall of Gainsborough, and a further 2000 foot were ordered to be raised in the Association, while new provisions were made for the payment of Cromwell's troops. The House also discussed an 'Ordinance and Instructions for the Committees of the Six Associated Counties'.[17] This legislation, in form little more than a ratification of Grey's commission of 21 April, had considerable importance. First, the personnel of the Cambridge Committee, which consisted almost exclusively of Cambridgeshire men in late July, was reinforced. Named commissioners, two from each county, were instructed to attend at Cambridge immediately, and, in consequence, the Committee again could claim to be the representative body of the Association. Further, the Committee's powers, which, when dependent solely upon Grey's commission, had been challenged by the counties and some M.P.s, were legitimized, clarified and enhanced; the Committee were given command over the forces raised by the counties, and were empowered to levy new troops and their pay from the latter according to the agreed proportions. This Ordinance passed the Commons on 8 August, the day that the House learned of Willoughby's retreat to Boston in the face of Newcastle's inexorable advance into Lincolnshire. Discussion of the new military situation lasted three hours, and it was agreed that money and supplies should be sent to Willoughby, and that Cromwell should be directed to assist him. But in addition to these piecemeal expedients the Committee of East Anglian M.P.s were ordered to discuss the raising of new forces in the Association. The results of their deliberations were presented to the House next morning, and the Commons agreed that 10,000 foot and dragoons, to include the 4000 infantry levied on the orders of 22 July and 4 August, and the 1000 dragoons mobilized in Essex for service with Sir William Waller, were to be raised in the Association, and that the Earl of Manchester should be commissioned as Major-General of the Association.[18]

Manchester's appointment gave the Association's army a powerful cavalry force. The 'flying army' first discussed on 18 July was originally designed to serve in four distinct bodies, each commanded by a noble field officer, but three of the Lords designated as commanders pleaded to be excused, and so overall command devolved upon the Earl of Manchester, who was originally to lead the London, Middlesex and Essex contingent.[19] For a time there was some confusion as to whether the entire force would operate in conjunction with Sir William Waller's new army, and whether as a complete body or as four separate contingents.[20] But by 9 August it appears to have been decided that the entire force was directly subordinate to Manchester, and thus was potentially available to serve with the Association's army. The legislative provision establishing the Association's new army was completed on 16 August with the passage of an Ordinance empowering the Committees of the constituent counties to impress up to 20,000 men for military service.[21]

But Manchester's army existed only on paper. Although the Earl was strenuously active, riding through the eastern counties pressing the local committees to hasten their levies,[22] his success in transforming votes into regiments can largely be attributed to the pusillanimity of his opponent, the Earl of Newcastle. After his initial success in Lincolnshire the latter pulled back the bulk of his forces to the interminable siege of Hull, and made no attempt to push south even when presented with an excellent opportunity by the seizure of King's Lynn by Royalist elements in the town and a group of neighboring gentlemen on 23 August. The assessment of one London journalist that had Newcastle marched to assist the Lynn Royalists he would soon have been at the walls of London, was an exaggeration, but certainly any attempt to relieve Lynn would have seriously embarrassed Manchester.[23] The countryside was sympathetic to the town's Royalist defenders, refusing to send in provisions to Manchester's forces, while many of the local trained-bands failed to obey the Earl's order that they should participate in the siege.[24] The number of troops which slowly assembled about Lynn was small, and their quality doubtful: deficiencies in their equipment and pay, and their poor discipline made them, in Manchester's words, 'far more dreadfull to me than any enemy'.[25] But Newcastle did nothing, and the defenders, despairing of the relief which they had expected,[26] surrendered the town on 15 September when Manchester threatened to storm.

With Lynn secured, and in the absence of any further thrust south by the northern Royalists, Manchester was able to concentrate on the organization of the newly raised levies that were being sent up from the constituent counties of the Association.[27]

Meanwhile Cromwell, who had commanded a cavalry screen in Holland while the Earl's infantry were besieging Lynn, scored a major success by linking up with the Yorkshire cavalry under Sir Thomas Fairfax. This force, which had been of limited utility bottled up in Hull during the siege, was ferried across the Humber, where their landing was covered by Cromwell's cavalry; then, despite the attentions of a large body of Royalist horse, the conjoined forces retired safely into Holland.[28] On 7 October Manchester brought his newly-embodied infantry to Boston, and two days later he, Cromwell and Fairfax marched against Bolingbroke castle, hoping that by besieging the place they would provoke the Royalists into mounting a relief column, and so precipitate a more general engagement. The cavaliers, encouraged by the success of a surprise attack which drove in Manchester's cavalry outposts, took the bait, but were routed at the battle of Winceby on 11 October.[29] This day saw another body blow to the Royalist cause in the north; Lord Fairfax sallied from Hull and over-ran Newcastle's siegeworks. In the face of these two defeats, and with the Scots preparing to cross the border, Newcastle fell back to York. Manchester immediately capitalized on the situation, taking Lincoln on 20 October.[30]

In January the Royalist commissioners at Newark informed the King of the desperate condition of their garrison. Since the fall of Lincoln their remaining outposts in Lincolnshire had been mopped up, and they were no longer able to draw supplies from that county, which the Parliamentarians 'enjoy . . . in quiet possession'.[31] Indeed, for the previous three months Newark itself had been blockaded by the Association's cavalry, which skirmished with fluctuating success with the Royalist horse.[32] Yet, despite these achievements, Manchester did not draw as substantial an advantage from his autumn campaign as the Royalists had feared, or the Parliamentary press hoped: the former expected the Earl to advance into Derbyshire or Yorkshire, the latter that he would besiege Newark.[33] In part Manchester's failure to fulfill these expectations was due to the success of Sir Lewis Dyve's diversionary raid against the western flank of the Association, which obliged the Earl to move south to cover the eastern counties.[34] But after the dispersal of this threat Manchester moved his infantry into winter quarters; he had decided, reported the Scots' commissioner, Robert Baillie, to undertake no major action until Parliament's new northern allies were fully mobilized.[35]

Strategic considerations were not the sole factor influencing Manchester's decision: deficiencies in the material and financial provision for his army, and in its administration, were as important. In the late summer and autumn of 1643 Manchester had two basic grievances. The slowness with which the impressed levies joined his army, and their quality, was the first.[36] But this was to be a recurrent problem during the existence of his army: on this particular occasion the local committees' difficulties in organizing the impressment of unwilling countrymen was compounded by the proximity of the harvest, the large number of men required for the burgeoning army, and their own inexperience in implementing the relevant Ordinances.[37] While the Earl took the opportunity provided by his army's early withdrawal into winter quarters to recruit and redeploy his force,[38] not all the difficulties that had reduced the effectiveness of his autumn campaign could be resolved merely by time and limited internal reorganization. Manchester's second complaint, of the inadequacies of the financial provision and organization upon which his army depended, could only be remedied by positive action by Westminster.

What, then, were the basic characteristics of the fiscal system employed in the Association in the summer and autumn of 1643? Initially Manchester's army raised by the series of orders and Ordinances culminating in that of 16 August was granted no new financial provision. Basically the counties still had to pay and equip their increased numbers of troops and meet the 'common charges' of the Army and the Cambridge Committee from their receipts upon the Ordinance of 18 May for the assessment of the Fifth and Twentieth part, supplemented in some areas by money raised upon special local Ordinances or dispensations.[39] But these resources were patently insufficient: the unpaid soldiers mutinied or deserted, while the requests of Manchester and the Cambridge Committee for money to meet 'common charges' went unanswered.[40]

In early September the pressing financial needs of the Association finally received some consideration in Parliament. On the 4th the Commons agreed that the arrears of the Earl of Essex's assessment owed from Norfolk, Essex and Kent might be collected by Manchester's agents and employed for the purchase of arms. Next day the House passed an Ordinance introduced by John Gurdon, the radical M.P. for Ipswich, allowing the counties (with the exception of Essex) to raise such sums as the Deputy-Lieutenants thought necessary, provided the total levied did not exceed the weekly tax for the army of the Lord General.[41] But, as Cromwell informed St John in his letter of 11 September,[42] what was needed was a permanent, fixed financial provision if the Earl of Manchester's army was not to melt away, and Gurdon's Ordinance was soon superseded. On 18 September Harbottle Grimston, probably acting as chairman of the Committee of East Anglian M.P.s, introduced a measure which passed the House on the 20th. By virtue of this Ordinance Lincolnshire was added to the Association,[43] new committees were named for all the constituent counties, and, most important, Manchester's army was allocated a definite sum for its maintenance; the counties were to raise £5630 a week. Further money was made available to the army of the Association with the passage of the Ordinance of 11 October. In debate the Commons were informed that many fiscal Ordinances had been either neglected or improperly executed in the constituent counties; accordingly Manchester was empowered to enforce such legislation as had 'not been put in due and speedy execution', paying the arrears so raised into the Treasuries designated in the original Ordinances.[44] In fact Manchester showed no interest in levying the arrears of the Lord General's weekly assessment for him, or in paying the contribution for Ireland into the London Treasury. The Ordinance was used solely to justify the reassessment of the Fifth and Twentieth part by the Earl's nominees; it was claimed that the execution of 18 May legislation by the local committees had been marked by partiality and inefficiency.[45] In addition the Ordinance of 11 October granted Manchester a third of the money raised by the sequestration of the estates and property of Royalists within the Association. Yet, despite the additional funds voted for the army of the Association in September and October, Manchester was still dissatisfied with his financial situation.

The most obvious reason for the Earl's concern is apparent in the chorus of complaints of his subordinates of the hardships which their troops had to undergo through the perpetual shortage of money. In late September, on his return from the rendezvous in northern Lincolnshire with Sir Thomas Fairfax, Cromwell 'wept when he came to Boston and found noe monyes for him from Essex and other countyes; he saith he regards mony as little as any man, but for his troopes, if they have not monyes speedely they are in an undonn condition'. There was no improvement in October. On the 24th Major Nathaniel Rich reported that the pay of his troop was nine weeks in arrear, despite his having disbursed money from his personal resources; morale was good, but the soldiers complained 'that when most service is done, least pay is coming', and he feared that the first experience of defeat would result in wholesale desertion.[46] In mid-November Cromwell was again in tears for want of money to pay his men 'which are in great want of clothes and other necesarys', and in December it was reported that his soldiers were refusing to march until they received some pay. About this time the commander of the Norfolk cavalry, Bartholemew Vermuyden, wrote that his men's arrears totaled £9000, and 'to see our troops goe barefoot and naked this winter wether, and thire horses unshodd for want of your assistance makes me write thus earnestly'; some of his troopers were dying of cold for want of adequate clothing.[47] Surviving accounts from this period verify the officers' complaints. In the seventeen weeks from September to the end of December 1643 Major Whalley, of Cromwell's horse, received only seven weeks' pay, and Alford and Rich, who commanded troops in Manchester's own regiment, approximately nine weeks. The infantry appear to have been slightly better paid: Major Holmes's company of Manchester's regiment, paid by the county of Essex, was only five weeks in arrear in this period.[48]

The development of substantial arrears in the pay of the army in the autumn of 1643 was primarily a function of the undertaxation of the constituent counties given the size of the army which they were expected to maintain. But another aspect of the financial system established by the September and October Ordinances, if not so immediately critical as the sheer shortage of funds, enhanced Manchester's difficulties as a General in this period: the failure of the legislators to establish central fiscal control. Although the Ordinance of 11 October enabled Manchester to set up a central Treasury for the collection and disbursement of the sequestration revenue and receipts upon the review of the Fifth and Twentieth part, the legislation upon which the Earl depended for the bulk of his revenue, the Ordinance of 20 September imposing the three months' weekly assessment upon the Association, made no reference to any central Treasury, and accepted and legitimized the system whereby the individual county committees paid and equipped the troops raised in their own localities.

From Manchester's perspective the decentralized system of finance operating in the autumn of 1643 had several objectionable features: it resulted in military inefficiency, it discriminated against certain counties, and it generally undermined central control of the army of the Association.

The responsibility of the local Treasurers for the pay and equipment of the troops which had been raised in their county resulted in a number of anomalies, individually perhaps little more than minor annoyances, but collectively damaging to military efficiency. Discipline was not strengthened by a system whereby the soldiers from one shire might find that their pay was further in arrear than that of troops from a neighboring county.[49] Nor had Manchester either the authority or the machinery of a central audit department to investigate suspected malfeasance in the payment of county troops, such as the accusations of the Hertfordshire cavalry that their commander, Colonel Sir John Norwich, had conspired with the treasurer appointed by the county committee to defraud them of some six weeks' pay.[50] Besides these potentially deleterious effects on morale, the decentralized system also led to a time-consuming complexity of accounting. By virtue of the Ordinance of 12 August the Essex committee had, with considerable reluctance, raised more than its proper proportion of horse and dragoons for the Association's army; accordingly it had to 'sell off' two dragoon companies to the other associated counties in order to avoid disbursing more than its correct proportion in weekly pay. Captain Poe's troop, blockading King's Lynn immediately after its revolt, was forced to requisition money and supplies in the vicinity of the town in order to subsist. In consequence, the Norfolk committee angrily demanded that the Suffolk treasurers should repay them the sums levied by Poe, arguing that as his troop had been raised in Suffolk its pay was the responsibility of that county.[51]

The individual local committees were also responsible for the equipment of their troops, and this was another aspect of the decentralized system which left much to be desired. The counties lacked the resources or the administrative experience to organize the provision of large quantities of arms or munitions, and were often unable to meet their responsibilities. So in September 1643 the Essex committee, caught between Manchester's demands for expedition in the dispatch of their newly raised forces to the siege of Lynn, and the inability of their harassed agents in London to provide adequate equipment, resolved their dilemma by sending their recruits to the Earl with 'noe armes, noe clothes, noe coulors, noe drums' – 'in so naked a posture, that to imploye them were to murther them'.[52] Further, cost economies and the standardization of equipment,[53] which could have been effected by the bulk purchase of munitions through a centralized system employing expert factors in London, were unavailable to the hard-pressed county committees buying supplies in small quantities from local craftsmen or in the city.[54] Finally, the system of local responsibility for the equipment of troops allowed the county committees to claim a proprietary right in the arms and munitions which they had purchased which resulted in further time-wasting complications of accounting.[55]

The county system of financial administration not only led to military inefficiency; it was inequitable. It placed a disproportionately heavy burden on the frontier counties, whose committees were expected to maintain forts and garrisons as well as their regiments with the field army. The Ordinance of 20 September had amended the ridiculous situation whereby the cost of maintaining Cromwell's 'Ironside' regiment fell solely upon Huntingdonshire, the poorest of the constituent counties, yet in November the county committee complained that their weekly charge for garrisons, alarms, their companies with Manchester and their proportion to the charge of Cromwell's horse came to £400 a week, while the assessment, their sole source of income as the Fifth and Twentieth was wholly expended, was a mere £220, and they petitioned Parliament 'further to enable us by some other means to leavie monies for the defraying our over great charge'. In the next month the committee of the Isle of Ely lodged a similar protest; they had to maintain four companies in garrison in addition to their men with Manchester's army, and asked that either the receipts from both the excise and the sequestration of Royalists' estates be allowed them, or that the charge be put on the whole Association.[56] The system was also weighted against a county that experienced a Royalist insurrection. During the siege of Lynn the Norfolk committee petitioned Parliament that all money raised in the county, upon any Ordinance, should be assigned to their Treasury to meet those 'extraordinarye charges which at this present wee are enforced to pay'. Parliament rejected the request in case it became a precedent for similar demands from other counties.[57]

The county system of decentralized fiscal administration was complex and inefficient, and it discriminated against those counties whose financial burden, either because of the proximity of the enemy or internal insurrection, was heaviest. But its major disadvantage was that it weakened overall central control of the Association. This is most apparent in the relations between the constituent counties and the Committee of the Association in the autumn of 1643.

As in the previous spring, the Committee still had no independent budget. Its expenses – the payment of the garrison, artillery, scouts, guards and other incidentals – still had to be met from the sums that could be extracted from the county treasuries according to the rule of proportion for 'common charges' established by the committee of East Anglian M.P.s. In mid-August the Cambridge Committee proposed to establish a 'competent Treasury' from which they could meet their necessary expenses as they occurred, and their chairman, Sir William Rowe, wrote to the Essex committee, 'Give me leave . . . to commend to your memory that some course may be resolved on, how wee may make good and maintaine by a constant supply off treasure, these our hopefull beginnings.'[58] But this was a pipe dream: no 'constant supply' was forthcoming. By 26 August only Essex had forwarded any part of the requested sum, and on 7 September the Norwich agent informed his city that Norfolk was considerably in arrear, and that 'the treasure here is much exhausted, they have noe money'. The next day the full Committee wrote to the Essex Deputy-Lieutenants complaining that their credit was so poor that they could scarcely borrow £50, and that 'the pressinge necessities are such that unles some speedyer course bee thought uppon to furnish the Treasurie . . . wee must not only discontynue this comission, but the Army must totally disband, many of them beinge att that point already, for that they comeinge to us for mony, wee are not able to furnishe them, but are soe much indebtted to them and others that wee are att a stand'. In early October the Committee informed the House of Commons that they were 'utterly destitute of mony', and that they had written frequently to the committees of the constituent counties to remit the sums they owed, but 'without effect in most of them'. Nor was money paid in any more eagerly at the end of the month.[59]

In November the Cambridge Committee, strengthened by Manchester's frequent presence in the town following the end of his autumn campaign,[60] made a serious effort to implement its reiterated financial demands. Claiming that it had disbursed £6916-10-4d between 20 April and 2 November, the Committee insisted that those counties who had not met their full share of this sum according to the proportional rate established by the Committee of East Anglian M.P.s should pay in their arrears immediately. The amounts owed by the three largest of the constituent counties were substantial; Essex, Norfolk and Suffolk should each have contributed £1679 to Cambridge – in fact, they had forwarded £238, £532, and £812 respectively. The Committee had only remained solvent because of its ability to borrow money from the Cambridgeshire county treasury, and the generosity of the Hertfordshire administrators.[61] This ultimatum immediately involved the Committee of the Association in an angry dispute with Norfolk, to whom, with the City of Norwich, it had sent a joint bill for £1393-5-2d. This claim was rejected out of hand by the county committee, who argued that they had paid in a great deal more than the sum entered in the official statement, that the revolt and subsequent siege of Lynn had put the county to considerable expense, of which the other members of the Association had borne no part, and, finally, that they had been at 'vast chardges of ammunition, artillery, shipping, and the frontiers, besides owre troops and 2 foot regiments'.[62]

The Norfolk committee's rejoinder to the demands from Cambridge is a microcosm of the deficiencies of the existing fiscal structure: the disparity between the two sets of accounts demonstrates the need for the establishment of a central audit agency; the claim that vast charges stemming from the Lynn revolt had been borne unilaterally reveals the inequity of the decentralized system. But the local committee's third point, the apparently innocuous argument that they had not responded to financial demands from Cambridge because they had expended huge sums on 'ammunition, artillery, shipping, and the frontiers', is perhaps most significant. For, in effect, the Norfolk committee were claiming that they were better qualified to decide to what purposes the money raised in their county should be allocated than were the Cambridge Committee, the body theoretically empowered by Parliament to 'order the affairs of the . . . Associated counties'.[63]

In the spring and early summer of 1643 the reluctance of the constituent counties to observe the dictates of the Cambridge Committee when they conflicted with the localities' assessment of their optimum individual interests was apparent. The financial difficulties of the Committee in the autumn indicate that Manchester's appointment and the passage of the Ordinance of 10 August whilst they temporarily strengthened the Committee, did not erase these sentiments; the counties swiftly reverted to their previous behavioral patterns. The financial crisis is not the only symptom of this phenomenon. By late August the counties were neglecting to observe the legislative requirement that they should send representatives to Cambridge,[64] and in early October the legitimacy of the Committee was again questioned. The challenge arose from the passage of the Ordinance of 20 September, which had imposed a weekly assessment for the maintenance of Manchester's army, added Lincolnshire to the Association, and named a new committee for each of the constituent counties, with specified powers: it was argued by some that this last clause, and the failure of the Ordinance to mention the existence of the Cambridge Committee, voided the previously established powers of the latter. A practical concomitant of this constitutional debate was the encouragement of the counties' reluctance to send representatives to Cambridge, and the Committee was 'in danger of dissolution through the non-appearance of Commissioners'.[65]

Shortly after the Committee had complained to the Commons of the damaging effects of the September legislation, their inability to exercise their theoretical authority to command the constituent counties was dramatically demonstrated. On 16 October Sir Lewis Dyve, in an effort to create a diversion which would force Manchester to withdraw forces from his successful Lincolnshire campaign to cover the Association, captured Bedford and Newport Pagnell, so cutting the lines of communication between London and the north and menacing the eastern counties – a threat which was emphasized when his raiding parties plundered the adjacent parts of Cambridgeshire and Hertfordshire. The immediate menace passed when Parliament instructed the Earl of Essex to move north against Newport Pagnell, which the Royalists abandoned to his army on 28 October.[66] During this crisis the Cambridge Committee endeavored to exercise its authority to co-ordinate the defense of the Association by the local militia units. On 17 October the constituent counties were instructed to send forces to Cambridge as 'our alarums come thicke upon us'. Next day Sir William Rowe, the Essex representative at Cambridge, who was acting as Chairman of the Committee, twice wrote to Chelmsford to inform the local committee that Dyve's men were at Potton threatening Cambridge and Huntingdon, and that the latter would be an easy prey as the local committee had already fled from the town: 'so . . . your forces must march night and day to gett into the towne to releife it, as you love religion, the laws, your country, the church off God and your true frend'. But the response of the Essex committee was negligible; three days after receipt of the first warnings no orders had been issued for the mustering of the local militia, nor were any other preparations made to reinforce Cambridge. The committee merely wrote to Parliament stressing the unreliability of the trained-bands, and entreating the Militia Committee of London to send assistance.[67] The supine behavior of the Essex administrators provoked Lady Judith Barrington, the wife of the most influential member of the committee, Sir Thomas, to write an angry denunciation, 'All the country in theas parts standes in amaze att the security you are in this time of soe certain danger; that you all at Chelmsford are still in security, delayes and expectance still of more news untill Cambridge be lost irrecoverably. When if in such tender cases you had erred in to much credulity, itt hadd been much more pardonable; to have sent assistance without need, rather then to late.' Lady Barrington implied that the other counties of the Association were as lax as Essex, and certainly the Hertfordshire trained-bands were defending their own county, while the Suffolk militia, though summoned on 18 October, were not fully mobilized for another five days. On the 23rd the Essex trained-bands were partially operational, and able to reinforce the 'twenty people with pichforkes' which, Lady Barrington had sarcastically suggested, was the full extent of Essex's contribution to the defense of Cambridge at the first alarm.[68] But by this date Sir William Rowe had tired of his fruitless task at Cambridge: in a letter to Barrington his pent-up frustration, a product not only of the failure of the counties to respond to his alarms during Dyve's attack but of his whole period as chairman, burst out, 'but what will now become off . . . anythinge . . . at Cambridge I am afraide to conjecture sinc you have beene deafe to so many letters off advertisment for so much as conduceth to the preservation off it for you, by forbearing so long to send men, money, or commissioners'.[69]

   In the autumn of 1643, as earlier in the year, the reluctance of the constituent counties to provide money, to send representatives, or to obey those commands relating to the defense of the Association, are symptomatic of their disinclination to subordinate their individual interests to the collective welfare of the Association as determined by the Cambridge Committee. This tension between the parts and the whole, apparent from the inception of the Association, could not be abolished by legislative fiat from Westminster, yet a Parliamentary reform could weaken the ability of the constituent counties to question the policies of the Cambridge Committee, and enhance the self-confidence of the latter – the establishment of a centralized fiscal system. 'Command, you, and be obeyed!' Cromwell had written: yet the constituent counties were not predisposed to obey nor could the Cambridge Committee command effectively, when the latter had to go cap in hand to the former for every penny in its treasury. There could be no effective central control as long as financial responsibility rested with the individual counties. A centralized financial organization was not a panacea which could eliminate all centrifugal tendencies within the Association, but its introduction was a precondition for any improvement in the status of the Committee of the Association at Cambridge.

Besides the difficulties stemming from the deficiencies in the financial provision for his army and the decentralized fiscal administration established by the September and October Ordinances, Manchester was hampered by two other problems in the autumn of 1643 which also required legislative solution.

The first was the question of the degree of control which the Earl of Essex could exercise over the forces of the Eastern Association. Manchester, who had received his commission as Major-General from Essex, was technically his subordinate: did this enable the Lord General to direct the army of the Association, or contingents of it, over Manchester's head? The issue had arisen at the inception of Manchester's command, when, on 26 August, Essex had ordered Cromwell and the Association's cavalry, which were covering the fenland frontier, to join his army as it moved to the relief of Gloucester. The committee of Huntingdonshire immediately petitioned Manchester 'to have a care of many thousands of soules that if the forces be gone are like to perishe by the 30 troopes of horse that . . . Newcastle hath in Lincolnshire', and clearly the removal of Cromwell's force with Lynn in revolt would have been suicidal. This immediate issue was settled in a mutually agreeable compromise, whereby Cromwell stayed put, while Essex was reinforced by some Association troops that had previously operated with Grey of Warke's old division, but this did not settle the fundamental constitutional issue of the legitimacy of the Lord General's attempt to command a detachment of the army of the Eastern Association without reference to Manchester. The issue lay dormant until December, when Essex ordered 600 of the Association's horse, quartered at Bedford, to leave the town and operate in conjunction with his army 'without the consent of the Earl of Manchester', but in mid-November the leaders of the Association were aware that the principle of whether their army had an independent status, or was directly subordinate to that of Essex, was a critical question which would require Parliamentary determination.[70]

In the same period Manchester was involved in a lesser jurisdictional dispute concerning his position in Lincolnshire, a conflict which stemmed from Parliament's carelessness, not unusual, in drafting its legislative enactments. By the Ordinance of 20 September Lincolnshire was added to the Eastern Association, and the Earl of Manchester, as Major-General of the Association – and hence of Lincolnshire – was empowered to commission a military Governor of Boston. The Ordinance completely neglected the fact that there already existed a Major-General in Lincolnshire, Lord Willoughby of Parham, who held a commission from the Lord General to command the forces of that county. The financial provisions of the Ordinance enhanced the anomalous situation, for it was uncertain whether the £3250 a month which the local committee were instructed to raise should be paid to the existing forces in the county commanded by Willoughby, or must go to new regiments to be raised in Lincolnshire which would be subordinate to Manchester. To complicate matters further, when, by the Ordinance of 11 October, the Earl was allowed to receive a third part of the sequestration revenues raised in the constituent counties, Lincolnshire was not specified as coming within the terms of the Ordinance. After Winceby, as control of the county was wrested from the Royalists, Parliament was forced to come to grips with the situation which their legislation had created in Lincolnshire, whereby both Manchester and Willoughby could claim supreme command in the county, and to control its newly accessible financial and military resources. On 18 October the Commons decided that the Ordinance of 20 September entailed the supersession of Lord Willoughby, to whom they offered as a face-saving alternative 'Honourable Command' in the main Parliamentary army. Willoughby was prepared to march his troops to join Essex on condition that some provision was made for the payment of his men's arrears and the debts which he had incurred in Parliament's service, but when no attempt was made to meet these demands he resolved to keep his forces in the county. As a result Lincolnshire became the scene of a fierce 'competition between two authorities to governe the affaires of this county', with the two putative Major-Generals and their agents struggling to monopolize the resources of the county, and pursuing disparate military strategies.[71]

It has been suggested that Manchester failed to capitalize on his military successes in the autumn of 1643 because of serious weaknesses in the organization of his army which had become apparent in the course of the campaign. The existing legislation did not produce a sufficient sum given the size of his army, and in consequence his men were unpaid, ill-equipped and starving. The lack of central fiscal control created military inefficiency, was inequitably weighted against certain counties, and undermined attempts, particularly those of the Cambridge Committee, to insist upon central control of the constituent counties. In addition, the jurisdictional dispute with Lord Willoughby, and the more important question of the status of the Association's army with reference to the powers of the Earl of Essex as supreme commander, had to be settled. This interpretation is strengthened by Manchester's actions in mid-November: having marched his force into its winter quarters he made a secret visit to Westminster. 'I learn', wrote the Venetian ambassador to his masters, 'that it is because he cannot supply his army which . . . has not the provisions and help it requires.'[72]

The journey did not provide immediate relief for the army of the Association, although it did serve to inform Parliament of the Earl's difficulties. These were discussed in the Commons on 10 November, and on the 18th a draft Ordinance 'for settling the affairs in the six associated counties; and for giving further power unto the Earl of Manchester' was introduced by Harbottle Grimston. Although the proposed legislation attempted to settle the dispute in Lincolnshire by paying Willoughby's forces a proportion of their arrears and instructing them to join Essex's army, most of its provisions dealt, in a piecemeal fashion, with peripheral matters – enforcing the counties to raise the men and money already voted by Parliament, for example, or granting the committee at Ely all sums to be raised in the Isle for its defense.[73] Eventually Grimston's draft was tabled, and although one of its clauses, that empowering Manchester to eject scandalous ministers from their livings and to purge Cambridge University, was revived in the form of a separate Ordinance on 12 December, that too became bogged down in Committee.[74] The failure of Grimston's proposed legislation was probably caused, not by any lack of Parliamentary sympathy for Manchester's predicament, but by a realization that only a fundamental reorganization of the Association's finances could obviate the causes of the Earl's complaints, and that no real changes could be undertaken until the expiration of the existing fiscal Ordinances in December.

Manchester had to wait for a legislative solution to his problems, but he did not wait in vain. On 20 January an Ordinance passed which both increased the assessments to be levied on the seven counties by an overall 50%, and established a centralized financial organization: local collectors were instructed to pay in the assessments they had levied 'at the place . . . where the Earle of Manchester, and the Committee for the said Association . . . shall appoint, and to the . . . Treasurers to be by them named', while no part of the sum raised by virtue of this Ordinance was to be disbursed without orders from the Earl, his Commissary-General and two of the Cambridge Committee. Besides improving the financial provision of the Earl's army and abolishing the 'county' treasury system, the Ordinance also settled Manchester's jurisdictional disputes with Essex and Willoughby. Against the pretensions of the former, Parliament categorically declared that the forces of the Association should be 'kept intire'; that no contingent could be commanded upon any service without the agreement of Manchester and the Cambridge Committee or 'particular direction of Parliament'. The Ordinance also effectively destroyed Willoughby's authority in Lincolnshire as his force was left without any financial provision by the clause which ordered that all sums raised in the county should be paid to Manchester's treasurers. Two days after the passage of this Ordinance, after an angry debate in the Commons in which Cromwell impugned Lord Willoughby's military ability and devotion to the Parliamentary cause, and denounced the indiscipline of his troops, it was voted that Essex should issue a commission for Manchester to command in chief in Lincolnshire. On the same day the Ordinance which had stuck so long in committee, empowering the Earl to purge the clergy of the Eastern Association and Cambridge University of men deemed 'scandalous', was passed.[75]

In the period immediately before the passage of these critical enactments Manchester and his aides had organized a well coordinated and powerful lobby. In November and December the press was employed to keep the Association's army in the eye of the public, even when the bulk of it lay idle in winter quarters. John Dillingham, the editor of *The Parliament Scout* who was later accused of being Manchester's 'pensioner', reported every petty cavalry skirmish, emphasized the growing strength of the Association's army and enthusiastically praised its excellent discipline and religious enthusiasm; the latter was obliquely contrasted with the unruly behavior of Essex's force, as was Manchester's successful generalship with Lord Willoughby's dismal record.[76] In December a series of petitions was organized in the constituent counties, in which the signatories, having stressed their devotion to the cause and to Manchester, pressed that the Earl might be empowered to reorganize the local militia and to purge ill-affected ministers. In Lincolnshire a petition questioning Willoughby's military competence, suggesting that the behavior of his forces was little better than that of the cavaliers, and pleading that Manchester be given sole command in the county, was organized. Signatures were canvassed by Colonel Edward King, whom the Earl had appointed to the Governorship of Boston, and by other officers in the army of the Association who, it was later claimed, insulted and threatened those that refused to sign.[77] In late December a deputation from the Cambridge Committee journeyed to London to present petitions to the Commons, one pressing for power to reorganize the militia within the Association, the other protesting bitterly against Essex's attempts o command a detachment of the Association's army without reference to the Earl of Manchester.[78] The ground well-prepared, in mid-January the Association's military leaders, particularly those that were M.P.s, gathered at Westminster determined to so arrange matters 'that for the future a constant pay may be had for them'. Cromwell's role in this final stage of the Parliamentary campaign is particularly impressive. He moved that the House accept the new fiscal Ordinance when it emerged from committee on 17 January, in a speech stressing the want of provisions, shoes, clothes and money which would hamstring Manchester's spring campaign unless some new financial supply was forthcoming: his attack on Lord Willoughby on the 22nd resulted in Manchester's securing an unchallenged command in Lincolnshire.[79]

The ease with which the program of reforms regarded as essential by the leaders of the Association was pushed through Parliament was a triumph for the carefully planned campaign which prefaced the debates.[80] But that such a lobby was necessary was a reflection of the complicated political situation at Westminster in the winter, as the supporters of Essex, of the local associations, of Scottish intervention, struggled for slices of the financial cake. The effect of this complex political conflict can be seen by studying the history of the legislation requested by the Earl of Essex and Sir William Waller for the strengthening and maintenance of their armies. On 22 November an Ordinance was introduced in the Commons for the Lord General's army to be recruited to the number of 10,000 foot and 4000 horse, to be financed by a monthly assessment upon the counties controlled by Parliament: it finally passed, in a severely attenuated form, on 26 March, having been delayed in committee for 'six or seven months', as Essex remonstrated with pardonable exaggeration.[81] Passage of legislation for the maintenance of Sir William Waller's army was also retarded. On 4 November, in the face of Hopton's advance into Sussex, Parliament had associated the four south-eastern counties under Waller's command, but the Ordinance made no firm provision for the raising of new forces, nor permanent fiscal arrangements for their maintenance. Legislation to remedy these defects was not introduced until 12 February, and then did not finally pass until 30 March.[82]

To a degree the political divisions in the winter of 1643 reflected those which had appertained in the summer debates in Parliament. The political group most virulent in their opposition to the passage of the Lord General's Ordinance were still those radical M.P.s who, in the summer of 1643, reacting against what they regarded as his over-cautious generalship and the inefficiency of his army, had endeavored to effectively reduce the Lord General to impotence by setting up Waller as a commander independent of his control with a better financed and supplied army. Neither the failure of this attempt, nor the Earl's relief of Gloucester and victory at Newbury, had reconciled the radicals to his generalship. His declared preference for a negotiated, compromise peace was anathema to the war party, who feared that 'a strong partie . . . which would ever have been at peace in any termes' would endeavor to strengthen Essex's army at the expense of other Parliamentary forces, so that 'by the power of the Generall's armie, when it had all the strength conveyed to it, they might command a peace'.[83] Accordingly the war party, in the winter session of Parliament, continually emphasized the inefficiency of Essex's army, in particular its high proportion of officers to the number of men in service, and its indiscipline.[84] More practically, the radicals put every obstacle in the way of attempts to strengthen Essex's army, or to establish an adequate financial provision for it. Sir Henry Vane the younger played a major role in a series of Committee meetings in December in which the size of Essex's army was cut to 7500 foot and 3000 horse, and its financial supply reduced to a sum which, in the opinion of the Lord General's supporters, would not even maintain this number. Lengthy disputes followed as to the sums which should be assessed upon the individual counties, which were only ended when it was decided that Essex's army should be funded from the excise, the monthly assessment from London, and a fixed sum from the revenues from the Fifth and Twentieth part. Yet, despite this decision, and the protests of Essex and his allies, the Committee sessions continued into February with discussion ranging from improvements in the collection of the excise revenue, to such trivia as the instructions which should be given to the agents that were to muster the army, and similar 'impertinencies'. In late February the radicals secured another weapon with which to harass the Earl of Essex. In response to a petition from the City of London denouncing some of the Lord General's subordinates as 'unfaithful, scandalous and prophane' a Committee, consisting almost exclusively of 'fiery spirits', was instructed to select, from Essex's existing cadre, the officers to command the seven regiments of foot and six of horse that had been voted. The Committee's investigation into the competence and devotion of Essex's officers was time-consuming, and the passage of the Ordinance was further retarded until the defeat of the brigade besieging Newark made the Commons realize the need for the mobilization of Essex's army.[85]

But while the radicals headed the campaign to obstruct the passage of the Lord General's Ordinance, legislation on behalf of Sir William Waller, their hero in the summer with whom they had proposed to supplant Essex, proceeded through the Houses with comparable slowness. In part this was due to a change in the attitude of the 'fierie spirits' towards Sir William. They were still willing to use him as a stick with which to beat Essex, angrily denouncing the Lord General for his failure to issue a commission to Waller in form similar to those given to the Major-Generals of other Associations, and, on 13 March, reversing a previous vote in the Commons to accept a House of Lords amendment implying Waller's subordination to the Lord General.[86] Yet a number of the radicals were disillusioned with Waller, largely, according to his own account, because of his refusal to act as their cat's-paw: in the summer he had rejected a suggestion by his sponsors that he should 'engage . . . to entertain none but godly officers, such as should be recommended to me', telling them that there was more to the make-up of an officer than godliness, and 'from that time forward I may date the expiration of their friendship'.[87]

The waning of the radicals' enthusiasm for Waller did not end the antipathy felt for him by Essex and his adherents. This feud, engendered in the summer of 1643, and subsequently reflected in and exacerbated by the quarrels of the two generals' subordinates, came to have a dynamic of its own, independent of political considerations. So Essex's friends in the Lords added three amendments to Waller's Ordinance stressing his subordination to the Lord General, although they had earlier felt no compulsion to make similar provisions in the legislation for the Eastern Association. The fierce, irrational, opposition to Waller displayed by Essex's supporters further retarded the passage of the former's Ordinance.

The group most strenuously opposed to Waller – 'the Generall's partie' – was led by Holles, who was also the most active spokesman for those who desired a negotiated peace. But the peace party were not united; while Holles's faction worked vigorously to secure the passage of Essex's Ordinance, so enhancing the radicals' fear that they intended to use his army to impose the compromise settlement they desired, some firm supporters of peace initially opposed the measure, arguing that it would increase an already intolerable financial burden. The discussion in Committee in December concerning the sums which were to be imposed upon the counties for the maintenance of the army gave men like D'Ewes an opportunity to bemoan the escalating costs of the war, and to demand an abatement of the sums assessed upon their own localities.[88] While D'Ewes was ultimately to realize that failure to pass the Ordinance was a false economy, in that without it Essex's army was unable to move into action and merely plundered the unfortunate inhabitants of Hertfordshire upon whom they were quartered,[89] the opposition of men of similar principles played into the hands of the enemies of Essex in the war party.

In the summer of 1643 the middle group, led by Pym, had carefully held the balance between the peace and war parties, reorganizing the Lord General's army despite the opposition of the radicals on the one hand, while refusing to sacrifice Sir William Waller to the resentment of Essex and his allies. On every occasion of friction the middle group endeavored to achieve a working compromise between the two commanders. Yet in the winter of 1643–4 the middle group was apparently powerless; Parliament was deadlocked on the issue of military supply as the supporters of Essex and Waller opposed and obstructed the legislation demanded by their respective opponents.

The sickness and death of Pym was in part responsible for this new situation: the loss of his leadership, mastery of Parliamentary tactics and skilled manipulation of the Commons was a severe blow to the middle group. But the group did not immediately disintegrate after the loss of their great leader,[90] and their vital impact on the formulation of the Ordinance establishing the Committee of Both Kingdoms has been demonstrated.[91] In the winter the group still endeavored to pursue Pym's old policy of supporting Essex's army, while strengthening the other Parliamentary forces in order to enhance the efficiency of the war-machine. On 1 January, during the 'most earnest and vehement debate' concerning Essex's refusal to grant Waller a commission as fully independent Commander of the South-Eastern Association, St John suggested a full examination of that and other commissions before apportioning blame, as the radicals Haselrig and Wentworth were only too willing to do, and Sir Walter Earle proposed a compromise which was acceptable to the House.[92] Their influence can also be discerned in the compromise which settled the dispute concerning the Lords' amendments to Waller's Ordinance,[93] and in the question which was eventually put following the debate on Lisle's addition to Essex's Ordinance, that the latter's army should be subject to the order and direction of the Committee of Both Kingdoms,[94] both affairs in which the radicals were endeavoring to embarrass Essex and further retard the passage of his Ordinance.

Yet despite these interventions, the members of the middle group were powerless to speed either the Lord General's or Waller's Ordinance in pursuance of their traditional policy of strengthening the military machine. This failure cannot be understood purely in terms of the political divisions which had existed in Parliament in the summer of 1643. The three general political divisions – war party, peace party and middle group – survived, but were complicated by the impingement of a novel pattern of political behavior whereby some M.P.s voted funds and supplies for the theater of war most agreeable to their local interests. In a discussion on 6 December with a fellow M.P. concerning the slow progress which the legislation for the Earl of Essex was making in committee, D'Ewes was informed of the existence of three groups in the Commons. First 'those that desired all that might possibly be spared for the satisfying of the Scotts' led by young Sir Henry Vane, and consisting chiefly of northern M.P.s, whose estates had been seized by Newcastle; the second faction consisted of western M.P.s, led by Prideaux and Trenchard, who worked 'to further Sir William Waller's expedition into the west for reducing of those parts'. These two groups combined just outnumbered the third, consisting of Essex's supporters, and were both 'loath that the Lord Generall's army should be too numerous or require too much money'.[95]

It was the support of M.P.s who feared that the provisions of Essex's Ordinance ran counter to their optimum local interests that enabled the radicals to wage their campaign of obstruction to the passage of the legislation, although the ultimate political ends of these allies differed widely. But the local dimension of Parliamentary divisions also frustrated Waller. While both the western and the northern regional groups were led by M.P.s associated with the war party, and could combine against Essex, their co-operation could shatter when their financial interests clashed, as they did over the question of the sequestration revenues of the south-eastern counties. In November when Sir Henry Vane the elder moved that Waller's treasurers might borrow £5000 out of this source, which had been previously allocated to the Scots, he was opposed by a group of M.P.s led by his son. In February the pro-Scottish group temporarily erased a clause in Waller's Ordinance giving him a third part of the sequestrations raised in Kent and Surrey, arguing that the money was earmarked for the Scots.[96] Waller's command was also weakened by another local lobby, that of the Militia Committee of the City of London, whose forces formed such an integral part of his army. The Commons were unwilling to offend their powerful allies, and not only did the Committee insist upon maintaining independent control of their forces, which led to a number of military anomalies, but endeavored to enhance their powers at the expense of Waller's control over the counties of his Association.[97]

The Eastern Association legislation sailed through this political maelstrom of conflicting interest groups swiftly, unscathed by the factional obstructionism which retarded the Ordinances of both Essex and Waller. The carefully co-ordinated lobby conducted by the leaders of the Association alone cannot explain this success, which must be accounted for in terms of the legislation's appeal to the various conflicting groups in Parliament.

Manchester's Ordinances received the support of the radicals of the war party. In the late summer Sir William Waller had jibbed at the group's request to 'entertaine none but godly officers, such as should be recommended to me' and dated the 'expiration of their friendship' from this refusal. But Manchester's army was increasingly thought of as the repository both of good discipline and godliness, a view most vigorously propagated by *The Parliament Scout*, but also appearing in other journals: so in December *Mercurius Civicus* wrote of the Association's troops, 'The best meanes to have a growing . . . Army, is to appoint . . . Commanders of godly and religous lives, . . . and such more eminently are the . . . Officers under this Noble Earle'.[98] Cromwell was playing a dominant role in the selection of officers for the Association, and a number of the godly, like John Lilburne, left their positions in Essex's army to join that of the Earl of Manchester.[99] We may also assume that the passage of the Ordinances was supported by the middle group: the maintenance of the Association was part of its policy of enhancing the efficiency of the war-machine, many of its members were East Anglian M.P.s, and they were joined by prominent middle groupers like St John, who had shown an interest in the Association's affairs.[100]

Although some members of the peace party, like D'Ewes, were horrified by the provisions of Manchester's 'fatal' Ordinance, especially the 'vast and unparaleld' taxation,[101] the group as a whole, in particular 'the Generall's partie' led by Holles, did not oppose its passage with the ferocity with which they obstructed legislation on behalf of Sir William Waller. Their quiescence stemmed from the fact that Manchester's command had not aroused, at its inception or in its subsequent history, the violent antipathies which poisoned relations between Essex and Waller and their respective adherents. The Lord General did have a number of grievances against the Eastern Association. He objected to the removal of the remnants of Grey of Warke's brigade from his army in the Thames valley 'when it was weakest' and his annoyance was enhanced by the fact that, in the absence of adequate supplies from the constituent counties, he had paid some of those troops from his own pocket, and then had the greatest difficulty in recouping the money from the local authorities.[102] He was involved in another squabble with the latter, when, after the appointment of Manchester, the committees of Essex and Hertfordshire put up a fiercer resistance to the activities of the officers whom the Lord General had appointed to requisition cavalry mounts, claiming that their seizures disenabled the counties from meeting the requirements of Manchester's army, now their first priority.[103] Further, Essex was said to be envious of the October legislation empowering Manchester to receive a third of the seques-tration revenues in the eastern counties when no such provision had been made for him, and there had been friction over his attempt to command the Association's troops without reference to the Cam-bridge authorities.[104] But the tensions had not developed into an outright feud, and Cromwell, in his speech on 17 January, went out of his way to placate the Lord General's adherents, moving the Commons to pass Manchester's legislation 'next after the Earl of Essex's Ordinance'.[105]

Finally the passage of Manchester's Ordinance was acceptable to the group of M.P.s who supported Scottish intervention in the hope of clearing the Royalists from the north, for it was generally believed that the Association's army would operate in conjunction with the Scots. Their support may not have been entirely a matter of increas-ing the force potentially available for the northern theater. As Baillie was aware, even 'the best of the English' were not enthusiastic to employ the services of the Scots, and a number, including young Vane, the architect of the alliance, were distrustful of the intentions of their 'brethren'.[196] A powerful army operating with that of the Scots might mitigate the dangers of Scottish intervention, serving as a check on the territorial, political or religious ambitions of the invaders.

It has been shown in the preceding chapter that the military achievement of the Association's forces in the period from the sitting of the first Bury conference to July 1643 was limited, and that the fundamental causes of this were weaknesses in the administrative and political structure of the Association. The forces at its disposal, dependent on a diminishing stream of volunteer recruits, and raised by a series of expedients based largely on the inefficient county militia system, were small, constantly depleted by desertion and disease, and their military effectiveness weakened by endemic mutinies caused by lack of pay. Although Parliament had come to realize that this force could not be maintained by the flagging generosity of the well-affected, the Commons had done little to provide a viable alternative; there was no grant of regular taxation producing a specified sum for the use of the Association's forces. Finally, the financial system, which placed all responsibility in the hands of the local governors, allowed the defensive, locally oriented aims of the latter to predominate. It negated any attempt at central direction of policy.

The period from July 1643 to January 1644 saw the creation of a system which obviated these major weaknesses. In August, when a willingness among the legislators to re-think their overall strategy coincided with the serious military threat posed by Newcastle's advance, the Association was empowered to raise a powerful body of horse and foot, and to levy the latter by impressment. In the following two months the attempts to finance the Association's force by a series of temporary and insufficient fiscal expedients was abandoned, and a monthly assessment was voted to be levied on the constituent counties for the maintenance of their army. Yet Manchester's success in the autumn of 1643, though encouraging, was still limited by the continued existence of flaws in the financial arrangements and political structure of the Association. The assessment was insufficient to meet the army's needs, and its disbursement was still controlled by the individual counties, which created a number of military anomalies and, in particular, limited the possibility of central control. In January these difficulties were partially overcome as the result of pressure from the military command, and through the broad-based support which Manchester could command in both Houses. It was the lack of similar support which Waller stressed when reflecting on his dismal military record in 1644: his enemies in the Commons refused to vote him an adequate financial supply, and were determined that he should not command 'an entire body of my own; but so compounded of city and country regiments that when they pleased they might take me to pieces, like a clock . . . these . . . borrowed forces, having no dependence upon me, but upon them that sent them, would not follow me further then pleased themselves, but would be ready to march home when they had pursued their point, as if they had don enough when they had don anything'.[107] Manchester was more fortunate. His allies in Parliament voted an increased financial provision, and, by the legislation establishing a centralized treasury and military administration, ensured that his forces would be dependent upon the Earl, not upon 'them that sent them'. The Ordinance of 20 January was the legal basis for the army which won Marston Moor and which, not only in its personnel, but in its centralized treasury, administration and supply system, foreshadows the New Model.

PART III

The hegemony of Cambridge: the financial and military organization established by the Earl of Manchester

The Ordinance of 20 January 1644 not only authorized the levy of the unprecedented sum of £33,780 a month upon the eastern counties for the maintenance of the forces of the Association, but empowered the Earl of Manchester, not the individual county committees, to supervise its disbursement. Manchester was given the opportunity to create a centralized fiscal and military administration, and thus to command an 'entire body of . . . [his] . . . own', to the lack of which Sir William Waller, with 'borrowed forces, having no dependence upon me', attributed his failures. The way in which the Earl transmuted the critical Parliamentary legislation into the Treasuries and supply departments based at Cambridge, which provided the fiscal and administrative backbone for the army victorious at Marston Moor, and the constitution of that army, must now be examined.

6

The Cambridge Committee

Ironically the linchpin of the system which the Earl established upon the basis of the January legislation was an institution previously neglected by the constituent counties and distrusted by Parliament.

In 1644 the Committee of the Association became the agency responsible for the supervision of the fiscal and administrative departments established at Cambridge. The Ordinance of 20 January ordered that the audited accounts of the Treasurers should be reviewed by the Committee each month, and that all warrants directed to the Treasurers for the disbursement of sums collected upon the assessment should be approved by Manchester, his Commissary-General William Harlackenden, and at least two of the Committee. In fact the system employed was that Gawsell and Weaver, the Treasurers who traveled with the army, issued money on the receipt of warrants from Manchester and Harlackenden, which were subsequently counter-signed by two of the Committee, while Leman, the Treasurer at Cambridge, accepted the Committee's warrants, which were later approved by the Earl and the Commissary-General.[1] Occasionally Manchester, when he was with the army or in London, would sign warrants which he then forwarded to Cambridge for payment, either for the convenience of the payee or because Gawsell was short of ready cash.[2] The Committee's independent initiative varied according to the type of warrant. Clearly the counter-signing of warrants which Gawsell or Weaver had already met was a rubber-stamp formality, but warrants forwarded to Leman were discussed and sometimes rejected.[3] Many of the warrants which the Committee issued to Leman were of a routine nature, particularly the payment of quarters bills and the issues upon debenture to the officers, but others, notably the payments to sick or recovered soldiers marching to their homes or back to the colors, involved some discussion and an investigation of the credentials of the claimant.[4]

It is regrettable that while the bulk of the records of the Association's Treasuries are available, none of the minutes or letter-books of the Committee have survived. In consequence the latter's largely routine role in central administration can be established in detail, but any account of its more important functions, as a lobby at Westminster and as an intermediary between the army and the constituent counties of the Association, is necessarily more impressionistic.

However, Parliamentary diaries and the Journals of the two Houses do enable the historian to present some account of the close working relationship between those M.P.s who supported the Association in the Commons, and Manchester, his immediate advisors, and the Cambridge Committee. In some instances the Earl wrote personally to Westminster, either to the Committee of East Anglian M.P.s or to the Committee of Both Kingdoms to press for the introduction of an Ordinance for the benefit of the Association.[5] But, particularly when asking for the passage of more contentious legislation, Manchester might enlist the support of the Cambridge Committee, in which case the request would be made to the House in the form of a petition from the Committee, presented by a deputation from that body. This practice was employed in December 1643 preparatory to the passage of the Ordinance of 20 January, and was used again in the attempts made from September to November 1644 to persuade Parliament that it was imperative for the Association to receive the excise revenues from the seven counties.[6] In the absence of the day-to-day records and correspondence of the Committee it is not possible to determine the degree to which that body played an active part in the creation of policy. During the attempt to secure the excise revenue in the autumn of 1644, a letter from Colonel Valentine Walton, M.P., the Governor of King's Lynn, to Manchester,[7] suggests that the Committee were not vitally involved in the inauguration of the legislation for which they subsequently lobbied. Walton writes that he and Dr Stane, the auditor of the Association, had come to Cambridge and met with the Committee and had pressed that they should petition Parliament for the excise revenue to be granted to the Association. Initially the Committee questioned the wisdom of the move 'making many objections against it'; Walton replied that some new source of revenue would have to be tapped if the army was to be maintained, that if they did not petition for the excise it would be put to some other use, and, finally, that if they collected the excise, it would ease the burden of the weekly assessment. These reasons convinced the Committee, and Walton's mention of the forthcoming Stourbridge Fair caused its members to 'strain who should contribute most in propounding commodities to be excise-able'. In this case, though the Committee's opinion was canvassed, its final petition for the excise was an exercise in public relations, designed to add weight and the appearance of a favorable consensus within the Association to measures previously determined upon by Manchester, his Treasury officials and military entourage. However, its endeavors to influence Parliament during the New Model Army and Self-Denying Ordinance debates demonstrate that the Committee could take a very independent line,[8] and the chance survival of Walton's letter is not conclusive evidence that they always performed only a passive, rubber-stamp function in relation to proposed legislation.

However they originated, when the petitions of the Cambridge Committee were presented to the Commons, local M.P.s were ready with support; on the presentation in October of the Committee's second petition desiring the excise revenue, Miles Corbett, burgess for Yarmouth, and other M.P.s rose to inform the House of the vast charge of the Association's army, and the sources of revenue at present available to it. It is probable that the exact timing of the presentation of petitions and the mobilization of the support of M.P.s was the work of the Westminster Committee of the Association, which consisted of those members from East Anglia. The Committee's official function was the discussion of proposed legislation concerning the Association referred to them by the House, but they also acted as a lobby and as a liaison between the Commons and Manchester and the Cambridge Committee.[9] In April 1644 the latter sent Thomas Cooke to Westminster with a proposed Ordinance and instructions to 'passe the same as he can gett it, not alteringe the substance'; to that end he was to discuss the matter with Speaker Lenthall, with the central Committee for Sequestration, and with the Committee of East Anglian M.P.s, in particular its chairman, Corbett. Cooke was employed in a similar function in August, and again in January 1645, when he was joined by Colonel Mildmay who also worked with the Committee of East Anglian M.P.s.[10] Besides commissioning its own members to attend at Westminster to press for the passage of legislation, the Cambridge Committee maintained an agent at London to solicit business, presumably of a more routine nature, concerning the Association.[11]

Parliamentary journals and diaries partially fill the gap left by the disappearance of the letter-books of the Cambridge Committee, and make it possible to give some account of the latter's communications and relationship with the Commons. But the lack of central records, and the scarcely better survival of similar documents for the county committees with whom the men at Cambridge corresponded,[12] make it more difficult to delineate the other major function of the Committee in 1644: their supervision of the local authorities in the constituent counties. However, certain areas of control and interference by the Cambridge Committee may be distinguished from the surviving evidence.

The Committee acted in an overall supervisory capacity with regard to the defense of the Association during the absences of the field-army in the north and the Thames valley, summoning the local trained-bands to the borders when Royalist raiders threatened the eastern counties. It endeavored to expedite the execution of legislation within the counties, pressing the local committees to hasten their assessments or recruits, and to inquire into the whereabouts of deserters; those individuals who persistently refused to pay their assessments could be summoned to Cambridge and imprisoned.[13] The Committee of the Association also played a part in the organization established by Manchester for the prosecution and sequestration of 'scandalous' ministers: it was particularly active in the purge of the University which the Earl had instituted, while legal disputes within the constituent counties, particularly concerning tithes, between the ousted ministers and their replacements were heard in Cambridge.[14] In addition the Committee decided common policy in certain military and fiscal matters in the interests of uniformity, as in its order concerning the arrangements to meet the charges of the county committees.[15] Finally, disputes within a county, such as the disagreement between the town of Ipswich and the committee of Suffolk concerning the apportionment of certain taxes, might be referred to the Committee for settlement.[16]

In 1644 the Committee of the Association had three major functions. As instructed by the Ordinance of 20 January, its members supervised the operations of the centralized administration established at Cambridge. They also represented the interests of the Association to the authorities at Westminster, discussing proposed legislation and then working with the Committee of East Anglian M.P.s to expedite its passage through Parliament. Finally they provided central direction to the local administrators, supervising their activities, and exhorting and cajoling the committees in the interests of uniformity and efficiency. Not only do these wide-ranging functions contrast with those which the Committee had sought to perform in 1643, but Manchester's Committee, in its relations with Westminster and with the localities, was acting with greater authority and far more self-confidence than had its predecessor. Both the hysterical appeals for military assistance, funds and delegates from the Cambridge Committee, and the neglect of their requests by the local authorities were things of the past. The Committee's new self-assurance owed much to the January legislation, which ended the debilitating financial dependence upon the local committees, and, by requiring the Committee to perform an important function in the administration of the army, ensured the growth of a formal institutional structure which enhanced the sense of corporate identity.[17] But the Committee's developing maturity was also a function of changes in its structure and personnel initiated unilaterally by the Earl of Manchester.

In the autumn of 1643, despite the instructions embodied in the Ordinance of 10 August, the constituent counties disregarded both the duty of providing commissioners to represent them at the Cambridge Committee, and the commands of the latter. However, after his November journey to London, Manchester settled at Cambridge, and his presence boosted the authority, prestige, and self-confidence of the Committee, which began to hold its meetings in the Earl's lodgings at Trinity College, their location throughout 1644. In November the Committee made its first serious effort to enforce the counties to pay in the long-overdue sums owed for common charges, and in December played an important part in the lobby for new legislation. In this period Manchester abandoned the system established by the August Ordinance whereby the county committees were responsible for the provision of a representative, and personally summoned men of his own choice to serve on the Committee.[18]

In the early spring, with the approach of the campaigning season, the Earl, recognizing the need to give structure to a system which had depended upon his presence for its effectiveness, formally reorganized the Committee. In a warrant of 2 March Manchester ordered that every Committee member 'that shall be sent for by my Lord' should receive 7/6d a day from the Treasury for his service, provided that he stayed for at least a month in Cambridge. Manchester firmly established the system whereby he, and not the local committees, who had always been very reluctant to pay their nominees the £1 a week fee established by Ordinance, was to select the commissioners, while the novel system of payment ensured a greater continuity of membership.[19] By the end of April, when military men who had previously served on the Committee had marched with the army, its membership had stabilized in a small caucus of seven, one from each of the counties of the Association, who sat fairly regularly until the end of the year, when, after the effective destruction of the Association by the New Model Ordinance, they ceased to attend and were replaced by new men who sat for shorter periods.[20]

The Cambridge Committee's efficiency and self-assurance stemmed not only from the continuity of membership and consequent sense of corporate identity, but from the quality of the men Manchester appointed to it. Biographical studies of the seven representatives reveal a number of common characteristics: none of them was heir to a major established county family, all save one were demonstrably Puritan, a majority had wide-ranging economic or social interests and ties. The sociology of the group suggests that none of them would be devoted to the ideal of the county community and persuaded of the impropriety of external interference in local affairs.

The chairmanship of the Cambridge Committee was held by Nathaniel Bacon, a grandson of Elizabeth's Lord Keeper who had established this leading East Anglian family. But Nathaniel was a younger son of a cadet branch which had settled at Shrubland in Suffolk. His family was famous for its Puritan zeal: his father had studied at Geneva with Beza, and his eldest brother Nicholas, who was sympathetic to the New England venture, was described by a contemporary as 'the greatest friend to pious ministers in all these parts' and his house as 'famous for religion and hospitality'. After being called to the Bar in 1617 Bacon settled at Langham in Essex and became a J.P. for the county; in 1628 he was reported as a forced loan refuser. In 1643 he returned to his native county, being elected recorder of Ipswich. The duties of this position were to conflict with his services at Cambridge in the next year: on at least two occasions the Committee had to write to the bailiffs of Ipswich to request them to postpone their local courts, so that Bacon might stay longer in Cambridge because of 'the importance of the present affaires heere':[21] a good illustration of the Committee's confidence in the chairman. During his periodic absences, presumably on local business, Bacon's position as Suffolk representative and his chairmanship were taken by his younger brother Francis, another lawyer.[22] Both the Bacons became recruiter M.P.s in 1645, Nathaniel for the University, Francis for Ipswich, and the former, while supporting Presbyterian legislation, was also associated with the party that favored the fullest prosecution of the war.[23] The brothers were secluded at Pride's Purge, and although they were formally re-admitted to the Rump in June 1649, and in 1652 Nathaniel was given legal office, both were unenthusiastic about the Commonwealth.[24] The brothers achieved greater prominence in the Protectorate; both became Masters of Requests, and, as M.P.s, supported a return to the 'Ancient Constitution' of government by two houses and a single person. Like many Puritan lawyers Nathaniel was a notable antiquary, compiling the 'Annalls' of Ipswich from the corporation records, and writing an historical discourse on the government of England, the ideals of which he propagandized in his speeches in Richard Cromwell's Parliament.[25]

If the Bacons were to advocate Presbyterianism after 1645 the Norfolk representative on the Committee was a staunch Independent. Like the Bacons, John Brewster had ties and contacts throughout East Anglia; born at Wrentham in Suffolk, he had married into a prominent aldermanic family of Norwich, as had two of his brothers, and was later to settle at Barking in Essex, representing that county in Barebone's Parliament. Independency was part of Brewster's family background; his father was patron of John Philip, who was influenced toward the 'Congregational Way' by his brother-in-law, Dr Ames. In 1638 the attentions of the ecclesiastical authorities had forced Philip to flee to New England, but in 1641 he returned to Wrentham and by 1644 had established an Independent church there.[26]

The Essex representative on the Committee, Colonel Henry

Mildmay of Graces in Little Baddow, came from another Puritan family with contacts throughout East Anglia and in New England. The son of the professional soldier Sir Henry, Colonel Mildmay's grandmother was a Winthrop, and his mother, a Gurdon; through the latter he was related to the Bacons of Shrubland. This group of families, bound tighter by common religious interests, maintained close personal relationships.[27] Colonel Mildmay was educated at Felsted school under the Puritan Martin Holbech 'whoe scarce bred any man that was loyall to his prince', and, at the beginning of the civil war, with the encouragement of the Earl of Warwick, he became captain of a troop under the Lord General. In August 1643 he was commissioned as captain of one of the Essex county troops which were being raised for service with Manchester, but the Earl, impressed by his enthusiasm for the cause, attached him to his personal staff and promoted him Colonel and Governor of Cambridge castle. Mildmay played little part in politics between 1645 and 1660, but achieved prominence again when he became one of the most able, if unscrupulous, Whig activists in the Exclusion crisis.[28]

The other four regular members of the Committee were men of less eminence than Mildmay, Brewster or the Bacons. The Cambridgeshire representative was Edward Clench of Grantchester; originally a Suffolk man, he had moved to manage the estates of his widowed sister, and possessed property in both counties, besides a share in an Ipswich ship. Clench had been a victim of Laud's High Commission, but the case, in which he was accused of attacking the local minister, seems to have stemmed less from differences of religious principle than from personal disagreements.[29] Clench took no further part in politics after 1645. The Lincolnshire representative, Humphrey Walcott, was more active. Descended from an ancient but impoverished minor gentry family, he settled in Boston in the 1630s where his family came under the influence of John Cotton, one of the most prominent of the future New England divines. In 1653 Walcott was returned to Barebone's Parliament for Lincolnshire, and in the next year was ordered to investigate the persecution of a group of sectaries by an intolerant J.P.[30] The religious beliefs of Isaac Puller of Hertford may also have tended to Independency; he was the son of the town lecturer and son-in-law of Gabriel Barbor, the most active Parliamentarian in the county, and an extreme Independent. Puller was returned as M.P. for Hertford in all the Protectorate Parliaments, but did not participate in debate.[31] The most surprising member of the Committee was the Huntingdonshire representative, Robert Vintner; whilst his fellows all sprang from gentry stock, he was the son of a yeoman of Godmanchester. In the 1630s he moved into the hierarchy of office of that agrarian corporation, and was accorded the coveted ascription 'gent'; by the time of his death in 1670 he was 'Esquire', but he seems to have been little more than a small farmer. He may have owed his position on the Committee to the patronage of the Earl of Manchester, who wielded great influence in the borough.[32]

One other man who, while he was not one of the semi-permanent members of the Cambridge Committee, worked in close conjunction with them as their agent in London, also merits some biographical description. Thomas Cooke was descended from a minor gentry family of Pebmarsh in Essex, but was related by marriage to the Bacons, Mildmay and the New England Winthrops. Like his relatives he was a Puritan; he won an unenviable reputation as a persecutor of Laudian ministers and their families on the outbreak of war, and in his will left money to those 'poore ministers' who were ejected for refusing to conform in 1662. Cooke became one of the leading Parliamentarians in Essex during the rule of the Rump; a militia colonel, he was given an honorary D.C.L. by Oxford University for his part in the battle of Worcester. Although a near contemporary Essex historian described him as 'a great Oliverian' he was less prominent during the Protectorate, and his radicalism led to his being considered a dangerous man after the Restoration.[33]

The Cambridge Committee was not an entirely homogeneous body. Its members differed in social and economic background, and their careers diverged after the formation of the New Model: the Bacons were Presbyterians, Brewster and Walcott Independents; Cooke became a firm supporter of the Rump, the Bacons disliked its rule, but became important functionaries under the Protectorate; Brewster, Puller and Walcott remained active in administration, Clench retired from public affairs. But in 1644 they were united in their Puritanism, and in that none of them came from that social group, the traditional rulers of the counties, for whom the maintenance of the autonomy of the county community was all important. Most were from lesser gentry families, but their horizons were not narrowly parochial; they had ties of interest and relations throughout East Anglia and in New England. It was this background, in addition to the sense of collective identity encouraged by Manchester's determination to secure continuity of membership and the formal powers granted them by the Ordinance of 20 January, that enabled the Committee of Cambridge, in its relations with Westminster and the local authorities, to act with an authority and self-confidence which had been so noticeably absent from the deliberations and pronouncements of 1643.

7

The Treasury

Buried in the Ordinance of 20 January 1644 is the critical clause 'the severall collectors shall pay the severall summes by them collected at the place . . . where the Earle of Manchester and the Committee of the Association . . . shall appoint, and to the Treasurers to be by them named'.[1] This was the legislative basis for Manchester's major innovation, the establishment of the centrally controlled Treasury system which he and his officials built up in the early months of 1644. Before discussing the institutional structure they developed, the personalities and careers of the leading bureaucrats will be examined.

Treasury officials

Those collective characteristics which emerge from the biographies of the members of the Cambridge Committee also appear in a study of the Treasury officials whom they supervised. The backgrounds and subsequent political attitudes of these five men differed widely, but, as with the Committee, none were members of old-established gentry families, and all had broad social and economic interests. Of the men Manchester appointed to Treasury posts Gregory Gawsell,[2] one of the Treasurers for the Monthly Assessment, came from the most prestigious background; educated at Cambridge, he had inherited the estates of an old but not particularly eminent gentry family: but his interests were not restricted to his native county – he was related to a number of the New England colonists, and in the 1630s had been a member of the Providence Island Company. The qualifications which recommended him to Manchester as a Treasurer are unknown; he was a proficient estate manager, and in the 1630s was agent for the Earl of Warwick's Norfolk lands, but he admitted in 1644 that he had no knowledge of or contacts upon the London money market. In this respect his colleague as Treasurer of the Monthly Assessment, William Leman,[3] was far better placed. Born in Beccles he became a successful city merchant and acquired considerable property in Hertfordshire and Huntingdon by purchase and by inheritance from his wealthy uncle, Sir John Leman, Lord Mayor of London in 1632. After the formation of the New Model Army the careers of the two men diverged. Gawsell, who had supported Manchester in his conflict with Cromwell, retired to political obscurity: Leman was elected Recruiter for Hertford, served on many central committees dealing with military administration and survived Pride's Purge to become Treasurer of the Army in 1650. He played little part in politics during the Protectorate, but was active as a member of the restored Rump in 1659–60; despite his radical record he made his peace with Charles II and was made a baronet in 1665.

Another of the Treasurers, John Weaver,[4] who headed the organization for the reassessment of the Fifth and Twentieth part, was also to become a Rumper, although he appears to have been a more committed political radical than Leman. Weaver was from Stamford, the son, so his enemies suggested, of an innkeeper, and certainly from a northern family which had been financially embarrassed in a series of lawsuits; before the civil war he had moved into the town government, and it seems probable from the office that he held *in commendam* in the army, that of Judge-Advocate, that he had some previous legal training. In 1645, having assisted Cromwell in attacking Manchester, he was elected as Recruiter M.P. for his home town. In Parliament he was identified with the extreme Independents; the vitriolic Clement Walker thought him a typical member of that group, both because of the radical causes he espoused and in his personal rapacity. He refused to sit as one of the King's judges, but continued as a member of the Rump, showing an especial interest in Irish affairs. Ludlow describes him as a protégé of Cromwell's in this period, but after 1653 he moved into opposition and in both Protectorate Parliaments and that of Richard Cromwell he was associated with Sir Henry Vane and the 'commonwealth men'.

The last two officials were Essex men in origin. Dr William Stane,[5] auditor of the Association and Treasurer of Sequestration, came from a minor county family and was educated at Emmanuel, from which he proceeded M.D. in 1641, and in the same year was elected a fellow of the Royal College of Physicians. Before the war began he settled in Coventry, and was acquainted with both Lord Saye and Manchester, who, in 1642, offered him the post of Physician to the Earl of Essex's army; he turned the post down, but in 1643 became Manchester's personal doctor. He retained his post as Auditor-General in the New Model, and, with his friend the freethinker Scoutmaster-General Leon Watson, became a fierce opponent of the intolerance of the Scots and their English Presbyterian allies; in 1647 the two men played a leading role in the negotiations between the army grandees and Sir John Berkeley, hoping to secure a settlement with the King along lines agreeable to the Independents. After the failure of this project, in the course of which he came to be regarded with suspicion by many of the army leaders, Stane retired to private life and to pursue a distinguished medical career which was rewarded by high office in the College of Physicians after the Restoration. The Commissary-General of the Army was William Harlackenden,[6] a younger son of a gentry family from Earl's Colne which was related to many of those involved in the New England venture; he was educated at Cambridge, and maintained the Puritan tradition of his family by marriage to 'a very religious person'. His career in military administration began in the summer of 1643 when he was appointed paymaster of the Essex troops stationed at Cambridge, and his efficiency soon led to his being employed in a similar capacity by the other counties of the Association. Working in this post, he came into contact with the Earl, and eventually became his indispensable personal assistant. This remained his role in 1644; his specific functions as Commissary-General, the organization of the musters and the payment of troops, was performed by deputies. Like Gawsell, Harlackenden retired from national politics and military administration upon the formation of the New Model.

As with the Cambridge Committee, though their backgrounds and, in particular, their subsequent careers differed widely, certain common characteristics emerge from the biographies of the officials whom Manchester had selected to develop and run the centralized Treasury. Those whose religious opinions before the war can be determined were Puritans; none of them came from the established county ruling class; all had wide-ranging contacts and interests. And it is interesting to note that two of the administrators, Dr Stane and John Weaver, both of whom subsequently were identified with political and religious radicalism, came from the professional groups in provincial towns who were most ready to serve as the agents of the central government in the localities in the 1650s.[7]

It will have appeared from the offices held by the Treasury bureaucrats whose careers have been discussed, that while it has been suggested that the establishment of central fiscal control was the major innovation of 20 January legislation, there was no single Treasury. The Association operated a system involving first three, then two distinct administrative entities: while the Treasury for Sequestration revenue was soon abolished, those for the Fifth and Twentieth part, and for the Weekly Assessment remained separate accounting units, with distinct sources of revenue and functions, throughout 1644. But central fiscal control was not undermined by the fragmented institutional structure. All the Treasuries were responsible to the same authority, that of Manchester and the Cambridge Committee, for the issue of money. Nor were they completely independent; by warrant from the Committee cash could be syphoned from one Treasury to another should the latter's resources prove temporarily inadequate to meet the demands upon it.[8] Control of the system was exercised by Manchester and the Committee, but, on a lower plane, their efforts were seconded by the audit department, whose agents operating both at Cambridge and with the army checked the bills of merchants and the village claims for payment for billets and provisions, and drew up the debentures upon which the troops were paid, for all the individual treasuries.[9] It is to the latter that we must now turn.

The collection of revenue

Sequestration revenue

In November 1643 Manchester established two central treasuries for the collection of revenue deriving from the exercise of the powers granted him in the Ordinance of 11 October, one for the receipt of the third part of those sums raised from the sequestered estates of Royalists in the constituent counties, the other for money levied by his agents who were reassessing the Fifth and Twentieth part. The former had a comparatively short history. Its revenues were not appropriated to any particular charge, and after the establishment of the Treasury for the Monthly Assessment upon the passage of the Ordinance of 20 January, its disbursements merely paralleled on a much smaller scale those of the latter. Indeed, the Treasurer for Sequestration, a post held *in commendam* by the Association's auditor Dr Stane, paid approximately 35% of the £4732 he received prior to 16 April directly to the Treasurers for the Monthly Assessment. After the end of April the use of a separate treasury for Sequestration revenue was discontinued, and the county collectors returned Manchester's third part of their receipts to Gawsell and Leman.[10]

The third part of sequestrations did not produce a great deal of money for the Association. The sums raised in Lincolnshire and the Isle of Ely were retained for the maintenance of local forces, and the Treasurers received only about £10,000 from the other counties by the end of 1644, and perhaps another £2000 in the following three months.[11] A large proportion of the revenue raised which should have been forwarded to Cambridge was retained by the counties, either to meet certain charges allowed by Manchester,[12] or diverted to purposes not indicated in the Ordinance, as were the sums requisitioned from the local sequestration agents, or raised by the exploitation of neighboring Royalist estates, by the Governor of King's Lynn, for which he never officially accounted.[13]

A more fundamental reason for the poor return was the defective nature of the entire system, which gave maximum opportunity for the exercise of local influence, and for corruption and peculation. Some of the county committeemen, with whom responsibility for the implementation of the Sequestration Ordinance lay, endeavored to protect the estates of friends, neighbors and relatives, while others were not averse to feathering their own nests.[14] But the worst abuses were perpetrated by the agents the county committees employed to manage sequestered property, who embezzled goods and rents, sold stock or let lands to their friends at an undervaluation, and then claimed exorbitant fees for their services. Perhaps the most spectacularly fraudulent of the local agents was Robert Hynde, an employee of the committee of Cambridgeshire, who managed an estate worth £400 for 2 years, but 'have not answered one penny to the state, but makes them by his accompt rather indebted to him'.[15]

The Fifth and Twentieth part

The second Treasury which had its legislative foundation in the Ordinance of 11 October was that for the receipt of money raised on the review of the Fifth and Twentieth part. A section of the October enactment empowered Manchester to appoint agents to supersede the county committees in cases where the latter had neglected, or proved remiss in, the execution of certain financial Ordinances. Although phrased in general terms the clause was obviously introduced with an eye to the reassessment of the Fifth and Twentieth, for the local committees' execution of the Ordinance of 18 May had been marked by partiality, and by the application of different standards of assessment from county to county.[16]

At the head of the organization for the reassessment was the Treasurer, John Weaver, who also acted as the Association's financial agent in a number of lesser transactions, receiving the fines levied on those Norfolk militiamen who failed to attend at the siege of Lynn, and selling goods seized from Lincolnshire delinquents in the autumn of 1643, or captured during the 1644 campaign.[17] Although Manchester did not commission Weaver as Treasurer until 1 February, he began to act in that capacity prior to that date; between late November 1643 and the end of the year north-western Norfolk was reassessed by Manchester's nominees, and £8104-3-4d collected and returned to Weaver. The activities of Weaver's subordinates provoked an official remonstrance from the committee of Norfolk, who, besides accusing them of oppression, complained more generally, with justice, of 'the evill and misery of two treasuries and two committees, one being altogether unacquainted with the actions of the other'; Manchester's agents were returning money to Cambridge which would otherwise have come to the Norfolk Treasury, and been used for the payment of the county's impoverished troops.[18] The passage of the Ordinance of 20 January, which ended the independence of the local Treasuries, removed the major objection to reassessment as expressed by the Norfolk committee, and Manchester's agents extended their operations into Suffolk and Cambridgeshire, and then into the other counties of the Association.

Initially the process of review was undertaken by officers seconded from the army,[19] but with the increased area to be reviewed, and perhaps in response to criticism of military personnel being engaged in the work of taxation, a more sophisticated system was established. The Association was divided into convenient administrative units, not necessarily following the county boundaries, each supervised by a commissioner, usually an outsider, who was assisted in the work of assessment by a group of agents, some of whom might be local men, each paid 10/– a day for their services.[20] The agents were a paid bureaucracy, responsible to Weaver, and with few contacts among, and thus little inclination to favor, the communities they were reassessing. Although their mode of operation differed from area to area, the commissioners generally appear to have been peripatetic, moving from town to town and assessing the surrounding villages.[21] Warrants were issued requiring the parish constables to summon all persons with an income of over £5 p.a. in rent, or property valued at £50, to appear before the commissioners, bringing with them their receipts for taxes previously levied; the constables were to provide valuations of all estates, both real and personal, in their villages, and copies of the rates for the monthly assessment. Based on this information, and the inquiries of their own agents, and taking into consideration the enthusiasm the individual under review had displayed for the Parliamentary cause, and his personal situation – the aged and impotent, and those with a large number of dependents were to be treated more leniently – the commissioners issued warrants to each village, setting down the sum to be charged on individuals, and instructing the latter to pay in the money to them, usually at a local inn, by a specified date. Failure to pay led to the distraint of the offender's goods by troopers attendant upon the commissioners, and the imprisonment of the recalcitrant.[22]

In all between November 1643 and 15 February 1645 Weaver received approximately £73,000 from the local commissioners for the review of the Fifth and Twentieth in the Associated counties.[23] Proportionally there were wide divergences in the amounts raised from county to county. In the two 'frontier' counties of Huntingdonshire and the Isle of Ely, on which the county system of finance in 1643 placed the heaviest burdens, only miniscule sums were collected on the review, presumably because financial necessity had enforced the local committees to assess the Fifth and Twentieth part strictly in the summer and fall of 1643; at Little Thetford on the Isle Manchester's commissioners did not make a new rate because 'it was found that the inhabitants of the . . . Hamblet were formerly assessed to the full'.[24] Hertfordshire and Essex produced substantial sums, but less proportional to their wealth than Cambridgeshire, Norfolk or Suffolk[25] – perhaps a reflection of the previous efficiency of the respective county committees, and of the fact that large areas of the former counties fell within the 20 miles radius from the center of

London which was assessed by the Committee at Haberdashers' Hall. In the absence of any detailed accounts of the commissioners it is impossible to state categorically which groups in the community were hit most severely by the review procedure. But from the Hertfordshire village returns it appears that the commissioners were prepared to re-rate the wealthy who had already paid substantial amounts at the first assessment, and that they were also mulcting small sums from those who had not been touched by the local committee,[26] presumably as being below the income qualification instituted by Parliamentary Ordinance, which Manchester had halved on his own initiative.[27]

The Fifth and Twentieth part had one obvious disadvantage as a source of revenue: it was a wasting asset. In the first four months of 1644 Weaver's local agents returned an average of nearly £10,000 a month to Cambridge, but in May the receipts began to dwindle, and by the summer were reduced to a trickle. And although Weaver accounted for the receipt of £12,427 between September 1644 and February 1645, over £7000 of this sum was raised in Lincolnshire and employed locally to meet the expenses of equipping the forces designed for the defense of that county. As Colonel Walton argued to the Committee of Cambridge in September, when proposing that the Association should endeavor to secure the use of the excise revenue raised in the seven counties, the Fifth and Twentieth was 'neere spent'.[28]

The Monthly Assessment[29]

While centralized Treasuries, those for sequestration revenue and for the Fifth and Twentieth part, had been established, on paper, by the Ordinance of 11 October, the provision of pay and the purchase of equipment for the bulk of the army remained the responsibility of the county treasurers who controlled the Monthly Assessment, and the money raised on the first levy of the Fifth and Twentieth tax. This combination of central and local fiscal control was obviously unworkable. As the Norfolk committee bitterly complained in December, the sums levied by the agents of Weaver's Treasury in the north-west of their county was money which would otherwise have come to their Treasury and been used for the pay of their troops:[30] the system robbed Peter to pay Paul. But this anomalous situation terminated with the passage of the Ordinance of 20 January. The counties lost their fiscal independence; they were instructed to forward their receipts on the Monthly Assessment to Cambridge, and the central Treasury so established became responsible for the pay of the army.

In the first two months after the passage of the crucial January legislation there was a fluidity of administrative personnel in the new

Treasury,[31] but from mid-March 1644 until April 1645 its chief officers were Gregory Gawsell and William Leman, who, after the beginning of the campaigning season, arranged a simple division of responsibilities. Leman remained based at Cambridge, where he supervised the collection of the Monthly Assessment by the county treasurers; although he was responsible for the issue of money upon the warrants of the Cambridge Committee, until the winter of 1644–5 the bulk of his receipts were forwarded to Gawsell, who traveled with the army and organized the payment of the troops. The disbursements of the two Treasurers will be discussed in the following section: here only the organization for the collection of the assessment which Leman supervised will be examined, and its performance evaluated.

Although the Ordinance of 20 January, by establishing a central Treasury at Cambridge, ended the previous local control of the expenditure of the assessment, the collection of the tax did not involve so obvious or, from the viewpoint of the county committees, so objectionable an intrusion of the agents of the central authority in local affairs as did the review of the Fifth and Twentieth. The county Treasurers who were responsible for the return of the sums due to Cambridge, although appointed by Manchester, were invariably local men who had served in the capacity prior to the Earl's appointment, as were their immediate subordinates, the divisional collectors. The county committees assigned the sum to be raised on individual parishes, and they supervised those members of the village communities who were responsible for the collection and assessment of the tax at the grass-roots level.

But while the basic process for the collection of the Monthly Assessment remained in the hands of the local authorities, they were not, as in the collection of sequestration revenue, virtually autonomous. Central supervision was maintained by the establishment of a number of agencies designed to improve the channels of communication between Cambridge and the localities, and to prod the committees into the swift return of their receipts to the Treasury. Manchester appointed an auditor and an agent for each of the constituent counties: the former were charged with the discovery and collection of sums outstanding upon the accounts of local officials;[32] the agents, while they too might check local account books, were primarily responsible for expediting the collection of the assessment, badgering the county committees and organizing the transportation of money to Cambridge.[33] Like the commissioners for the review of the Fifth and Twentieth part, it would appear that these officials of the Cambridge Committee were not natives of the counties for which they were responsible.[34] Manchester also commissioned the captains whose troops were employed to collect outstanding taxes from the recalcitrant, arresting the latter and distraining their goods. A number of these officers were local men who had been employed in a similar capacity prior to the summer of 1643 under the direction of the county committees, but after the issue of Manchester's commission their troops were subject to central control, and might receive their instructions direct from Cambridge.[35]

For the collection of the Monthly Assessment Leman developed an organization in which the routine procedures were performed by the parochial authorities under the direction of the local committees, but the Cambridge Committee supervised the latter, and could mobilize troops to enforce the payment and return of money. How successful was this system? The surviving accounts of the Cambridge Treasuries and those of local officials, although very far from complete, enable us to construct some figures indicative of the efficiency of Leman's organization.

But before presenting this information, two important points must be noted. First, while each of the three assessment Ordinances was designed to raise £135,120 for the Association, Leman could expect to receive only £112,080 as none of the money levied in Lincolnshire and the Isle of Ely was returned to Cambridge. The assessment of the Isle was utilized locally for the payment of the garrison and the building of fortifications, and that part of the Lincolnshire assessment which was collected was also appropriated for local use – the maintenance of Rossiter's horse, Rainborow's infantry regiment, and the garrison of Grantham.[36] The Treasuries of the Isle and of Lincolnshire, though obliged to account to the Cambridge Committee, were effectively autonomous institutions, disbursing the sums raised in their counties for local defense.[37]

Second, not all the money collected by the local officials in the other six counties and accounted for at Cambridge was actually received by the central Treasury. Occasionally the county Treasurers would be instructed by the Cambridge Committee to pay certain detachments of the army, or the Association's creditors, themselves; sums disbursed in this manner were accounted as having been paid to the Treasury. This system was frequently utilized in the early months of 1644, when the central Treasury was still in embryo and lacked large cash balances. In consequence the Association's most importunate creditors were often sent to collect their debts directly from the county Treasurers, while a number of the regiments quartered within the Association could be paid most conveniently by the local authorities.[38] Receipts upon the second and third Ordinances for the Four Months' Assessments were less frequently paid out directly by the county Treasurers,[39] except in Hertfordshire and Huntingdonshire. The army marched through both counties in the autumn, taking free quarter: bills for the latter were met directly by the county Treasurers, and, by Manchester's orders, their acquittances were accepted by Leman in part payment of the sums charged upon the counties by the Ordinance.[40]

In January 1645 Leman produced an account of the sums which he had received to that date from the county authorities upon each of the three Ordinances for the Four Months' Assessment. Correcting his totals in those cases where the local Treasurers had not yet presented accounts of the money which they had paid out locally on the warrants of the Cambridge Committee, a table can be constructed in which the sum received from each of the counties is expressed as a percentage of the sum due upon each Ordinance.

TABLE 1   *Money accounted as received by Leman on 1 January 1645,*
expressed as a percentage of the sum due upon each Ordinance

| County | Four Months Assessment Ordinance | | |
	First: Jan.–April	Second: May–Aug.	Third: Sept.–Dec.
Cambridge	95.7	94.5	20.6
Essex	89.3	88.2	26.4
Hertford	97.8	97.7	14.8[a]
Huntingdon	100.0	82.7	0.0[a]
Norfolk	92.0*	93.4*	24.1
Suffolk	100.0	95.3*	32.4
Total	94.7	92.7	24.6

Source: P.R.O. 30/15/3 no. 561; S.P. 28/144 no. 3. The figures marked * have been corrected by comparing Leman's account with those of the local Treasurers which indicate the sums disbursed locally upon the warrants of the Cambridge Committee. (*Norfolk* – S.P. 28/26 ff. 314–21; *Suffolk* – S.P. 28/24 f. 74.)

[a] These figures do not indicate the sums disbursed locally to pay the quarters bills of the army in the winter of 1644; a considerable sum was spent in the two counties for this purpose, but none of the surviving accounts states the date at which the money was collected.

The table shows that Leman never received more than 95% of the money due from the six counties, while the third column indicates another problem which faced the central Treasury: the time-lag between the expiration of the relevant Ordinance and the date at which the money was brought to account at Cambridge. The few surviving accounts of local Treasurers and collectors suggest that this time-lag was growing in the course of the year (see table 2).

But while the arrears and the slow return of money to Cambridge adversely affected the Association's ability to pay its troops and to meet the bills of its creditors, the positive achievement of Leman and the organization he headed should be stressed. In 1644 Parliament's financial demands upon the Association were unprecedented, both

TABLE 2 *The percentage of money due returned to Cambridge within two months of the expiration of the relevant Ordinance*

Area	First Assessment	Second Assessment	Third Assessment
Suffolk	100.0	74.9	71.3
Cambridgeshire (western division)	98.2	87.3	no figure
Hertfordshire (western division)	88.0	71.7	70.4

Sources: *Suffolk* – S.P. 28/143, unfol., the Suffolk Treasury Book, ff. 124v, 125v, 130v; *Cambridgeshire* – S.P. 28/152 part 21; *Hertfordshire* – S.P. 28/22 ff. 352–389; 38 ff. 589–90.

in extent and duration. In 1639 the inhabitants of Suffolk had resisted the collection of the £8000 demanded from the county in ship-money, arguing that so exorbitant a sum would ruin the trade, industry and agriculture of the area,[41] yet in 1644 the three Four Months' Assessments should have realized £90,000 in the county. In late 1643, when the assessment had stood at £5000 a month on Suffolk, Sir Simonds D'Ewes had claimed that taxation was draining off two-fifths of every man's income, while the county committee, totaling up the assessment, the excise, the Fifth and Twentieth and the sums owing on several minor Ordinances, calculated that the burden was nearer one-half, and demanded an easing of future charges.[42] Parliament's response to these representations was to raise the monthly assessment upon Suffolk to £7500. In 1644 the protests of D'Ewes and the Suffolk committee were echoed by a number of East Anglian townsmen, in particular the inhabitants of the ports whose trade was dislocated by privateers and by the Royalists' control of Newcastle,[43] and gentlemen, who found that their own ability to pay assessments was curtailed by their tenants' difficulties under the pressure of taxation; rents were in arrears, and farmers were refusing to re-hire their properties without abatements.[44] Many gentle families must have been enforced, as was Lady Denton,[45] to curtail both their conspicuous consumption and their charitable giving, by a rate of taxation which devoured from a fifth to as much as a third of their incomes as rentiers.[46]

Although on one occasion the authorities' attempts to assess a town provoked a riot, and there were a number of violent assaults upon local collectors, there was little overt resistance to the payment of taxes by comparison with the resistance to the collection of ship-money in 1639–40.[47] Payment may have been encouraged by Manchester's mobilization of pulpit propaganda to arouse popular enthusiasm for the war. From the outbreak of hostilities the pro-Parliamentary ministry in East Anglia had roused their congregations to arms, or to contribute liberally to the cause,[48] and Manchester continued to encourage and employ this channel of communications. Lecturers were financed from public funds, and, in periods of military crisis, the East Anglian members of the Assembly of Divines were desired to return to their counties 'to stir up the People'. The Earl appointed 7 April 1644 as a special day of Thanksgiving in the Association, and instructed the ministry to read publicly *A catalogue of remarkable mercies conferred upon the seven Associated Counties*, a tract printed at Cambridge and published at the expense of the central Committee.[49]

But perhaps more important were the Earl's endeavors to remove those ministers who opposed Parliament's proceedings, and to replace them by men sympathetic to the cause. This process had begun at the outset of the war with the establishment of the Parliamentary Committee in London, chaired by John White, which had prosecuted and sequestered 'Malignant Priests'; but the influence of White's Committee was geographically limited to the home counties, and ministers in more remote parts of East Anglia were little affected by its investigations. The situation changed dramatically with the passage of the Ordinance of 22 January, which empowered Manchester to nominate local committees charged with the collection of evidence against 'scandalous' or 'maligant' ministers, and, after evaluating the testimonies and report forwarded by the committees, to eject the unacceptable from their livings.[50] While the Earl's investigations were partly concerned with the religious opinions and moral life of the accused, the latter's political attitudes were also examined in detail. Had the incumbent preached against Parliament? or failed to read its propagandist declarations, whilst publishing the similar literature that came from Oxford? had he taken the Covenant, and generously contributed to the cause?[51] Many ministers were accused of openly dissuading their parishioners from serving in the army or paying their rates, and their example and instruction was influential in formulating the political attitudes of the village community: the petition from the 'well-affected' of Suffolk in December 1643 pressing that Manchester should be given power to sequester the 'ill affected clergie' emphasized the 'prevailinge influances theire bolde advices . . . have had and still have into the mindes and affections of instable and weake people'.[52] The control over the pulpit which Manchester gained by the Ordinance of 22 January might have lessened local opposition to Parliamentary legislation, particularly the payment of taxes.

But certainly more influential than pulpit oratory in securing the collection of the assessment were the heavy penalties which the recalcitrant risked, given that the local committees controlled instruments of unprecedented efficiency to implement their threats of distraint, imprisonment and sequestration. The village constables were instructed to return the names of defaulters to the county committee, and were smartly rebuked and fined by the latter if they failed to do so.[53] Those reported as offenders were distrained, not by the parish officers who might not dare to act against 'men of . . . qualitie', but either by the sequestrators, or by the troops at the disposal of the local committees. Upon the passage of a new financial Ordinance the Colchester committee noted cynically, 'Wee only want Captain Hatcher to bring in the harvest': Hatcher commanded the troop employed by the Essex committee to assist in the collection of assessments. In the Isle of Ely 21.8% of the sum due upon the first Four Months' Assessment was collected by troopers.[54] Indeed, the degree to which the local committees relied upon military force to ensure the collection of taxes may be judged by the hysterical reaction of the Essex authorities when the Committee of Safety ordered Hatcher and the local troop to join the field-army in August 1643: Sir Thomas Barrington wrote a letter of protest in which he conjured up a vision of the 'malignant insolencyes' that would inevitably follow when 'we have no meanes left to compell the refractorie to complye with any rates . . . when our meanes of fearinge into obedience is gone'.[55]

While direct resistance to the payment of assessments was rare, given the force available to Manchester and the local authorities to 'compell the refractorie', opposition to the heavy burden of taxation could still manifest itself. It is apparent in the protracted rating disputes which occurred throughout the Association, and which partly explain the slow return of money to Cambridge. Hertfordshire constantly complained that it was over-rated by comparison with the other constituent counties, and a number of East Anglian towns squabbled with the county committees over the rates imposed upon them by the latter.[56] Relations between Norwich and Norfolk were particularly bad. In addition to continuing their earlier controversy concerning the respective proportions which the city and the shire should bear in any general levy, the two authorities feuded over the degree to which the city was financially responsible to the county committee, specifically whether the latter might audit the accounts of the corporation, and over the status of Thorpe; the citizens argued that the parish lay within the liberties of Norwich and so should be rated towards any tax required from them, a claim fiercely resisted by the committee.[57] This boundary conflict was paralleled at the parish level: in both Essex and Norfolk villages disputed whether certain lands lay within their own or a neighboring parish for the purposes of taxation.[58]

The unprecedented demand also encouraged the local committeemen, motivated either by considerations of equity or by sectional

interests, to revise the accepted conventions of local assessment.
Such alterations invariably led to disputes, as in Suffolk, when a rate
supposedly based on the relative prosperity of the Hundreds, rather
than the traditional proportions, was introduced, and in Hertfordshire, where the local committee rated certain 'ancient demesnes',
previously free from taxation, and endeavored to lighten the tax-
load borne by St Albans by increasing their demands upon the
surrounding parishes.[59] The most spectacular conflict of this nature
was that which arose between the Hundred of Becontree and the
Liberty of Havering. In 1641 it had been claimed by the former that
an equitable division of the sum assessed upon them jointly would
be for the men of Havering to pay a third; the latter pressed that the
traditional arrangement, whereby they paid a quarter, should be
retained. Both sides refused to concede defeat, and a substantial
arrear built up while the matter was debated at Romford and
Chelmsford and before various committees at Westminster. The
problem was still not resolved at the Restoration.[60]

The burden of taxation also resulted in a series of rating disputes
at the grass-roots level: a good deal of the time of the Romford
committee was taken up with hearing the chorus of complaints from
aggrieved villagers against the local assessors and collectors. Some
of these protests were found to be frivolous or malicious, but a
number of assessors, like John Radley of Shenfield who had consistently over-rated his neighbors' property and grossly under-valued
his own, were dismissed for their 'partiall and unequall assessments'.[61]
Not all the village assessors whose rates were challenged were as
flagrantly self-seeking as Radley, but many endeavored to avoid
unpopularity in the village community by rating outsiders heavily
for lands held in their parish, or by over-taxing those who were
locally unpopular, or who might not be expected to receive much
sympathy from the committee should they complain: in this respect
those of suspected Royalist sympathy, clergymen and foreigners were
fair game.[62] Class interests also impinged on the question of local
rating. A common complaint against the assessors was that they
rated land alone, the tax burden of which fell upon the landlord if
the property was let at a rack-rent, and neglected to rate tenant-
farmers for the stock which they owned.[63]

Despite the loud protests of the inhabitants at the enormous
burden of taxation upon the constituent counties of the Association
in 1644, nearly 95% of the sum due upon each of the three Monthly
Assessments was eventually accounted for at Cambridge. The county
committees, under continuous pressure from Leman and his local
agents to expedite the return of money to the Treasury, were not
solely reliant, as had been the sheriffs in the 1630s, upon local
assessors and constables, who might be reluctant to offend 'men of

. . . qualitie', for the collection of taxes but could enforce payment from the localities by 'fearinge into obedience' with troops. But although the greater part of the sum due was eventually accounted for at Cambridge, there were substantial, perhaps growing, delays between the expiration of the Ordinances and final payment which hampered the efficient operation of Leman's Treasury, as protracted rating disputes, a natural response to the unprecedented demand, retarded the local collection of the money.

With the reorganization of the central institutions of the Association upon the passage of the Ordinance of 20 January 1644, Manchester established three Treasuries for the collection of the sums assigned to him from the eastern counties. One of the Treasuries, that for sums raised by the sequestration of delinquents' estates, a comparatively unimportant source of income, was soon abandoned and its revenues paid into the Treasury controlled by William Leman. The latter's major responsibility was the collection of the Monthly Assessment, and he developed a system involving a considerable degree of central intervention in matters which had previously been the responsibility of the local governors: the routine of assessment and receipt was still handled by the traditional parish officers under the direction of the local gentry of the county committees, but they were closely supervised by Leman's agents, and their accounts were subject to central audit. Bureaucratic centralization is even more apparent in the third Treasury, that headed by John Weaver for the collection of sums raised on the review of the Fifth and Twentieth part. The local authorities played a negligible role; assessments were made by committees of outsiders responsible directly to Weaver, who enforced payment of the sums demanded by troopers who attended them as they toured the country.

Disbursement of revenue

After January a simple division of financial responsibility was envisaged between the two major Treasuries: Weaver's revenues were allocated to the purchase of munitions and the costs of certain military departments, notably the train of artillery and the intelligence service,[64] while Leman's Treasury was to meet the pay of the army. In practice this division was never maintained. In the early months of 1644, as Leman awaited the receipts from the counties from the first Four Months' Assessment, £15,470 was transferred from Weaver's Treasury and employed for the payment of the army; initially it was intended that the sum should be repaid when money began to flow into Leman's Treasury, but this idea was eventually discarded. By the end of the summer the situation was reversed. As Weaver's receipts dwindled bills for the purchase of munitions which he had previously met were being paid by Leman.[65] But, although it ultimately proved unrealistic in practice, the contemporary accounting division between the pay of the army and the purchase of supplies is useful for the purposes of analysis.

The pay of the army

The previous analysis of the system developed for the collection of the Monthly Assessment emphasized Leman's comparative success in securing the return of money to Cambridge, given the general unpopularity of the quite unprecedented burden. But Leman's achievement was not so well regarded by his colleague, Gregory Gawsell, who, during the 1644 campaign, traveled with the army and supervised its payment with the sums forwarded to him by Leman from Cambridge. In the summer of 1644 Gawsell informed Leman that his want of money disenabled him from paying the troops, and that he was enforced to 'please them as well as I can with good words'. The latter were less welcome than cash, and on one occasion Gawsell's frustration burst out: 'Sir, I am sicke with the importunitye and the unworthy use of the souldyers', he wrote to Leman, 'if you pay moneyes at Cambridge . . . and leave me to be tormented with the souldyers I shall desire you to change places.' In 1655, recalling his experience as Treasurer a decade before, Gawsell informed the central Committee of Accounts 'Gentlemen, you must know that wee wer ever in want.' Gawsell's remarks which suggest that the army was not well paid are supported by other literary evidence. In mid-December Dillingham, the editor of the *Parliament Scout*, wrote of the army receiving only six weeks' pay in six months, and, a fortnight later, of the soldiers 'crying out, that they have had but nine weeks' pay since Candlemas'.[66]

But before examining those statistics which can be produced of the number of days' pay issued to the army in 1644 and early 1645 to evaluate the complaints of Gawsell and Dillingham, it must be noted that there were supplementary sources of income available to the soldiers. 'Lawful plunder' – the money or valuables which could be seized from the enemy dead or prisoners, or from the inhabitants of a captured town – could be highly profitable to fortunate individuals;[67] less haphazard were the gratuities given the soldiers in lieu of plunder or for some particularly good service.[68] More dubious methods of raising money were employed. Some commanders forcibly levied assessments upon the area in which the detachments were temporarily quartered, and the sums thus illegally raised were never brought to account. Finally, for most of the year the soldiers did not meet the costs of their accommodation and provisions from their pay, but took 'free quarter'.[69] Within the Association the bills of the inhabitants with whom they were quartered were met by the Treasury, and put to the account of the troop or company in question: in this case the sum disbursed can be expressed in terms of daily pay, and be added to the number of days' actual pay issued to the troops. But outside the Association repayment to the villagers who billeted the soldiers was the exception rather than the rule, and in these areas 'free quarter', along with plunder, gratuities and arbitrary exactions, swelled the troops' official pay to a degree which cannot be computed. Real income diverged substantially from that officially received, and the historian can only estimate the latter – 'estimate' rather than 'ascertain' owing to the fragmentary survival of the accounts of the Association's Treasurers.[70]

The officers. In 1644 Parliament endeavored to limit the immediate costs of the war by paying the officers only a proportion of the sum due to them. A clause in the Ordinance of 20 January instructed that all officers and specialist personnel, with the exception of the regimental ministers, whose pay exceeded 10/– a day were to receive half-pay, and those who received from 5/– to 10/– a day, two-thirds of their established pay; for the remainder they were to accept certificates promising repayment 'on the Publique Faith' after the termination of the war.[71]

The pay of officers below the rank of Colonel was included with that of their companies, but the higher ranks were paid by the issue of personal debentures. The auditors calculated the sum owed to the officer for a given period, and a debenture was issued for this sum; payments made to the officer in the period covered by the debenture by the Treasurers 'on account' were totaled up and deducted from the sum owed, and the remainder was paid off, usually in instalments, on the Treasurers' receipt of a warrant from Manchester. In general the superior officers were reasonably well paid,[72] probably because of the necessity of their loaning money to captains under their command: in October Major-General Crawford desired the Treasurers to pay him the £100 outstanding on his debenture, as 'I am extremlie in want of money, by reason I have lent my regiment what I had.'[73] A similar system of personal debenture was employed to settle the accounts of those men who died or left the service; debentures were drawn up, sums already paid deducted, and the remainder paid off in instalments by the Treasurers.[74]

The cavalry. Initially the troops of cavalry, like the higher officers, were paid by the issue of debentures, the first series of which were issued in mid-April 1644.[75] The sum owing to each troop was calculated by the auditors from a muster taken earlier in the month, for a set period either of 12 weeks from 1 January to 25 March, or, for certain troops of Cromwell's regiment, which had already received six weeks' pay upon a muster taken about 20 February,[76] of six weeks from 12 February to 25 March. As the troops which had served in the Hilsden House campaign had been paid prior to their advance into Buckinghamshire, and again upon the successful completion of their mission, while those troops that had remained quartered in the Association had received about five weeks' pay in March, these sums were deducted from the totals owing on the debentures.[77] A further three weeks' pay was issued by the Treasurers in mid-April, and the remainder of the sum outstanding upon the debenture was finally cleared, in most cases, by payment in June.[78]

The second series of cavalry debentures was issued in late September: they stated the sums owed for the twenty-two-week period from 25 March to 26 August, calculated upon the numbers present at the muster of 20 September.[79] Again those sums issued to the captains in the period since the clearing of the previous debenture were deducted from the total outstanding, but these did not represent a large amount.[80] Upon the issue of this debenture most troops were given six weeks' pay, although Crawford's troop received nothing, because 'the Treasury is so empty' and the Major-General was forced to borrow the money to pay his men. Another victim of the impoverishment of the Treasury was Lilburne's regiment; when they received only three of the six weeks' pay promised them the dragoons mutinied, and were only appeased when Lilburne and his officers distributed the pay that they had received amongst them.[81] This six weeks' pay was the last substantial payment made to the cavalry in 1644, although the debentures record the receipt of small sums by the captains in October and November. When the cavalry was paid in 1645 the system of debentures, with its wholly unrealistic pretense that, for example, the six weeks' pay given the troopers in September was the sum due for their services from 25 March to 5 May, was abandoned, and the captains were paid 'on warrant'. The troops were mustered in late December or early January, and upon this muster were given three weeks' pay on the 16th of that month, and a further two weeks' pay in mid-February. Those troops which were not embodied in the New Model Army on 1 April were given pay for a further week or fortnight in the course of that month.[82]

From this examination of warrants, debentures and accounts, it appears that the Association's cavalry officially received eighteen weeks' pay in 1644 (discounting the week's pay given the troopers as a gratuity for their good service at Marston Moor), and a further five to seven weeks' pay in 1645. But these figures do not accurately reflect the Association's total expenditure for the cavalry, in that the Treasurers did not only pay the troops, but met bills for clothing, quarters within the Association and other necessaries for which the troopers were financially responsible, and so should have been deducted from their pay. But sums disbursed in this manner were not taken into account by the auditors when the debentures were drawn up, and could represent a substantial amount: in the first three months of 1645 Leman paid £315-3-7d to villagers within the Association who presented unpaid bills for food and provender requisitioned by Major Alford's troop in winter quarters, a sum approximately equal to a further twenty-one days' pay for each of his troopers.[83]

The infantry.[84] The period before the army's advance north, as new companies were embodied and the old recruited, was marked by some confusion in the organization of the pay of the infantry.[85] But in May a uniform system was in operation. On the 8th of that month, as the foot rested about Gainsborough and Lincoln, unable to advance north because of the heavy rains which had swollen the Trent, they were mustered and debentures were issued for either four, seven or eight weeks' pay, so that, when the sums set out in the debentures had been issued, the infantry would be uniformly paid up to the middle of May. Half of the sum was paid to captains at the time of the muster and the remainder about 14 June, later than Manchester had hoped, after the army had joined the forces engaged in the siege of York.[86] The second series of debentures for the infantry, with the exception of Palgrave's regiment,[87] was issued on a muster taken about 23 July, when the army was resting in the Doncaster area after the victory at Marston Moor and the fall of York.[88] The debentures were for four weeks' pay, which was issued immediately to the captains. The final series of infantry debentures was made out on 18 September upon a muster taken about that date at St Albans; the debentures were for six weeks' pay, and with their issue all the regiments that had fought at Marston Moor were fully paid up to 15 July.[89]

In the intervals between musters, the issue of debentures and payment upon them, captains borrowed money to meet the immediate needs of their companies. Gawsell loaned money from his Treasury to certain captains to be technically repaid by deduction from the sum due upon debenture when the latter was made out: on 14 September two officers in Manchester's regiment noted that they would effectively receive only a week's pay upon the St Albans muster, as a sum equivalent to the other five weeks' pay had already been borrowed from Gawsell. John Weaver would also loan money to captains to pay their companies 'in this theyre greate need', to be repaid 'when money comes', while other officers borrowed from civilian money-lenders. The officers would pay these borrowed sums to their men, or use them to meet the charges for the quarters, provisions or clothing of the latter, and then recoup themselves and reimburse their creditors when the infantry was eventually paid.[90]

By September 1644 the issue of debentures, and the system of loans, involved a growing complexity of accounting. Not only were the infantry two months in arrears, but the rate of turn-over of common soldiers in the individual companies was extremely high.[91] So at St Albans the captains received money supposedly covering the pay of their companies for a period two months earlier, yet issued upon a muster at which their numbers were significantly lower than those actually present in July. The debentures made no allowance for money borrowed by the captains and issued to men present for the period for which payment was formally made, but who had died, deserted or been invalided out of the army between July and September, and the officers were obliged to return separate accounts to the Treasurers to recoup these sums.[92]

The time-consuming complexity of this system, the shortage of money in the Treasury, and the difficulty of holding a formal muster of the army, which until mid-December was constantly on the move as it participated in the second Newbury campaign, led to the abandonment of the debenture system after the St Albans muster, and the captains were issued small sums for the use of their companies, paid far more frequently, 'on warrant'. The sums paid individual captains in this way in the final three months of 1644 varied considerably: Johnson acknowledged receipt of sums totaling forty-nine days' pay for his company; Holmes, in the same regiment, was issued forty days' pay, while most captains appear to have received about five weeks' pay for the common soldiers, less for the officers. In 1645, with the regiments in garrison at Abingdon, Aylesbury and Henley, or quartered near Cambridge, new musters were held, and in January and early February six or eight weeks' pay were issued by the Treasurers in two or three instalments,[93] but by warrant not debenture. Between February and the disbandment of the Association's army in mid-April the experience of the companies differed widely, ranging from the fourteen days' pay received by Captain Barnes[94] to the fifty-two days' pay for Holmes's company.

In the course of their service in 1644 and 1645 the infantry were far better paid than the Association's cavalry, and it is clear that the jeremiads of Lilburne and Dillingham refer to the latter, not to the army as a whole. The considerable divergence between the pay of the two arms is explicable in that the foot were less disciplined than the horse, and were prone to mutiny or desert if their pay fell too far in arrear. But as Table 3 shows, comparatively the army of the Association was well paid, and even the troopers did better than their counterparts in the other major Parliamentary armies.

But while the men of the Eastern Association were better paid than

TABLE 3 *Days' pay received in 1644 and in 1645 until the formation of the New Model by the armies of the Association, the Earl of Essex and Sir William Waller*

	1644	1645
Cavalry		
Eastern Association	126[a]	35
Earl of Essex[b]	91	28
Sir William Waller[c]	77	(21?)[d]
Infantry[e]		
Eastern Association	231–259	56–91
Earl of Essex: men[f]	161–175	63–70
Earl of Essex: officers	140–147	42–49

[a] I have included only sums formally paid to the Association's troopers, excluding the money disbursed by the Treasurers for quarters, provisions and clothing.

[b] Based primarily on the account of Colonel Sheffield (S.P. 28/140 part 15) and confirmed by totals in other officers' and troopers' accounts (S.P. 28/33 f. 480; 140 part 2; 267 ff. 71–2, 225; E. 315/5 pp. 28–9) and by the warrants of Essex's Treasurers scattered in the series S.P. 28.

[c] Based on the account of Captain Greville (S.P. 28/265 f. 393) and confirmed by some troopers' accounts (E. 315/5 pp. 80, 89, 123, 131, 142).

[d] Greville does not acknowledge the receipt of any money in 1645; the troopers' accounts suggest that three weeks' pay was received – but perhaps only when the troop was disbanded.

[e] It is not possible to give an accurate account of the pay of the foot in Waller's army: there are no surviving warrants, and the few individual accounts drawn up by his officers are very confused. Between August 1643 and March 1644 Waller's men received only sixty-three days' pay (E. 315/5 pp. 34–5), and the officers perhaps seventy-seven days' pay between that date and April 1645, although some may have received more (S.P. 28/265 f. 401; 267 ff. 396–403, 475).

[f] Based on Essex's warrants to his Treasurers in S.P. 28/12–21, 27–8, and certain officers' accounts (S.P. 28/40 ff. 24–5, 214–15; 140 part 6; 265 ff. 427, 524; 266 ff. 25–6, 59–60, 143, 442–3; 267 ff. 486–7).

any other army on foot before the foundation of the New Model, their arrears were substantial and proved to be damaging to military discipline. In the autumn Lilburne's dragoons, and in February 1645 the garrison of Henley, mutinied when the Treasury proved unable to supply them with the promised number of weeks' pay. In September Ireton informed Manchester of the poor condition of the cavalry resulting from the deficiencies of their pay, and noted that few of the troopers were very well-disposed towards the prospect of military action. Indeed, the growing disparity between the pay of the cavalry and that of the infantry aroused the jealousy of the former, and became one of the sub-issues in the primarily religious dispute between Crawford and Cromwell, who felt that the cavalry's necessities had been deliberately neglected and money 'partially disposed'.[95]

The growing arrears also generated conflict between the army and the civilian population. Not only were the soldiers forced to requisition supplies and take free quarter, but some officers endeavored to extort money from the villages in which they were billeted; in the winter of 1644–5 two captains were accused of systematically plundering markets in, respectively, Bedfordshire and Rutland, and of compelling the countrymen to redeem the goods which they had seized for cash. More sophisticated, but no less arbitrary, were the methods employed by the governors of Henley and Aylesbury, who levied assessments on those towns and the surrounding countryside for the maintenance of their garrisons. Major-General Crawford, the governor of Aylesbury, who enforced the payment of his tax by distraint and imprisonment, became involved in a fierce dispute with the local committee, which clearly reveals the antipathy between civilians and the military: the committee denounced Crawford as 'sole plunderer and oppressior of the county'; he described them, more laconically, as 'fooles'.[96]

Not only did the shortage of money undermine the morale of the army but it impaired its fighting efficiency as the Association's supply system proved unable to adequately equip, provision and clothe the soldiers.

The supply of the army

Before discussing the system instituted for the purchase or requisition of horses, arms and food, and its deficiencies, it must be noted that, as with their pay, the troops were not completely dependent upon official agencies to procure necessary supplies. All could be captured from the enemy: Lilburne boasted that he had received no equipment 'but what I won with my sword', and that his dragoons had been 'recruited . . . over and over, both with Horse and Armes, with our industry and resolution, without 6d charge to the state'. Marston Moor enriched the stores of the Association's army by 4500 muskets, 800 pikes and 40 barrels of powder, besides ordnance, shot, swords and bandoleers, while the garrisons that surrendered to the Earl's forces in July and August brought in smaller quantities of arms and ammunition, and some horses and victuals.[97] Less gloriously, there was theft. In all the counties through which the army marched, and for which parish accounts survive, there are accusations of the seizure of clothing, provisions and horses, particularly the latter, by the troops.[98] The offense was punishable by death, but the only Association soldier known to have been punished was a corporal in Bushell's troop, who, while engaged in an orgy of plunder, was unwise enough to rob the servant of a regimental officer – and he was merely imprisoned and cashiered. The victim might expect redress or financial reparation if he had the courage to arrest the offender, or to appeal to one of the staff-officers, but clearly most cases went unpunished and there was no restitution. Manchester's forces were never as given to 'disorder and outrage' as were the armies of Essex and Waller, but in the winter of 1644–5 when the Treasury and supply organizations were increasingly unable to meet the army's needs, some detachments took the law into their own hands: one troop was accused of plundering the Buckingham area, pretending that they were cavaliers.[99]

Horse. The army of the Association was insatiable in its demand for horses, not only for equipping newly-raised troops, but for the replacement of those lost in action or through disease. It would seem that horses were more vulnerable to the chances of military service than their riders: Captain Griffen, whose troop strength never exceeded sixty-five men, lost a total of forty-two mounts between March 1644 and May 1645. Theoretically the horse issued to a trooper at the commencement of his service became his full financial responsibility, a provision instituted to prevent unscrupulous cavalrymen from selling their horses, but of Griffen's losses only one could be ascribed to the negligence of the rider 'which hee is to make good'. Of the remaining forty-one, twelve were captured by the enemy, five killed in action, and the rest either lamed out of service or incapacitated by disease.[100]

The legislation passed in the summer of 1643 for the raising of a large body of cavalry in East Anglia empowered the local committees to raise the necessary numbers of horses. Every person who had been charged with a horse for service in the militia was instructed to provide one for the new army, or money in lieu of it. The remaining horses required were levied upon the villages: the county committees instructed each constable to requisition a certain number of horses, which were valued by 'two well-affected neighbours', and their owners reimbursed by a parish rate. In Essex, required to raise far more horses than the other constituent counties and given a more definite financial provision by the Ordinance of 12 August, the committee both employed the methods already outlined and bought large numbers of cavalry mounts from dealers.[101] Parliament hoped that the levies would be made 'with such indifferency and equality, that as little offence may be given to the well-affected party as may be', and although payment was often considerably delayed and it was claimed that some officers had requisitioned horses and then refused to issue receipts,[102] the system was preferable to the indiscriminate seizures from 'malignants' which had been employed in the first half of 1643.

With the centralization of the Treasury the raising of horses became the responsibility of the Cambridge authorities, and between January 1644 and April 1645 £14,712 was spent; initially Weaver's

Treasury provided the money, but in the summer Leman took over this function.[103] The Committee's agent for the purchase of horses was Lieutenant Russell, and throughout the year he bought horses in the markets of Cambridge, Huntingdon, Bedford, Stamford and Northampton, and, more occasionally, requisitioned horses in the constituent counties with the assistance of the local committees.[104] The horses which Russell bought were usually stabled in Cambridge inns, or sent into the fens to graze on sequestered pastures, until they were issued out for the recruit of an existing troop or at the embodiment of a new one.[105] But the purchase and issue of horses were not entirely centralized, and individual captains might buy recruits for their troops locally and would be reimbursed for their outlay by the Treasurers.[106] Officers might also exercise an independent initiative by exchanging their unserviceable horses for fresh ones with farmers on the line of march. With proper safeguards this could be a perfectly fair arrangement,[107] but in many cases the countryman was substantially the loser by the deal, and the practice was not far removed from outright theft: parish accounts are full of tales like that of John Hull of Bozeat, who had to follow the army to Abingdon before he could get a horse in exchange for the one taken from him, and then he was given 'a pore spitle jade, that could scarce drive to Bozzat'.[108]

But despite the efforts of the centralized organization headed by Russell and those, more or less legal, of the individual captains, in the winter of 1644–5 there was a severe shortage of cavalry mounts: troopers were sent home by their captains 'for want of horses'.[109]

Arms. As with his horse, the trooper was officially responsible for his equipment and arms, and met the bills for their repair by the sadler or gunsmith who rode with the troop.[110] But worn-out equipment or that damaged in service was replaced at the charge of the Treasury. After January the purchase and issue of arms and munitions was highly centralized; captains might make small purchases on their own initiative,[111] but, with the exception of those by commanders of garrisons or detached brigades of the army,[112] larger transactions were handled by qualified officials responsible to the Cambridge Committee. Until early in September 1644 the main depository for the arms and ammunition of the Association was the garrison town of King's Lynn. The town was certainly chosen as the center for the distribution of munitions because its position as a port and focal point of a network of inland waterways enabled the authorities to take advantage of the greater security and cheapness of water transport as against cartage by land.[113] The bulky cargoes of munitions were shipped from London or the continent, off-loaded at Lynn under the supervision of the clerk of the stores,

William Botterell, and from there distributed according to the needs and position of the army, while damaged arms were returned to Lynn for repair. A store at Cambridge, to which arms were also sent by carriers from London at far greater expense, was supplied by keelboats plying down the rivers Ouse and Cam; keels crossed the Wash to Boston, and sailed up the Witham to Lincoln. During the siege of York, Lynn vessels freighted munitions and other supplies to Hull or Selby, where their cargoes were put aboard barges which were hauled up the Ouse to the besiegers. After September, as the army marched into the Thames valley, Lynn's importance as the central munitions distribution center waned; its stock was eventually sent to Cambridge, while new supplies of munitions were sent direct from London to the Lieutenant-General of the Ordnance or his deputies, who supervised the issue of equipment from the magazine which traveled with the army.[114]

Before January the counties had made their own arrangements for the purchase of arms, and initially Manchester continued to deal with the small local traders they had employed; Botterell and Colonel Walton, the governor of Lynn, who appears to have acted in a supervisory capacity with regard to the store, bought small quantities of supplies from such men throughout 1644.[115] But the major contracts fell to larger operators. Early in 1644 a Lynn merchant, Bartholemew Wormell, provided munitions from the Netherlands valued at nearly £8000.[116] But after May there were no further transactions with the Low Countries.[117] With the costs of shipping and customs charges the goods were marginally more expensive than those which could be obtained in London, and there were difficulties concerning relative continental and English specifications.[118] Probably foreign merchants were approached only when the foundation of the centralized depot system and the preparation of the army for the new campaigning season in the beginning of 1644 created a very immediate need which could not be met by domestic purchases.

In the early months of 1644, when large-scale purchases of munitions had been made on the continent, London had also been a major source of supply. Captain West, assistant to the Lieutenant-General of the Ordnance, represented the Association in the City, and between February and mid-April 1644 he bought arms to the value of £6665.[119] Although West rejoined the army in April, almost all subsequent purchases of arms were made in London;[120] the Association dealt with a number of businessmen, but its chief supplier was Edward Barker, a city merchant, with whom West had worked in the spring.[121] Altogether nearly £39,000 was spent on arms after the centralization of the Treasury.[122]

Despite a shortage of munitions in August 1644, probably occasioned by the capture of a supply ship by a Royalist privateer, the organization responsible for the provision of arms and ammunition appears to have been the most successful of the supply departments. On his arrival at the siege of York, Manchester was able to lend his Scottish allies powder, bullet and pistols, and in the winter of 1644–5, when the deficiencies of the other departments became most apparent, the supply of munitions was adequate.[123]

Clothing. By Ordinance the parish authorities were required to provide adequate clothing and shoes for the men they impressed; the central Treasury only provided the coats which, by their color and facings, distinguished the soldiers of the respective regiments. These coats were purchased from manufacturers in Cambridge and Suffolk, where the Treasurer to the local committee, Samuel Moody, a clothier, was the major supplier.[124] But after being fitted out at the beginning of his service, the soldier had to meet all his subsequent necessities from his own pay.[125] Individual soldiers might negotiate personally with a draper, but the usual practice was for the captain to contract with a supplier, issue the clothing to his company, and deduct the cost from their pay.[126] The captains might pay for the goods immediately, or send the creditor to Leman at Cambridge who met the bills, and put the sum paid to the captain's account, to be deducted from the pay owed to the company.[127] Direct negotiation between captain and merchant, which was the rule in the early months, continued to be employed throughout 1644, but in the summer a parallel, more centralized system developed. The earlier method proved inadequate during the northern campaign as the growing arrears in the pay of the army disenabled the captains from direct purchase, and most had long ago exhausted their personal credit, while the necessary goods were difficult to obtain in an area where trade and industry were dislocated by war.[128] More central initiative was required, and was first undertaken during the siege of York when an agent was employed in Norfolk to buy up shoes. From August to the end of 1644, Treasurer Gawsell employed a number of men to purchase boots and shoes in bulk, which he issued to the captains deducting the cost from the sums owed to their companies for pay.[129] In September the Treasury bought breeches and doublets from Cambridge, and stockings from Richmond, and in December stocks of clothing were obtained in London.[130] These supplies were transported with the army on its marches, and an official was appointed responsible for their issue to the troops.[131]

The commissariat. The basic system employed for the accommodation and feeding of the army was of quartering the soldiers on the civilian population. On arrival at the town or village selected by the Quarter-Master-General of the army, the quartermaster of the troop or regiment, with the assistance of the parish constable, would assign the soldier a billet with one of the inhabitants, who was obliged to provide shelter and food, for which his enforced guest paid according to a fixed schedule of rates, depending upon his rank.[132] This system, involving an invasion of individual privacy, was much resented by the civilian population. When the soldiers had money they might refuse to pay their bills, theft was common, and careless or wanton damage to property could occur – at least two disastrous fires were caused by the carelessness of billeted troops.[133] In addition to providing quarters villagers in the line of march were frequently required to provide carts and teams to transport provisions, supplies or the sick; this was an expensive business at best,[134] and was frequently rendered even more burdensome by the failure of the soldiers to return the requisitioned horses and wagons.[135] The presence of the army might be unpopular for reasons other than the physical damage and expense entailed; the inhabitants of Yaxley were horrified by the crude horseplay with which a company of Manchester's dragoons, billeted upon them, displayed their contempt for infant baptism. Probably the constables of Baldock were not the only parochial authorities who bribed a company 'that should have staid here, to have them gone'.[136]

The system of quartering on the civilian population not only led to antagonism between the latter and the soldiers. It also engendered feuds between various Parliamentary commanders, as each strove to keep the area which supplied his forces free from the demands of others for accommodation and provisions. Sir Samuel Luke waged a ceaseless struggle to keep the Association's forces from poaching in the region which supplied his garrison at Newport Pagnell, and regarded the prospect of a skirmish developing between his men billeted at Chicheley and one of Manchester's troops sent to quarter there with both equanimity and confidence in the outcome.[137]

But the unpopularity of the system with the civilian community, and its complexity, was compounded by the growing arrears in the pay of the army, and the soldiers' consequent inability to meet their charges. From this arose the necessity of taking 'free quarter', a system of deferred payment. The householder should have received, in lieu of money, a ticket specifying the number of men he had accommodated and the length of time they were so quartered, signed by an officer or the soldiers themselves.[138] Occasionally the soldiers would refuse to sign tickets, in which case an affidavit under the hand of the constable and other parishioners might be deemed sufficient.[139] The money due was to be paid by the soldier, or by the Treasury which would then deduct the sum from the man's pay, at an unspecified date. Within the Association the prospect of repayment was not too remote. In the early months of 1644, although the foot paid their individual bills for accommodation,[140] the horse were generally in receipt of free quarter in Cambridgeshire and Huntingdonshire.[141] The individual householders' bills were sent to Cambridge, verified by the audit office, and the sums owed to each village were totaled and paid by Treasurer Leman to the parish constables.[142] 1/4d had already been deducted from the daily pay of each soldier in those troops stationed permanently in Cambridgeshire and Huntingdon from January through March when they had been paid in April, and the sum thus retained by Leman was used to meet the village bills when they were finally received at Cambridge.[143] But those troops which had been on active service outside the Association for any length of time in early 1644 had received full pay in April; in these cases Leman entered the sums paid to meet the village bills in his account, to be deducted from the troops' pay at a future muster.[144]

In August and September 1644, and again in the following winter when substantial bodies of Manchester's horse and foot took free quarter in the counties of the Association, the Earl instructed the local committees to receive, audit, and pay the claims from parishes in their counties from their receipts on the third Four Months' Assessment; they were to forward the bills and acquittances to Leman at Cambridge, who was to set the sums paid against the arrears owed the troops and regiments involved.[145]

Within the Association, with the exception of the inhabitants of Lincolnshire and of King's Lynn,[146] the householders seldom had to wait for more than a year for payment of their bills, and in cases of necessity payment could be speeded, as it might for villages with good records in their payment of Parliamentary assessments.[147] For them free quarter was a temporary financial inconvenience. But for residents outside the Association it was a much more serious burden: though some of the infantry paid their bills in Yorkshire, and partial repayment or the payment of tickets in especially deserving cases is recorded in some south midland parishes,[148] the village accounts of Northamptonshire and Buckinghamshire, drawn up in 1646, suggest that free quarter with no subsequent repayment was the rule, particularly in the autumn of 1644, and could fall with particular severity on some communities.[149]

Free quarter, though the backbone of the system of provision and accommodation of the army of the Association, was, however, not in itself sufficient to meet the requirements of the cavalry, or of the army when it was on the march and the regiments forced to quarter in close proximity to one another, often in country already devastated by the passage of armies. In these cases the system of free quarter was supplemented by the efforts of regimental commissaries, and increasingly by a growing centralized supply network.

When a troop was quartered for any length of time on a village, as in the winter of 1643–4, it became impossible for the inhabitants to provide the necessary horse provender. While some captains purchased the requisite commodities on the open market, more usually these were requisitioned from neighboring parishes, which were required to provide a stipulated amount of hay, oats, and beans weekly: so from January–March 1644, Major Alford's troop, quartered at Hartford, was supplied with forage by levies on the neighboring villages in the Hundred of Hurstingstone.[150] Such arrangements were supervised by the commissaries attached to each regiment. A similar system was employed when the army was operating in territory already wasted by the movement of troops and where the prospect of enemy activity necessitated the troops being billeted close together. When Cromwell launched a force against Hilsden House in March 1644, his regimental commissary Richard Lawrence was responsible for its supply, and requisitioned not only forage, but bread and cheese from a number of villages in Buckinghamshire and southern Northamptonshire in the rear of Cromwell's area of operations: at the same time Commissary James was organizing the supplies for the force besieging Newark.[151] During the siege of York the regimental commissaries and sutlers toured the surrounding area, occasionally purchasing on the open market, but more usually requisitioning supplies.[152]

When the army operated as a body, rather than as a number of small independent units, the efforts of the regimental commissaries and sutlers were of less importance than those of the Commissary of the Army, a post held by Edward Orpin,[153] in obtaining the provisions required to supplement the system of quartering on the civilian population. As the army prepared to move into Yorkshire, a major center of the war occupied already by three substantial armies, Orpin requisitioned supplies from a huge area; in late April parishes in northern Northamptonshire were ordered to bring stated amounts of beef, bacon, mutton, cheese, wheat, oats, and malt to Stamford, a month later Orpin was raising supplies in East Lindsey to be brought to Gainsborough.[154]

Whilst the army was engaged in the siege of York, Orpin established a more sophisticated supply network to meet its necessities. Working in conjunction with William Mumford of King's Lynn and some Hull merchants, he organized the purchase of supplies in East Anglia, which were then transported to Selby and York by sea and river, often in the same vessels as Botterell's munitions.[155] When the army marched south Orpin was unable to use the system of navigable waterways which had been so advantageous during the York campaign and was forced to rely more on the purchase of supplies from local merchants and manufacturers. However, some provisions were bought in London by the Association's agents and by the Committee of Both Kingdoms, to be shipped up the Thames to the army.[156]

The provisions provided by the commissaries should have been purchased from them by the captains, and the sums expended by the latter deducted from the soldiers' pay.[157] But, as with billeting, the system was complicated by the substantial arrears in the pay of the army which developed in 1644. Two methods of deferred payment were used. Occasionally the regimental commissaries were given cash balances by the Treasurers, with which they bought provisions and issued them to the troops, returning lists to the Treasury of the value of the goods given to each troop; this sum was entered in Leman's account to be deducted from pay at a later date. But more frequently the commissaries requisitioned provisions, and gave a ticket to the merchant or farmer stating the value of the goods; this bill would be paid by the Treasury and the sum entered on the account of the regiment involved.[158] Requisitioning supplies and payment by ticket involved the same abuses from the point of view of the village community as did the system of free quarter. Within the Association repayment, if delayed, was usual, but those Buckinghamshire and Northamptonshire parishes which brought provisions to the commissaries at Buckingham or Stamford in March and April were never paid. Indeed, villages instructed to bring provisions to Stamford were given the option of making a monetary composition in lieu of meeting the commissaries' full requirements in kind. In this form the system was little more than a thinly disguised additional assessment on areas where Manchester had no legitimate authority to raise money: it was obviously regarded as such by Major-General Crawford's brigade in the winter of 1644–5.[159]

With the exception of the organization for the provision of munitions, the Association's supply system was never adequate. Despite the efforts of Lieutenant Russell, there was a shortage of horses in the winter of 1644–5, and troopers lacking mounts had to be sent home. But the organizations for the provision of food and clothing were most deficient. Immediately after Marston Moor one of Manchester's captains reported that victuals were 'very scarce amongst us: and our soldiers hungry and tired with a lingering siege', while in the next month the Earl ascribed the outbreak of sickness in his army to the lack of adequate food and clothing both during and after the siege.[160] But it was the Newbury campaign, when the Association's army was operating with the two other major Parliamentary forces in territory already ravaged by the frequent passage of armies, in winter, which most fully displayed the weakness of the system. Major-General Crawford reported of the infantry that 'they were but so many ghosts for want of provisions and other accomodations', and the cavalry were in little better condition, their horses weakened by hard duty and lack of forage. When Manchester ordered Cromwell to bring the cavalry to a rendezvous preparatory to action, the latter remonstrated that the horses 'will fall down under the riders . . . you may have their skins, but you can have no service', and the King's relief of Donnington Castle was in part achieved because the Parliamentary cavalry were 'through scarcity of provisions, quartered a great distance from one another', and so could not be drawn into a body swiftly enough to oppose the Royalist army. Three times the inability of the army to secure supplies forced their withdrawal from strategically advantageous positions, culminating in the retreat from Newbury on 17 November.[161]

By the autumn of 1644 the army of the Association was no longer the well-ordered military machine that it had been six months previously. Its ranks had been thinned by desertion and disease, the common soldiers were ill-equipped and worse provisioned, its morale was poor; the impoverishment of the Treasuries was a factor, although not necessarily a determining factor, in all these difficulties. The alarming rate of desertion from the infantry regiments might have been limited had the men been better paid, and the ravages of disease controlled had they been adequately clothed and fed. Morale was adversely affected by the burgeoning arrears, which resulted in feuds between infantry and cavalry, and the crude exploitation of the country people in areas through which the army was passing.

The conclusions of the two previous sections may appear contradictory: in 1644 the Earl established a number of financial agencies at Cambridge which collected the unprecedented burden of taxation from the eastern counties with considerable efficiency, yet the army was badly weakened by deficient financing. The paradox struck at least one informed contemporary, John Lilburne. Writing in 1645 he recalled the privations suffered by his dragoon regiment in the previous year as a result of the shortage of pay and supplies, and questioned the reason for this: 'my Lord of Manchester's provision of money by Ordinance . . . was very large, and the countreys made us beleeve that they made very good payment, and yet . . . we received but a very small proportion of it, which makes me wonder what is become of the rest; surely it is either in those men's pockets that have no right to it, or else it is sunke into the ground'.[162] The following section will seek to answer Lilburne's question; why, if some 95% of the money due upon the Monthly Assessment was accounted for by Leman and the Association also had the revenues administered by Stane and Weaver, was there a financial crisis?

The balance of accounts

Already, early in 1644, both the Commons and the central administrators of the Association were troubled by the growing arrears in
the pay of Manchester's army. They also agreed as to its cause: the
recalcitrance of the taxpayers within the eastern counties, and the
consequent slowness with which the local Treasurers returned money
to Cambridge. In July both Parliament and the Committee of Both
Kingdoms sought to inspire the counties to quicken their payments
by hymning the benefits that would accrue to the Parliamentary
cause in general, and the eastern counties in particular, from the
Association's victory at Marston Moor. In August, having learned
from Manchester of the financial difficulties of his army Westminster
again pressed the counties to hasten their returns of the money due,
and this demand was repeated in December.[163]

But by this date the earlier agreement between the Commons and
the Cambridge Committee in casting the blame for the arrears in the
pay of the army upon the local officials had been undermined. The
greater part of the receipts upon the first two Four Months' Assessment Ordinances had been returned to Leman, and the receipt of
part of the outstanding sum had been anticipated by borrowing on
the London money market or from wealthy individuals in those
towns where the army was operating,[164] yet there was little improvement in the financial situation of the army. Further attempts to bully
or cajole the county authorities into hastening the return of money
to Cambridge were obviously an insufficient remedy, and other
explanations of the deficiencies in the financial system of the Association had to be found.

In Parliament some members began to express their suspicions of
the integrity of the officials of the Association's Treasury. Suggestions
that the Treasurers were distributing the available funds partially and
diverting sums to their own use probably emanated from the cavalry,
months in arrears, and would have been brought to the notice of the
Commons by Cromwell's visit to London in September.[165] Such
suspicions lay behind the new clause in the Ordinance for the third
Four Months' Assessment, appointing a committee which was to
travel with the army and oversee the musters and payment upon
them, and the order of 11 October that Cromwell's regiment should
receive a quantity of new equipment from London armorers, the cost
of which was to be met by the county Treasurers forwarding money
direct to the city: the Treasurers at Cambridge were excluded from
the transaction. The accusation of corruption was openly voiced
in the Commons' order of 10 December, ordering an investigation of
the 'complaints . . . of the misemploying the monies raised . . . and
diverting them from the pay of the soldiers', and would appear to be

implicit in the House's interference in the Association's fiscal affairs in 1645.[166]

The surviving documentation provides no evidence to substantiate these charges of the misapplication of funds, except that a divergence did develop in the regularity with which the cavalry and the infantry were paid – a phenomenon as typical of the other Parliamentary armies. If the Treasurers can be faulted it is that their priorities were wrong: the Cambridge Committee, its officers and the local garrison[167] were fairly regularly paid, and the fact probably enhanced the antagonism between the military and the Treasury bureaucrats. But the pay of the former would not have improved notably had the officials been forced to undergo the same privations, as sums disbursed on administration were infinitesimal by comparison with the pay of the army.

In late 1644 in reply to the Commons' suggestions that the growing arrears of the army stemmed from corruption and the misappropriation of funds, the Cambridge Committee argued that the revenue made available to them by Ordinance was totally insufficient for the maintenance of the army they had on foot. By September the Treasury officials had realized that the Fifth and Twentieth was 'neere spent', and Gawsell, who was so desperate for money that he was prepared to sell wealthy Royalist prisoners of war their freedom, was pressing 'that Parleament would do something for our Army; to make us travell from South to North, and from North to South without taking care of us, I thinke . . . is strange'.[168] The Treasurer concluded that without legislation enabling the Association to tap new sources of revenue 'we must sitt still', and in the next months he and the Committee addressed a series of appeals to Parliament for additional funds – that they might receive the excise, or a larger proportion of the sequestration revenues from the constituent counties, or that other counties should be added to the Association, thus increasing the area within which assessments could be raised.[169]

These appeals did not produce the desired legislation, and in November[170] the Cambridge Committee prepared a vigorous Remonstrance, arguing that the 'provision of the weekly assessment is not sufficient to discharge the charges of theire proportion of the warre' because a substantial proportion of the sum voted never reached their Treasury, and, even had the full sum been received, the army's expenses far exceeded it. They concluded, with a bitterness perhaps engendered by the charge that the corruption and inefficiency of their administration was culpable, that they were not to be blamed if 'after five monthes sollicitinge for reliefe, the souldiers still cry out for want of cloathes, food and pay, and contract diseases and dye upon the guards, to the daily greife of all that are true-harted and well-affected'.

In the autumn of 1644 the Cambridge Committee announced that their expenditure was £12,000 a month greater than their income from the assessment, while, in the course of a debate instigated by one of the Committee's petitions, the East Anglian M.P., Miles Corbett, put the arrear as high as £15,000 a month.[171] How accurate were these gloomy pronouncements?

Not until the very full September 1644 muster return can the monthly pay which the army should have received be calculated with reasonable accuracy. Comparable figures cannot be constructed for the earlier period because the army was still being recruited and reorganized until May 1644, and the muster material is less complete. But in February the London press wrote of the build-up of the Association's army to an operational strength of 10,000 foot, 2000 dragoons and 3000 horse, and that this was not just a journalist's pipe-dream appears from some calculations in the papers of the Essex M.P., Sir Thomas Barrington.[172] The cost of paying the officers and men of this 'ideal establishment' would have been approximately £34,277, a figure which does not take into account the upkeep of the army's train of artillery or its intelligence service, the expenses of administration or the cost of the purchase of munitions. To meet this Gawsell and Leman should have received £33,780 a month, while in the first third of 1644 Weaver received about £10,000 a month from the Review of the Fifth and Twentieth part. Theoretically the financial situation appeared viable.

By September 1644 the Treasurers faced grim reality. The assessments raised in Lincolnshire and the Isle of Ely had been allocated for local defense, so Gawsell and Leman's possible maximum monthly receipt was only £28,020, without considering the arrears which had developed in the counties' payments to the Treasurers; no help could be expected from the Fifth and Twentieth, which was 'neere spent'. The Treasury had to meet the pay of the army, at £31,521 a month, and the expenditure, previously born by Weaver, of approximately £6197 a month in munitions and horses, and £1351 a month for the upkeep of the Cambridge bureaucracy.[173] Further, Gawsell and Leman had to meet a series of outlays unforeseen in February – the pay of small garrisons and isolated detachments, the higher cost of medical services as sickness ravaged the army, the expenses of the third siege of Crowland after its seizure by the Royalists in November 1644.[174] A calculation based on the January 1645 muster of the army shows that the situation of the unfortunate Treasurers was as desperate as four months before; although fewer men were in service than in September – indeed a number only 56% of that envisioned in the previous February–the proliferation of troops and companies, each with its expensive cadre of officers and n.c.o.s, still held the pay of the army at £30,917 a month.

In the light of these figures the Committee's estimate of a £12,000–£15,000 monthly arrear does not appear unduly pessimistic, and the difficulties of the Treasurers, and the army's poor performance in the autumn of 1644, must be understood in terms of an over-riding fiscal crisis.

The army of the Association

By virtue of the powers granted him in the Ordinance of 20 January 1644 the Earl of Manchester re-organized the army of the Association and led it to victory at Marston Moor. This success owed much to the system which Manchester instituted to raise and recruit his infantry regiments, to the ability of the army of the Association to attract a leaven of well-motivated, committed volunteers to serve in its cavalry troops, and to Manchester's insistence upon certain personal qualities when choosing and promoting officers. These questions of military organization and the social structure of the army will now be examined. Such an analysis will also add to an understanding of the serious decline in the efficiency of Manchester's force so apparent during the Newbury campaign. The crisis of the autumn was not only a product of inadequate financing and the concomitant difficulties in the provision of supplies already discussed: it will be shown that the system of impressment ultimately proved inadequate as the infantry regiments were ravaged by disease, while morale was weakened by the politico-religious rift among the officers of the army, which stemmed in part from the criteria employed by the Earl in their selection.

The infantry

By the end of the summer of 1644 eleven infantry regiments had been raised in the eastern counties for service with Manchester. For four, those on permanent garrison duty,[1] no muster rolls have survived, but the number of men serving in the seven regiments of the field army can be calculated from the muster returns given in the Treasury warrants and debentures, and these are tabulated in Appendix 8. The figures show that by mid-September Manchester had only about 60%, and by January 1645, 45% of the infantry strength with which he had prepared to move into Yorkshire in June 1644. But the crude figures, which take no account of recruits sent up to the army in the course of the year, conceal even more startling losses. Captain Harvey of Hobart's regiment mustered 107 men on 30 March 1644, ten months later his company totaled 46; in this period he lost 80 of his original 107 soldiers, and 61 of the 80 recruits sent to him on two occasions.[2]

Before discussing how the foot soldiers were raised and the reasons for the disastrous decline in the strength of the Association's infantry in the course of the year, a related development, with important financial repercussions, must be noted. Despite the dramatic fall in the numbers of common soldiers, the cost of maintaining the infantry did not fall proportionally.[3] In part this was occasioned by an increase in the number of n.c.o.s in each company,[4] but far more significant financially was the proliferation of companies and regiments. Crawford's and Pickering's regiments were both embodied in mid-March, before the decline in the number of common soldiers in the army, although the Cambridge Committee cannot have given much thought as to how they intended to raise their pay. Rainborow's was raised in June, but it was designed for service in Lincolnshire and was paid by the local committee.[5] The embodiment of these regiments can be justified, but subsequent developments are quite incomprehensible, for in the late summer, when the infantry's strength was spiraling down, new companies and regiments were raised.

The fault was not entirely that of the Association's administrators and commanders. In late June the King's sudden push towards London had been met by a hastily raised army under Major-General Browne, consisting of trained-band detachments from London and the home counties, which had subsequently behaved with their usual mutinous inefficiency. In consequence the Commons agreed, in the Ordinance of 12 July, to raise a new permanent force for service in the vicinity of Oxford under Browne; its soldiers were to be impressed in the southern, midland and eastern counties.[6] Manchester protested bitterly against the Ordinance, arguing that the levies for Browne's brigade were interrupting the essential recruiting of his battered regiments. After some delay Parliament accepted the Earl's argument, and the men raised in East Anglia for service with Browne, with the exception of those from Essex, were diverted to recruit the army of the Association.[7] However, at least in Suffolk and Hertfordshire, the levies for Browne's force had been organized in complete companies, each with a full cadre of officers and n.c.o.s, and these companies were incorporated into Manchester's army as they stood; the newly levied men were not used to recruit depleted companies, but to form new ones.[8] This folly was compounded in November. Alone among the eastern counties, Essex had swiftly raised its full quota of men for Browne, and, organized as a regiment under Colonel Sparrow, they were serving as part of the garrison of Abingdon.[9] The regiment had been paid by a special levy on the county, but by early November both the relevant Ordinance and the willingness of the Essex committee to meet this extraordinary expense had expired. The Committee of Both Kingdoms thereupon wrote to Manchester blandly informing him that Sparrow's regiment should be incorporated into the army of the Association and be paid from its Treasury. This, they suggested, would recruit his shattered army. But, in effect, the Association had to bear the charge of another regiment with its expensive officer corps intact, and its fighting strength decimated.[10] In January 1645, as a result of the policy of the Committee of Both Kingdoms with respect to Sparrow's regiment, while the number of infantrymen in Manchester's army had fallen by 15% since September, the cost of its officer cadre had increased by 8%.

Although Manchester and his aides were not entirely responsible for the ridiculous policy of embodying new companies, they may perhaps be faulted for failing to merge 'broken' companies. In September six companies of Montagu's regiment had less than 30 men – two had only 11 apiece! – yet all had a full cadre of officers and n.c.o.s.[11] Such companies could have been combined and costs cut by canceling the commissions of superfluous officers or reducing them to 'reformado' status. In any case such remodeling would have presented administrative difficulties, but it may not have been undertaken for political rather than pragmatic reasons. As will be seen, by the autumn the officers of the army were polarized into factions centering on Crawford and Cromwell, each of whom sought to advance his own adherents and secure the dismissal of those of his opponent. In these circumstances any attempt to combine companies and remove superfluous officers would have presented almost insuperable political difficulties to Manchester.

Recruits

A nucleus of Manchester's foot was provided by the brigade raised in the Association that had served under Lord Grey, and which was withdrawn from Essex's army in the Thames valley in July 1643. But these old volunteer regiments were pitifully weak and many of the remaining soldiers deserted when their companies returned to their counties of origin in the summer to be recruited up to full strength.[12] Accordingly the Earl's infantry consisted chiefly of levies raised in the Association by impressment. A few other, less productive, sources of men were available to the Earl. Some foot soldiers transferred from other Parliamentary armies to that of the Association,[13] and a small number of men joined Manchester as volunteers.[14] Captured Royalist soldiers might enlist, and the Earl's subordinates endeavored to impress men in the counties where the army was serving, although they had no legal authority to do so, and in the face of considerable local resistance.[15] But by far the major part of the infantry were conscripts from the seven counties of the Association.

Impressment of men within the Association was a fairly continuous process, but three major periods of activity may be distinguished.

Firstly the two months after the passage of the Ordinance of 16 August 1643 when men were rushed to the siege of Lynn; secondly while the army lay in its quarters about Cambridge in the winter of 1643–4 and was built up to its full operational strength; and finally in the summer of 1644 when recruits were sought to replace the losses incurred in the York campaign. In each case the demand emanated from Manchester, who endeavored to raise recruits from the county in which the regiment had originally been embodied, as this 'made the soldiers more united among themselves'.[16] On receipt of Manchester's directive, often backed by exhortations from Westminster,[17] the county committees proportioned out the required number of men upon the hundreds and parishes, dealt with complaints concerning the latter, and supervised the constables who were responsible at the village level.[18]

Hostility to the system of impressment was universal, both among those liable to conscription and their relatives and employers. The combination of self-interest and a genuine moral revulsion against impressing 'any man to take awaie his liffes', led one group of draftees to arm themselves and stand on their own defense, and more regularly revealed itself in a willingness to accept imprisonment or a £10 fine instead of the press money.[19] Another group of potential conscripts displayed a sudden eagerness to serve in the trained-bands, the members of which were excluded from impressment by the Ordinance. The local authorities were well aware of this loophole, and the Chelmsford committee instructed the constables to impress any trained-band soldier who had failed to attend the previous muster.[20] But the committees themselves were not above a little log-rolling, and the release of impressed servants or laborers could be secured by those whose friends were committeemen.[21]

As in Parliament's demands for unprecedented sums in taxation, both the burden and the concomitant unpopularity of impressment fell upon the wretched village constable. In the execution of his duty he was subjected to a variety of manifestations of communal or individual hostility, ranging from abuse, like the imprecations Mrs Bateman hurled at the constable of Barking who had impressed her servant – 'such Roundheaded Rascalls . . . were the causers of these warres, and bid him goe him selfe which was one of the cawsers of it', through a contemptuous disregard for his authority and refusal to assist him in the execution of his duty, threats and vindictive lawsuits, actual physical violence, to the bewitching of the constable of Upwell and his assistants, who were rash enough to attempt to impress the son of a notorious local sorceress.[22] Victimized by his neighbors on the one hand the unfortunate constable was subject to the pressure of the committee on the other. Any failure to produce the number of men charged on the parish would render the constable liable to a swingeing fine, and the threat that he himself might be drafted.[23]

Some constables abused their powers, and impressed men from the households of their personal enemies, whilst others took the opportunity to demonstrate their dislike of the local committee, impressing their servants, or of the whole Parliamentary cause, as did the constables of Burrow Green who, remarking that 'they had but few Roundheads in the town', resolved 'to rid the town of them, whereupon they pressed one which was the best affected man in theire Towne'.[24] But if the constable had no axe to grind, a natural reaction was to seize a traveler or the inhabitant of another parish. This both met the committee's numerical requirements and avoided disturbing the village community. The Chelmsford committee absolutely forbade this practice, and the Romford committee released two carters impressed while on journeys, but despite official disapproval the practice continued. No one challenged the impressment of a demented laborer from Surrey in West Ham, and the incident is only recorded because of an official investigation of his subsequent blasphemous pronouncements, while in Norwich 9% of those impressed came from parishes outside the city.[25] If forced to impress within the village the constables endeavored to take bachelors, who had no dependents to become a charge on the parish, or the socially undesirable: 'have an especiall care', a Norfolk high constable advised his subordinates, 'to take idle servingmen and such other able persons as live dissolutely or idly without any imployment'.[26] The raid on an unlicensed alehouse must have been a common event, nor is the impressment of the criminal class, even direct from prison, surprising. The constables of Coggeshall must have leapt at the chance to draft so notorious a local ne'er-do-well as William Yorke, who had a record of convictions for theft, receiving stolen goods and riot dating back to 1625.[27] The constable also might seize the opportunity to rid the parish of potential charges on the poor rate: having impressed a poor man the constables of Nevendon pulled down his house, and refused to allow him to re-settle in the parish when he returned from the army.[28] But rogues and vagabonds had considerable previous experience of avoiding parish officers, while the county committees did not always look with favor on the constables' efforts to cut their parishes' poor rate; demanding that conscripts be 'as neare as may bee, able bodied', the local authorities rejected boys, the sick and the aged.[29] This, in addition to the sheer size of the demand, enforced the constables to impress from a wider cross-section than had been necessary under Elizabeth, when 'the dregs of society' had been sufficient to fill the ranks.[30] The surviving records from rural East Anglia suggest that servants and laborers were most frequently impressed, although householders, husbandmen or men of some property were occasionally drafted.[31] Within the urban setting of Norwich the pattern is similar: the names of 140 conscripts are known, and the status of 34 is given – 16 were servants, 7 apprentices, 4 served in local hostelries, 5 were workmen, and there was a butcher and a husbandman.[32]

Having impressed the requisite number of men in his village, the constable was responsible for clothing the conscripts adequately. This was to be performed at the charge of the parish, and could represent a considerable expense.[33] Accordingly it was often neglected: in August 1643 the Cambridge officials had never seen 'worse tattered soldiers' than the Essex conscripts, while a year later, when Silas Titus took command of his newly raised Hertfordshire company, he found them 'extreamlie ill provided for a march, without shooes, stockings, coates; in conclusion . . . they wanted nothing but all'.[34] The constable was also responsible for bringing his contingent to the local rendezvous on the stipulated day, where they would be handed over to a captain or 'conductor' to be marched to Cambridge or directly to the army. Should an impressed man escape before the constable brought him to the rendezvous, the latter had to find a replacement, and in consequence some parishes employed a number of men to guard the unwilling conscript and 'keep him in awe',[35] an additional expense. Bringing the men to the rendezvous might not always end the constables' responsibility. In September 1643, when the large numbers of recruits required, the urgency of the occasion and the inexperience of the central and local officials combined to create chaos, the constables arrived at the rendezvous only to find that the officers who were to convey the men to the army had not yet come; the constables, eager to return to their harvest work, were forced, 'in the nature of so many gaolers', to guard their men at the rendezvous until the captains turned up.[36]

Even when handed over to the officers at the rendezvous, the levies still posed a problem for the local committees. Warned by their experience of the Bishops' war, the gentry were chary of combining reluctant lower-class conscripts into companies and arming them. So in September 1643 the Essex committee sent their levies to Lynn without weapons, while Sir Thomas Honeywood suggested that the trained-bands should be mustered on the day when the recruits were marched out. This would give a morale-boosting indication of the county's readiness to second the efforts of the newly raised troops, and, more practically, would 'prevent all mutinies'.[37] But, to the genuine surprise of the local governors, the trained-bands and troops of horse which stood ready to suppress the expected riots, proved superfluous. However, though the levies did not ravage the countryside, they did desert by the score; approximately half of the Essex recruits disappeared between their coming to the rendezvous and their arrival at King's Lynn.[38] Inexperience and the haste required by the military situation partly explain the huge losses from desertion in the autumn of 1643. Thereafter a more sophisticated system was developed whereby small parties of men rather than entire companies[39] were marched to the army under the charge of a conductor with several assistants.[40] Smaller numbers lessened both the potential dangers and the extent of desertion, though it could eradicate neither; Robert Dall lost 8 of the 34 men he conducted from Norwich to Reading, and had to seek the assistance of a cavalry troop to get the remainder of them out of Maidenhead on the last stage of their journey.[41] Impressed men gathered at Cambridge prior to their being sent to the army were liable to mutiny, incited by the students, or to desert: between 3 June and 15 July 209 recruits were quartered in Cambridge and 75 deserted whilst in the town. Of the remaining 134, only 95 eventually reached Manchester's army.[42]

Losses

There were three major reasons for the sharp decline in the Association's infantry strength in 1644, despite the formation of new companies and the recruiting of old: battle casualties, desertion and disease. The first was the least important. Losses were surprisingly light at Marston Moor, more substantial in assaults on towns or fortified positions. The greatest number of casualties occurred during the siege of York, in particular at the assault on the Manor and Bootham Bar.[43] But such losses were unimportant by comparison with those from desertion and disease.

As has been shown, the foot were victims of impressment, and would frequently endeavor to escape the clutches of the constable or the conductor before they were embodied in the regiments of the Association. In the army their morale and discipline remained poor: they occasionally refused to fight, would neglect a military opportunity in favor of plundering,[44] and frequently deserted. In the five infantry companies for which reasonable estimates can be made, one-tenth of the soldiers present on 7 June had run away by 1 October.[45] The offense could be punished by death, but, although he exacted the full penalty at least once, Manchester preferred to get deserters back into the army. Officers were employed to round up runaways, and heavy fines were levied on those towns which harbored them.[46]

But disease was the major cause of the swift reduction in the strength of the infantry regiments. Men had been absent from the May muster through illness, but sickness became more prevalent during the siege of York and hit some companies badly: two captains alone sent 28 men into the Isle of Axholme where a hospital camp for the sick and wounded had been established. By July the epidemic had a firm hold – on the 22nd Manchester reported that 'my men fall sicke dayly' – and continued to decimate the army in the next two months; in early September the Royalist diurnal *Mercurius Aulicus* gloated over the 'strange sickness' consuming the Association's army.[47] The autumn brought some relief, but another outbreak in the winter of 1644–5 thinned the ranks of the regiments garrisoning Henley.[48] The disease was a 'feaver and flux', possibly typhus, which rendered the victim susceptible to secondary infection, and was probably caused by the privations endured by the infantrymen during the siege of York and by the deficiencies of their clothing and provisions subsequently.[49]

When, in November 1644, the Earl of Manchester complained to Westminster that his foot were 'so weakened and wasted that I may truly say they are not sufficient . . . to guard the train of artillery here with me', this was not just a rhetorical flourish.[50] Despite the formation of new companies and the recruiting of old, battle losses, desertion and disease had decimated the unwilling conscripts, and seriously weakened the fighting strength of the Association's infantry.

The dragoons

Most of Manchester's dragoons were raised in Essex by the Ordinance of 12 August, but were subsequently assigned to other counties for the purposes of payment until the centralization of the Treasury in January.[51] It was intended that these companies should be filled by volunteers, but the latter were not forthcoming, and the Essex committee were enforced to mount impressed men to make up the numbers.[52] This, and examples of dragoons reverting to infantrymen, suggests that their social status was on a par with that of the foot, rather than the cavalry.[53] In March 1644, while some dragoon companies were reasonably strong, others were short of both men and horse – Captain Miller's company consisted of 20 men with horses, and a further 18 without. As a result of such deficiencies a number of companies were disbanded in early April, and the dragoons were re-organized into a regiment of five companies under John Lilburne.[54] Regrettably the dragoons were not mustered with the rest of the army in the summer of 1644, but in January 1645 the regiment, presumably recruited up to 100 men in each company at the re-organization, contained only 263 men.[55] Disease and desertion must have taken their toll, but Lilburne's own account of his men's service, 'constantly quartered in the van of the whole armie; where constantly in a manner, we fought for both horse meat and man's meat, or else with a great deal of vigilancy stood upon our guard', suggests the likelihood of a proportionally higher casualty rate than in the cavalry or infantry.[56]

The cavalry

By January 1645 Manchester had forty-four troops of horse under
his command, the bulk of which had been raised prior to the
commencement of the 1644 campaign. They had been embodied in
two distinct ways. First, there were those troops raised by the efforts
and independent initiative of certain individuals, who received little
legislative assistance from Westminster. Such were the troops of
Cromwell's regiment embodied early in 1643, and at least two troops,
those of Swallow and Margery, raised after Manchester's appointment. The first owed its existence to the willingness of the young men
and maids of Norwich 'to cast in their mite', their subscriptions
being used to purchase equipment; Margery, who 'hath honest men
that will follow him', raised his troop in his native Suffolk without
official assistance, indeed, in the face of the hostility of the committee.[57] But the necessity for raising men in this way was ended by
the legislation passed at the time of Manchester's appointment, and
the bulk of his cavalry was raised by the 'flying army' Ordinance of
25 July, and the particular Ordinance of 12 August for Essex.[58] The
former empowered the Earl to command 6500 horse to be raised in
the eastern, southern and midland counties, and from London and
Middlesex. But, with two exceptions,[59] Manchester eventually
received only those troops raised within the Association, as Parliament, in the face of local pressure, ordered the horse from other
areas to join Waller or the Lord General.[60]

The advantage in terms of morale and enthusiasm of troops raised
by individual initiative over those embodied by the Ordinance were
considerable. While there is no evidence of men being impressed to
serve in the troops raised in the summer of 1643,[61] and many of
Manchester's cavalrymen had previously served with Lord Grey
of Warke,[62] clearly the 'honest men' prepared to follow Margery of
their own volition were preferable to those raised by the parishes on
receipt of a warrant to provide a horse and 'an able sufficient man'.
As Sir Thomas Nightingale wrote to the Essex committee, 'wee are
to finde men well affected . . . but where wee shall finde them god in
heaven knowes, for wee doe not'.[63] The slowness with which the men
were raised,[64] and their subsequent behavior, suggest that the
answer was never found. One of the local committee wrote of the
troopers raised in Essex that he had never seen 'such an indisposition
in men to the service in my life'; Cromwell had an equally low
opinion of the Essex men, and complained of the Suffolk troops
'they are so mutinous, that I may justly fear they would cut my
throat'.[65]

How did these men, so closely related to the 'old decayed serving
men and tapsters' Cromwell despised, become the psalm-singing

victors of Marston Moor? The transition in part may be ascribed to the discipline imposed on the troopers and the infectious attitude of religious and moral purpose inculcated by Cromwell and his officers. But a more mundane reason may be suggested. An examination of comparable cavalry muster returns shows that, unlike the infantry or dragoons, there was little decline in the size of troops in 1644.[66] But it is probable that these crude figures conceal a substantial turnover of men.[67] This certainly occurred in one troop in 1643–4: when Captain Sparrow rode from Romford in September 1643 his troop numbered 83 men; in December only 58 of these remained, and in April he had only 42 'old soldiers'. Yet his troop was still 80 strong at this date.[68] As there was no Ordinance instructing the counties to raise horsemen, obviously as losses occurred Sparrow's troop was recruited piecemeal. This conclusion is also suggested by a study of the arrears claimed by troopers for service in the army of the Association later set off against the sale of Royal or capitular lands. For example, Captain Grove's troop was embodied in early 1644, and 26 of the 50 claimants for arrears are credited with a sum consonant with their having served since the first embodiment of the troop; the remaining 24 claim sums ranging between £18-3-6d and £6-3-0d.[69] As it appears that in most cases the amount of pay in arrears is proportional to the service performed,[70] this suggests a considerable turnover of men and piecemeal recruitment to make up the losses.

Whilst the troops contained some men escaping from social or family pressures, and those more interested in plunder, or whose devotion to 'the Cause' was limited,[71] the piecemeal system of the recruitment of volunteers after the initial formation of many troops probably secured a leaven of the 'honest godly men' Cromwell demanded.[72]

From which geographical areas and from which status groups did these troopers come? Certainly not just from the Fens, or from the class of 'Freeholders and Freeholders' sons', as Whitelock, too often followed by historians,[73] suggested of Cromwell's own troop.

First it must be noted that many of the cavalry had served previously in other armies. Captains like Fleetwood and Harrison, who had commanded under the Lord General, brought a nucleus of men from their old troops and troopers who had served with other officers in Essex's army, when they were commissioned in the army of the Eastern Association.[74] Other troopers 'swapped' armies independently of their captains; of the 34 troopers of Cromwell's personal troop whose claims for arrears survive, at least 6 had served previously elsewhere – 3 in Yorkshire, 2 in the Midlands, 1 with Waller. Other arrears certificates show that troopers joined the army of the Association having served previously not only with Essex, Waller, the city brigade or Fairfax, but with forces as remote as the garrison of Liverpool, or Brereton's Cheshire division.[75] Some gravitated to Manchester's command because of the destruction of the armies with which they were originally serving,[76] others were attracted by the prospect of promotion or more regular pay and better conditions.[77] But a powerful factor must have been the desire to serve in a sympathetic religious environment. 'Independency' had emerged in all the Parliamentary armies in 1643,[78] but only in Manchester's force was it favored by a significant or influential number of the higher officers. So, as Baillie wrote, 'all sectaries who pleased to be soujors, for a long time casting themselfe from all other [armies], arrive under his command'.[79] The Lord General was particularly intolerant of religious deviation, and it is notable that the troops of Harrison and Fleetwood, both of which contained a high proportion of men who had originally served in the Earl of Essex's army, were centers of sectarian zeal; 'what a cluster of preaching offecers and troopers ther is'.[80]

This analysis of the pre-Association careers of some troopers reinforces an idea suggested by the practice of piecemeal recruiting. That is, that the cavalry were drawn not just from the Fens but from an area far wider than the Association itself. Whilst the bulk of the cavalry probably were East Anglians, if the theory of piecemeal recruiting is correct we would expect a significant proportion to be raised in those counties through which the army was marching, and a number of troopers to be drawn from farther afield by the army's religious reputation: certainly an Independent pamphleteer thought that Manchester had 'culd out all the honestest youth in the Kingdome'.[81] But this must remain a speculation for, while it is possible to re-construct lists of the troopers serving under the Association's captains, the paucity of the materials which would allow us to determine the specific parish from which an individual trooper came, does not admit of a categorical conclusion. But the surviving evidence does reinforce the suggestion: wills for three of Disborough's troopers who served with the Association survive – one came from Cambridge, one from Lincoln and the third from Beverley.[82]

A similar lack of documentary evidence confronts the historian concerned with the status group from which the cavalry were recruited. It is indefensible to infer, from literary evidence or wills relating to the Protectorate when military service, regularly paid and against national enemies, was respectable, that men of some substance were serving in 1644. Only one Association troop, the Earl of Manchester's lifeguard, undeniably contained men of substance: 'the gentler sort of rebels' noted *Mercurius Aulicus* sourly.[83]

However, some indication of status can be derived from the claims emanating from the cavalry in the political ferment of 1647. The grievances of Rich's regiment are of interest in this respect; many of them, they claimed, had been apprentices in London, but were now denied their freedoms by ill-affected masters, despite the terms of a Parliamentary Ordinance by which time spent in military service was to be counted as part of their apprenticeship. A number of individual petitions from men who had served with Manchester verify the general complaint, and clearly a fair number of the Association's troopers had been London apprentices.[84] Secondly, it is clear that the agitator program, which received its strongest support from the cavalry, was designed to appeal to status groups lower in the social hierarchy than the freeholders, both in its proposals for the franchise and in its suggested social reforms; it was directed to the tenant farmers and copyholders, and to the small businessmen and crafts-men excluded from corporations.[85] Sexby, a Suffolk man who had served in Cromwell's troop, argued from his own social position at Putney and assumed that it was the common experience of many of his comrades; 'there are many thousands of us soldiers that have ventured our lives; we have had little property in the Kingdom as to our estates'.[86] If Sexby was speaking for the majority of his fellow troopers, then cavalrymen like Thomas Ormes, the copyholder of Felbrigg, and John Fitch, the Radwinter husbandman, or Browne, the Cambridge tailor, Hurt the mason, Oliver the carpenter and Seman the son of a blacksmith of Bury St Edmunds, were typical figures. It was to these status groups that the Essex committee looked in August 1643, when they contemplated the impressment of cavalry-men – 'men of able bodyes, tradesmen and apprentices and the like'.[87] But service in the cavalry was not the prerogative of any one social group: a Cambridge scholar, foreigners, and a man of 'not any estate to the value of five shillings' also served.[88]

Other military departments
Artillery

The Association's train of artillery, under the charge of the Lieutenant-General of the Ordnance Thomas Hammond, was comparatively small, and contained few heavy guns; Manchester had to borrow artillery from the Scots during the siege of York, and when Crawford decided to invest Sheffield Lord Fairfax had to provide the siege-guns.[89] Hammond was also responsible for the issue of arms and ammunition, which were carried with the train of artillery, and commanded the pioneers who served 'in a double capacity', as both sappers and firelocks to guard the artillery. The Lieutenant-General, whose ingenuity was to win praise when he held the same post in the New Model, was an efficient administrator, whose innovations secured substantial savings to the Association.[90]

Medical facilities

The medical arrangements for the army were supervised by two 'physicians general', Doctors Emsley and Glisson, and an apothecary, all paid at the rate of 10/– a day. Beneath them were the regimental chirurgeons, each assisted by two mates; in addition to their pay of 4/– a day and the allowance they received for medicines and instruments, the chirurgeons were granted additional sums to meet the expenses they incurred in the course of the campaign.[91] The quality of medical attention provided by this system is doubtful; a number of chirurgeons were unqualified and at least one regiment lacked any medical services.[92] During the campaigning season sick and wounded soldiers were carried with the army in carts, while those too ill to be moved were billeted on the civilian population, as were the sick when the army marched into winter quarters,[93] and a local apothecary or chirurgeon made responsible for their medical needs.[94] The 'walking wounded', particularly at the end of the campaigning season, might be sent home to recuperate; they were given money by the Cambridge Committee to bear their charges to their native villages, and their medical expenses were then borne, often reluctantly, by the parish.[95] Manchester periodically sent officers into the counties to round up those men sent home who had recovered, and to conduct them back to the army.[96]

The sickness which first struck the army during the siege of York, and decimated its ranks in the following months, forced the Association to institute novel medical measures. During the siege a hospital camp was established on the Isle of Axholme, and, as the army marched south, another was set up at Horncastle.[97] In this period a number of officials were employed to buy provisions for the sick, supervise the issue of their pay, and arrange their return to the army after their recovery.[98]

Intelligence service

The intelligence service of the Association was directed by Scout-master-General Leon Watson, who was to hold the same post in the New Model; a goldsmith of Lincoln, he had begun his military career as Treasurer to Lord Willoughby's force.[99] The work of his department is best described in his own account, in which he charges for 'fouer and twenty men and horses . . . imploied dayly as spies into the enemyes armyes and garrisons'. The information gleaned by his agents was forwarded to the generals, and he also corresponded with the commanders of other forces and garrisons, exchanging news.[100]

Police

The police authority in the army was exercised by the regimental provost-marshal, under instructions from the Provost-Marshal General. The provosts were not only responsible for the maintenance of discipline according to the Laws and Ordinances of War promulgated by the Lord General, but for the guarding of Royalist prisoners.[101]

The officers

Prior to Manchester's appointment the prevailing sentiment among the authorities of the constituent counties of the Association was that the local levies should be officered by local men, and that the chain of command should mirror the social hierarchy. Hence the objection of the Suffolk committee, for whom gentility was the essential criterion of fitness for office, to 'honest, godly' Ralph Margery, the 'plain russet-coated captain that knows what he fights for and loves what he knows', whose promotion was defended by Cromwell.[102] In fact the need for some professional expertise and the frequent reluctance of men from the approved status groups to undertake military responsibility forced the county committees to commission outsiders or men of limited social prestige,[103] but wherever possible they sought to realize the ideal of an officer corps consisting almost entirely of local worthies. So the higher posts in the Norfolk foot regiments raised early in 1643 were filled by men from the county's traditional ruling gentry elite; their captains were the cadets of major families, lesser gentlemen, or from the urban patriciate.[104]

However, with the raising of new forces under Manchester's command in the autumn of 1643, the complexion of the officer cadre, in terms both of its local and its social origin, steadily changed. In the formation of new regiments the Earl selected his officers without reference to the county within which the men were raised. Of the nine Colonels appointed after August 1643 only one, John Sparrow, commanded a regiment raised in his native county, and he was selected for the post by the committee of Essex before it was decided that the regiment should join the army of the Association.[105] A similar development occurs with respect to the junior officers of both infantry and cavalry. Montagu's regiment of foot was raised in Cambridgeshire in the winter of 1643–4, but its first Lieutenant-Colonel was a west-countryman, and his replacement came from Essex; the Major was a Scot, and the captains included men from Surrey, Worcestershire and Montgomery. The Lieutenant-Colonel, the Major, a captain, and some junior officers of Rainborow's regiment were all New Englanders.[106] Manchester's own regiment of horse appears to have contained only one East Anglian officer, Major Rich; Dendy came from Westminster, Dingley from Worcestershire, Thomlinson from Yorkshire, Knights from Berkshire, and Thomas Ireton from Nottingham. The London contingent was also very strong; Bethell, Browne and Grove, who became captains in Cromwell's regiment in early 1644, were all from the city.[107]

Manchester's appointment also resulted in a significant change in the social composition as well as the local origin of the Association's officer cadre; the higher posts were no longer purely the preserves of substantial country gentlemen. Four of the new Colonels came from families of equivalent status to the commanders of the Norfolk regiments, Sir Miles Hobart and Sir John Palgrave, but while Edward Montagu would inherit the 'ample means' of the Hinchinbrooke branch of the Montagu clan,[108] Fleetwood, Pickering and Sidney were younger sons.[109] The fathers of both Montagu and Fleetwood were career 'King's Servants', and two other high-ranking officers commissioned by Manchester, Thomas Hammond, Lieutenant-General of the Ordinance, whose father was physician to James I, and Colonel Thomas Rainborow, son of one of Charles I's most experienced naval commanders, came from similar, if less elevated, *officier* backgrounds.[110] Colonels Walton, Sparrow and Ayloffe were all members of the lesser gentry, the last from a family in financial difficulties.[111] Nor were Manchester's Lieutenant-Colonels uniformly from a gentry background, as they had been in 1643: Henry Warner was the son of a Cambridgeshire minister, John Hewson had been 'an honest shoemaker in Westminster'.[112]

The most obvious reason for Manchester's disregard for the previous local and social norms in his appointment of officers was his determination to secure the services of men with some previous military experience. The French Colonel and thirteen Scots commissioned by the Earl were almost certainly professional soldiers, the New England contingent in Rainborow's regiment were the 'best military men in the colony', and three of the new Colonels had served with the English army in Ireland.[113] But the experience of most of the new officers was less exotic than warfare against Spinola or Wallenstein, the Confederate Catholics or the Pequot Indians. They had served in other civil war armies or brigades: with Essex, Waller, Fairfax, or Willoughby, or in the garrison of Bristol.[114] To attract the experienced officers he required Manchester could offer promotion. Although some of the commanders the Earl commissioned were temporarily unemployed, having previously served with forces which had been destroyed or disbanded,[115] most transferred from existing armies, and the prospect of rapid professional advancement must have been a lure. Of eight officers who had held captaincies in the Earl of Essex's army, one became Manchester's Lieutenant-General of the Ordinance, two were promoted to Colonelcies, three to Lieutenant-Colonelcies, and two became Majors. Ten of the Association's captains had previously been lieutenants, cornets, or gentlemen of the life-guard with the Lord General.[116]

But the recruitment of the officer cadre of the army of the Association involved factors other than a simple market-place exchange of promotion for military experience. The qualification of professional expertise, as that of social status, was always subordinate to the Earl's requirement of certain moral and religious qualities in his officers; like his Lieutenant-General, Cromwell, he sought men who 'know what they fight for and love what they know'. The Earl did not hesitate to cashier those whose absolute devotion to the Parliamentary cause was suspect,[117] or disreputable professionals like the French Colonel, Mazères, who found service in an army without the usual diversions of dice, cards, drink and women intolerable.[118] And if the Earl sought qualities other than experience in his subordinates, a number of officers probably transferred to the army of the Association not only to obtain preferment[119] but attracted by its discipline and godliness hymned in the press:[120] a reputation which contrasted with the 'debauched' behavior typical of the Lord General's army.[121] In particular, Independents gravitated to Manchester's command. The Earl's ideal of 'the godly' was ecumenical, comprehending all who 'love Christ in sincerity' though 'differing in judgement to what I profess', and, in consequence, as Cromwell announced on his superior's behalf, appointment and promotion did not depend upon a narrowly defined religious orthodoxy. The army of the Association alone provided a sympathetic religious environment for those who espoused Independency, and John Lilburne was probably not alone in surrendering his commission with the Earl of Essex 'for his persecuting for non-taking the Covenant', and accepting a post under 'my then two darlings', Manchester and Cromwell.[122]

The officer corps of the army of the Association took on a new complexion after the appointment of the Earl of Manchester. Commanders were chosen and promoted without respect for origin or social status, for their military expertise and their religious fervor and devotion to the Parliamentary cause. The cadre of experienced and zealous officers established by Manchester was one of the strengths of the Association; the army's operations were not hampered by 'timidious' local officers whose strategic visions were no wider than those of the county committees who had appointed them, nor its morale undermined by the activities of mercenary professionals, whose commitment to personal advantage rather than the cause led them to plunder the populace indiscriminately, make false claims upon the Treasury, or even to betray their paymasters.[123] But the Earl's major criterion for the selection and preferment of officers – godliness – was not entirely a source of strength to the army; in the late summer of 1644 the growing sectarian religious strife among his subordinates shattered the Earl's ecumenical vision and led eventually to the supersession of the army of the Association.[124]

Conclusion

The politicians at Westminster who had supported the passage of the legislation of January 1644 had sought to create an army free from the defensive and localist demands of the county authorities and capable of participating in a national strategy: the victory at Marston Moor justified their faith in Manchester's organizational skills. From the conglomerate body of local levies directly financed by, and thus responsible to, the individual county committees, which he had inherited in August 1643, the Earl had built up a unified force. Officered by men chosen for their military ability and politico-religious zeal rather than their local prestige, it was supported by a centralized system of treasuries and supply departments which was controlled by bureaucrats who were equally independent of local pressures.

But the Earl's success as a military administrator was not un-qualified. After the abortive Newbury campaign one of his officers complained that the army 'are more broken with the last eight weeks expedition, then with all the seidge of York and fight at Marston Moore, and yet have done the enemy no harm . . . there is so many differences, discontents, discouragements, that the most and ablest men are weary and thinking every day to withdraw'.[125] And some aspects of the physical weakness and demoralization of the Association's forces apparent in December 1644 can be attributed to flaws in the administrative system established by Manchester. Throughout 1644, despite the efforts of the Cambridge Committee and its agents, the landowner could not be persuaded to pay his taxes without procrastinatory rating disputes, nor the laborer to undertake military service with enthusiasm. And during the Newbury campaign the commissariat had proved unequal to the task of provisioning and clothing the army during the winter season in an area which had been fought over since the beginning of the war. The medical system had no more success in checking the ravages of the epidemic which decimated the army in the months following the fall of York. But Manchester can scarcely be held responsible for these failings; desertion, disease, poor supplies and the slow return of money to the central Treasury were to hamper Fairfax's operations in 1645–6, and were generally endemic difficulties in seventeenth-century armies.

Manchester and his advisers were more culpable with regard to the basic miscalculation which underlay the fiscal crisis in the winter of 1644. At its inception the financial resources which the Earl con-trolled were only barely adequate for the needs of the army, and, as new regiments and companies were formed in the course of the year, the expenses of the latter grew, while, with the exhaustion of the Fifth and Twentieth, the money available for its maintenance declined.

By December 1644 Manchester was trying to maintain 10 regiments of infantry and 40 troops of horse on exactly half the sum which Fairfax was given to maintain 12 regiments and 60 troops in 1645. But Manchester was not wholly responsible for this situation. The army of the Association was expanded to enable it to perform a central role in the national military strategy of the Earl's political allies; but to perform that role adequately required greater resources than those which could be provided by the eastern counties alone. The rational solution was a military reorganization designed to establish a national army, utilizing the legislative and administrative innovations forced by the experience of two years' warfare, the lack of which had partly occasioned the failure of Parliament's first national army, the Lord General's force. In the winter of 1644–5 such a reorganization was undertaken – but not solely as a rational response to the failures of the existing military machine in 1644. The New Model legislation and the Self-Denying Ordinance were equally the product of political developments, both national and local.

PART IV

The supersession of the army of the Association

The politics of the Earl of Manchester's command, February–August 1644

The defense of Manchester's authority at Westminster

The Parliamentary legislation of January 1644, which enabled the Earl to build the powerful army victorious at Marston Moor, had freed Manchester from the interference both of the Lord General, to whose commands he was no longer subject, and of the authorities in the constituent counties, who were prevented from dictating military policy by the removal of the control of the purse-strings which they had previously exercised. But the independence of the army of the Association was not unchallenged. Those in the Commons who had secured the passage of the January Ordinance, the war party and the middle group, had to defend Manchester from local complaints and from the more serious challenge posed by the Parliamentary supporters of the Earl of Essex through the summer of 1644.

Opposition to Manchester's authority was first voiced in March when the Commons heard a protest against the activities of the Earl's agents for the re-assessment of the Fifth and Twentieth part. M.P.s like Sir Simonds D'Ewes were appalled by the 'horrible exactions' of the latter, particularly the rating of those worth less than £10 a year in land or £100 in goods, an innovation of the Earl's without legislative warrant.[1] They also took offense at the employment of soldiers and other outsiders as local assessors and collectors. On this occasion members of the peace party were joined by some East Anglian M.P.s who normally supported measures designed to further the war-effort,[2] and many 'spake freelie' against the re-assessment. But to no avail. Although the Commons voted that its previously established minimum income limits for rating should be observed, and that a letter should be sent to Manchester expressing the House's concern with the policy of review, a motion that would have forbidden re-assessment altogether and another against the employment of soldiers as local agents were re-committeed and then forgotten. Even the innocuous official letter was never sent to the Earl.[3] In June the issue was raised again by the peace party man, Sir Thomas Dacres, who presented a complaint to the House from Huntingdonshire detailing the 'horrible oppressions of certaine persons of meane ranke and strangers in the countrie who came and assessed men over againe . . . by which the countrie was like to be ruined'. Other peace party adherents seconded Dacres, but found that they 'could not inhibit these harpies' in the face of the opposition of members of the war party and the middle group, who spoke 'to maintaine and countenance these oppressions'. Finally it was agreed only to send another letter to Manchester again expressing the Commons' concern in the matter.[4]

Between the two debates on the activities of the Earl's agents involved in re-assessment Manchester's authority was subjected to a more serious challenge, which was successfully beaten off by his adherents in the Commons. The fiscal legislation for the Association of 20 January expired at the end of April, and on the 27th the Commons passed an Ordinance renewing the Earl's powers. It was hardly discussed in the Commons, but the Lords refused to ratify the new enactment without the addition of a clause in which Manchester's subordination to the Lord General was acknowledged, arguing that their powers, as established in their existing Ordinances and Commissions, clashed. The Lords had not opposed the Ordinance for the Association in January, but the objectionable fact that, as a result of its passage, Manchester commanded a 'greater and better paid armie than the Generall' had been driven home by the war-party's attempt to hamstring Essex's army in February and March, first by cutting its fiscal provision and size, and then by retarding the passage of the necessary legislation in a series of filibusters over administrative trivia, and by the erosion of Essex's powers as supreme commander with the establishment of the Committee of Both Kingdoms.[5]

The determination of the majority of peers to defend the substance of Essex's office as Lord General, which they feared was being deliberately whittled to a mere shadow title by the radicals in the Commons, was categorically stated on 1 May. The previous day the lower House had set out their reasons for desiring the passage of Manchester's Ordinance without the additional clause: having reminded the Lords of the need for expedition as Manchester's army was on active service and required financial support, the Commons explained that the independence of the Earl's army from the Lord General's authority had been one of the demands of the Committee of the Association in January, who had claimed that it was a pre-requisite of their ability to raise so large a force. In their response, in addition to questioning a number of the Commons' assertions, the Lords argued that Essex, as Captain-General by virtue of Parliamentary Ordinance, had granted Manchester his commission, and that this necessarily implied the subordination of the latter to the Lord General's authority. If this were denied 'it doth apparently abridge his [Essex's] power, who hath done such eminent service to the Kingdom'. This, the Lords suggested, could be construed as a breach of the Protestation to live and die with the Lord General taken by the members of both Houses in 1642. Their answer aroused a furore in the Commons, who claimed that the implication that they had broken their Protestation was 'derogatory to their honour and integrity, and destructive to the essential privileges of Parliament'.[6]

The ill-feeling between the two Houses generated by this quarrel was enhanced by the Lords' contemporaneous refusal to pass Ordinances excluding those peers and M.P.s who had fled to Oxford but subsequently returned, and for the renewal of the Committee of Both Kingdoms. Of these three contentious enactments, that for the Association was settled first. On 8 May the Lords accepted the Commons' contention that only the financial provisions of the Ordinance of 20 January had expired at the end of the four-month period, not the powers granted to Manchester in that enactment, and on the 13th an Ordinance was passed enabling the Earl to raise taxes within the Association for a further four months.[7]

Throughout this debate, as in the contemporary conflict over the Committee of Both Kingdoms, members of the war party and the middle group in the Commons resisted the Lords' proposals. When the upper House first added their proviso the war party leader, the younger Sir Henry Vane, and the middle group men, St John and Barrington, moved that a letter be written to Manchester instructing him to levy money even though the Ordinance had not passed, as the dispute between the Houses did not involve the sum to be assessed. On 1 May St John led the attack on the Lords' reasons for adhering to their proviso, and some war party radicals moved that 'we go on by our selves and pass the Ordinance without them'. St John and the other middle group men, Crewe and Barrington, and the war party M.P.s, Vane junior and Lisle, drew up the Commons' answer to the reasons presented by the House of Lords, and when some of the peace party – D'Ewes, Holles, North and Stapleton – suggested that their draft was too aggressive, putting the worst construction on the expressions used by the Lords, St John 'pressed it vehementile' and Vane openly attacked the Earl of Essex.[8]

Besides backing Manchester in the major issues of the Fifth and Twentieth, and the renewal of his assessment, those M.P.s who favored the fullest prosecution of the war supported the Earl's command in a number of lesser matters. When in June Lord Willoughby successfully prosecuted Colonel King, Manchester's agent in Lincolnshire in the previous winter, before the House of Lords, Strode led the Commons in their defense of the Colonel. In the same month St John moved the passage of the Ordinance for the Posture of Defence in East Anglia, and Glynn that for the raising of new forces; in July

Vane reminded the House of its obligation to protect the eastern
counties while Manchester's army was engaged in the north.[9]

But while the middle group and the war party were in fundamental
agreement in supporting Manchester's command, their attitudes
toward the Association can be distinguished. Members of the
middle party, besides expressing themselves with more moderation
and demonstrating a greater readiness to compromise,[10] also viewed
the army of the Association as a part of the Parliamentary war-
machine, not as a complete replacement for Essex's force. This
appears from the House's rejection of a proposal of the Committee
of East Anglian M.P.s that all taxes raised in the Isle of Ely should be
employed for the maintenance of the local garrison. The opponents
of the scheme argued that the excise raised throughout England had
been assigned to the Lord General and allowing the local authorities
to syphon off the sums raised on the Isle might encourage other areas
'upon the pretence of necessity [to] make the like motion' and so
'prejudice the Lord Generall's army'.[11] This was hardly a consideration which would have troubled Sir Henry Vane or his allies of the
war party, and the rejection of the proposal suggests that the middle
group voted with Essex's adherents in the Commons to ensure that
his army would be adequately financed.

In the first six months of 1644 the army of the Eastern Association
was the pampered brainchild of those groups in Parliament who,
although they differed as to what would constitute acceptable terms
for an eventual settlement, agreed on the need for the development
of a military machine capable of defeating the King's forces. But St
John, Vane and their supporters at Westminster did more than
provide Manchester with the necessary sinews of war; they also
established a new relationship between the central administration of
the Association and the local authorities.

The Earl and the constituent counties

In May, in response to the Lords' attempt to subordinate Manchester's force to the Earl of Essex, the Commons argued that the
constituent counties of the Association would not tolerate such an
alteration in the constitutional status of *their* army.[12] But this was a
debating point. The army as constituted after January 1644 owed
little to any input from the local committees in East Anglia, and the
role of the latter relative to the central authority was downgraded
from master to servant. The situation which had appertained in 1643,
encouraged by the federalist fiscal system, whereby the county
committees could neglect the Cambridge Committee and dictate
the strategic priorities to which they would direct their men and
money, terminated with the passage of the January legislation. The
local authorities were subordinated to Manchester and the Com-

mittee of the Association. Manchester commissioned the county Treasurers; local account books could be examined by the Earl's auditors; his agents badgered the committees to hasten money to Cambridge, while others, frequently outsiders, re-assessed the Fifth and Twentieth tax. And, as a last resort, the Earl was empowered to replace any Deputy-Lieutenants or committeemen in the counties who 'have been negligent and remisse in the due execution' of Parliamentary legislation. The county committees were reduced to the status of administrative agencies forwarding men and money for the use of an army in the control of which they had very little say.

Naturally this situation was resented by the local authorities and frictions developed between them and the Earl in a number of areas. Particularly disliked were those central agencies which were empowered to interfere in matters which had previously been the prerogative of the committees. The requests of Manchester's auditors for assistance in the examination of accounts were neglected in some counties,[13] and his commissioners for the re-assessment of the Fifth and Twentieth part were universally detested. Norfolk first experienced their attentions, and in early December the county committee lodged a formal protest with the Earl, complaining that his assessors operated in competition with their agents, so diverting much needed funds to Cambridge which would otherwise have been used to pay the Norfolk forces, and denouncing the rapacity and the low social status of his nominees – they beseeched the Earl to consider 'the danger of our treasures coming through such indigent hands'.[14] The centralizing legislation of 20 January answered the first part of the complaint, but the second, the commissioners' extortion and the fact that they were 'persons of meane ranke and strangers in the countrie',[15] was the subject of the bitter protests of the local authorities throughout 1644. When the latter were thwarted in their attempts to secure the censure of Manchester's agents in the Commons they resorted to local obstruction. Peter Fisher, a leading member of the Suffolk county committee, was arrested and carried before Manchester, then at York, for leading the opposition to the review commissioners in Ipswich. At Aldeburgh the authorities, including some of the county committee, argued that their ancient corporate privilege 'that none but of our towne have ever sat to rate tax . . . and noe others have medled therein', protected them from reassessment, and rejected a compromise suggested by Manchester whereby one of the bailiffs would assist his commissioners. Two of their number should sit with the Earl's assessors; on these conditions the latter would be welcome to the town, 'and not otherwyse'.[16]

A similar antipathy to the interference of agents responsible only to Manchester in their internal affairs was displayed by the local authorities in areas subject to military government. The feud between the Lincolnshire committee and Colonel King, Manchester's nominee as Governor of Holland and Boston, was particularly fierce: King, his opponents complained, 'did quarrel with and slight the committee ... who were men of the best estates, quallity and integrity ... publickly villifying them and their actions and assuming their power without any authority'.[17] Cromwell, too, as Governor of the Isle of Ely, and Ireton, his deputy, were involved in a number of less heated jurisdictional disputes with the committee of the Isle.[18] A particularly well-documented incident indicative of the county authorities' concern to maintain local autonomy and their consequent objection to the intrusion of military government is provided by the resistance of the Norfolk and Suffolk committees and the corporation of Great Yarmouth to the establishment of a garrison to defend the port and its hinterland.

From the beginning of the war the corporation of Yarmouth had sought to obtain financial assistance for the maintenance of troops and fortifications for the defense of the town and of the two adjacent island Hundreds of Flegg and Lothingland, and upon Manchester's appointment in August 1643 they successfully petitioned that they might be allowed to raise a company for garrison duties, which was to be paid for from the weekly assessment for Norfolk. But in December the Earl embarked on a more grandiose scheme for the defense of the area which proved far less acceptable to the local authorities. Manchester took up the town's plea for a substantial garrison to be maintained at the expense of the entire Association, but he put the area under a military governor, Colonel Russell, whose authority entrenched deeply into that previously exercised by the corporation and the local committees. Not only was Russell empowered to rate and levy assessments within the area but to employ martial law against the recalcitrant. The corporation was horrified. The Colonel's commission was denounced as 'much prejudiciall to our liberties and ancient government within our selves', and when it was learned that the suggestion that the town be put under military government had originated in a petition to the Earl from some townsmen, the corporation voted that all its members should swear that they had not promoted the project. It was decided to employ 'all convenient meanes for the stopping and hindering the coming downe of such a governour hither', and accordingly Manchester was barraged with petitions and deputations until he agreed to put some leading men of the town in commission with Russell as joint commanders-in-chief. Even this did not satisfy the Yarmouth authorities, who added other members of the corporation to the commissioners without the Earl's consent. In February Russell finally left his post at Yarmouth and rejoined his regiment in the field army. Throughout this period the major role in opposition to his authority had been played by the corporation of Yarmouth, but the Norfolk committee were no more amenable to the establishment of an independent military authority in the area, and absolutely refused to obey a warrant from Russell to raise horse for his garrison.[19]

In April Manchester again considered appointing a military governor, on this occasion Colonel Fleetwood, and troops were sent to the area. The implacable hostility of the Yarmouth authorities continued unabated, and their opposition was actively supported by the county committees of Suffolk and Norfolk. In May the Committee of Both Kingdoms was presented with a series of objections against the scheme by a deputation of M.P.s and gentlemen from the two counties, while Manchester was petitioned by the 'well-affected' of Suffolk. The petitioners argued that the cost of a regiment of foot would exhaust the Association; far better that the defense of the town and the islands be left to a force of local volunteers, financed by the Cambridge Treasury, who would be supported by the neighboring trained-bands should danger threaten. Further local pressure at Westminster and upon the Earl to get the project shelved was ultimately successful; Fleetwood's commission was not confirmed and in July his troops were withdrawn from the area.[20] When the leading local proponent of the garrison project endeavored to get it reconsidered in early 1645 he was arrested on a trumped-up charge by the Suffolk committee and his papers were seized.[21]

The affair of the garrison of Yarmouth is also indicative of another objection which some of the local committees had to the army of the Association after January 1644. Fleetwood was opposed by the Norfolk and Suffolk authorities not only because his appointment would have represented a gross intrusion in local affairs, but because he and some of his captains were convinced Independents, and men who maintained 'strange opinions' like Lawrence Clarkson and John Boggis had been attracted to their troops.[22] The fear that the garrison would become a sectarian enclave explains the involvement of two influential Suffolk ministers in the behind-the-scenes maneuvering of the opponents of the scheme, and why it was expected that 'some of the Scotish nation' on the Committee of Both Kingdoms would support the abandonment of the project. The powerful position which religious radicals had attained in the army of the Association under Manchester's command was profoundly disturbing to the conservative county authorities.[23]

The proliferation of Independents and sectaries within the army must have reminded the local governors of another transformation in their relationship with the central authorities at Cambridge since the appointment of the Earl of Manchester. Not only could the Earl's agents now interfere in their internal affairs, but the county committees' influence over the troops which they raised and for which they paid had been destroyed. In the spring of 1643 the local committees had nominated the officers of their regiments, but at the outset of his command Manchester demonstrated that he intended to exercise that prerogative. Although his own regiment was formed from the remnants of the Essex county brigade which had served with Grey of Warke, and was recruited with conscripts from that county, the Earl refused to use the officers previously employed by the local committee, and insisted that men of his own nomination should take command. His decision caused considerable ill-feeling in Essex. A committeeman wrote to Sir Thomas Barrington 'this part of the countrye doth much strange that Captaine Gowers, a man of knowne fydellitie should be put by his companie and others admited whose zeale to the cause hath not so much apeared'. Indeed, the county eventually took the law into its own hands and, to the Earl's annoyance, neglected his nominees, and sent its recruits to the siege of Lynn under captains of its choosing.[24] This dispute was eventually settled by a compromise, whereby the county officers were to be employed once the Earl's nominees had received companies, but thereafter the Earl insisted upon his right to commission all officers; in the winter the Norfolk committee found themselves unable to dismiss a captain who had offended them, even though they had originally appointed him,[25] and in 1644 the choice of outsiders, men of limited status and religious radicals to positions of responsibility in the army of the Association demonstrates that the county committees no longer had a powerful voice in the selection of officers.

But the local authorities probably objected less to the loss of military patronage than to the limitation of their ability to influence the strategy to be pursued by the army. Manchester's backers in Parliament intended the army of the Association to be a key element in a national military strategy, and in the January Ordinance they clarified the previously disputed question of the location of constitutional authority, declaring that the Association's forces were subject only to 'the particular direction of Parliament' or the commands of Manchester and the Cambridge Committee,[26] who, while technically representing the constituent counties, were the Earl's nominees. At the same time the establishment of a centralized fiscal system prevented the county authorities from unofficially influencing strategy by allocating funds to the schemes which they favored as they had done in 1643. Deprived of their ability to influence the strategic priorities of the army, the local authorities resented its employment in a role determined by Manchester and his allies at Westminster to the neglect of the original purpose of the Association as they saw it, local defense. In June the Essex committee, instructed to raise their trained bands as the King threatened East Anglia from Buckingham, having protested the expense involved, pointedly informed the Commons of their readiness 'to silence . . . the remembraunce of *our* forces at York at this tyme'.[27] The committee's obsession with local security also appears in their endeavors to secure authority to raise troops designed to serve 'only for the safety of the county', which would be wholly responsible to them.[28]

Given the position of subordination to which the county committees in East Anglia were reduced after the passage of the January legislation, no longer possessing an influence in the formulation of military policy, and subject to the control and interference of agents appointed by Manchester in local affairs, it might be asked why the county authorities co-operated with the Earl. For, despite the refusal of some committeemen appointed by Parliament in 1643 to serve in 1644,[29] the bulk of them continued to act, supervising the collection of money to be forwarded to the Cambridge Treasury and the impressment of men for Manchester's army, accepting the reduced role to which they had been relegated. They may have done so because they recognized that some local authority was better than none. Manchester was empowered to dismiss those who were 'remisse', and the county committeemen knew that they were not indispensable; others of greater enthusiasm, if lower social position, were ready to implement Parliamentary legislation to which the traditional governors of the localities objected.

In Norfolk the reluctance of the leading gentlemen to engage in the work of sequestration had led to their replacement in that function by men of lesser status. On 13 September 1643 Miles Corbett, the radical M.P. from Yarmouth, attacked the Norfolk committee in the Commons as 'remisse and careles' in the execution of the Ordinance of Sequestration, and argued that their reluctance to undertake the service was encouraged by the refusal of two of the county M.P.s, Sir John Holland and Framlingham Gawdy, to play any part in the work of sequestration. When the House voted that the two men should go down into the county to supervise the proper execution of the Ordinance, Holland explained that he could not be expected to implement legislation against which he had spoken in debate, and which involved the seizure of the property of those 'to whome I have the neerest relations of blood and obligation of friendship'; he concluded, 'I could as easily perish under such rigour as performe this office against those to whom I had soe great obligations.'[30] When the radicals insisted upon the execution of the Ordinance Holland managed to obtain the permission of the House to visit his sick wife in the Netherlands for six weeks: he stayed abroad for two years. Although Holland was the most vocal in his opposition to the Ordinance, it is clear that his dislike of proceeding against friends, relatives and neighbors was shared by his fellow gentry on the county committee. In November the central Committee of Sequestration were again commenting on the 'lukewarmness' of the local authorities, and by 1644 all sequestration business had fallen into the hands of a group of citizens of Norwich and parochial gentry.[31] With the latter, whom they sneered at as 'indigent and meane persons', the county committee engaged in an extended feud throughout the year in their efforts to protect the estates of those to whom they were bound by 'relation of kindred and friendship', from seizure by the sequestrators.[32] A similar pattern occurred in Cambridgeshire. 'The gentlemen would not, or durst not, act', and the task of sequestration devolved upon 'persons of low and mean condition'.[33] As in Norfolk the two bodies were soon in conflict over the county committee's attempts to protect 'their friends and brothers'. When the sequestrators refused to accede to their requests for selective leniency, the county committee arrested them, and imprisoned one on a specious charge of high treason. The central Committee of Sequestrations blocked these prosecutions, and rebuked the county committee, but the latter continued to harass and obstruct the sequestrators throughout 1644.[34]

In Hertfordshire the authority of the local gentry was even more seriously undermined by an influx of the 'mean men' who had taken control of the sequestration machinery in Cambridgeshire and Norfolk to positions of responsibility. In mid-August 1643 two Hertfordshire M.P.s, Sir Thomas Dacres and Edward Wingate, informed the House that they had not disarmed those who had not taken the Vow and Covenant as some of the recalcitrant were, in their opinion, 'very honest men'; this infuriated the radicals, and Strode used the occasion for an attack on the general lethargy of the county committee, particularly in the matter of sequestration. A few days later the committee were again assailed in the Commons 'as if they were not trustie but favourers of malignants'.[35]   In September the House, having learned of the 'many suspicious actions' of the county authorities, voted that the raising of a volunteer force in Hertfordshire should be entrusted to a new body, modeled on the London Militia Committee, and, with the extension of their power in the Ordinance of 18 December, this group was given effective control of all local forces.[36] The old local governors – 'the principal gentlemen of the county' – most of whom were excluded from the new structure, deeply resented the intrusion of the rival committee whose members they denounced as 'persons of mean condition', of 'Anabaptisticall and independent opinion'.[37]

The experience of the committees of Norfolk and Cambridgeshire in the matter of sequestration, and of Hertfordshire with the local militia, must have made it apparent to the East Anglian gentry that they had to co-operate with Manchester, however much they might dislike those aspects of the January legislation which undercut the powers which they had previously exercised, unless they were prepared to be forced from their positions of local authority by men of lesser status who would be more responsive to the demands of Parliament or the Committee of the Association. But, for his part, the Earl did his best to encourage the co-operation of the local gentry. Although firmly insisting upon exercising the powers granted him by Parliament, he invariably treated the county authorities with courtesy and consideration. Clarendon's judgment is apposite in this respect: Manchester was 'never guilty of any rudeness towards those he was obliged to oppress, but performed always as good offices towards his old friends, and other persons . . . as the nature of the employment he was in would permit him to do'.[38] So Manchester endeavored to persuade the counties of the benefits which would accrue to the Association by the army's operations in the north, and, recognizing that the degree of centralization entailed by the Ordinance of 20 January would be unpalatable to the county authorities, he tried to sugar the pill by instructing his Treasurers at Cambridge to provide the local committees with statements of the use to which the monthly assessments from their county had been put. He also ordered the much-hated commissioners for the review of the Fifth and Twentieth part to make their account books available to the local authorities and forbade captains to commandeer horses without prior consultation with the committees. When, as with the quarrels over the garrison of Yarmouth or the assessors for the review, conflict arose, the Earl, although he might not abandon his demands, treated those complaining with 'noble respects'. He always endeavored, as he wrote to Sir John Potts in the course of a dispute with some of the Norfolk committee, 'to expresse my selfe tender off the reputation of those that are for the service of the publicke'.[39]

Besides consciously endeavoring to work harmoniously with the county authorities, and to minimize potential friction, Manchester also shared a number of the social presuppositions of the local gentry, and this helped to make his authority more acceptable to the latter. In particular the Earl sympathized with the gentry's objections to the sequestration of friends and neighbors, and used his authority to mitigate the rigors of the relevant legislation in many cases.[40] His attitude appears in a letter written after he had arranged Sir William Paston's escape from a threatened sequestration; 'I am glad to have any occasion to expresse any respecte to persons off quallitye, and esteeme itt a great happines to be understood as one that desires to win by civillitye then by harshnes.'[41] Manchester also shared some of the gentry's objections to the 'persons of inferior ranke' upon whom the work of sequestration had devolved in many counties. The sequestrators of Norfolk and Cambridgeshire eventually protested to London that malignants were abusing the Earl's 'loving and milde disposition'; he was 'to favor'able to malignants; . . . it was to no purpose for them to take paines if he had power to discharge . . . at his pleasure'.[42] On this question Manchester broke with those M.P.s who had worked to secure and defend the legislation which had established his army; in April members of the war party and the middle group in Parliament were, like the local sequestrators, expressing some exasperation at the Earl's lenience.[43]

So in the first part of 1644 the local governors in the constituent counties of the Association reacted to Manchester's authority with mixed emotions. They resented their subjugation to the Earl's central administration, and the interference of its agents in local affairs. They objected to paying for an army which they no longer effectively controlled and which was visualized by its Parliamentary backers not in terms of local defense but as a major instrument of national strategy. Yet Manchester personally did much to reduce the potential tensions between his central administration and the local gentry: he endeavored to establish harmonious relations with the latter, was responsive to their complaints, and his social status and outlook were attractive to them. This ambivalent relationship explains the ease with which, when he broke with his Parliamentary supporters in the late summer and autumn of 1644, Manchester could secure the enthusiastic support of the local authorities in the Association.

The triumph of Westminster: the creation of the New Model Army, August 1644–March 1645

In January 1644 the legislative foundation upon which Manchester's army was subsequently erected had been pushed through Parliament by the efforts of those M.P.s who agreed on the need to develop a powerful force capable of participating in a national strategy. Thereafter, until the summer of 1644, these political groups had fiercely resisted the efforts of the peace party and of the local committees within the constituent counties of the Association to undercut or restrict the Earl's authority. But in the autumn and winter of 1644–5 the enthusiasm of St John, Vane and their Parliamentary allies for the army of the Association cooled, and ultimately they came to pin their political hopes upon the product of a further military re-organization: the New Model Army.

The changed attitude of the war party and the middle group to Manchester's command was essentially a product of their disappointment at the diminishing returns from his forces in late 1644. In July their commitment to the army of the Association had been triumphantly vindicated by the crushing defeat inflicted on the northern Royalists at Marston Moor and by the fall of York, but in the next four months that army's record was far less impressive. In August a few minor garrisons in Yorkshire and Nottinghamshire were captured, but nothing had been done against Newark, an obvious objective which the London press had expected the forces of the Association to besiege or blockade;[1] instead the bulk of the army was allowed to 'lye idle' at Doncaster for ten days and at Lincoln for over three weeks. In September the military failings of the army of the Association became more apparent to the central authorities. On the first of the month the Committee of Both Kingdoms, informed of the Lord General's desperate plight in Cornwall, ordered Manchester to begin 'a speedy march . . . with all the forces you can' to the west. But on 17 October, despite the issue of fourteen letters from the Committee of Both Kingdoms and three orders from the Commons, all insisting upon the need for expedition to prevent the King's army from regaining the circle of fortified positions surrounding Oxford for its winter quarters, the bulk of the Association's army had advanced no further west than Reading.[2]

In part the limited achievements of the autumn of 1644 were a product of those institutional and structural weaknesses in the army of the Association already discussed: the insufficient fiscal provision, and consequent arrears in the pay and deficiencies in the supply of the troops; the difficulty of recruiting the army, its ranks decimated by disease and the hardships of the long northern campaign. However, this was not the whole story: worse conditions did not prevent Sir William Waller's army from playing a far more vital role than that of the Association in the autumn campaign. We must agree with Cromwell when, in late November, he argued that the lethargic generalship of his superior, the Earl of Manchester, was responsible for the dismal record of failures, delays and lost opportunities.[3]

Manchester, although not deserving all the obloquy that Cromwell heaped upon him, was certainly culpable. In August, with a series of flimsy excuses, the Earl had blocked all the efforts of his subordinates to take action against Newark, while the few minor successes which had been obtained owed little to his initiative.[4] From the first Manchester had opposed the central orders for his army to march into the west, telling his subordinates that 'if any should persuade him to goe westward he would hange him', and in mid-September he publicly attacked the policy at a meeting of the Committee of Both Kingdoms: given 'that condition that I see these armyes in, you doe expose us to scorne, if not to ruine'.[5] Thereafter, in his correspondence with the Committee, while stressing his readiness to obey their commands, the Earl continued to express his doubts as to the wisdom of marching west, and to avoid doing so by deliberate procrastination. From 29 September to 17 October the Association's foot stuck at Reading while the Earl answered the preremptory commands of the Committee and the urgent requests from Waller for infantry support for his men, who were retreating through Dorset and Wiltshire in the face of the superior Royal army, with a barrage of excuses – his force was weak; he needed more supplies; he must await the city brigade; he needed more cavalry. His obstructionism culminated in his letter of 9 October, when he claimed that his instructions were imprecise and required clarification; he had often received orders for 'my marching westward, but they never designed any place to which I should march'.[6] As Waller was begging the Earl for immediate assistance, only a man who was willfully blind could fail to see the import of the orders of the Committee and the House. The Earl's hostility to the demands of the Committee of Both Kingdoms was openly expressed to his officers while the army lay at Reading. 'He would rather adventure a cashiering' than advance into the west; the expedition had been organized solely to gratify those M.P.s whose estates lay in that part of the country.[7]

Nor was the Earl's military record after the conjunction of the three Parliamentary armies on 21 October any more impressive.

Cromwell's ascription of both the failure to win a total victory at Newbury and the King's subsequent relief of Donnington Castle solely to the Earl's poor generalship is by far the least convincing part of his charge against his superior, but it is clear that Manchester had opposed engaging the Royal army at almost every juncture during the campaign. Haselrig later testified that he could not remember 'that the Earl . . . did ever declare any opinion att any time for fighting with the King's army but hath often declared his judgement att the councell of warre against it'.[8]

After the fall of York John Lilburne thought that Manchester 'visibly degenerated'. From July 1644 the Earl demonstrated, in Cromwell's words, a 'continued backwardness to all action', an 'aversenes to engagement or what tendes thereto . . . neglecting of opportunityes and declineing to take or pursue advantages upon the enemy'.[9] What had caused this shift in the attitude of the General who had been the nominee of the more radical elements at Westminster earlier in 1644?

The Earl of Manchester and the conflict within the army of the Association

One dimension of the Earl's changed attitude was apparently a growing sense of the futility of the conflict. The fighting seemed pointless: even a resounding success like Marston Moor brought the end of the war no nearer. That 'this war would not be ended by the sword', as Manchester concluded, was evidently God's will, which He had declared 'by not suffering us to take the opportunityes we had on of another'; 'god did never prosper us in our victories to make them clere victories'. Accordingly, the war should be terminated at the earliest opportunity by a negotiated settlement.[10] The Earl's war-weariness may have stemmed from his experiences during the siege of York. Manchester's good nature, his 'generous . . . soft and obliging temper', was apparent throughout his short military career. He was attentive to the welfare of his troops, and to their morale: he marched with them on the muddy road from Selby to York, rode around the camp thanking them and trying to provide for their needs after Marston Moor, and instructed his subordinates to be careful of 'hazarding the lives of the soldiers'. He also insisted on the proper care of Royalist prisoners, and frequently displayed his sympathy for the civilian victims of the war: after the sack of the upper town of Lincoln, Manchester bought up goods seized by the soldiers and distributed them among 'the poore plundered people'.[11] It is possible that by the summer the Earl, 'that sweet meek man', was revolted by the carnage, suffering and waste that he had witnessed. Certainly the Earl's influential personal chaplain, Simeon Ash, was deeply moved by his experiences during the siege of York;

he wrote to a friend, 'Had thine eyes yesternight with me seene Yorke burning, thy heart would have been heavie. ... Truly, my heart sometimes is readie to breake with what I here see. ... Pitie, pitie and pray for poore people, oppressed with the pride and cruelty of the inhumane prevailing souldier, ... my hardship is nothing, nothing to that which thousands here suffer.' Ash concluded by beseeching God to 'speedily, mercifully end our combustions'.[12] His patron, too, may have become less enthusiastic with regard to the war as a result of his first-hand experience of bloodshed and misery.

But there was more to Manchester's changed attitude than a negative sense of the futility of further hostilities. As Cromwell argued, the Earl's reluctance to play an active role in the prosecution of the war was deliberate and purposive. His 'backwardnes was not (meerely) from dulnes or indisposednes to engagement, but ... from some principle of unwillingness in his Lordshipp to have this warre prosecuted unto a full victory, and a designe ... to have it ended by accommodacion (and that) on some such termes to which it might be disadvantageous to bring the King too lowe'.[13] Manchester's demand for an immediate settlement because 'this warr would not be ended by the sword' concealed a more fundamental conviction: 'that it would not be well for the Kingdom if it wer ended by the sword'.[14] It was this fear that led Manchester to avoid a confrontation with the Royal army, lest its destruction should end the prospects for a negotiated peace on acceptable terms.

By the autumn of 1644 Manchester, who, both as commander of the forces of the Association and in the Lords,[15] had played a major role in building the machinery designed to enable Parliament to undertake the efficient prosecution of the war, had identified with the program of the peace party, and favored an immediate compromise settlement based on mutual concessions.[16] How can this shift in attitude be explained? His chaplain, Ash, argued that from the first the Earl had favored a negotiated pacification, but only upon one important condition, peace 'with the perfecting of the Reformation which is hopefully begun'. After Marston Moor Manchester supported an immediate termination of the war not because the promised Reformation had been secured, but because he had come to recognize that war 'was not the way to advance religion'. Indeed, the continuance of hostilities and an absolute Parliamentary victory would establish, not the New Jerusalem, but an anarchic confusion in which the only certainty was further strife.[17] The Earl's gloomy prognostications were a product of the bitter divisions within his own army in the summer of 1644.

In the autumn of 1643 Manchester had endeavored to establish a force officered by 'the godly'. Appointment and promotion were to be dependent upon enthusiasm for the Parliamentary cause and religious devotion, the latter defined without respect to sectarian difference. The Earl sought to command an army in which the Independent 'should close with the honest Calvinest and Scot and go on unanimously against the common enemy'.[18] But a year later his ideal had shattered. The army of the Association was divided into two factions, the Independents led by Cromwell, the Presbyterians aligned with the Earl's Scottish Major-General, Lawrence Crawford, each bitterly antipathetic to, and seeking the destruction of, the other.

The major reason for the Presbyterian faction's opposition to Cromwell was voiced by Crawford and another high-ranking commander, Lieutenant-Colonel Dodson, in the winter of 1644–5.[19] Both accused the Lieutenant-General of seeking to pack the army of the Association with officers sympathetic to the sectaries. Dodson, a native of the Isle of Ely who had served with Cromwell since the outbreak of the war, argued that in choosing officers for his own regiment, he had dismissed 'honest gentlemen and souldiers that ware stout in the cause', and replaced them with 'common men, pore and of meane parentage, onely he would give them the title of godly pretious men'. After the passage of the Ordinances in the summer of 1643 establishing a powerful force for the Association, Cromwell continued to pursue his earlier policy on a wider scale, controlling appointments throughout the whole army by ingratiating himself with Manchester, and when 'some new upstart Independent did appeare ther must be a way mayd for them by cashiering others, some honest commander or other, and thos silly peopell putt in ther command'.

After the fall of York the argument of Dodson and Crawford that Cromwell sought to officer the army of the Association with Independents, and to secure the removal of those who opposed this policy, can be validated. In August 1644, as the army rested at Lincoln, the Lieutenant-General and his allies made a vigorous attempt to purge their antagonists. Lilburne pressed for the court-martialing of his intolerant Presbyterian superior, Colonel Edward King, for supposed military ineptitude; Captain Armiger, who had refused to sign a petition favoring toleration, was discharged and his troop given to the extreme sectary Paul Hobson; Captain Taylor of Montagu's infantry was cashiered by his Independent Colonel, unjustly in Manchester's opinion;[20] the dismissal of a number of junior officers, members of Crawford's faction, was also sought for alleged plundering and presenting false musters.[21] Finally, and most critically, Cromwell insisted that his rival, Major-General Crawford, be cashiered for 'a number of pretended faults', including a blunder he had committed during the siege of York which had resulted in the loss of many men.[22]

But if the accusation that Cromwell deliberately sought to turn the army of the Association into an Independent enclave can be substantiated for the period after the fall of York, were such 'sinister endes' as apparent in the appointment and promotion of officers prior to the siege? Crawford and Dodson assert that this was the case, but their argument is less plausible. From the first, Cromwell believed that religious fervor and devotion to the cause were the essential attributes of an officer, not social status or even military experience; his ideal was the 'plain russet-coated captain that knows what he fights for and loves what he knows'. But he also felt that the qualities he sought were not the monopoly of any one religious group. In February he warned Crawford to 'take heed of being sharp . . . against those to whom you can object little but that they square not with you in every opinion concerning matters of religion', and argued that 'the State, in choosing men to serve them, takes no notice of their opinions, if they be willing faithfully to serve them, that satisfies'. In these respects Cromwell's position is similar to that of Manchester: both the Earl and his Lieutenant-General hoped to build up an army commanded by godly officers without respect of sectarian difference. It was probably because of this fundamental agreement that Manchester gave Cromwell such an important voice in 'the choice and approbacion of most of the comaunders in the army'.[23]

That Cromwell was not merely making a debating point when he informed Crawford that enthusiastic service, not religious partisanship, was the major criterion of a man's capacity to serve as an officer appears in his handling of the case of Colonel King in the winter of 1643. In October a new Lincolnshire regiment was formed as part of the Association's army and its command given to Edward King, who soon demonstrated his intolerance of sectarian deviation by breaking up a private religious gathering at Boston and imprisoning the congregation, which included some of his own officers and a number of Cromwell's troopers. The aggrieved Independents complained to Cromwell, his troopers threatening to leave the army unless their persecutor was cashiered. Yet, far from rebuking the Colonel, Cromwell 'apprehending . . . King the activest and fittest man that he knew in Lincolnshire', secured a commission from Manchester appointing the Presbyterian as commander of all the Association's forces in the county. King's faithful and enthusiastic service to the Parliamentary cause recommended him to Cromwell, despite his hostility to the Independents. If the King affair shows that Cromwell was prepared to promote a Presbyterian officer, his dealings with Lieutenant-Colonel Dodson demonstrate that he had no intention of purging those opposed to the sectaries from the army. Dodson, a Presbyterian, found service with the Independents in the

Association's army increasingly intolerable and sought to resign his commission in the early summer: yet far from welcoming this development, Cromwell twice tried to persuade Dodson to retain his post, offering him further promotion if only he would try to work with the Independents in the army.[24]

No other case of the promotion or dismissal of an officer is as well documented as those of King and Dodson, but examination of the available evidence, largely circumstantial, does not suggest that Cromwell pursued a deliberate and consistent policy of appointing Independents and purging those who opposed them. The fact that in the spring of 1644 the Independents Fleetwood, Harrison, Bethel, and Neville[25] were commissioned as captains of horse while at least three commanders left the Association's cavalry might be seen as confirming Crawford and Dodson's accusation, but in only one case of a captain leaving the army is it clear that the man was dismissed;[26] the other two may have resigned their commissions voluntarily.[27] The reorganization of the dragoon regiment in April and May 1644 also involved the dismissal of some officers from their posts and the appointment of a number of Independents. In February a force of two thousand dragoons had been projected, but nothing had come of this and at the spring muster of the cavalry a number of the existing dragoon companies proved to be in a very bad state, with few men and less horses.[28] Accordingly, in April and May the dragoons were consolidated and reorganized into a regiment of five full-strength companies. Only two of the previous eight dragoon captains were retained,[29] and the vacant posts were given to three newcomers, two of whom were Independents: the command of the regiment was given to John Lilburne, fresh from his extended religious feud with his old Colonel, the Presbyterian Edward King, while one of the captains was Richard Beaumont, like Lilburne a transfer from the army of the Earl of Essex, who was a radical sectary with Anabaptist leanings.[30] Again the question arises as to whether the six captains of the old dragoon organization who were not retained were purged or voluntarily resigned their commissions. In two cases the evidence perhaps suggests the former: it appears that neither Major Sackville Moore nor Captain Holcroft welcomed retirement, for, after leaving the army of the Association, both accepted commissions in the force raised by the county of Essex in July, and Moore appears to have been financially dependent upon military employment.[31] But overall the evidence cannot support Crawford's contention that from the first Cromwell had sought to realize a sinister design to pack the army with sectaries. The well-documented cases of Colonel King and of Dodson, and the fact that a number of posts were given to men who were certainly not Independents, in particular thirteen Scottish officers,[32] suggest that

before August 1644 the Lieutenant-General was prepared to promote
men without respect to their beliefs, provided they 'be willing faithfully to serve'. However, experienced officers of Independent
principles, like Lilburne, did gravitate to the army of the Association
which alone provided a sympathetic religious environment, and so
were on hand to take up new posts as they became available,[33] a
circumstance which, in itself, certainly enhanced Crawford's fears
of a sectarian conspiracy.

Early in 1644 Cromwell had shared Manchester's ecumenical ideal
of an army of the united godly, but in the summer of that year his
attitude underwent a radical change. The Earl reported that his
Lieutenant-General had told him 'that he desired to have none in
my army but such as were of the Independent judgement',[34] and his
attempt to purge the army of the leading Presbyterians in August
demonstrates his commitment to this policy. What occasioned this
change in Cromwell's attitude? We may distinguish three major
developments.

First was a growing resentment at the hostile attitude of the
Presbyterian officers under Manchester's command to the employment of Independents. The toleration which flourished in the army
of the Association was anathema to committed Presbyterians, and
their outrage was enhanced by the occasional excesses of the
sectaries. The baptism of a horse in urine by dragoons from the
company of the radical Captain Beaumont in Yaxley parish church[35]
was the sort of incident which did little to improve relations between
Presbyterians and Independents. Dodson was horrified that soldiers
'have gonn up into the pulpitts . . . and preached to the whole parish',
Colonel King amazed by the 'bitter invectives against the Church
and ministers of England' of his Independent subordinates. If the
religious opinions of the sectaries were offensive to the orthodox,
their socio-political radicalism was equally unacceptable: 'such as
have filld dung carts' had been made officers, and attacks launched
on the principle of social and political hierarchy.[36] Accordingly a
number of Presbyterian officers sought to rid the army of the
Independents. Colonel King, encouraged by his chaplains, began
to persecute 'all the honest zealous and conscientious men' under
his command, and cashiered one of his officers solely for his religious
opinions; shortly after his appointment Major-General Crawford
also sought to oust two sectaries, arresting Lieutenant Packer and
his own Lieutenant-Colonel, Henry Warner.[37] Although unsuccess-
ful in this attempt to rid the army of those 'who square not with you
in every opinion concerning matters of religion', Crawford's Presbyterian zeal was undiminished, and in the spring and summer he 'got
a great hand . . . with all the army who were not for sects',[38] becoming
the focus of opposition to Cromwell and the Independents. The

intransigent hostility of Presbyterians like Crawford and King, to whom he had offered equal opportunity if they would 'be but conformable to pretious godly men', was one factor which decided Cromwell to purge the army in August.

The second factor which influenced Cromwell to seek to create an army consisting solely of 'such as were of the Independent judgement' was his realization of the inflexible determination of the Scots to secure the establishment of their fully-fledged, rigid Presbyterian system in England. He knew of their 'pressing for their discipline' not only from the reports of his colleagues at Westminster, but from his own experience of their hostile attitude after the Association's conjunction with the Scottish forces at the siege of York. Baillie in London had warned the ministers with the Scottish army of the dangers of the contamination of their men, 'silly simple lads', by Manchester's pestiferous army of ungodly heretics, and in June it was affirmed that an agent had been sent from the city to encourage General Leslie to 'make Brownists, Anabaptists and Independents the common enemy'.[39] Whatever the truth of this story, it is probable that an attempt was made to persuade the Scots to consider some measure of toleration during the siege. In early June, Sir Henry Vane journeyed to York, ostensibly to bring new instructions to the generals from the Committee of Both Kingdoms. The Venetian ambassador was convinced that so important a political figure would not have been sent on a trifling military mission, and while his suggestion that Vane's secret purpose was to discover the generals' opinion of a plan to depose Charles seems highly improbable, it is likely that Sir Henry discussed the religious question, seeking to 'feel the pulse of the Scots to try if they were plyable to their phantasies and opinions'. Cromwell's endeavors during the siege to get subscriptions to a petition favoring toleration may have been designed to the same end.[40] But the Scots were unyielding, remaining 'constant to their principles, and firm unto the Covenant'.[41] After the fall of York the three Parliamentary generals wrote to Westminster pressing that every effort should be made to settle the church according to the provisions of the Solemn League and Covenant. What Fairfax and Manchester intended by this is uncertain, but the Scots were not content with the rhetorical expression of general principles: an agent was dispatched to London with detailed, practical demands and with orders to emphasize the Scots' 'discontent, grieff and discuragement that there is so litle progresse as yit made in the setlement of the effaires of the hous of God'.[42]

From his contact with the Scots during the siege of York, Cromwell recognized that they would not compromise their demand for the establishment of a rigid, intolerant Presbyterian system; he was reported as bursting out, in his anger, that 'in the way they now carried themselves, pressing for their discipline, he could as soon draw his sword against them as any in the King's army'. Cromwell also feared that the Scots would be willing to sacrifice anything to obtain the religious system upon which they insisted. Accordingly he sought to purge the army of the Association of the Scots and their adherents, 'that in case there should be . . . any conclusion of a peace such as might not stand with those ends honest men should aime at, this army might prevent such a mischeife'.[43]

The third determinant in Cromwell's hardened attitude toward the rigid Presbyterians was *his* victory at Marston Moor. In London the Scots were furious at the propaganda that the battle had been won by 'Cromwell alone, with his unspeakablie valorous regiments', assiduously trumpeted about the city by the Lieutenant-General's partisans, realizing that such claims strengthened the Independents' political position, as Parliament would be reluctant to pass measures directed against a group who had so signally demonstrated their military utility.[44] But for Cromwell the victory involved more than an accretion of political strength: it was a divine sanction of the religious cause which he espoused. The battle 'had all the evidences of an absolute victory obtained by the Lord's blessing upon the godly party principally. We never charged but we routed the enemy.'[45]

In August 1644 Cromwell, antagonized by the campaign of harassment and persecution conducted by officers like Colonel King and by the hostility and obduracy of the Scots, his determination strengthened by the 'great favour from the Lord' he and 'the Church of God' had obtained at Marston Moor, finally abandoned his earlier attempt to work with the Presbyterians and sought to purge Crawford and his adherents. While the army rested at Lincoln, Manchester was presented with an ultimatum whereby Cromwell and 'his Colonells' threatened to resign unless their opponents were dismissed. The demand was wholly unacceptable to the Earl who still strove to maintain his original ideal of the Association as an army of the united godly and who recognized that the military reasons given for the cashiering of Crawford were merely a façade for a religious purge. The Earl was unable to reconcile Cromwell and Crawford, and in mid-September brought both men before the Committee of Both Kingdoms, where the immediate dispute was patched up and both returned to their posts. But the hostility between the two factions in the army remained. Independent regiments would not obey Presbyterian officers, some companies came to blows, and junior officers were dismissed and reinstated for reasons of faction.[46] The army was rent by suspicion and hostility – 'pitifullie divided'.

Manchester's 'known meeknesse and sweetnesse of disposition'[47] was not well suited to deal with a situation whereby he had become an isolated arbiter between two fiercely hostile groups, and the frustrations of seeking unsuccessfully to 'quiett those distracions' must have combined with the more mundane difficulties of the army of the Association – shortage of pay, lack of provisions, the ravages of disease – to enhance his war weariness. But the critical determinant of his lethargic generalship in the autumn was the realization, as a result of the dispute within his army, that a continuation of the war 'was not the way to advance religion', for it could only intensify the bitter hostility between Presbyterians and Independents, and 'be an occasion . . . of a further quarrel'.[48] To prevent this Manchester believed that an immediate compromise peace should be negotiated with the King, in which no party would be strong enough to dictate the terms of the settlement.

After the fall of York the Earl of Manchester's attitude to the war underwent a profound change: disillusioned and frightened by the religious divisions within his own army, the Earl sought to secure a compromise negotiated peace and, to obtain this, refused to bring the King's army to a conclusive engagement, or even to improve the military balance in Parliament's favor by capturing a few enemy garrisons. The political repercussions of his *volte face* were ultimately to lead to the supersession of the army of the Eastern Association by the New Model.

Central politics in the autumn and winter of 1644: the New Model and the Self-Denying Ordinance

In essence an analysis of the politics of the supersession of the army of the Association in the winter of 1644–5 is simple. The army had been the chosen agent of groups who sought either the total defeat of the King or to negotiate only from a position of military predominance. But its dismal performance after the summer of 1644, a product of Manchester's changed attitude to the war and his consequent refusal to play the military role designed for him, disillusioned its political backers. Their growing dissatisfaction is apparent in the sharp reprimands sent to the Earl for his failure to obey central orders, and in the relaxation of the efforts of the war party and the middle group on behalf of the army of the Association: suspicions were voiced in the House about the administration of the Cambridge Treasury, and the additional sums which the Committee of the Association insisted were necessary for the maintenance of their army were never voted.[49] Ultimately the Association's erstwhile supporters began to think in terms of alternative military structures better designed to execute their policies. When, on 19 November, the Cambridge Committee presented yet another petition insisting on their inability to maintain their army without further financial provision, the Commons instructed the Committee of Both Kingdoms to consider the state of all the armies, and the possibility of re-organization; four days later the Committee was directed to 'consider of a frame or model of the whole militia'.[50] In the next months both the Earl and the army of the Association were abandoned, and their ex-supporters at Westminster diverted their energies to securing the passage of the New Model legislation and the Self-Denying Ordinance.

But while the general outline is clear, some of the maneuvers at Westminster which resulted in the ousting of Manchester and the creation of the New Model Army illuminate the nature of the divisions within the Parliamentary camp in this period, and deserve more detailed analysis. Particularly important to an understanding of central politics in the winter of 1644–5 are the immediate circumstances surrounding Cromwell's bitter denunciation of Manchester in the Commons on 25 November 1644.

After the battle of Newbury, heralded as a Parliamentary victory, the capture of the ordnance which the King had left at Donnington Castle upon his hasty retreat was confidently expected both in official circles and the press.[51] Accordingly, when the Royal army relieved the castle on 9 November, and drew off the guns without even token opposition from the three Parliamentary armies massed at Newbury, there was an immediate, shocked outcry – 'we had the saddest news that ever came in a great while' lamented *The Parliament Scout*.[52] In the face of such 'clamours and censures' the Parliamentary commanders involved in the campaign initially strove to maintain a united front in public; on the 14th Haselrig vigorously defended his and his colleagues' generalship in the Commons.[53] But the apparent unity was only a façade. As the criticism against all the general officers involved continued unabated, individuals strove to salvage their own tarnished reputations. Manchester's chaplain Ash wrote an account 'for the satisfaction of private friends' defending his patron, and it is clear that similar letters were circulating in London on behalf of other officers.[54]

Finally some of the generals involved at Newbury and in the subsequent campaign decided to channel the fierce current of resentment. When on 25 November Waller and Cromwell made their report to the Commons of the 'proceedings of the armies since the conjunction', their intention was clearly to cast the blame for the failures of the previous month solely upon Manchester and thus to vindicate their own behavior. This intention colors their account of the entire Newbury campaign. They underplay or fail to mention certain critical decisions, such as those of 9 and 10 November when it was decided not to engage the Royal army, which had been agreed collectively at a Council of War, and emphasized the importance of incidents where Manchester had made unilateral decisions: his failure to synchronize the assault on Shaw house with the attack on Speen; his not ordering an immediate pursuit of the Royal army after the battle; his removal of the army from Compton Downs into Newbury on 6 November.[55] The Earl was to be the scapegoat for the disappointments of the autumn campaign.

The concern with which the commanders involved in the Newbury campaign strove to protect their reputations, first by letters to 'private friends', then by attacking Manchester as solely responsible for the wretched performance of the conjoint armies, suggests that the criticism to which they were subjected involved more than the dissatisfaction of the London press. It had greater political significance, I believe, because it was part of an attempt by the Earl of Essex to re-assert his claims as commander-in-chief.

The Lord General was the only leading Parliamentary commander not present during the Newbury campaign, as he was sick in London. Immediately after the relief of Donnington he had expressed his 'resentment touching the miscarriage of this affair' in a letter to Skippon,[56] and thereafter his officers and his friends in London led a chorus of criticism in the city against the other generals. It was said that if Essex had been present the King would never have been allowed to recover his guns without interruption; that the failure to engage the enemy stemmed from having 'the commanders in chiefe to be godly men, which is not always a character of wisdom or valour'; that Essex and his subordinates were 'the only men to conduct an army, the rest novices and incapable'. Essex, whose own military abilities had been the subject of the jibes and abuse of his political opponents since early 1643, in particular after the fiasco in Cornwall in the summer, must have relished the opportunity to denounce with righteous indignation the incompetence of those who had commanded during the Newbury campaign. But his criticism was more than a malicious turning the tables on his rivals. He hoped to create, in the words of the Venetian ambassador, 'an opening for himself and a way to employment'.[57]

The one obvious lesson of the battle of Newbury and the relief of Donnington was that the Parliamentary armies would require a thorough overhaul at the end of the campaigning season. The forces of Waller, of Manchester, and of the Lord General were ill provisioned and poorly armed; all were over-burdened with a top-heavy officer corps as desertion and disease drastically cut into the number of private soldiers; their pay was months in arrears as the taxes allocated for their maintenance proved insufficient. That ideas for some sort of re-organization were circulating at Westminster in mid-November appears from the votes of the Commons on the 19th and the 23rd instructing the Committee of Both Kingdoms to consider 'a frame or model of the whole militia'.[58] But any re-organization of the armies would require a re-consideration of the high command. Essex must have hoped that if he could emphasize the ineptitude of those generals who had been patronized by Parliament at his expense in 1644, he might assert his claims to the position of supreme commander in any re-organization of the armies.

The Lord General's aspirations may have been enhanced by an accession of political strength in the autumn. This did not result from any alteration of English 'party' configurations, which as the debates following the surrender of Essex's army at Lostwithiel demonstrated, were similar to those that had appertained in the previous winter. The 'violent spirits' of the war party still sought to secure the Earl's relegation to a position without real military responsibility, while he was supported by his allies of the peace party, and also by members of the middle group, who did not wish to weaken Parliament's military machine by discarding the Lord General in the middle of the campaigning season.[59] The change was in the attitude of the Scots.

The employment of the Scots to swing the military balance heavily in Parliament's favor had been a project favored by Pym and after his death was implemented by Vane, St John, and their allies of the war party and the middle group; it was vigorously opposed by the peace party in Parliament. After their entry into the war the Scots worked closely with those who had engineered the alliance and who continued to defend their interests in Parliament, and viewed the peace party and their favored general, Essex, with an intense suspicion, which, according to Holles, was assiduously fostered by Vane and his friends.[60] However, by the summer, the Scots and the groups that had encouraged their intervention became increasingly disillusioned with the alliance. From the point of view of their English allies the vaunted Scottish forces had proved a paper tiger; the expected victories had not materialized as their army bogged down in tedious sieges at York and Newcastle. For their part the Scots found that their hopes of establishing a theocratic Presbyterian system in England made little headway against the opposition of Independents and Erastians in the Assembly of Divines and the Commons. The Scots recognized that their ability to insist upon their religious program depended upon a dramatic military success, but when their army finally obtained a victory at Marston Moor they found to their chagrin that the Independents claimed that 'all the glory of the night' belonged to Cromwell 'with his unspeakablie valorous regiments' and that the Scots had played a very minor role.[61]

In July Baillie recognized that the importance claimed for Cromwell's part in the Marston Moor victory might strengthen the Independents' demands for toleration and lead the 'politick part in the

Parliament', those who were not committed to the Presbyterian settlement, 'to conclude nothing in the matters of religion that may grieve the sectaries, whom they count necessatie for the time'. Yet, when on 13 September, with the passage of the Commons' order instructing a committee to consider 'how far tender consciences . . . may be borne with', his earlier analysis proved correct, he was still profoundly shocked. His outrage stemmed from the identity of those who proposed the order – St John, 'our most trustie friend', and Vane, 'our most intime friend . . . whom we trusted most', the joint architects of the Scottish alliance. St John and Vane had acted 'without any regard to us, who have saved their nation'.[62]

As the Scots came to recognize that many of those M.P.s who had been previously thought 'our greatest friends' were either conscientiously opposed to Prebyterianism, like Vane, or would not risk alienating the Independents, who had demonstrated their military utility at Marston Moor, by insisting upon subscription to a fully-fledged Scottish discipline at a critical juncture of the war, so they tentatively began to develop a new alliance designed to secure the religious settlement they desired: an alliance with the previously suspect peace party, and the Earl of Essex. In September they played a major role in securing the rehabilitation of the Earl of Essex following the surrender of his army at Lostwithiel. By November the Scottish Chancellor, Loudon, and Essex's supporters, Holles and Stapleton, were conjointly negotiating with the French ambassador, proposing that he should use his influence at court to persuade Charles to consider terms which would be offered as a basis for peace; only one concession was required – some appearance of his readiness to abandon episcopacy.[63]

It was this development, whereby the Scots, Essex, and the latter's adherents in the peace party 'came to a better understanding',[64] which encouraged the Lord General to endeavor to realize his own claims to supreme command by indiscriminately attacking the commanders involved at Newbury. Conversely, Essex's enhanced political strength, and the threat which it posed to the other generals, explains their desperate efforts to defend themselves, a process culminating in their attempt to cast the Earl of Manchester as the scapegoat for the failures of the campaign.

But if Waller and Cromwell expected Manchester, that 'sweet meek man', to surrender tamely, they were mistaken. On 28 November in the Lords[65] the Earl not only responded to their charges of military incompetence, stressing the communal responsibility of the generals for the critical decisions, but hit back hard at his Lieutenant-General. Manchester emphasized those incidents which had caused his breach with Cromwell in the summer: the latter had attacked the principle of hereditary peerage; he had vilified the Assembly of

Divines; he had displayed a violent animosity against the Scots.[66] The Lords immediately appointed a committee to investigate these charges, but a more dangerous product of the Earl's counter-attack was a secret meeting held within the next three days at Essex House, where the Scottish commissioners, the Earl of Essex himself and a number of peace party M.P.s discussed the possibility of proceeding against Cromwell, 'that darling of the sectaries', as an incendiary between the two Kingdoms according to the terms of the Solemn League and Covenant on the basis of Manchester's charge.[67]

Although the participants at the Essex House conference finally decided not to press the extreme 'incendiary' charge against Cromwell, the meeting itself reveals the extent of his and Waller's initial miscalculation. Far from diverting the charges of Essex and his adherents against all the generals by stressing Manchester's sole guilt, the effect of their accusation had been to draw the Scots and the Lord General into a closer alliance and so improve the latter's chances of making political capital from the Donnington Castle debacle, 'seeing an opening for himself and a way to employment'. Essex and his allies could still argue that the responsibility for the failure of the Newbury campaign 'was common to all the generall officers then present', while Manchester's counter-accusation against Cromwell had given the Scots the ammunition and the enhanced determination to secure 'his removeall from the armie'.[68] Neither Manchester nor Cromwell could hope to survive the damaging charges laid by the other: the way was still open for Essex to reassert his claims to overall command.

When Cromwell launched his attack on Manchester in the Commons one of the better-informed Parliamentary journalists, Dillingham of *The Parliament Scout*, refused to divulge the details to his readers, hoping that 'it may be all buried in the grave of oblivion'. What was needed was not investigation and recrimination, which could only advantage the enemy, who 'are . . . much joyd in our division', but the building up of a 'brave, valiant, resolute, active, faithfull and unanimous army', designed to terminate the war swiftly.[69] A number of M.P.s shared Dillingham's fears and hopes. When Cromwell and Waller first laid their charges these had not been welcomed by many M.P.s who feared that they 'might tend to the increasing of division', and in early December Agostini noted that some 'leading Parliamentarians' were striving to restore unity at Westminster.[70] Their efforts culminated in the first Self-Denying Ordinance.

The Ordinance was an inspired move, which reversed the glissade into the morass of long-drawn-out investigations, internecine ideological division and bitter personal feuds where the Parliamentary cause seemed inevitably to be slipping in early December. The details of its introduction do not need repetition,[71] but its general appeal should be emphasized. The reception of the legislation by the press was overwhelmingly favorable,[72] and it was greeted with general enthusiasm in the Commons. The Ordinance had features attractive to all political groups. For those favoring the vigorous prosecution of the war the incompetent generals who had damaged Parliament's efforts in 1643 and 1644 would be removed without tedious and divisive investigations of individual culpability, and the necessary re-organization of the army could proceed without hindrance from the squabbles of the old commanders for posts in the new force. On the other hand, the peace party had frequently claimed that M.P.s holding lucrative military posts were deliberately spinning out the war 'lest their own power should determine with it'; the removal of all M.P.s from offices of profit would silence that charge.[73] Perhaps a measure of the general support that the notion of the Self-Denying Ordinance received in the House is the constitution of the committee appointed to draft the legislation after the debate: it included only one war party man, Lisle; Maynard and Reynolds of the peace party; and four men attached to the middle group, Glynn, St John, Crewe and Pierrepoint.[74]

The only contentious issue during the passage of the Ordinance through the Commons was raised on 17 December, when Reynolds moved a proviso excluding the Earl of Essex from the effects of the legislation. The debate raged from 'morn till night' and ended with the defeat of Reynolds's motion by seven votes, 100 to 93.[75] The Lord General's ambition, first apparent in November, to secure the supreme command of the re-organized Parliamentary forces was finally thwarted by the desertion of some of his previous supporters. From 1643 the war party had sought the Earl's dismissal, while the peace party had defended him from these assaults; they had succeeded in retaining Essex, despite the fierce hostility of Vane, Haselrig and the other 'fierie spirits', through the assistance of the middle group, who continued to pursue the policy of Pym in the summer of 1643 in supporting Essex, whose status and his popularity in the army were thought to add strength and respectability to the Parliamentary cause. But on 17 December some middle group men – Crewe, Pierrepoint, St John – while stressing their high regard for the Lord General, voted with Vane's party to ensure the defeat of the proviso. It was later argued that they did so having recognized Essex's poor generalship in Cornwall, but it may be suggested that Essex's developing rapport with the Scots, and their fears that the latter, now they had broken with their old political allies and had 'entered into privacy and intimacy' with those who 'carried on the Court design', would conclude a 'sell out' peace with the King provided Presbyterianism was established, decided the Lord General's erstwhile supporters of the middle group to desert him and vote for the passage of the Self-Denying Ordinance.[76]

During the critical debates in the winter of 1644–5 on the question of military re-organization, the Earl of Manchester was virtually forgotten, an irrelevance to the new disputes and alignments at Westminster. His old allies of the war party and the middle group had discarded him, and were supporting the legislation revamping the Parliamentary army, while the peace party, previously the opponents of the Association, still distrusted the Earl and reserved their energies for their attempt to secure the exemption of the Lord General from the provisions of the Self-Denying Ordinance. The Commons quickly suppressed an attempt by some officers in the army of the Association to present a petition favoring the retention of the Earl in command,[77] and Lisle's committee continued to hear the testimony of those who blamed Manchester for the failures of the autumn campaign, but the bitter charges which he and Cromwell had exchanged were virtually forgotten in the excitement aroused by the proposed program of military reform.[78] However, despite his political isolation at Westminster, 'the owl of this Commonwealth, wherein every bird hath a peck at him',[79] the Earl's stand in the autumn of 1644 had won him new allies: the authorities in the constituent counties of the Association.

The Earl of Manchester and the constituent counties: August 1644–March 1645

As has been shown, the January 1644 legislation, by firmly establishing the central authority of the Earl of Manchester and the Cambridge Committee, relegated the local governors of the constituent counties of the Association to an inferior position to that which they had previously enjoyed. They became merely the executors of policies in the making of which they had little influence; they were subjected to the intrusion of outsiders in county affairs; and their army participated in a national strategy, to which the needs of local defense, their essential priority, were subordinated. But while the most objectionable features of the new system were resisted in the counties, the local governors never lost their personal respect for Manchester: his prestige as a wealthy local magnate, his good nature, his readiness to hear their complaints sympathetically, and his subscription to a number of their social prejudices were attractive to the county gentry, and prevented any complete breakdown of relations between the central authority and the local communities. In the autumn of 1644 this ambivalent attitude of the county governors, of esteem for Manchester combined with serious misgivings concerning the centralized organization he headed, was exchanged for one of whole-hearted support for the Earl. The enthusiasm was a product of one aspect of Manchester's changed attitude to the war apparent after August 1644: his acknowledgment of his predominant obligation to provide for the defense of the Association.

On 10 August, while at Lincoln, Manchester presented a series of objections to the Committee of Both Kingdoms to a plan for his forces to march into Cheshire in pursuit of Prince Rupert. One was the responsibility of his army to provide the Association with 'the protection for which wee were designed'. It was a theme he constantly reiterated in the next three months, both in his letters to the Committee of Both Kingdoms, and in his remarks to his subordinates: 'it is a pity', he told Lieutenant-Colonel Rich, 'we should leave those countys who have paide us and parted with their money so willingly to us all this while, and now by our absence be exposed to the incursions of an enemy'. And in December, in his fullest statement of what he understood to be his military obligation to the constituent counties, Manchester argued that as 'a servant to the Association' he was 'obliged both in honor and conscience in regard to the great trust they have reposed in mee to bee sub servient to their desires'.[80]

In the autumn of 1644 there was no Royalist threat to the territorial integrity of the Association sufficient to explain the Earl's desire to give priority to its defense in preference to pursuing the strategy ordered by the Committee of Both Kingdoms. Upon the removal of the army of the Association from Lincoln in September the garrisons of Newark and Belvoir again raided deep into Lincolnshire, and on 4 October succeeded in surprising the fortified town of Crowland.[81] But the Newarkers hardly represented a serious challenge to the Association. Colonel Rossiter's local levies, supported by Fleetwood's regiment, routed a large Royalist force at Denton on 28 October, and thereafter, although Crowland proved difficult to recapture in the wet weather, the Parliamentarians were clearly dominant in southern Lincolnshire.[82] If the military situation scarcely warranted the Earl's concern with his responsibility to provide for the defense of the Association, the latter also post-dated the fall of York. Manchester had not objected to marching his army to join the Earl of Essex at the proposed general rendezvous at Aylesbury in April, even though the Royalists, as a result of their victory at Newark, had occupied most of Lincolnshire and were threatening Boston.[83] In the early summer the Earl did not feel obliged to request his army's removal from the siege of York to protect Lincolnshire from the depredations of the Newarkers, or to defend the Association in late June, when the King's army advanced to Buckingham and threatened the eastern counties.[84]

Manchester's obsessive sense of his duty to guarantee adequate protection for the Associated counties, a concern which had not apparently troubled him unduly prior to the capture of York and which owed little to any increased Royalist pressure upon East Anglia in the autumn of 1644, was obviously a rationalization, designed to justify his personal reluctance to obey the orders of the Committee of Both Kingdoms to march west and bring the King to a conclusive engagement. However, for whatever subjective reasons it was made, the Earl's acknowledgment that he was 'a servant to the Association', and that its defense was his major priority, was very gratifying to the authorities in the constituent counties.

Throughout the York campaign, as in 1643, the counties had resented the national role designed for the army of the Association by its Parliamentary backers. They objected to the employment of the forces which they had raised, and for which they were paying unprecedented sums in taxation, in distant parts of England, leaving them exposed to the attacks of the enemy. Their protests were neglected until the autumn of 1644, when they found Manchester suddenly responsive to their viewpoint. Thereafter the relationship between the Earl and the county authorities was mutually sustaining. The counties, aware of the General's new sympathy for their demands, bombarded him with letters and petitions pressing for the return of their forces to the defense of East Anglia, and such pressure reinforced Manchester's sense of his obligation to the Association. By 30 September the Earl could inform Westminster that he was receiving 'dayly lettres' from the constituent counties, 'expressing their great trouble that their forces are drawne soe farre from them', and that he had been presented with a statement of the objections of the Suffolk committee to the westward march. A few days later the Earl received a similar formal protest from the Norfolk authorities, whose delicate hint of fiscal blackmail he reported to the Committee of Both Kingdoms: the local committee feared that if the army was 'carryed soe farre from them ... they should be disabled as to further recruites or payments of money'.[85] In November the Earl wrote of the 'many letters' he had received from the committees reminding him that 'I should act as a protection to those counties which both raised these forces and still pay them with this intent'.[86] The Norfolk committee, besides pressing the Earl to return to the defense of the Association, also organized a county-wide petition, insisting that the army should 'not be drawne fourth beyond the reach of our safetye' but 'be imployed nere the confines of our Association'. Their intention, the committee stated in its letter soliciting subscriptions, was to ensure 'that our owne troopes may be imployed for the safety of our owne countyes'. The petition was presented to the Commons on 8 October, where it was coldly received.[87]

The *rapprochement* between the Earl and the constituent counties in the autumn of 1644 was not only a product of mutual agreement concerning the proper functions and priorities of the Association's forces. The committees could also identify with other aspects of Manchester's change in attitude. His desire for a speedy negotiated settlement mirrored that of the county gentry,[88] and his open breach with Cromwell and the Independent faction in the army of the Association was equally welcome. As the local opposition to the project to garrison Yarmouth demonstrates,[89] some of the county committees had been disturbed by Manchester's acquiescence to the appointment and promotion of religious radicals. But after the autumn they clearly felt that the Earl's religious position was more akin to their own;[90] a number of petitions denouncing 'Antinomians and Anabaptists' were presented to Parliament [91] which, while in part a reflection of the increasingly fierce religious debate in London, were also informed by an awareness of the divisions in the army of the Association, and were a demonstration of the counties' solidarity with Manchester in his conflict with Cromwell.[92] In October, when petitions pressing Parliament to require a general subscription to the Covenant and to pass legislation for the settlement of the Church in accordance with the recommendations of the Assembly of Divines were being canvassed in Norfolk and Suffolk, it was reported that the Independents in Manchester's army were being denounced in these counties as 'men not to be trusted', who 'will, if they be not prevented, get a power together, [and] joyn with the King against the Parliament for Liberty of Conscience'.[93]

By the winter of 1644–5, although 'the owl of this Commonwealth' at Westminster, the Earl's breach with the Independents, his hopes for a negotiated settlement, and his stress on the defense of the Association as the primary obligation of his army, had won him the complete confidence of the constituent counties. In Essex Ash's vindication of the Earl from Cromwell's charges of military negligence was read in churches, while the Norfolk committee eulogized the 'noble speritt which dwell in your Lordshipp, of wisdome and constancie'. As Colonel Mildmay, one of the Cambridge Committee, wrote in late January, 'Your Lord shipp's faightfullest friends and simple-est eniemise are in this Assotiation.'[94]

In fact the development of an harmonious relationship between Manchester and the committees of the constituent counties owed much to the efforts of Mildmay and his colleagues at Cambridge. Not that the central administration was politically homogeneous. The Treasury officials, in particular, were divided. Gawsell favored the return of the army to the defense of the eastern counties, and was regarded with suspicion by the Independents, while Weaver testified against the Earl during the investigation of Cromwell's charges; that 'juggling knave,' Dr Stane, sat on the fence.[95] The Committee of the Association was also split,[96] but the major part of its members supported Manchester, and their demands for the return of the army to the defense of the Association probably encouraged the local committees to voice their own resentment at the westward march.[97] Upon Cromwell's presentation of his charge against Manchester, Mildmay wrote that the majority of the Committee 'wold bee forward to serve yor Lordship': their efforts included the circulation of a petition for the retention of the Earl in command among the officers of the army of the Association, and the organization of the Bury conference.[98]

In late January the Cambridge Committee, warning that 'the Associacion was in danger of disturbance', invited the local authorities to send representatives to a general meeting to discuss the political and military situation. Thirty-three men from the seven counties gathered at Bury on 30 January, and, after the election of one of the Suffolk representatives as chairman, the conference was begun by the reading of extracts from the legislation of 20 December 1642 which had first established the Association, designed to demonstrate that the seven counties must have a common army, which should 'serve for the mutuall defence of the said counties'.[99] Having thus reminded the delegates of the original and essential purpose of their union, the chairman invited them to consider 'whither is not the Associacion impaired' by the proposed New Model legislation. After some debate, in which only a single dissenting opinion was voiced when one of the Hertfordshire delegates argued that the New Model might benefit the Kingdom as a whole, and thus the eastern counties as an integral part of the larger entity, it was agreed that the 'ends and purposes' for which the counties had originally banded together were negated by the projected military reorganization, and that every effort should be made to 'indeavoure the repaire and preservation of the Association'. To this end it was decided that a deputation of two men from each of the constituent counties should go up to Westminster, and present the Committee of Both Kingdoms with a 'letter with instructions' from the conference. The 'instructions' consisted of seven specific but peripheral requests concerned with the settlement of a number of recurrent administrative problems that had troubled the Association.[100] The essence of the discussions at Bury was set out in the letter, signed by all the delegates, which, in opposing the incorporation of Manchester's force into the New Model Army, contained a powerful re-affirmation of the insular ideal of the Association which the constituent counties had maintained since its inception. The army of the Association was described purely as an instrument of local defense, 'designed, promised and by ordinance settled for theire mutuall assistance', its sole function to protect the eastern counties from 'secret malignants at home and . . . the watchfull enraged enimy abroade', and to secure 'generall peace . . . to theire borders'. The representatives at Bury made no mention of the national role which those M.P.s who had backed the legislation establishing Manchester's army had envisaged it as playing: 'The safety of the Kingdome', it was remarked in the course of the discussion at Bury, 'was not our worke.'

After his breach with Cromwell in the autumn of 1644 and the consequent transformation of his attitude to the war which was to lose him the support of his previous allies at Westminster, mutual interest had led to the development of a close understanding between Manchester and the local authorities in East Anglia. The Bury conference, with its stress on the defensive function of the Association and its expression of loyalty to the Earl, 'whoe hath been and yet is the chiefe of all the Associated forces', was the climactic affirmation of the solidarity of the constituent counties and their General.

Yet the unanimous determination of the constituent counties to preserve the army of the Association expressed at Bury had virtually no effect on the decisions reached at Westminster. The New Model legislation was passed without regard for their 'sadd apprehensions'. On 4 February, the deputation from Bury was received by the Committee of Both Kingdoms, who agreed that their representations should be reported to both Houses. The Lords, obviously hoping that the protest of the Association would strengthen their own rear-guard action against the passage of the New Model Army legislation, responded with alacrity. On 5 February, they discussed the letter and instructions from Bury, which they entered in their official journal, and voted to establish a joint committee to consider the matter further. But the attentive concern of the upper House for the views of the constituent counties was not mirrored in the Commons. No report was made from the Committee of Both Kingdoms, and the Lords' proposal, twice repeated, for the establishment of a joint committee was disregarded. On 13 February, the Commons acknowledged the deputation from Bury to the extent of issuing a vaguely-worded order to the Committee of East Anglian M.P.s to 'consider of all things tending to the good and safety of the Association', but their effective reply to the 'feares' expressed at the conference was to continue to discuss and push through the Ordinances establishing the New Model.[101] Despite the receipt of further, more specific requests from the Association and a protest from Bury at the House's neglect,[102] it was not until 7 April that the Commons finally heard the 'humble petition . . . and . . . desires of the Eastern Associated Counties'. On that date three infantry regiments of the Association were being formally incorporated into the New Model Army.[103]

In 1645 the counties of the Association were still of critical importance to the Parliamentary war-effort: their force was to provide the backbone of the re-organized army, and they would bear over half the national burden of taxation required for its up-keep. Given their apparently strong bargaining position, the Commons' complete disregard of their protest against the projected military re-organization is surprising. The determinants of the Commons' inflexible attitude are uncertain, but one of the factors which may have convinced the leaders at Westminster that their neglect would not result in the complete alienation of the Association may have been the hesitancy detectable in the deliberations and conclusions of the delegates at Bury: an uncertainty concerning the constitutional propriety of their action in holding the general conference and lobbying Parliament. Professor Everitt has written of the Bury conference, 'it is difficult not to detect . . . a veiled claim to some share in sovereignty along with the Lords and Commons'.[104] This was precisely the impression the representatives sought to avoid. They hastened to deny, in a formal protestation, the least intention of challenging Parliament's authority or proceedings. They would only 'represent our feares . . . unto those that are betrusted with power to provide remidy', and the policies they suggested 'were allwayes intended to be uppon hipotheses, submitting to the wisdome of Parliament'. So they voted to lobby the Committee of Both Kingdoms in case a petition to the Commons might be thought to be an attempt to pressure Parliament in a matter under consideration, and so 'might seem to intrench uppon the priviledges of the Houses'. In their letter, having expressed their objections to the New Model Army proposal, they immediately announced that 'none of these discouragments or any private regarde shall withdraw our zeale from the service of . . . the Parliament and Kingdome', and stressed that they would waive their request for the retention of the army of the Association if it were not thought to be 'in consistence with the publiq' by the Houses. The delegates, in their determination to avoid giving the impression that they were challenging the sovereignty of Parliament, undermined any force that their objections might otherwise have had at Westminster.

From the outset of the civil war, a friction had been apparent between the local priorities of the counties forming the Association and the nationally-oriented demands of Parliament. But the opposition of the county committees to the latter had been inchoate, a pragmatic neglect of, or resistance to, specific Parliamentary demands when they conflicted with local interests, not a rejection on principle of the authority of the central government. In the autumn of 1644, however, the counties' common grievance at the westward march of their army, which they were encouraged to voice by Manchester's newly responsive attitude, resulted in a heightened tension between the center and localities, an open 'clashing betwixt the commands of the Parliament ... and the desires of the Association',[105] which culminated in the carefully organized meeting of the representatives of the local authorities at Bury to formulate a general statement of their conception of the proper function of the Association. In this respect the conference may indeed, as Everitt argues, mark the high point of 'the claims of "the county community" ',[106] but it also exhibits their fatal weakness. The delegates at Bury could not articulate their powerful localist sentiment into a justification of opposition to Westminster which would be intellectually acceptable. The counties might resist specific Parliamentary orders, but when confronted with the general problem of the relationship between the center and the periphery they were unable to develop a coherent constitutional theory to dispute the acknowledged sovereignty of Parliament.

The Association in eclipse, 1645–8

Upon the incorporation of the army of the Association into the New Model in April the centralized Treasury and supply system which Manchester had established at Cambridge was dismantled. The Committee of the Association, too, was preparing to discontinue its meetings at Trinity College with the expiration of the Ordinances that had provided for the stipends of its members and other charges, when the Commons hurriedly voted it the necessary funds to remain in session.[1] Thereafter the Committee met regularly until 1646, performing a number of the functions which it had undertaken in the period of Manchester's ascendancy. It still decided common administrative policy for the counties, and the co-ordination of the defense of the region remained its responsibility – it controlled the Cambridgeshire garrisons, and during the Naseby campaign and again when the King surprised Huntingdon in August 1645 the Committee summoned the county militia regiments to protect the frontiers of the Association.[2] The Committee also retained a limited role as the central financial agency for the Association, supervising the collection of assessments for the maintenance of the forces raised in the counties to check the Newarkers.[3]

But, despite these activities, 1645 was a sunset period for the Committee at Cambridge. It had lost the authority and prestige which Parliamentary Ordinances, Manchester's commission and control of a nationally important army had conferred upon it in 1644, and its remaining administrative responsibilities were being steadily eroded by the Committee of the Eastern Association at Westminster. In 1643 and 1644 this body, which was attended by those Lords and M.P.s with interests in the region, had been the forum for the debate and drafting of enactments affecting the Association. It continued to perform this latter function in 1645, discussing the proportion which each county should raise of the force designed to besiege Newark, and proposing legislation to raise money for the maintenance of the East Anglian garrisons. But in this period the Committee at Westminster also began to extend its range of operations, and increasingly involved itself in the *minutiae* of routine local administration, supervising the raising of men and the collection of revenue, which had previously been the responsibility of the Cambridge Committee.[4] With the encroachments of the Westminster Committee further weakening its already uncertain status,[5] the situation of the Cambridge Committee in 1645 is reminiscent of that of its predecessor in 1643 prior to Manchester's appointment. The local authorities in the constituent counties were unresponsive to requests for money, and, as in 1643, the Cambridgeshire county treasurers found themselves footing the bill for supposedly 'common' charges. And, when the Royalists threatened the frontiers of the Association, the Committee's appeals for assistance were neglected by the counties, whose priority remained local defense.[6] Consideration of its growing impotence may have led the representatives of the constituent counties at a general meeting at Bury in February 1646 to question the value of further meetings of the Committee at Cambridge, and shortly thereafter the Westminster Committee smoothly took over the remaining administrative responsibilities which had been located at Cambridge.[7] Trinity College gave way to Dutchy Chamber, the meeting place of the Committee of East Anglian M.P.s, as the headquarters of the Eastern Association. The change was of more than symbolic significance. The members of the Westminster Committee were not completely indifferent to the local interests of the constituent counties,[8] but, obviously subordinate to Parliament and regarded by the latter as little more than a convenient administrative agency,[9] they were unlikely to encourage a direct 'clashing betwixt the commands of the Parliament . . . and the desires of the Association' as had the Cambridge Committee in the autumn and winter of 1644.

With the passing of the Cambridge Committee one vestigial manifestation of the privileged semi-autonomous status the eastern counties had once enjoyed survived: the general meeting of the representatives of the constituent counties. Three such meetings, similar in form, ironically, to that which had heralded the inception of the Association in February 1643, were held at Bury between 1646 and 1648. These conferences, or at least the two for which some record of the discussion has survived,[10] also provided a muted echo of the tensions between the central authorities and the local rulers of the Associated counties which had been so apparent in late 1644.

At the Bury conference held in February 1646 the delegates, who agreed on a list of twenty proposals for presentation to Parliament,[11] were primarily concerned with fiscal issues. They insisted that money loaned to Parliament 'upon the Public Faith' and sums owed for free quarter should be speedily repaid, and that the weekly assessment should be reduced. It was claimed that the tax burden on the Association could not be maintained at its present level without 'apparent destruction to trading and husbandrie', and the delegates moved that a large proportion of the costs of the army now borne by the land tax in the eastern counties should be taken up by areas newly won from the Royalists and by the excise. Relative to the latter it was suggested that revenue could be improved if the abuses of the much-hated, London-appointed excise officers were investigated,[12] and it was moved that the county committees might be instructed to take over the administration of that tax. Only in one area did the delegates seek additional taxation – to secure revenue to meet the running costs of local administration. The emphasis on local interests in these financial propositions is equally apparent in the other requests. Redress of two long-standing grievances of the country gentry, the exactions of the Court of Wards and the exorbitant fees demanded of the sheriffs upon the audit of their accounts, was desired, and it was proposed that the Assizes should be kept in the counties to avoid the expenses of litigation at Westminster. Claiming that East Anglia was not as well defended as the north or west, the conference also pressed for the navy to guard the coasts against pirates and foreign invasion. In their one proposition concerned with national affairs rather than local interests, the delegates of the constituent counties, as hostile to the sectaries as they had been in late 1644, requested a settlement of church government, universal subscription to the Covenant, and the punishment of lay preachers.[13]

The final Bury conference was held on 10 August 1648, after the suppression of most of the Royalist insurrections in East Anglia but before Colchester had fallen to Fairfax. The representatives agreed to a series of propositions of which no complete list survives, but which involved the raising of 2500 horse for the defense of the eastern counties, and the reconvention of the Cambridge Committee of the Association. Their proposals were forwarded to Parliament through the Essex M.P., Sir Henry Mildmay, who requested further consideration of two key issues: whether the counties would agree to the choice of officers being entrusted to Sir Thomas Fairfax, and whether the force would be subject to the latter's overall command. The delegates assembled again at Cambridge on the 22nd, and, after much debate, voted to retain local control. All commissions were to be issued by the Committee of the Association and their nominee as commander, the Presbyterian Colonel Rossiter, and the latter would only be subordinate to Fairfax when the General was present in the Association, or when Rossiter's brigade served outside East Anglia, which it could only do 'with the consent of the . . . committee of the association'.[14] In addition to the improved military situation after the fall of Colchester and the victory at Preston, it may have been the counties' firm determination to raise a force largely independent of external control which decided the Commons to shelve their proposals.

The August 1648 Bury conference was the last. These meetings, summoned upon the initiative of the local authorities in the constituent counties and a sounding board for their localist demands, survived the incorporation of the army into the New Model, and the erosion of the power and the eventual disappearance of the Cambridge-based institutions, to be the final relic of the strength of, and the tensions within, the Earl of Manchester's Association. But they could not survive the political revolution of 1649. Thereafter the Eastern Association became a mere administrative convenience, a handy regional division for the supervision, by a Parliamentary Committee under the Rump, by Major-General Hezekiah Haynes during the Protectorate, of the execution of the commands of the central government.

12

Conclusion

This work began by posing the historical problem presented by the peculiar role of the Eastern Association in the civil war. We are now in a position to answer the question, and to suggest some more general conclusions from this study.

Most immediately, the success of the Association was a function of the powerful force which the Earl of Manchester was able to build up in the winter and early spring of 1643–4, and which was to smash Prince Rupert at Marston Moor. Although East Anglia was its financial base and the bulk of its infantry was impressed in the seven counties, it was an army which had many of the characteristics of a national force. Manchester could attract recruits for its crack cavalry regiments from 'the honestest youth in the Kingdome'; its officers were selected for qualities of military experience and enthusiasm for the Parliamentary cause without deferring to considerations of local connection or traditional definitions of social prestige; its logistical support was provided by a series of bureaucratically organized, centralized administrative agencies designed to raise unprecedented sums from the taxpayer. As appeared in the autumn of 1644, Manchester's force was not ideally suited to play the national role designed by its Parliamentary backers, but the experience gained in its establishment and administration was a vital element in the military reorganization of early 1645. In its sophisticated central administration, as in the make-up of its officer cadre, the army of the Eastern Association was the precursor of the nationally oriented New Model.

The power of this military organization contrasts markedly with that of the other regional Associations. Previous explanations of Manchester's success in constructing and maintaining it have stressed the individuality of East Anglia: that a common ideology or homogeneous social structure bound the area together in enthusiastic support of the policies of Parliament, and muted the county-centered localism which flourished elsewhere. However, such explanations neglect a necessary intermediate stage of analysis. When Sir William Waller sought to account for his military failures he did not stress the localism of the south-eastern counties as the determining factor: rather he emphasized his want of legislative authority which enabled that localism to flourish. This study has shown that Manchester's military and administrative achievements stemmed very largely from central political support which Waller claimed had been denied him.

Manchester was backed by a number of interest groups in Parliament. Some M.P.s voted funds and material for the army of the Association from considerations of local interest – for example, those with estates in the north supported the force which seemed most likely to smash Royalist dominance in their region; others were troubled by the political and religious programs of their new allies, the Scots, and hoped that a powerful army, in particular one in which Independents held some key posts, would provide a very necessary counterweight to the ambitions of their 'brethren'. Most support for Manchester came from those who sought to force the King to make the substantial concessions upon which they insisted in any negotiations. But even these M.P.s were not a united party. In 1644, while the middle group viewed the Association's force as a desirable addition to the Parliamentary war-machine, Sir Henry Vane the younger and the 'fierie spirits' sought to strengthen Manchester's command at the expense of, and as a replacement for, the army of the despised Earl of Essex, and, as was to emerge in 1646–8, the two groups could not agree upon the optimum politico-religious settlement.

Yet, however they might differ on ultimate issues, those at Westminster who refused to contemplate the peace party's policy of an immediate settlement on any terms, recognized the need for military predominance. They had initially pinned their hopes on the Lord General's army to swing the balance of advantage against Charles, but in the summer of 1643, in part as they grew dissatisfied with Essex's poor showing, in part in response to Newcastle's onslaught in Lincolnshire and the threat of a further push south, they had developed the numerically small and poorly organized forces of the Eastern Association into a powerful body under Manchester's command. In January 1644, impressed by the Earl's conduct of the campaign clearing Lincolnshire and by the morale and discipline of his army, both of which suggested that he might provide more dynamic and effective generalship than had Essex, they worked to iron out those difficulties which had limited the efficiency of the Association's army in the previous autumn.

In a flurry of legislative activity Manchester's financial provision was increased, and, more important, he was given the requisite authority to develop a centralized military administration, free from interference by the Lord General and independent of the fiscal control of the constituent counties. Both Essex and the local gentry resented the diminution of their authority, and, until the summer of 1644, those groups in the Commons who had pushed through the critical January legislation were forced to protect the army of the Association from their counter-attacks. However, after August 1644 the enthusiastic support which had previously been accorded Manchester by the majority in Parliament waned, as the Earl's attitude to the war 'visibly degenerated'. Manchester's bitter sense of futility was largely the product of the impassioned religious feud within his own army. His growing belief that the absolute defeat of the King's forces promised, not 'the perfecting of the Reformation which is hopefully begun', but only 'a further quarrel' within the Parliamentary party, surfaced in deliberate procrastination in his response to military orders from Westminster. He rationalized this by stressing his constitutional obligation to defend the Association, a consideration which had not troubled him in the previous months. Accordingly the groups in Parliament headed by Vane and St John, which a year previously had brought the army victorious at Marston Moor into being, forsook Manchester, dismantled the forces of the Eastern Association, and transferred their energies to ensuring the thorough military reorganization entailed in the Self-Denying and New Model Ordinances.

What must be emphasized, therefore, is the determining influence of the politicians at Westminster in creating, supporting and, ultimately, discarding the army of the Earl of Manchester. It is a dimension of the history of the civil war in East Anglia which has gone largely unobserved and it invites a re-evaluation of the role of the counties in the development of the Eastern Association. Recognizing the critical role of central politics in the evolution of the military organization, the historian is no longer forced to postulate an atypical constructive enthusiasm in the eastern counties to account for the success of the Association, or to relate that enthusiasm to the supposed social or ideological patterns of the region. In fact, the ruling elites in East Anglia, with the possible exception of that of Essex, were the passive recipients of legislation passed by factions at Westminster, and their innate attitudes, far from being characterized by active enthusiasm, were similar to those of the south-eastern counties which hampered Sir William Waller in the organization of his army. Their outlooks were marked by hesitation, uncertainty and defensively-oriented localism.

In the autumn of 1642 the ruling gentry of the eastern counties, in so far as they had considered an Association, sought a defensive alliance; when Parliament passed legislation based upon the divisive Covenant-Shibboleth favored by the radicals at Westminster and in the City of London the majority of the local governors neglected it for two months until finally persuaded of the immediate danger of invasion and internal insurrection. In 1643, when the Association was ordered to send its forces under Lord Grey to assist the Lord

General's army in the Thames valley, the defensively-oriented localism, apparent at the inception of the Association, persisted. The counties were reluctant to surrender their individual autonomy. They hesitated to allow the troops they had raised to serve other than in the immediate defense of their localities; they placed a higher financial priority upon local defense projects, such as the building of fortifications, than on the maintenance of their contingents with Grey or Cromwell; they neglected the Cambridge Committee, disregarding its instructions, its appeals for supply, and their duty of providing commissioners. These policies survived the supersession of Grey by Manchester and the rapid build-up of the army of the Association in the autumn of 1643: money was still not forwarded to Cambridge, and, as their response to Dyve's October raid demonstrated, the counties refused to subordinate local defense to the collective welfare of the Association as defined by the central Committee.

The Parliamentary legislation of January 1644, by which Manchester's army was established as a major national force, severely restricted the independent authority which the individual counties had previously been able to exercise. They could no longer influence policy and lost control of military appointments; worse, the agents of the centralized administration established by the Earl increasingly interfered in local affairs, traditionally the bailiwick of the county gentry. Yet, although an organization like that headed by Weaver was anathema, opposition in the constituent counties was restricted to ineffectual protests to Westminster and limited local resistance until the late summer of 1644. At this time Manchester's disillusionment with the progress of the war and his justification of his refusal to contemplate decisive military action in terms of his primary obligation to defend the eastern counties gave the gentry the opportunity to reassert, in his support, the localist ideal of the function of the Association upon which they had always insisted: 'that our owne troopes may be imployed for the safety of our owne countyes' – 'the safety of the Kingdome was not our worke'. However, despite the unanimity displayed by the representatives of the counties at Bury in January 1645 in opposition to the proposed military reorganization which 'dothe impaire the Associacion', their protests were completely neglected by Parliament as the New Model legislation was pushed through. Further Bury conferences voiced the eastern counties' dissatisfaction with aspects of Westminster's policy, but the local gentry never directly refused to execute the legislation to which they objected.

The gentry of the eastern counties were not enthusiastic proponents of the vigorous prosecution of the war. Throughout the period they viewed the Association as an organization designed primarily to secure their counties from invasion or insurrection, and, as appeared in 1643, even their enthusiasm for collective security was limited by their prior concern for the immediate defense of their own localities. They objected to the organization of a semi-national force under Manchester in 1644, as they did to the New Model a year later, because both involved increased demands for men and supplies, the interference of centralized agencies designed to secure the latter, and the subordination of local defense to the broader war aims of the majority at Westminster. The East Anglian gentry, like their counterparts in the south-eastern counties, sought to retain local control over local resources for local needs. The major reason for the success of the Eastern Association was that Manchester was granted a legislative authority never allowed Denbigh or Waller, which enabled him to override the localism of the indigenous authorities within the region. But this suggests that there were limits to the local particularism of the gentry; as appeared in January 1644 and again in the wake of the Bury conference, localism was a visceral not an intellectual sentiment. The gentry's personal social ties, administrative experience, economic and intellectual interests, and hence their immediate loyalties, might focus on their county/country, but when faced with the categorical demands of the central legislature they could not transmute insular sentiment into an intellectual justification of privileged local or regional autonomy. The Tudors had done their work well: although its practical manifestations might meet limited resistance, the theoretical sovereignty of the nation state was unchallenged.

Appendix 1

The marriage connections of the East Anglian gentry in 1640

County	No. in group	A	B	C	D	E	F	G	H	I
Essex										
Knights and barts.	46	28.3	2.2	X	4.4	–	6.5	10.9	15.2	32.6
Gentry	263	43.3	1.6	X	3.4	–	3.4	10.6	16.4	20.5
Hertfordshire										
Knights and barts.	16	31.3	–	–	X	6.3	6.3	6.3	25.0	25.0
Gentry	123	37.4	1.6	4.9	X	–	3.3	2.4	20.3	30.1
Norfolk										
Knights and barts.	34	44.1	8.8	–	2.9	–	X	20.6	5.9	17.6
Gentry	282	71.6	1.4	5.0	0.7	–	X	10.3	2.5	8.5
Suffolk										
Knights and barts.	21	42.9	4.8	4.8	–	–	14.3	X	9.5	23.9
Gentry	329	69.0	3.4	6.7	0.3	0.3	12.2	X	3.1	5.2
Huntingdonshire in 1613	54	24.0	7.4	1.9	3.7	X	3.7	1.9	1.9	55.5
Cambridgeshire in 1619	129	36.4	X	9.3	3.9	1.6	10.9	11.6	2.3	24.0

Key: A = percentage of marriages within the home county: B = with Cambridgeshire: C = with Essex: D = with Hertfordshire: E = with Huntingdonshire: F = with Norfolk: G = with Suffolk: H = with London: I = with other counties.

Sources: Essex: W. C. Metcalfe (ed.), *The Visitations of Essex*, 2 vols. (1878, 1879). Hertfordshire: W. C. Metcalfe (ed.), *The Visitations of Hertfordshire* (1886). Norfolk: A. Campling and A. W. H. Clarke (eds.), *The Visitation of Norfolk 1664*, 2 vols. (1933, 1934); A. Campling (ed.), *East Anglian Pedigrees*, 2 vols. (1939, 1945). Suffolk: W. C. Metcalfe (ed.), *The Visitations of Suffolk* (Exeter, 1882); J. J. Muskett, *Suffolk Manorial Families*, 3 vols. (Exeter, 1900–10). Huntingdonshire: Henry Ellis (ed.), *The visitation of the County of Huntingdon ... A.D. MDCXIII* (1849). Cambridgeshire: J. W. Clay (ed.), *The Visitation of Cambridge* (1897).

Manorial holdings in East Anglia in 1640
(see pages 12–15)

County	A	B	C
Essex	780	63 (8.1%)	65 (8.3%)
Hertfordshire	323	17 (5.3%)	28 (8.7%)
Norfolk	755	64 (8.5%)	36 (4.8%)
Suffolk	780	87 (11.2%)	39 (5.0%)
Huntingdonshire	121	9 (7.4%)	27 (22.3%)

Notes: A. The number of manors in the respective counties where the ownership can be recognized in this period. I have corrected this total to exclude all manors held by the King, the Church or other corporate bodies, and, for Norfolk and Suffolk, the manorial holdings of the Earl of Arundel.

B. The number and percentage of manors held by persons not resident in the county in question, but living in East Anglia.

C. The number and percentage of manors held by outsiders.

Sources: Essex: P. Morant, *The history and antiquities ... of Essex*, 2 vols. (Colchester, 1768); *V.C.H.*, *Essex*, vols. IV and V (1956, 1966). Hertfordshire: *V.C.H.*, *Hertfordshire*, vols. II, III and IV (1908, 1912, 1914). Huntingdonshire: *V.C.H.*, *Huntingdonshire*, vols. II and III (1932, 1936). Norfolk: F. Blomfield (completed by C. Parkin), *An essay towards a topographical history of the county of Norfolk*, 11 vols. (1805–10). Suffolk: W. A. Copinger, *The manors of Suffolk*, 7 vols. (Manchester, 1908–11).

Appendix 3

The antiquity of the East Anglian gentry of political eminence in 1642[a] (see pages 12–15)

| County | No. in group | The percentage of those whose families had settled in the county in question | | |
		before 1485	1485–1603	after 1603
Essex	59	15.25	50.85	33.90
Hertfordshire	40	10.00	47.50	42.50
Norfolk	59	42.37	44.07	13.56
Suffolk	59	30.51	50.85	18.64

Sources: those listed in Appendices 1 and 2.

[a] The group consists of those gentlemen who were either appointed by Parliament to serve on the local committee before 1 April 1643 (from *Firth and Rait*, I), or were named by the King to execute the Commission of Array (from Northamptonshire Record Office, Finch-Hatton Ms., no. 133).

Appendix 4

Receipts and disbursements of the Committee of the Association, April–November 1643 (see pages 101–2)

Total disbursement = £6916-10-4d for 'common' charges

County	Sum owed by each of the constituent counties, according to the 'rules of proportion' established by the Committee of East Anglian M.P.s (£s)	Sum paid (£s)	Difference (£s)
Cambridgeshire	559-10-2d	2327-3-4d	+1767-13-2d
Isle of Ely	279-15-1d	698-1-11½d	+ 418-6-10½d
Essex	1678-10-6d	238-7-8d	−1440-2-10d
Hertfordshire	559-10-2d	1672-16-0d	+1113-5-10d
Huntingdonshire	202-8-5½d	78-0-0d	− 124-8-5½d
Norfolk	1678-10-6d	531-13-10½d	−1146-16-7½d
Norwich	279-15-1d	33-6-6d	− 246-8-7d
Suffolk	1678-10-6d	811-12-0d	− 866-18-6d

Sources: P.R.O. 30/15/3 no. 522; Tanner 62 ff. 70, 353.

Appendix 5

Sums raised upon the review of the Fifth and Twentieth part in the Eastern Association (excluding Lincolnshire) (see pages 131–3)

County	Sum raised (£s)	Percentage of total	Percentage of estimated total wealth of the eastern counties[a]
Cambridgeshire	7,802	11.90	8.0
Isle of Ely	43	0.01	4.0
Essex	12,397	18.91	24.0
Hertfordshire	3,925	5.99	8.0
Huntingdonshire	232	0.35	4.0
Norfolk	19,770	30.16	28.0
Suffolk	21,375	32.61	24.0

Sources: S.P. 28/139 unfol., the account of John Weaver, ff. 11, 32v–36v. As Weaver gives no total for the Isle of Ely, I have calculated the sum from the parish accounts in S.P. 28/152 parts 5 and 6.

[a] These are the proportions which the Committee of East Anglian M.P.s felt would be equitable for every county to bear in a general levy upon the Association.

Appendix 6

Sources for the account of the pay of the army
(see pages 142–5)

Any attempt to determine accurately the amount of pay officially received b
troops and companies in the Association's army, and the times at which the
were paid, from the centralization of the Treasury in January 1644 to the forma
tion of the New Model in April 1645, is hampered by the only partial survival o
the accounts of Gawsell and Leman. In 1645 the officials of the central Com
mittee of Accounts held three distinct series of account books for the Association
that of Gawsell, those of Leman, and the 'Red Book' (S.P. 28/267 ff. 50, 300
The former, in which was entered every individual sum paid to each captain b
Gawsell while he was in attendance upon the army in 1644 has disappeared, b
an abstract, in which is entered merely the *total* amount paid to each troop an
company has survived, and has been transcribed by Godfrey Davies, 'The Arm
of the Eastern Association', *E.H.R.*, vol. 46 (1931), pp. 88–96. Leman's disburse
ments in the same period were entered in 'county' books, of which two surviv
that for the Association (S.P. 28/128 unfol.), in which were entered all paymen
for arms, fortifications, the expenses of the Cambridge Committee, and to troo
not raised in any particular county, and that for Suffolk, containing an accoun
of his receipts from that county and disbursements upon forces raised the
(S.P. 28/143 unfol.). The remaining county books, with the exception of thr
pages from that for Hertfordshire badly damaged by damp (S.P. 28/6 ff. 46–7
and the 'Red Book', in which all payments made in 1645 by Gawsell or Lema
were recorded, have been lost; but fortunately an 'Alphabet Book' exists in whic
a clerk wrote the totals from each of the Treasury Books (S.P. 28/197 part 2,
26–47). Equally patchy are the surviving debentures and warrants signed by th
Cambridge Committee, and using them is not made easier by the failure of tho
who arranged the S.P. 28 class to agree upon a uniform system. Originally the
warrants were kept on files, of which one survives in its original state (S.P. 28/2
unfol., the bundle marked 'Mr. Leman's vouchers, 29th April–20th May'); t
files were broken up when the collection was organized in its present form, a
while some were arranged by Regiment (S.P. 28/25 ff. 1–114; 26 ff. 524–9
602–88, 700–4) most were arranged by date and are now scattered in volum
15–26 of the S.P. 28 class. The Treasurers appear to have retained their acqu
tance books (S.P. 28/18 f. 392), but one has found its way into the collecti
(S.P. 28/26 ff. 115–33).

The partial survival of the account-books and warrants of the Treasurers mak
it extremely difficult to determine the exact date at which pay was disbursed to
individual troop or company, and the sum paid on each occasion. But this di
culty can be overcome to a degree by supplementing the existing Treasury recor
with the claims filed with the central Committee of Accounts by ex-officers
the army of the Association seeking the payment of their arrears. However, the
statements must be handled with great caution. The central Committee dema
ded that officers' claims for arrears should be validated by the production o
complete account of all the sums that had passed through their hands prior
their disbandment or taking commissions in the New Model. But the offic
probably had little technical ability to undertake this task and less inclinatic
and many made no attempt to present a coherent or accurate account, usua
with the excuse that the relevant documents had been mislaid, stolen or captur

by the enemy (S.P. 28/36 ff. 300–6; 171 unfol., account of Captain Harvey; 257 unfol., accounts of Captain Porter and Major Jubbs): Lieutenant-General Hammond claimed that his accounts were irreparably damaged when a wagon overturned in a river! (S.P. 28/359 unfol., undated letter to central Committee of Accounts.) Other Captains merely account for their personal pay, making no mention of sums issued them for the use of their troops (S.P. 28/33 ff. 390–2; 49 ff. 67–8; 265 ff. 335–41, 405–14). This general reluctance to produce accounts must be borne in mind when interpreting documents produced by Captains who purport to account for all their receipts. Generally aware of the total sum charged against their account from the books of the Treasurers of the Association, they acknowledge receipt of the money, but their statements of when and how they received it, often demonstrably fictitious (S.P. 28/267 ff. 258–68), must be qualified by consideration of Captain Silverwood's ingenuous 'the . . . monies . . . was received to the best of my remembrance and paid out as hereafter' (S.P. 28/267 ff. 290–300). But such accounts, if used with caution, can illuminate the system of payment used in the Association's army, and the historian is assisted in his critical assessment of their validity by the survival of two near-perfect accounts, produced by the Scottish professional soldiers, Major Holmes (S.P. 28/42 ff. 637–51) and Captain Johnson (S.P. 28/265 ff. 114–23, 126, 166–7, 196, 209).

Appendix 7

Estimates of the pay of the army (see pages 158–61)

I. **The 'ideal establishment'** (the cost of the army which the Association was expected to raise and maintain in the spring of 1644: 10,000 foot, 2000 dragoons and 3000 cavalry).

A. *Infantry:* the press believed that 10,000 foot were to be raised; using the figures of the Barrington estimate (Egerton 2651 ff. 163–4), the infantry would consist of 9 regiments, each of 8 companies (72 companies), a total of 9340 men.

    Monthly pay of the officers = £3668-5-0d
    Monthly pay of the men = £9469-14-6d

B. *Dragoons:* 2000 dragoons, assumed to be organized in 2 full regiments, each of 10 companies.

    Monthly pay of the officers = £1533-0-0d
    Monthly pay of the men = £4562-10-0d

C. *Cavalry:* 3000 horse, assumed to be arranged in 4 regiments, 2 of 10 troops each, 2 of 5 troops each (thus approximating to the actual situation in the army of the Association in early 1644).

    Monthly pay of the officers = £3637-16-8d
    Monthly pay of the men = £11,406-5-0d

Total = £34,277-11-2d

II. **The September 1644 muster of the army**

A. *Infantry:* 9 regiments (Manchester's, Crawford's, Russell's, Montagu's, Pickering's, Hobart's, Palgrave's, Walton's, Ayloffe's: Rainborow's is excluded as it was paid directly by the committee of Lincolnshire); 95 companies (on the assumption that Walton's and Ayloffe's regiments, for which no muster rolls survive, each consisted of 9 companies). Average no. of common soldiers per company in the regiments mustered = 51.82. Therefore estimated no. of soldiers in pay = 4923 footmen.

    Monthly pay of the officers = £5027-14-11d
    Monthly pay of the men = £4991-7-6d

B. *Dragoons:* only one company of the dragoons was formally mustered in September. In January 1645 the dragoons were organized in a regiment of 5 companies, and totaled 263 men; Mercer's company, which was 74 strong in January, totaled 77 men in September, and this close correlation suggests that it would not be unreasonable to use the January figures as an indication of the cost of the dragoon regiment in September.

    Monthly pay of the officers = £371-16-10d
    Monthly pay of the men = £599-19-4d

C. *Cavalry:* In September 40 troops of horse, including one of 'Reformadoes', were in service, organized in 5 regiments. Average no. of men in each troop mustered = 99. Therefore estimated no. of men in pay = 3960 troopers.

    Monthly pay of the officers = £5474-4-10d
    Monthly pay of the men = £15,056-5-0d

Total = £31,521-8-5d

III. **The January–February 1645 muster of the army**

A. *Infantry:* 10 regiments (as September + Sparrow's); 103 companies. Average no. of common soldiers in a company of the regiments mustered = 40.78. Therefore estimated no. of soldiers in pay = 4200.

    Monthly pay of the officers = £5440-8-0d
    Monthly pay of the men = £4258-6-8d

B. *Dragoons* (as September totals)
    Monthly pay of the officers = £371-16-10d
    Monthly pay of the men = £599-19-4d

C. *Cavalry:* at the beginning of 1645 44 troops, including one of Reformadoes, organized in 5 regiments, were in service. Average number of men in each troop mustered = 85.10. Therefore estimated no. of troopers in pay = 3744.

    Monthly pay of the officers = £6009-11-5d
    Monthly pay of the men = £14,236-10-5d

Total = £30,916-12-8d

Appendix 8

Infantry strength of the army of the Association (see pages 162–9)

(A) The four major musters of the field army

Regiment	(1) May 1644	(2) July 1644	(3) September 1644	(4) January 1645
Manchester	1628	1053	1111[a]	984
Crawford	850	608	396	267
Pickering	738	524	362	243
Hobart	883	593[b]	400	(254)[c]
Montagu	759	418	307	(285)[c]
Russell	932	662	771	422
Palgrave, then Hoogan	804	741[d] 801[d]	633	526[e]
Total	6594	4629[f]	3980	2981

Sources: S.P. 28/15 ff. 255–89; 16 ff. 135–53, 163–5; 17 ff. 183–201, 204–8, 310–314; 23 f. 341; 24 ff. 365, 392; 25 ff. 1–114, 252–4; 26 ff. 295–7, 341–5, 455–8, 466–9, 483–6, 524–96, 602–88, 700–854; 27 ff. 262–3, 290–9, 310–14.

[a] Manchester's regiment was mustered on 26 August, not in mid-September, as were the other regiments.

[b] Hobart's regiment was not mustered in July, but upon 12 August.

[c] No musters survive for Hobart's and Montagu's regiments in January; I have calculated the approximate no. of men present from the sum paid to the two regiments by the Treasury.

[d] Palgrave's regiment, on garrison duty in Lincoln during the summer months, was twice mustered between June–August; the actual dates of these musters are uncertain.

[e] Hoogan's regiment was mustered in February.

[f] I have used a figure of 771 men for Palgrave's regiment.

(B) Detailed muster returns for the companies of Major Holmes and Captain Johnson, of Manchester's regiment

Muster	Holmes	Johnson
1644 25 February	87	87
11 April	123	90
8 May	115	94
21 July	71	46
26 August	(72)[a]	43
1645 1 January	64	51
17 February	41	38
31 March	34	26

Sources: S.P. 28/42 f. 643; 265 ff. 121–2

[a] Holmes's return omits this figure; I have taken it from the relevant debenture (S.P. 28/17 f. 186).

(C) **Muster rolls of Captain Harvey, of Hobart's regiment**

In March 1644 Harvey commanded a company of 107 men (A). On 8 May he received a recruit of 25 men (B), and a further body of 55 recruits about 1 October. The number of these men present at subsequent musters can be tabulated:

Muster	(A) original company	(B) May recruits	(C) October recruits
	(107)	(25)	(55)
30 March 1644	107	X	X
25 May	66	25	X
25 August	57	17	X
19 September	41	5	X
13 December	29	5	35
3 January	27	2	17

Source: S.P. 28/171 unfol., the account of Richard Harvey.

Appendix 9

The returns for those cavalry troops which were mustered on three occasions (see pages 170–3)

| Captain | Number of troopers present | | |
	April 1644[a]	September 1644[b]	January 1645[c]
Alford	98	113	106
Dingley	87	107	85
Griffen	42	43	60
Hammond	72	88	62
Knights	63	68	78
Samuel Moody	81	106	96
Rich	114	122	123
Vermuyden	100	108	119

Sources:
  [a] S.P. 28/13 f. 220; 14 ff. 145, 161–2; 24 f. 355; 25 ff. 437, 448; 28 f. 198.
  [b] S.P. 28/17 ff. 382–6, 389, 391–2, 396.
  [c] S.P. 28/26 ff. 8, 63, 71; 27 ff. 124, 128, 136, 138, 141.

Notes

In citation from contemporary documents punctuation has been modernized and abbreviations have been extended. Dates are given in the old-style calendar, except that the year is regarded as beginning on 1 January, not 25 March.

Introduction

1. This and the previous quotations are taken from Alfred Kingston, *East Anglia and the Great Civil War* (1897), pp. 2, 3.

2. Lord Grey's Association has not been studied in depth, but from A. C. Wood's work, *Nottinghamshire in the Civil War* (Oxford, 1937), pp. 31–2, 44–8, it appears that he concerned himself almost entirely with the forces of his native Leicestershire and allowed the local commanders in Nottinghamshire and Derbyshire virtually complete freedom of action. The peripheral counties acted with even less respect to their obligation to the Midland Association: in February 1643 the Buckinghamshire Committee made a unilateral attempt to join the Eastern Association (Alan Everitt, *Suffolk and the Great Rebellion* (Ipswich, 1961), pp. 40–1) and in May Huntingdonshire was detached from Grey's authority and brought within the Eastern Association (*C.J.*, III, p. 102).

3. For a general discussion of Denbigh's difficulties, see D. H. Pennington and Ivan Roots, *The Committee at Stafford 1643–1645* (Manchester, 1957), pp. lxxiv–lxxxiii; D. H. Pennington, 'County and Country: Staffordshire in Civil War Politics, 1640–1644', *North Staffordshire Journal of Field Studies*, vol. 6 (1966), pp. 17–18, 20–3. For the Earl's abortive attempts to assert his authority, see *H.M.C.*, 4th Report, Appendix 1 (1874), pp. 262, 263, 264, 269, 270; Add. 18779 ff. 19, 20v, 28, 28v. For the huge arrears of his forces, see S.P. 28/257 unfol., the account of Captain Smith; 265 f. 352.

4. John Adair, *Roundhead General* (1969), *passim*; Alan Everitt, *The Community of Kent and the Great Rebellion* (Leicester, 1966), pp. 149, 186–7, 201–2, 208–11; G. N. Godwin, *The Civil War in Hampshire, 1642–1645* (Southampton, 1904), p. 71; Sir William Waller, *Vindication of the character and conduct of Sir William Waller* (1793), p. 17.

5. See Ian Roy, 'The Royalist Army in the first civil war' (unpub. D.Phil. thesis, Oxford, 1963), pp. 66–8.

6. Everitt, *Suffolk*, p. 21.

Chapter 1

1. Christopher Hill, *The Century of Revolution* (1961), pp. 121–3.

2. *C.S.P.D.*, 1633–4, p. 298; 1637, p. 64; *A.P.C.*, 1619–21, pp. 79–80; *The clothiers petition to His Majestie* (1642), *passim*. See also *The humble petition of the bailifes . . . of Ipswich* (1641), pp. 2–3; B. F. Supple, *Commercial crisis and change in England, 1600–1642* (Cambridge, 1964), pp. 25–6, 62, 100–2, 128–31.

3. Tanner 68 ff. 147, 151–2.

4. F. J. Fisher, 'The development of the London food market, 1540–1640', *Economic History Review*, 1st series, vol. v (1934–5), p. 51.

5. Joan Thirsk (ed.), *The Agrarian History of England and Wales*, vol. IV (Cambridge, 1967), pp. 50–3; *C.S.P.D.*, 1625–6, p. 107; 1629–31, p. 485.

6. Lord Francis Hervey (ed.), *Suffolk in the XVIIth Century: the Breviary of Suffolk by Robert Reyce (1618)* (1902), pp. 13, 41; *C.S.P.D.*, 1629–31, pp. 202, 206; N. J. Williams, 'The maritime trade of the East Anglian Ports, 1550–1590' (unpub. D.Phil. thesis, Oxford, 1952), pp. 7, 175–89; Fisher, 'London food market', p. 47.

7. *C.S.P.D.*, 1634–5, p. 252; 1640, pp. 622, 634, 647; S.P. 16/327/101; Peter Heylyn, *Cyprianus Anglicus: or the history of . . . Laud* (1669), p. 288; Tanner 68 ff. 88, 90; E.R.O., T/B 211/1 no. 18.

8. Thirsk (ed.), *Agrarian History*, pp. 12, 173–4, 526; *A.P.C.*, 1623–5, p. 44; 1628–9, pp. 353–4; 1629–30, pp. 128–9; Add. 5508 f. 13.

9. C. B. Jewson (ed.), *Transcript of three registers of passengers from Great Yarmouth to Holland and New England, 1637–1639* (Norwich, 1954), *passim*; Tanner 68 f. 157.

10. S.P. 16/148/40; Tanner 68 f. 82.

11. Heylyn, *Cyprianus Anglicus*, pp. 276–81; *C.S.P.D.*, 1635, pp. 340–2; Harold Smith, *The Ecclesiastical History of Essex under the Long Parliament and Commonwealth* (Colchester, n.d.), p. 52; Raymond P. Stearns, *Congregationalism in the Dutch Netherlands* (Chicago, 1940), *passim*; C. B. Jewson, 'The English Church at Rotterdam and its Norfolk connections', *Norfolk Archaeology*, vol. 30 (1952–4), pp. 324–37.

12. Tanner 68 ff. 277, 279, 283, 285. For a similar affair in 1633, see *C.S.P.D.*, 1633–4, p. 113.

13. S.P. 29/6/53.

14. Everitt, *Suffolk*, p. 100; Christopher Morris (ed.), *The journeys of Celia Fiennes* (1949), p. 145; H. C. Darby, *The Draining of the Fens* (Cambridge, 1940), p. 23. For co-operation between the Fen villages to resist the drainers, see S.P. 16/230/50; 16/392/45, 54.

15. Lawrence Stone, *The causes of the English Revolution, 1529–1642* (1972), p. 56.

16. Professor Everitt (*Suffolk*, p. 21) argues this case.

17. P. J. Bowden, *The Wool Trade in Tudor and Stuart England* (1962), pp. 64–5; Thirsk (ed.), *Agrarian History*, pp. 33, 41, 508, 526.

18. Williams, 'Maritime Trade', pp. 63–4; *A.P.C.*, 1621–3, pp. 486–8.

19. The seminal work in this respect was Peter Laslett's 'The gentry of Kent in 1640', *Cambridge Historical Journal*, vol. IX (1947–9), pp. 149–64. Laslett's thesis has since been developed in detail by Alan Everitt see his *Kent*, pp. 13–35; *Change in the Provinces: the Seventeenth Century* (Leicester, 1969), pp. 5–35; *The Local Community and the Great Rebellion* (1969), *passim*), from whose work the following discussion is largely derived.

20. Besides the works of Professor Everitt, cited in note 19, see David Underdown, *Pride's Purge* (Oxford, 1971), pp. 22–44, 297–335.

21. Everitt, *Suffolk*, pp. 21–2.

22. See Appendices 1–3 for a discussion and tabulation of these figures.

23. For example, though in Yorkshire and Leicestershire only approximately two-fifths, and in Northamptonshire just over a quarter of the gentry could trace their family's tenure of their estates into the pre-Tudor period, yet in none of them was there any move to surrender county autonomy to a centralized regional Association (see J. T. Cliffe, *The Yorkshire Gentry* (1969), p. 13; Everitt, *Local Community*, p. 21).

24. For the settlement of courtiers and civil servants in Essex and Hertfordshire, see G. E. Aylmer, *The King's Servants* (1961), pp. 268, 271: B. W. Quintrell,

'The government of the county of Essex, 1603–1642' (unpub. Ph.D. thesis, London, 1965), pp. 12–13, lists some of the major gentry families who owed their estates in that county to wealth accumulated in London.

25. The marriage alliances of the Cambridgeshire gentry can be constructed for 1613, but not for 1640 (see Appendix 1); the *V.C.H.* for the county (vol. IV (1953)) covers the manorial history of the Isle of Ely, but it would obviously be illegitimate to generalize from the peculiar patterns of the Fenland to those of the county as a whole.

26. *C.S.P.D.*, 1625–6, p. 139. The statistical information is from *V.C.H.*, *Huntingdonshire*, vols. II and III (1931, 1936), *passim*, and Sir Henry Ellis (ed.), *The visitation of the county of Huntingdon . . . A.D. MDCXIII* (1849), *passim*.

Chapter 2

1. Smith, *Ecclesiastical history of Essex*, p. 33.

2. See Wren's 1639 visitation, as reviewed in *V.C.H.*, *Cambridgeshire*, vol. II (1948), pp. 180–1, and the Bishop's report to Laud (W. Scott and J. Bliss (eds.), *The works of . . . William Laud*, vol. V (1853), pp. 365–7). For Huntingdonshire, see *V.C.H.*, *Huntingdonshire*, vol. I (1926), pp. 366–8.

3. Excellent detailed accounts of the strength of Puritanism in the Norfolk boroughs are provided by K. W. Shipps, 'Lay patronage of East Anglian Puritan clerics in pre-Revolutionary England' (unpub. Ph.D. thesis, Yale, 1971), pp. 216–42, 267–99, 304–13.

4. H. of L.M.P., 9 June 1641, the petition of Matthew Brooks; S.P. 16/124/81; 16/171/9; Tanner 68 ff. 88, 90; N.R.O., VIS/6 *sub* Yarmouth.

5. S.P. 16/531/134; Egerton 2716 f. 263; Tanner 68 ff. 147, 149, 151–3, 157, 162, 180, 236, 238, 240, 267, 271.

6. *Ibid.*, ff. 232, 234, 236, 242, 312; S.P. 16/382/16.

7. For prosecutions, see D. W. Boorman, 'The administrative and disciplinary problems of the church on the eve of the civil war in the light of the extant records of the dioceses of Norwich and Ely under Bishop Wren' (unpub. B.Litt. thesis, Oxford, 1959), pp. 61–88. For gentry patronage, see Shipps, 'Lay patronage', pp. 142–50.

8. Scott and Bliss (eds.), *Works of Laud*, vol. V, p. 339; Tanner 68 f. 113. For Wren's difficulties with Ipswich, see Shipps, 'Lay patronage', pp. 243–66.

9. For the appointment of Puritans, see *ibid.*, pp. 144–7; Boorman, 'Administrative and disciplinary problems', pp. 85–8: for appeals on behalf of suspended ministers, see Tanner 68 ff. 96, 121, 127: for chaplains and schoolmasters, *ibid.*, f. 207: for lectures, *ibid.*, ff. 92, 113, 207: for refusal to observe, and protests against, the ceremonies, *ibid.*, ff. 200, 221v; R. F. Williams (ed.), *The court and times of Charles I* (1848), vol. 2, p. 277.

10. *V.C.H.*, *Hertfordshire*, vol. IV (1914), pp. 336–40.

11. See Shipps, 'Lay Patronage', pp. 141–4, 379–81 for prosecutions; *ibid.*, pp. 185–6, 206, 409 for Warwick's patronage.

12. Smith, *Ecclesiastical history of Essex*, pp. 66–7, 413–16; S.P. 16/427/30.

13. Cotton Mather, *Magnalia Christi Americana* (1702), book 3, p. 60.

14. S.P. 16/175/104; Lord Braybrooke (ed.), *The autobiography of Sir John Bramston* (1845), p. 124.

15. Smith, *Ecclesiastical history of Essex*, pp. 30–5; Mather, *Magnalia Christi*, book 3, pp. 43–4; R. P. Stearns, *The Strenuous Puritan* (Urbana, 1954), pp. 30–3, 41, 44; E.R.O., T/B 211/1 no. 39; Jeremiah Burroughes, *A vindication of Mr*

Burroughes against Mr Edwards (1646), pp. 18–19. For another Puritan minister who took refuge at Warwick's house, see (Samuel Butler), *A letter from Mercurius Civicus to Mercurius Rusticus* (Oxford, 1643), p. 8.

16. Edmund Calamy, *A patterne for all* (1658), p. 36. See also *C.S.P.D.*, 1640, p. 278.

17. Percentages are calculated from M. D. Gordon, 'The collection of Ship-Money in the reign of Charles I', *T.R.H.S.*, 3rd series, vol. 4 (1910), pp. 141–62. R. W. Ketton-Cremer, *Norfolk in the Civil War* (1971), pp. 89–103, has detailed the experiences of the sheriffs of Norfolk in the 1630s.

18. V. A. Rowe, 'Robert, Second Earl of Warwick and the Payment of Ship-Money in Essex', *T.E.A.S.*, 3rd series, vol. 1 (1964–5), pp. 160–3; *C.S.P. Ven.*, 1636–9, pp. 124–5; Quintrell, 'Government of Essex', pp. 337–44.

19. S.P. 16/449/48. See also Egerton 2646 f. 142; Harleian 454 f. 30 for accounts of the election. For Neville's Laudian sympathies, see *A True and Perfect Diurnal*, no. 11 *sub* 2 September, and Smith *Ecclesiastical history of Essex*, p. 53.

20. M. F. Keeler, *The Long Parliament* (Philadelphia, 1954), pp. 97, 198; Shipps, 'Lay Patronage', pp. 107–13, 151–2.

21. For another minister's electioneering efforts on Warwick's behalf, see P.C. 2/52 f. 217v; E.R.O., T/B 211/1 no. 23.

22. Smith, *Ecclesiastical history of Essex*, p. 51; Keeler, *Long Parliament*, pp. 268–9.

23. Morant 43 f. 51. See also *ibid.*, f. 89; 47 f. 73; 48 f. 53.

24. Harleian 454 f. 36; W. D. Macray (ed.), *Clarendon's History of the Rebellion and Civil Wars in England* (Oxford, 1888), book 3, para. 5. For Warwick's influence in the borough, see E.R.O., D/B 3/3/149 f. 5; 3/3/205 f. 21.

25. Harleian 97 ff. 9, 11.

26. Tanner 69 f. 47; Add. 15084 f. 4; *C.S.P.D.*, 1640, pp. 333, 471; Clive Holmes, *The Suffolk Committees for Scandalous Ministers 1644–1646* (Ipswich, 1970), pp. 78–80.

27. Boorman, 'Administrative and disciplinary problems', p. 86; Tanner 68 f. 221v.

28. G. W. Robinson and others (eds.), *The Winthrop Papers* (Boston, 1929–47), vol. 4, p. 217. For Burrell, see S.P. 18/76/7; for Fairclough, see Samuel Clarke, *The Lives of Sundry Eminent Persons in this later age* (1683), part 1, pp. 162–4, 170; Shipps, 'Lay patronage', pp. 65–104.

29. Thomas Carlyle, *Critical and Miscellaneous Essays* (1869), vol. 7, pp. 61–74. See also Harleian 97 f. 8; 158 ff. 292–5; 286 f. 318.

30. Holmes, *Scandalous Ministers*, pp. 41, 50, 98.

31. Sir Robert Crane, William Waldegrave, John Clench and John Hobart of Weybread (see, in addition to the election narratives, Tanner 65 f. 124; 115 f. 131).

32. S.P. 16/437/91; William Prynne, *Newes from Ipswich: discovering practices of domineering lordly prelates* (Edinburgh, 1636), p. 3; Tanner 220 f. 7; Wallace Notestein (ed.), *The journal of Sir Symonds D'Ewes* (New Haven, 1923), pp. 327–8.

33. E.S.R.O., EE 1/01/1 f. 85.

34. Harleian 384 f. 65; Robinson (ed.), *Winthrop papers*, vol. 4, p. 243; Notestein (ed.), *D'Ewes's journal*, p. 119.

35. Keeler, *Long Parliament*, pp. 51, 126, 130, 172, 233–4; Lawrence Stone

'The Electoral Influence of the second Earl of Salisbury, 1614–1668', *E.H.R.*, vol. 71 (1956), pp. 384–400; Tanner 65 f. 164.

36. Keeler, *Long Parliament*, pp. 36, 56, 57. For Percivall and Toll's involvement in the Lynn lectureship, see Shipps, 'Lay patronage', pp. 304–13.

37. N.R.O., Norwich Court Book 1634–46, ff. 297v–299; Keeler, *Long Parliament*, pp. 56–7. The radicals returned for the city in the spring were Thomas Atkins (see Valerie Pearl, *London and the Outbreak of the Puritan Revolution* (Oxford, 1961), pp. 311–13), and John Toolie (Tanner 68 ff. 149, 162, 238). Besides Catelyn, Alderman Harman was elected in October; he was not involved with, either for or against, the 1636 petition, and was respected by Bishop Wren (Tanner 68 f. 336).

38. Tanner 65 f. 164.

39. Ketton-Cremer, *Norfolk in the Civil War*, pp. 104–13, provides transcripts of the relevant material from the Tanner Mss.: see also Egerton 2716 ff. 333, 335; 2722 f. 90.

40. John Vicars, *Jehovah-Jireh* (1642), pp. 78–9; Macray (ed.), *Clarendon's History*, book 4, paras. 200–3.

41. *L.J.*, IV, pp. 523, 539; *Three petitions: the one, of the inhabitants of . . . Colchester* (1642), *passim*. The rolls of signatures for the county petition to the Lords (H. of L.M.P., 20 January 1641/2) were constructed by cutting up the original village subscription lists, and then combining the cut pieces promiscuously. This makes it difficult to determine the location of support, or its organization. But a number of village lists, headed by the parish minister, have survived intact – e.g. Finchingfield (headed by Stephen Marshall); West Bergholt; Chipping Ongar; Ramsden Crays; Castle Hedingham; Marks Tey; Felsted; Braintree; Rochford; Earl's Colne.

42. *L.J.*, IV, pp. 535–6, 540; Harleian 162 f. 347v.

43. *L.J.*, IV, pp. 537–43; Macray (ed.), *Clarendon's History*, book 4, paras. 247–52.

44. *L.J.*, IV, p. 573; *C.J.*, II, pp. 404, 412; Harleian 162 ff. 360v, 367v. Ipswich presented a separate but generally similar petition on 12 February (*The humble petition of the bailifes . . . of Ipswich* (1641), *passim*).

45. Tanner 66 f. 181.

46. *C.J.*, II, pp. 428, 449; Harleian 162 f. 398v.

47. *C.J.*, II, pp. 466, 480, 497; *L.J.*, IV, p. 648.

48. *C.J.*, II, p. 466. No complete copies of the Norfolk or Huntingdonshire petitions survive: the pamphlet *The fovre petitions of Huntington shire* (1642) which purports to give copies of both is an obvious fraud.

49. C.U.L., Buxton Mss., Box 97 c. 69, 71, 115.

50. *The remonstrance and petition of the county of Huntingdon* (1641), *passim*; *L.J.*, IV, pp. 467, 469.

51. Calamy, *A patterne for all*, p. 34.

52. In 1636 the Puritan group on the corporation of Norwich who were petitioning the King against Wren consulted with the Ipswich Puritans (Tanner 68 f. 147).

53. Harleian 384 f. 21. See also Egerton 2645 f. 124.

54. Keeler, *Long Parliament*, pp. 263–4; Add. 15520 ff. 21–2.

55. Providence Island Company: Barrington, Gurdon, Barnardiston (A. P. Newton, *The colonising activities of the English Puritans* (New Haven, 1914), pp. 59, 127–8). Interested in the Massachusetts Bay settlement: Barrington, Eden,

Harlackenden, Mildmay, Gurdon, Barnardiston (*Massachusetts Historical Society: Collections*, 5th series, pp. 13, 83, 212). Patrons of non-conformists: Barrington, Harlackenden, Gurdon, Parker, Barnardiston, Soame (Shipps, 'Lay patronage', pp. 107–13, 120–2; Boorman, 'Administrative and disciplinary problems', p. 86; Smith, *Ecclesiastical history of Essex*, p. 33).

Chapter 3

1. *The Knyvett Letters*, p. 102.

2. Macray (ed.), *Clarendon's History*, book 6, para. 239; Everitt, *Kent*, pp. 84–124: local pacifications are examined in detail by Dr B. S. Manning in his unpublished Oxford D.Phil. thesis, 'Neutrals and neutralism in the English Civil War' (1957), chap. 2.

3. P.M., *True intelligence from Lincolne-shire* (1642), *passim*. For a narrative, see J. W. F. Hill, *Tudor and Stuart Lincoln* (Cambridge, 1956), pp. 148–52.

4. A number of pamphleteers who pressed the King and Parliament to come to an accommodation stressed the horrors of war as displayed in Germany and Ireland: see, for example, *Considerations upon the present state of the affairs of this kingdom* (1642), p. 3; *The grand plunderer* (1643), *passim*; *The miseries of war* (1643), pp. 10–11.

5. This is the leitmotif of the speeches of Sir Simonds D'Ewes favoring peace in the spring and summer of 1642 (see below, pp. 49–50), and it is to be found in a number of pamphlets on the same theme (e.g. (Thomas Povey), *The moderator, expecting sudden peace* (1642), pp. 7, 14). For a general discussion of the fear of popular insurrection, see Christopher Hill, 'The Many-Headed Monster' in *From the Renaissance to the Counter-Reformation* (ed. C. H. Carter, 1966), pp. 296–324.

6. Everitt, *Change in the Provinces*, p. 8.

7. The phrase is taken from Maurice Ashley, *The greatness of Oliver Cromwell* (1957), p. 98.

8. Egerton 2643 f. 7; *A true relation of the army set out by the county of Essex* (1642), no pagination. Other commentators stressed the county's primacy in support for the Parliamentary cause: see Morant 44 f. 81; *L.J.*, IX, pp. 71–2; Vicars, *Jehovah-Jireh*, p. 97; *A new found stratagem* (1647), p. 4; *The Essex watchmen's watchword* (1649), p. 2.

9. *L.J.*, IV, p. 707; V, pp. 85, 86; *C.J.*, II, pp. 586, 602.

10. *Ibid.*, pp. 597, 602, 605; *L.J.*, V, p. 96; Harleian 163 f. 141v; Tanner 63 f. 43; (Chestlin), *Persecutio undecima. The churches eleventh persecution* (1648), p. 34.

11. *L.J.*, V, pp. 117–18, 141–2, 143; *C.J.*, II, pp. 616, 629; *Some Speciall Passages*, no. 4, *sub* 17 June; (John Brookhaven), *A letter sent to Mr Speaker, from the commissioners in the county of Essex* (1642), *passim*; Egerton 2651 f. 123.

12. *L.J.*, V, pp. 203–4, 313; *C.J.*, II, pp. 666, 681, 711, 718, 730, 758; Stowe 189 f. 5; E. Hockliffe (ed.), *The diary of the Rev. Ralph Josselin, 1616–1680* (1908), p. 13; *An exact and true diurnall of the proceedings in Parliament* (15–22 August 1642), *sub* 17 August.

13. *C.J.*, II, pp. 705, 814; Harleian 163 f. 164v; Tanner 64 f. 15; *Remarkable Passages, or a Perfect Diurnall*, no. 11, *sub* 2 September; H. of L.M.P., 8 August 1642, petition of the volunteers of Rochford hundred.

14. Hockliffe (ed.), *Josselin's diary*, p. 13; John Wenlock, *To the most illustrious, high and mighty Majesty of Charles the II* (1662), p. 25.

15. The case of Edward Symmons is the best documented: see the introductory

epistle to his *A loyall subjects beliefe* (Oxford, 1643); his *Scripture vindicated* (Oxford, 1644/5), sig. A 3; (Bruno Ryves), *Mercurius Rusticus: or, the countries complaint* (1685), pp. 18–22; *L.J.*, v, p. 635. Other Essex ministers arrested or imprisoned in this period for anti-Parliamentary expressions were Cherry of Great Holland (Add. 34523 ff. 7, 11, 12); Browning of Easton (Harleian 162 f. 365; *C.J.*, ii, p. 408); Nicholson of Stapleford (*ibid.*, pp. 782, 878, 893; *A Perfect Diurnall of the Passages in Parliament*, no. 16, *sub* 26 September; Smith, *Ecclesiastical history of Essex*, p. 131); Withers of Kelvedon (*ibid.*, pp. 91–2; *C.J.*, ii, p. 829). This list may not be exhaustive as the earliest records of the Committee of Scandalous Ministers, before which many of these cases were heard, have disappeared.

16. Ryves, *Mercurius Rusticus*, pp. 1–7, 13, 14, 17, 33; *H.M.C.*, 10th Report, Appendix vi (1887), p. 147; Harleian 163 ff. 307v–308; C.U.L., Patrick Ms. 33 ff. 19–21; H. of L.M.P., 29 August 1642, petition of Elizabeth, Countess of Rivers.

17. Ryves, *Mercurius Rusticus*, pp. 2, 28–9; S.P. 16/539/100; S.P. 28/1 D f. 486; 17 f. 273; 145 f. 244v; 147 ff. 242–50; *A Perfect Diurnall of the Passages in Parliament*, no. 13, *sub* 7 September.

18. *L.J.*, v, pp. 406, 415–17; *C.J.*, ii, pp. 818, 823; Add. 31116 f. 3v.

19. *The valiant resolution of the seamen* (1642), *passim*; *C.J.*, ii, p. 838; *A Perfect Diurnall* (31 October–7 November); *ibid.* (7–14 November); *Speciall Passages*, no. 13, p. 112; S.P. 28/39 f. 122; *England's Memorable Accidents* (17–24 October); *Exceeding true and happy newes from the Castle of Windsor* (1642), *passim*; (Thomas Jordan), *London's ioyfull gratulation* (1642), *passim*.

20. *A true relation of the army set out by the county of Essex* (1642), *passim*; Hockliffe (ed.), *Josselin's diary*, p. 13. The meeting can be dated from the entry in Sir Humphrey Mildmay's diary (Harleian 454 f. 54), who drove to Chelmsford 'to see the foolery and impiety of the Earl of Warwick and his rabble'.

21. *C.J.*, ii, p. 859; *L.J.*, v, p. 454; *Speciall Passages*, no. 16 *sub* 22 November.

22. *Ibid.*, no. 12, p. 99; *C.S.P. Ven.*, 1642–3, p. 188; Morant 48 f. 11; *C.J.*, ii, p. 849.

23. Morant 46 f. 73; 47 f. 39; 48 ff. 71, 347; S.P. 28/263 f. 63.

24. P.R.O., 30/15/3 no. 506.

25. *L.J.*, v, pp. 280, 362; Vicars, *Jehovah-Jireh*, p. 149.

26. Neville collected munitions at his Cressing Temple house in the summer of 1642, and was eventually captured in arms in Leicestershire in early 1643 (*C.J.*, ii, pp. 814, 953; *A True and Perfect Diurnal*, no. 11 *sub* 2 September).

27. For some contemporary comment on the theme that Barrington's 'power in the county is greate', see Egerton 2643 f. 7; 2646 f. 255; 2647 f. 114; *The Kingdomes Weekly Intelligencer*, no. 76, p. 611.

28. Tanner 63 f. 43; *C.J.*, ii, p. 737. A further indication of the respective influence of Warwick and the M.P.s is provided by an otherwise unremarkable incident at Halstead in early 1642. The Bishop of London had appointed John Webb vicar of the parish, but the congregation, desiring to nominate their own minister, resisted his induction. Barrington and some other M.P.s wrote on Webb's behalf, but not until Warwick seconded the letter were the villagers pacified (Egerton 2646 f. 205).

29. *Exceeding true and happy newes from the Castle of Windsor* (1642), *passim*; *A Collection of Speciall Passages and Certaine Informations* (17 October–1 November), *sub* 27 October.

30. Richard Harlackenden, for example (Egerton 2646 f. 171), or the unnamed

J.P. with whom Wenlock debated politics in the spring and summer of 1642 (Wenlock, *To Charles the II*, pp. 21–2).

31. *A true relation of the army set out by the county of Essex* (1642), no pagination.

32. *L.J.*, v, p. 446; S.P. 28/3 B ff. 471, 501; Warwick, Robert Rich, earl of, *A most worthy speech* (1642), *passim*; *England's Memorable Accidents* (7–14 November), p. 73; (14–21 November), pp. 84–5; *A Perfect Diurnall of the Passages in Parliament* (21–28 November), *sub* 22 November; *Speciall Passages*, no. 16, p. 133; *The English intelligencer shewing* (1642), p. 6; Hockliffe (ed.), *Josselin's diary*, p. 13.

33. *L.J.*, v, p. 445; Morant 47 ff. 37, 45, 177.

34. *Ibid.*, ff. 37, 173; S.P. 28/3 B f. 471.

35. *Speciall Passages*, no. 16, p. 133; Morant 44 f. 99; 46 f. 75; 47 ff. 37, 43, 45, 64.

36. (Henry) Farre, *A speech spoken* (1642), *passim*. The newly appointed professional captains and adjutants are listed in S.P. 28/3A ff. 8–121.

37. *C.S.P.D.*, 1641–3, p. 349.

38. Egerton 2651 f. 118; *C.S.P.D.*, 1641–3, pp. 357, 362; *A Perfect Diurnall of the Passages in Parliament* (18–25 July), *sub* 23 July. It would be interesting to know who refused to sign the petition; the counter-petition, which Sir Thomas Barrington immediately put on foot, implies that a number of J.P.s and grand-jurymen did not sign (Egerton 2651 f. 119). Unfortunately the assize rolls, which could determine the point, are missing for this period.

39. The eight sequestered were Sir William Wiseman (recusancy), Sir John Tyrell, James Altham, John Greene (flight to areas controlled by the Royal armies – though none of them fought for the King), Sir Benjamin Ayloffe, Sir Thomas Bendish and Sir Francis Cooke (for anti-Parliamentary expressions or actions in Essex in early 1643). The six men who signed but later served on the county committee were Edward Eltonhead, James Herne, Sir Robert Kemp, Oliver Raymond, Robert Smith and William Toppesfield. (See *C.C.C.*, pp. 847, 848, 879, 885, 891, 3216; *C.J.*, ii, p. 994.)

40. Such an explanation may be appropriate to Robert Smith. As High Sheriff, Smith was in a particularly exposed position, and seems to have gone out of his way to avoid giving offence to either side: a month before presenting the 'loyal' petition at York, Smith had refused to read the King's Proclamations against the Militia Ordinance and surrendered the documents to Parliament. He was later one of the most active members of the Romford committee (*L.J.*, v, pp. 146, 149; B. W. Quintrell, 'The divisional committee for southern Essex during the Civil Wars, and its part in local administration' (unpub. M.A. thesis, Manchester, 1962, p. 172).

41. *C.S.P. Ven.*, 1642–3, p. 231; *L.J.*, v, p. 529; *The humble petition of the inhabitants of the County of Essex* (Oxford, 1642/3), *passim*.

42. *Ibid.*, p. 5; *Mercurius Aulicus*, no. 2, p. 13; *L.J.*, v, pp. 526, 530.

43. H. of L.M.P., 4 January 1643, the Essex petition for peace. The first organizational meeting appears to have been held at Chelmsford on 23 December (Harleian 454 f. 55v); the petition was presented twelve days later.

44. The six groups center on Clavering (9 parishes); Pentlow (7); Canfield (10); Gt Baddow (8); Hempstead (14); and Braxsted (33). The Baddow group centered on the estate of Sir Henry Mildmay of Moulsham; Canfield was the home of Sir William Wiseman, and the very full subscription from the adjacent town of Dunmow was headed by Sir Andrew Jennour; the Hempstead area contained

the estates of Sir Thomas Bendish (Steeple Bumpsted), the leading spirit behind the petition, and Sir William Halton (Little Samford); the large Braxsted group contained the homes of Sir Benjamin Ayloffe (Braxsted), Sir William Maxey (Bradwell), Sir Edward Bullock (Faulkbourn), Sir Thomas Wiseman (Rivenhall) and the wealthy Thomas Darcy Esq. (Pattiswick).

45. Add. 5828 ff. 30, 55–62.

46. *Gardiner*, i, pp. 86–8, 90–6; Pearl, *London*, pp. 254–8.

47. This point can only be illustrated by reference to certain men's behavior; diaries and correspondence do not survive. So on 11 July 1642 Parliament nominated 45 men as commissioners charged with the collection of money loaned upon the Propositions (*L.J*, v, pp. 203–4); 13 of these men, who were presumably thought sympathetic to the cause when appointed, signed the petition for peace. John Gawden of Bocking (see *D.N.B.*) may be representative of a number of ministers who initially supported Parliament, but then signed the petition for peace.

48. C.U.L., Patrick Ms. 33 f. 19; *C.J.*, ii, pp. 734, 736, 758; *L.J.*, v, p. 337; Harleian 163 ff. 307v–308.

49. *H.M.C.*, 10th Report, Appendix vi (1887), p. 147; C.U.L., Patrick Ms. 33 ff. 19–21. It was claimed by a London journalist (*An Exact and True Diurnal* (23–30 August 1642), *sub* 26 August) that in parts of Suffolk the rioters denied any religious motivation, saying that they were for the King, 'and would not be governed by a few Puritans'. No other source confirms this report, however.

50. *A Perfect Diurnall of the Passages in Parliament*, no. 14, *sub* 14 September; *Speciall Passages*, no. 3, p. 22; no. 7, p. 50; E.S.R.O., FB 19/I 2/1, warrant of 26 October; Harleian 454 f. 54v; Harleian 164 f. 273v; *C.J.*, ii, p. 881; *A Continuation of Certain Speciall and Remarkable Passages*, no. 21, p. 6. Besides the activities of the Stour valley mob there were enclosure riots in the west of the county (*C.J.*, ii, p. 759; *L.J.*, v, pp. 376, 526) and affrays in the Royal forests in the south (E.R.O., Q/SR 318 nos. 34–42; 319 nos. 23–40, 102–3; Q/SBa 2/48, 2/49, 2/55).

51. *L.J.*, vi, p. 21; H. of L.M.P., 28 June 1643, affidavit of John Parish and John Flaske.

52. The Sheriff of Essex refused to call out the *posse comitatus*, despite the pleas of some J.P.s, without first seeking Parliament's approval (*C.J.*, ii, p. 747); the Sheriff and J.P.s of Suffolk did mobilize forces but there was some debate about the propriety of this action (Harleian 163 f. 325; M. A. E. Green (ed.), *The Diary of John Rous* (1856), pp. 121–2).

53. H. of L.M.P., 2 May 1642, the affidavit of John Peacock. Wilson believed that the psychological effects of the political disputes were most important (C.U.L., Patrick Ms. 33 ff. 19–19v).

54. B.L., Firth Ms. C 4 pp. 488–500; *A.P.C.*, 1628–9 no. 1319; 1629–30 nos. 12, 77, 80; *C.S.P.D.*, 1628–9, p. 521; Supple, *Commercial crisis*, pp. 128–31.

55. (Harbottle Grimston), *Mr Grimstone, his Speech in Parliament on Wednesday the 19th of January* (1642), *passim*; John Pym, *A speech delivered at a conference ... January XXV, MDCXLI* (1642), *passim*. For some comment on these speeches, see Perez Zagorin, *The Court and the Country* (1969), pp. 298–9.

56. *The clothiers petition to His Majestie* (1642), *passim*; *C.J.*, ii, pp. 429, 528. It is possible that Parliament's success in recruiting in the Stour valley area was a function of the dislocation of the clothing industry.

57. *A message sent to the Parliament from the members* (1642), pp. 1–4; *A Continuation of Certain Speciall and Remarkable Passages*, no. 21, p. 6. See Robin Clifton, 'Popular fear of Catholics in England, 1640–1660', *Past and Present*, no. 52 (1971), p. 41 for further comment.

58. *L.J.*, v, p. 545. There had been enclosure riots in that county in August and September (*A Continuation of Certain Speciall and Remarkable Passages*, no. 5, p. 6).

59. Thomas Bayles of Witham (*C.J.*, II, p. 881); Sir Humphrey Mildmay of Danbury (Harleian 454 f. 54v).

60. Stowe 189 f. 7. See also Morant 47 f. 39; Wenlock, *To Charles the II*, pp. 25–6. The Parliamentary instructions of 3 October empowered the Deputy-Lieutenants to seize the arms of 'dangerous and ill affected persons' (*L.J.*, v, pp. 382–4).

61. *Ibid.*, v, p. 530. For the Association, see pp. 62–6.

62. *Gardiner*, I, pp. 95–6, 103–26.

63. For Cooke's and Bendish's cases, see *C.J.*, II, pp. 944, 998; Smith *Ecclesiastical history of Essex*, p. 184; Add. 18777 ff. 134, 143; Harleian 164 f. 282; S.P. 20/1 ff. 100v–101.

64. *C.J.*, II, pp. 941–2; *Certaine Informations*, no. 2, p. 13; Egerton 2646 f. 249; Harleian 454 f. 56; H. of L.M.P., 1646/7 (January), the petition and case of Sir Benjamin Ayloffe; *C.C.C.*, p. 848; P.C.C. 136 Laud.

65. Egerton 2646 f. 311. See also Egerton 2647 f. 70; *Speciall Passages*, no. 36, p. 291.

66. E.R.O., Q/SBa 2/48. For similar cases see 2/55, 57, 58, 59; Q/SR 322 nos. 74, 75, 77, 78, 115; 323 no. 80.

67. *L.J.*, v, p. 233; Ryves, *Mercurius Rusticus*, pp. 29, 98; Harleian 163 f. 285v; H. of L.M.P., 1 October 1642, the petition of Frederick Gibb.

68. Tanner 63 f. 110; *Two petitions the one to the King's most excellent Majesty. The humble petition of the Grand-Jury . . . Southampton* (1642), pp. 6–7.

69. *L.J.*, v, pp. 245, 290; *C.J.*, II, pp. 714, 726.

70. *Ibid.*, pp. 714, 736; Nalson II no. 57.

71. On 11 August the House ordered the Suffolk M.P.s to prepare an order similar to that for the execution of the Ordinance in Northamptonshire (for which see *C.J.*, II, pp. 612, 633), but, despite this, the Earl of Suffolk was still being pressed to act in late August.

72. The county returned 16 M.P.s to Parliament, but Rainborow of Aldeburgh was dead and I have also excluded Bedingfield of Dunwich, who was a London merchant with only limited influence in the county (Keeler, *Long Parliament*, pp. 102–3, 320; Egerton 2717 f. 7).

73. Coke was disabled in September for refusing to acknowledge a summons from the House; LeGros, although frequently absent, managed to avoid the same fate (*C.J.*, II, pp. 716, 779; Keeler, *Long Parliament*, pp. 136–7, 248–9; Tanner 64 f. 84).

74. *C.J.*, II, pp. 716, 807, 871, 902, 907; *Speciall Passages*, no. 3, p. 22; *A Perfect Diurnall of the Passages in Parliament*, no. 18, p. 6; Harleian 164 ff. 274–274v; Add. 31116 ff. 16v–17.

75. Tanner 63 f. 125; 66 f. 298; *Notes and Queries*, 1st series, vol. 12 (1855), p. 360. See also Harleian 163 f. 27v; Wenlock, *To Charles the II*, p. 25.

76. Harleian 163 ff. 324–324v. For D'Ewes's major speeches and letters on the same theme in 1642, see *ibid.*, ff. 128–129v, 134, 135, 140–140v, 148–148v, 153v–154v, 207v, 210v, 271–3, 291; J. O. Halliwell (ed.), *The autobiography and correspondence of Sir Simonds D'Ewes, Bart.* (1845), vol. 2, p. 290.

77. *Notes and Queries*, 1st series, vol. 12 (1855), pp. 358, 360; *C.J.*, II, p. 726; Harleian 164 f. 315; 165 f. 222.

78. For Bence's identification with the proponents of war measures, see Harleian 164 f. 346. Cage's involvement in the central administrative machinery established by Pym is noted by Lotte Glow, 'The Committeemen in the Long Parliament, August 1642–December 1643', *Historical Journal*, vol. 8 (1965), p. 4. Gurdon displayed his zeal by bringing the activities of his less enthusiastic Suffolk colleagues to the attention of the Commons (Harleian 164 ff. 274, 332).

79. *Notes and Queries*, 1st series, vol. 12 (1855), p. 338. For Barnardiston's earlier career, see pp. 22–3.

80. Hervey (ed.), *Reyce's Breviary of Suffolk*, p. 59.

81. There were difficulties at Bury, where the example of conscientious refusal by the town's deputy-recorder to contribute upon the Propositions was followed by some inhabitants (Add. 31116 f. 2; *C.J.*, II, p. 811); there was also a dispute between the town's governors and a Parliamentary Lieutenant who claimed that the former would not permit him to raise recruits for Essex's army – but this affair seems to have been a product of the local worthies' reaction to his heavy-handed self-importance, rather than of political opposition (*ibid.*, pp. 767, 774; Nalson II no. 74). In other Suffolk towns there were angry verbal attacks on Parliament, but little more (Nalson II no. 103; H. of L.M.P., 6 October 1642, the information of Samuel Crossman). For general comment on the success of the Parliamentary committee, see Harleian 164 f. 12; *C.J.*, II, p. 825.

82. Tanner 63 f. 149. Crane, who had assisted the Catholic Lady Rivers to escape from the mob, had to garrison his house with a militia detachment 'to secure himself from the fury of the rable' (C.U.L., Patrick Ms. 33 f. 20v).

83. Green (ed.), *Rous's diary*, p. 121; Tanner 63 f. 146; Harleian 163 f. 325.

84. Peter Fisher, *For the right worshipful the Knights . . . of Suffolk* (1648), p. 11.

85. Harleian 163 f. 325; E.S.R.O., FB 19/I 2/2 warrant of 17 September 1642.

86. I have not used the official list of those who were instructed to assist Barnardiston (*L.J.*, V, pp. 337, 342), which is virtually a catalog of those of wealth and influence in the shire, but only the names of those who can be shown, from the sparse records of the local administration, to have actually participated in the Parliamentary Committee in the autumn of 1642 (Tanner 64 f. 107; S.P. 28/263 f. 63; E.S.R.O., FB 19/I 2/1–2).

87. Harleian 164 ff. 332, 340; Alfred Suckling, *The History and Antiquities of the county of Suffolk* (1848), vol. 2, p. 48.

88. S.P. 28/263 f. 63; Tanner 64 f. 107; E.S.R.O., FB 19/I 2/2; FB 130/I 1/8; HD 53/2786 f. 1.

89. In Hertfordshire, as will be seen, money was collected upon the Propositions in June and July in some localities; but although a committee was appointed for the general receipt of subscriptions in late July (*L.J.*, V, p. 207) it appears from the surviving parish accounts (see p. 258 note 56) that money was not collected on a countywide basis until August and September. See also H.R.O., Miscellaneous IX no. 46351, article I.

90. *C.J.*, II, pp. 720, 743; *England's Memorable Accidents* (19–26 September 1642), *sub* 21 September.

91. Zagorin, *Court and Country*, pp. 325–7; *H.M.C.*, Salisbury (Cecil), vol. XXII (1971), pp. 370–3; *L.J.*, V, p. 193; *C.J.*, II, pp. 712, 733.

92. *C.J.*, II, pp. 579, 646, 679, 696, 712; *L.J.*, V, pp. 173, 221, 274; S.P. 28/4 ff. 64–5; 16 f. 206; 17 ff. 263, 266; 154 unfol., parish account of Royston.

93. *C.J.*, II, pp. 597, 696; Harleian 163 f. 141v; S.P. 23/82 f. 775; Nalson XIII no. 79. The vicar of Hertford was also hostile to Parliament (*C.J.*, II, p. 488; *L.J.*, V, p. 663).

94. S.P. 23/82 f. 775; Harleian 384 f. 94; R.E., *A perfect diurnal of the proceedings in Hartfordshire* (1642), *passim*; *A true relation of a wonderfull and strange passage* (1642), pp. 1–2.

95. *L.J.*, v, pp. 545–6. Regretably, unlike the Essex petition, no list of the names of the subscribers survives, so the strength and location of popular support, and the organization behind the petition cannot be determined. The Parliamentary committee for the county later wrote of the 'multitudes' of signatories (S.P. 16/502/56 I).

96. A good account of the incident is provided by Kingston, *East Anglia*, p. 87. See also S.P. 23/82 f. 775; Tanner 64 f. 121; *Mercurius Aulicus*, no. 2, p. 18.

97. C. H. Cooper, *Annals of Cambridge* (Cambridge, 1842–52), vol. 3, pp. 326–7; F. J. Varley, *Cambridge during the Civil War* (Cambridge, 1935), pp. 63–4, 73–7. The county, however, was not entirely quiet (*L.J.*, v, p. 226).

98. P.R.O., 30/15/3 no. 503; *C.J.*, II, pp. 717, 726, 732; S.P. 23/99 ff. 713, 715; *L.J.*, v, p. 250.

99. Varley, *Cambridge*, pp. 77–83, and Kingston, *East Anglia*, pp. 55–61, provide good general accounts; but see also S.P. 16/540/364; S.P. 19/21 f. 87; S.P. 23/80 ff. 649–55; 223 ff. 609–13; S.P. 24/30 Almon *v* Crouch. The final fate of the plate is problematic: Varley dismisses the 'Royalist' accounts of Barwick and Clarendon, which state that a large amount of the plate reached the King, as fabricated propaganda, and argues that Cromwell seized, or prevented the movement of, the entire amount. Yet a number of the 'Parliamentarian' accounts read as though some of the plate got through to the King, either before Cromwell's seizure of the Castle or in piecemeal fashion thereafter (*L.J.*, v, p. 334; Add. 15672 ff. 48v–50; Tanner 63 f. 116).

100. Kingston, *East Anglia*, pp. 53–4. See also Add. 15672 ff. 33–4; S.P. 20/1 ff. 106v, 259, 313; *L.J.*, v, p. 242; *Quarrel*, p. 71; James Whinnel, *Matters of Great Concernment* (1646), pp. 15, 46–7.

101. Vicars, *Jehovah-Jireh*, p. 149; *A True and Perfect Diurnal*, no. 11, *sub* 1 and 3 September 1642; *Remarkable Passages from Nottingham* (1642), no pagination; *A Continuation of Certain Speciall and Remarkable Passages*, no. 5, p. 5; *Joyfull newes from the Isle of Ely* (1642), *passim*; Add. 15672 f. lv; Add. 18777 f. 44v; S.P. 28/128 unfol., Sir Thomas Martyn's account of money received on the Propositions; *L.J.*, v, pp. 334, 338, 342, 348, 362.

102. P.R.O., 30/15/3 no. 503; *Speciall Passages and Certain Informations*, no. 25, pp. 205–6.

103. R. W. Ketton-Cremer, in his *Norfolk in the Civil War*, provides a good account of events in late 1642 in the county and transcriptions of a number of the most important documents from the Tanner Mss. However, whilst his narrative is reliable, I disagree with the emphasis of his account in a number of particulars.

104. *C.J.*, II, p. 514; G.Y.C., 19/6 f. 512; King's Lynn, Assembly Book VIII f. 96v; *L.J.*, v, p. 243; Add. 22619 f. 40; *The humble petition of many thousands of the inhabitants of Norwich* (1642), *passim*; Nalson XIII nos. 80, 82, 83; N.R.O., Norwich Court Book 1634–46, f. 355; Norwich Assembly Book 1613–42, f. 373.

105. Ketton-Cremer, *Norfolk in the Civil War*, p. 145; *C.J.*, II, p. 697; N.R.O., Norwich Court Book 1634–46, ff. 355–7.

106. Harleian 164 f. 257v; *L.J.*, v, pp. 249, 251–3, 265–6. The press carried reports that the King himself intended to visit Norfolk to execute the Commission of Array (*A Perfect Diurnall of the Passages in Parliament*, no. 7, p. 3).

107. Keeler, *Long Parliament*, pp. 128, 203–4; Harleian 164 f. 257v.

108. The six were Sir Edmund Moundeford, Sir John Potts, Sir John Holland, Sir Thomas Wodehouse, William Heveningham and Framlingham Gawdy; only the first two went to Norfolk in early August. However, Heveningham's absence is probably a function of his involvement in Suffolk rather than his lack of enthusiasm.

109. *Notes and Queries*, 1st series, vol. 12 (1855), p. 359. For Holland's convenient illnesses, see Harleian 165 f. 190.

110. Tanner 63 f. 121.

111. *Ibid.*, f. 116. Taken ill at Newmarket, Moundeford went to Cambridge for medical attention; he was involved in the administration of Norfolk in early September (Tanner 64 f. 8; King's Lynn, Assembly Book VIII f. 96v), but played little part in events thereafter. He died in May 1643.

112. *The Knyvett Letters*, p. 102; Harleian 163 f. 293v; Tanner 63 ff. 32, 43.

113. *Ibid.*, ff. 117, 126, 132; Harleian 383 f. 206.

114. In a draft of a letter to Holland Potts first wrote 'the people are well affected to the Parliament'; thinking better of this he erased 'well' and qualified further by adding 'generally' after 'the people' (Tanner 63 f. 117).

115. Harleian 386 f. 223. His fears were not altogether misplaced. In November and December there was mob action in the Lynn area; initially directed against the Catholics it became an anarchic plundering of the propertied (N.R.O., Quarter-sessions Box 34, the information of Richard Barrett; *An extract of severall letters which came* (1642), p. 5).

116. *L.J.*, v, p. 101; *A true and exact relation of the present estate of the city of Norwich* (1642), *passim*.

117. Tanner 64 f. 145; Harleian 383 f. 206.

118. Harleian 386 f. 234. See also Tanner 64 f. 10 for a further comment on the Commons' distrust of their representatives in Norfolk.

119. Tanner 63 ff. 151–2.

120. *Ibid.*, ff. 151–2, 165; 64 ff. 9, 95–7, 102–4; 69 f. 200; 311 f. 29. See Ketton-Cremer, *Norfolk in the Civil War*, p. 154.

121. Tanner 64 ff. 99, 101, 106; N.R.O., Aylsham Mss., 198 unfol., warrant of 2 December 1642. See also N.R.O., Bradfer-Lawrence collection, vol. v no. 10; King's Lynn, Assembly Book VIII f. 105v.

122. Tanner 64 ff. 30–1, 50–2. Ketton-Cremer, *Norfolk in the Civil War*, pp. 151–3 provides a good account of the divisional meetings for raising money upon the Propositions in late September; for organization at the village level in the following month, see the papers of William Doughty of Hanworth, collector for the Hundred of North Erpingham, in N.R.O., Aylsham Mss., 198 unfol.

123. *C.J.*, II, p. 769; Tanner 64 ff. 10, 96v.

124. *Ibid.*, ff. 94–6, 111, 200; Add. 22619 f. 29; *C.J.*, II, pp. 813, 884; Harleian 384 f. 183.

125. See Tanner 64 ff. 114, 122, 123, 124–5 for military preparations in early January.

126. Ketton-Cremer, *Norfolk in the Civil War*, pp. 167–9. See also Tanner 55 f. 151 for further evidence of Spelman's disillusionment in early 1643.

127. Ketton-Cremer, *Norfolk in the Civil War*, pp. 166, 170–1; Tanner 64 f. 93; Add. 18777 ff. 139, 143; Add. 22619 f. 25; *The English Intelligencer shewing* (1642), p. 5; *The Kingdomes Weekly Intelligencer*, no. 6, p. 43.

128. Harleian 384 f. 183; *C.J.*, II, p. 930; Harleian 164 f. 294v. The Norfolk peace petitions themselves only survive in rough copies among the papers of

William Doughty of Hanworth (N.R.O., Aylsham Mss., 198 unfol.); these give no indication of the degree of support which the petition commanded, nor of its organization.

129. Add. 22619 ff. 29, 33; *C.J.*, III, pp. 129, 158; *The Knyvett Letters*, p. 105.

130. Kingston, *East Anglia*, p. 78.

131. *C.J.*, II, pp. 649, 666.

132. *A Perfect Diurnall of the Passages in Parliament*, no. 12, *sub* 1 September 1642.

133. This clause first appears in the Instructions issued for the Deputy-Lieutenants of Kent on 27 August (*L.J.*, v, p. 331); it was repeated in subsequent sets of Instructions, including those for Essex, Cambridgeshire and Suffolk (*ibid.*, pp. 340, 384).

134. *Ibid.*, p. 403; *C.J.*, II, pp. 814, 854; Add. 31116 f. 2v; *Firth and Rait*, I, pp. 49–51.

135. Add. 18777 ff. 34v–35, 36, 38v–39; Harleian 164 ff. 40, 324v, 381; *L.J.*, v, pp. 411, 417–18; *C.J.*, II, pp. 816, 817, 819; Edward Bowles, *Plaine English or, a discourse* (1643), p. 27. See J. H. Hexter, *The reign of King Pym* (Cambridge, Mass., 1941), pp. 28–9.

136. Tanner 64 f. 95; *L.J.*, v, p. 306. Norfolk and Suffolk had been ordered to work in conjunction for the defense of Yarmouth; Norfolk and Cambridge for the defense of Lynn (*ibid.*, pp. 319–20; 369–70).

137. Tanner 64 f. 96v; G.Y.C., 18/7 f. 39v; 19/7 ff. 2, 3v–4.

138. Add. 18777 f. 78; Tanner 64 ff. 99, 100v; Morant 46 f. 291; *C.J.*, II, p. 871; *A Perfect Diurnall of the Passages in Parliament*, no. 25, *sub* 28 November.

139. See *A remonstrance and protestation of the gentry and commonalty of . . . Buckingham* (1642), *passim*; *A glorious and happy victory obtained by the vollun-tiers of Buckingham* (1642), sig. A 3. It is obvious that in both these tracts, filled with non-existent victories, the authors' enthusiasm warped their accounts. Yet Morant 48 f. 237 shows that the proposed Association was not altogether a figment of the journalistic imagination.

140. *L.J.*, v, pp. 471, 474, 476; *C.J.*, II, p. 881; Add. 18777 f. 87; Harleian 164 ff. 243–244v.

141. *C.J.*, II, pp. 865, 867, 883, 889, 894, 897; *L.J.*, v, pp. 499, 503, 505–7; Nalson XIV no. 168.

142. Harleian 164 f. 174v; Tanner 64 ff. 97, 109. The actual oath was not introduced on 28 November, but Yonge's account of the proposed Declaration (Add. 18777 ff. 74v–75) shows that a personal commitment to the Association was envisioned at that stage.

143. *L.J.*, v, pp. 505–7; *C.J.*, II, p. 942.

144. *Ibid.*, pp. 910, 942; *L.J.*, v, p. 530; Tanner 114 f. 98.

145. Add. 18777 f. 94v, 110v; *L.J.*, v, p. 523; Everitt, *Suffolk*, pp. 40–1.

146. *Mercurius Aulicus*, no. 6, p. 76; Add. 18777 f. 140v; *C.J.*, II, p. 951; Harleian 164 f. 312v. See also H.R.O., Miscellaneous IX no. 46531, article XIV.

147. Tanner 64 ff. 39, 118, 122v, 130; Tanner 114 f. 98; *C.J.*, II, pp. 934, 956.

148. Tanner 64 ff. 118v, 125; *Abbott*, I, pp. 211, 212; *Norfolk Archaeology*, vol. 2 (1849), p. 45; I. G. Philip (ed.), *The Journal of Sir Samuel Luke* (Banbury, 1950), pp. 10–11.

149. Tanner 64 f. 157.

150. Everitt, *Suffolk*, p. 39 gives the final version. In addition three drafts of the declaration of intention of the Bury assembly survive (Tanner 114 f. 96).

151. N.R.O., Aylsham Mss., 198 unfol., warrants of 11 February, 15 March 1642/3.

152. No copy of Grey's commission survives, but this power was not established in the Ordinance of 20 December.

153. N.R.O., Norwich Court Book 1634–46, ff. 377v–378; G.Y.C., 19/7 ff. 8v, 10; Add. 22619 f. 29; Ketton-Cremer, *Norfolk in the Civil War*, p. 174; *Certaine Informations*, no. 8, p. 59. In the autumn and winter there had been a considerable body of anti-Parliamentary sentiment in the City, both popular (Nalson II no. 45) and among the ruling group (*C.J.*, II, pp. 884, 896; S.P. 24/66 City of Norwich *v* Cory; N.R.O., Norwich Court Book 1634–46, ff. 378, 381–381v).

154. Harleian 386 f. 236.

155. Ketton-Cremer, *Norfolk in the Civil War*, pp. 176–8, 180–4, 187–9. For Lynn see also *Certaine Informations*, no. 10, p. 78; no. 12, p. 95; *Speciall Passages*, no. 36, p. 291; *The Kingdomes Weekly Intelligencer*, no. 13, p. 101.

156. *C.J.*, III, p. 129.

157. William Bridge, *A sermon preached unto the voluntiers* (1643), p. 14; Add. 28930 f. 1; Add. 5829 f. 28.

Chapter 4

1. *The Knyvett Letters*, p. 109; *Abbott*, I, pp. 219–20; *Certaine Informations*, no. 12, pp. 92, 93; N.R.O., Norwich Court Book 1634–46, ff. 381–381v. No copy of the Lord General's commission to Grey survives, but the general tenor of his instructions is apparent in Morant 48 f. 87.

2. *Certaine Informations*, no. 12, p. 93; no. 14, p. 109; *The Kingdomes Weekly Intelligencer*, no. 16, p. 128; *Speciall Passages*, no. 35, p. 286; no. 37, p. 300; *Mercurius Aulicus*, no. 15, p. 188; C. Coates, *The History and Antiquities of Reading* (Reading, 1802), pp. 31–9.

3. *L.J.*, VI, p. 53; S.P. 28/11 ff. 143–6.

4. Egerton 2646 ff. 209, 229, 259, 291; Egerton 2647 ff. 31, 91, 207, 269; *C.J.*, III, pp. 63, 116; *Mercurius Aulicus*, no. 18, p. 228. For the condition of Essex's army in general, see Godfrey Davies, 'The Parliamentary Army under the Earl of Essex, 1642–5', *E.H.R.*, vol. 49 (1934), pp. 40–1.

5. Egerton 2646 f. 269; 2647 ff. 45, 49, 87. The strength of the dragoon companies was equally depleted (*ibid.*, ff. 47, 118).

6. H. of L.M.P., 21 June 1643, the information of Thomas Williams; S.P. 28/43 ff. 921–2; S.P. 28/196 unfol., paper book entitled 'Sir Thomas Martyn his Answeres'; S.P. 28/222 unfol., book of testimonies against Martyn. For desertion from an Essex troop, see Egerton 2647 f. 47.

7. So Gardiner writes of the minor clash near Grantham, 'The whole fortune of the Civil War was in that nameless skirmish.' (*Gardiner*, I, p. 167.)

8. Tanner 64 f. 157; *Speciall Passages*, no. 28, p. 229; no. 35, p. 285; no. 36, p. 292; *A relation of a fight in the county of Lincolne . . . neere Ancaster* (Oxford, 1643), *passim*; *A Continuation of certain Speciall and Remarkable Passages*, no. 41, no pagination.

9. Stowe 807 ff. 117–118v; *Speciall Passages*, no. 36, p. 294; *Abbott*, I, p. 224.

10. *Quarrel*, p. 73; *Divers remarkeable passages of Gods Good Providence* (1643), *passim*; *A true relation of a great victory obtained . . . by Lord Willoughby* (1643), pp. 4–6.

11. *C.C.C.*, pp. 978–9; *Abbott*, I, pp. 225–6; *Certaine Informations*, no. 15, p. 120; *Speciall Passages*, no. 36, p. 294.

12. Ryves, *Mercurius Rusticus*, p. 213; *Mercurius Aulicus*, no. 17, p. 218; *Abbott*, I, p. 226; *Divers remarkeable passages of Gods Good Providence* (1643), *passim*.

13. *Abbott*, I, p. 236; *The Kingdomes Weekly Intelligencer*, no. 27, pp. 212–13; *A true relation of Colonell Cromwels proceedings* (1643), *passim*.

14. Tanner 62 f. 220. See also *ibid.*, f. 192; Add. 22619 f. 90.

15. Morant 46 f. 27; Add. 31116 f. 63v; *Speciall Passages*, no. 30, p. 244; *Certaine Informations*, no. 18, p. 143; *A Continuation of certaine Speciall and Remarkable Passages*, no. 46, p. 1; Egerton 2646 ff. 212, 214; Tanner 62 f. 117; S.P. 28/222 unfol., warrants for the payment of troops and the building of fortifications.

16. Nalson XI no. 292; *C.J.*, III, pp. 153, 167, 186; Egerton 2647 f. 34; Add. 31116 f. 63v.

17. Nalson XI no. 243; *C.J.*, III, pp. 67, 82; *L.J.*, VI, p. 43; *Gardiner*, I, pp. 155–6.

18. *Abbott*, I, pp. 228–9; Harleian 164 f. 384; Nalson XI no. 253. For Cromwell's operations in Huntingdonshire and Northampton, see *ibid.*, no. 248; *Mercurius Aulicus*, no. 19, pp. 236, 237.

19. *Speciall Passages*, no. 40, p. 325; no. 41, p. 335; *The Kingdomes Weekly Intelligencer*, no. 19, p. 147; *Certaine Informations*, no. 18, pp. 141, 144; *Mercurius Aulicus*, no. 20, pp. 361–2. The best modern account of the skirmish near Grantham is provided by A. C. E. Welby, 'Belton Fight', *Lincolnshire Notes and Queries*, vol. XIII (1915), pp. 38–47. But no commentator has noticed that although Cromwell's wing routed the enemy, the Lincolnshire troops made no effect on the cavalry facing them. For this, see *Rushworth*, part III, vol. 2, pp. 799–801.

20. *L.J.*, VI, p. 67; Robert Bell (ed.), *Memorials of the Civil War, comprising the correspondence of the Fairfax family* (1849), vol. 1, p. 45; *Abbott*, I, pp. 231–2.

21. Bell (ed.), *Fairfax correspondence*, vol. 1, pp. 46–7; Harleian 165 f. 112; Nalson XI no. 271; *Mercurius Civicus*, no. 4, p. 31; *Mercurius Aulicus*, no. 24, pp. 312, 321; *The Kingdomes Weekly Intelligencer*, no. 24, p. 119; *A Perfect Diurnall of the Passages of Parliament*, no. 53, no pagination.

22. *Abbott*, I, pp. 235–6; Mss. in the possession of the dowager Lady Hastings at Melton Constable (hereafter Melton Constable Mss.) – letters of Sir Edward Astley to his wife, of 20 June and 1 July 1643; *Mercurius Aulicus*, no. 25, p. 327.

23. *C.J.*, III, p. 138; Harleian 164 f. 234v; 165 f. 107; *H.M.C.*, Hastings, vol. II (1930), p. 103; *Gardiner*, I, pp. 186–8.

24. *Mercurius Civicus*, no. 81, p. 749; *Mercurius Aulicus*, no. 27, p. 352; no. 28, p. 369.

25. Egerton 2647 f. 34; *Mercurius Civicus*, no. 8, p. 58; *Wednesday's Mercury*, no. 1, no pagination; *The Parliament Scout*, no. 5, p. 35.

26. For Cromwell's discipline see the contemporary accounts cited by C. H. Firth, 'The Raising of the Ironsides', *T.R.H.S.*, new series, vol. XIII (1899), pp. 57–8.

27. *Ibid.*, p. 28; *Speciall Passages*, no. 41, p. 335; *Abbott*, I, p. 230.

28. *Ibid.*, I, p. 232; Egerton 2651 ff. 140v–141; S.P. 24/45 Dodsworth *v* Hardmett; C.U.L., Cholmondeley (Houghton), Pell Papers, Correspondence no. 138; Melton Constable Mss., letter of 17 June 1643 from Sir Edward Astley to his wife; Tanner 62 f. 181.

29. Egerton 2646 f. 269; 2647 f. 28; see also *ibid.*, ff. 45, 49, 78; 2648 f. 28.

30. Egerton 2646 f. 207; 2647 ff. 45, 288; S.P. 28/7 ff. 80, 403.

31. *Abbott*, I, pp. 218, 247; Egerton 2647 f. 51; 2651 f. 140v; Morant 46 f. 27; S.P. 24/45 Dodsworth *v* Hardmett; S.P. 28/14 f. 155; 267 ff. 92–102.

32. *Firth and Rait*, I, pp. 51–2. See pp. 64–5.

33. Holmes, *Scandalous Ministers*, pp. 38, 83; *C.J.*, II, pp. 834, 956. There is an hilarious account of the general meeting at Ipswich in *Mercurius Aulicus*, no. 9, p. 118.

34. Tanner 284 ff. 41–7; Egerton 2647 f. 301; Hockliffe (ed.), *Josselin's Diary*, p. 13. For the Norfolk arrangements, see p. 66.

35. Tanner 284 ff. 42, 43, 45; G.Y.C., 19/7 ff. 8v, 10.

36. Everitt, *Suffolk*, pp. 38–9; E.S.R.O., HD 53/2786 f. 1; *Abbott*, I, p. 218; Fisher, *For the knights of Suffolke* p. 11; Morant 47 f. 7.

37. *Abbott*, I, p. 220; N.R.O., Aylsham Mss., 198 unfol., warrant of 26 March 1643; Egerton 2647 ff. 207, 209, 287. However, four companies in Palgrave's regiment from Norfolk were still seconded from the trained-bands in mid-June (Melton Constable Mss., letter of 17 June 1643 from Sir Edward Astley to his wife).

38. Treated in detail in Firth, 'The raising of the Ironsides', *passim*. The following account corrects Firth's error in suggesting that the five 'Ironsides' troops were all embodied by the time of the Lowestoft rising.

39. *Abbott*, I, p. 225; P.R.O., 30/15/3 no. 525; S.P. 28/128 unfol., the account of Sir Thomas Martyn; S.P. 28/267 ff. 92, 98; E. 315/5 p. 145; S.P. 28/234, the account of Gervaise Fullwood; Harleian 164 f. 340; *Certaine Informations*, no. 10, p. 78; Tanner 62 f. 348.

40. To meet the financial needs of the Hertfordshire contingent Parliament passed special Ordinances empowering the county committee to raise a weekly assessment and to utilize those sums raised upon the Propositions which were still in their hands. Why Hertfordshire was accorded such preferential treatment is uncertain (*Firth and Rait*, I, pp. 117–23; *C.J.*, III, p. 54; *L.J.*, VI, p. 13).

41. In March Cromwell believed that 'one month's pay may prove all your trouble' (*Abbott*, I, p. 221).

42. N.R.O., Norwich Assembly Book 1642–68, f. 6; Norwich Court Book 1634–46, ff. 377v–378; G.Y.C., 19/7 ff. 8v, 10; Egerton 2646 f. 188.

43. Compare Tanner 284 ff. 41–7 with V. B. Redstone (ed.), *The ship money returns for the county of Suffolk, 1639–1640* (Ipswich, 1904), pp. 188, 202–4. For Essex, see Egerton 2647 f. 44; Morant 41 f. 225; 47 f. 109; *Mercurius Civicus*, no. 2, sig. B 2: in Suffolk, too, some persons failed to pay the sums subscribed – Tanner 62 f. 642.

44. Egerton 2646 f. 299; Tanner 62 f. 35. See also Nalson III no. 98.

45. *C.J.*, III, pp. 93, 94; Egerton 2646 ff. 233, 236; 2651 ff. 146v–147.

46. S.P. 28/8 f. 34; 28/128 unfol., the certificate of the Cambridgeshire committee of accounts.

47. Tanner 66 f. 2; *Mercurius Civicus*, no. 6, p. 47; *Firth and Rait*, I, p. 132; S.P. 28/173 unfol., the Oundle account; S.P. 28/267 ff. 92–102.

48. *Firth and Rait*, I, pp. 145–55, 160.

49. In Essex there were complaints of 'a great deale of uneven carredg in some' (S.P. 19/94 f. 277. See also Egerton 2647 f. 312). See also Egerton 2651 f. 155 for an attempt by the Essex committee to develop a uniform procedure for assessment.

50. This section is based on the excellent series of warrants and assessments in N.R.O., Aylsham Mss., 198 unfol.; in Norwich and Essex the committees began the work of assessment slightly earlier than in Norfolk (N.R.O., Norwich Court Book 1634–46, ff. 386v–387; Egerton 2646 f. 256).

51. Tanner 69 f. 92. In western Suffolk nearly a quarter of the 439 persons assessed were subsequently discharged from payment upon appeal (S.P. 28/234 unfol., the account of John Thrower).

52. Nearly £29,000 in Suffolk (Fisher, *For the knights of Suffolke*, pp. 18–20); just over £10,000 in Hertfordshire (S.P. 28/155 unfol., the account of William Hickman; 156 unfol., the account of Humphrey Packer); and £3517 in the Isle of Ely (S.P. 28/152 ff. 1–197). I have not found estimates for the other counties of the Association.

53. Add. 33572 f. 302; Egerton 2647 ff. 269, 312; S.P. 28/353 unfol., 'the reporte upon the accompt of Robert Hynde'; N.R.O., Aylsham Mss., 198 unfol., receipt of 3 November 1643; *C.J.*, III, p. 206; *A briefe and true relation of the siege and surrendering of Kings Lyn* (1643), p. 2.

54. S.P. 28/259 unfol. the account of Thomas Girling; Tanner 62 f. 325; 66 f. 2; *C.J.*, III, p. 170 (in this order of 17 July the Commons noted first that the weekly assessment had not been collected in Huntingdonshire 'because of the fears and distractions in that county', and, second, that the county was now a 'frontier to the associated counties' and so enforced to make an extraordinary provision of troops for its defense. The committee was then instructed to levy the money and use it to maintain forces 'for the safeguard of that county'. As the county had been occupied by Cromwell since early April, I suspect that this was retrospective legislation designed to straighten out the accounts).

55. For Parliamentary orders, see *L.J.*, v, pp. 313, 387–8, 427; *C.J.*, II, p. 896; Add. 22619 f. 31. Warrants of the Committee of Safety are S.P. 28/263 ff. 62–3, 168; E.S.R.O., FB 19/I 2/2, warrant of 17 November 1642; Morant 48 f. 71; see also Morant 46 f. 65. For unsanctioned use of the Propositions money, see Fisher, *For the knights of Suffolke*, pp. 6–15.

56. In Hertfordshire there was a second wave of donations upon the Propositions in April 1643 (see the county's village accounts, scattered in S.P. 28, in particular S.P. 28/7 ff. 516–17; 9 ff. 376–77; 13 ff. 65–6; 197 part 1 ff. 142–6; 230 unfol., account of Clothall; 231 unfol., account of Little Hadham), and the less complete evidence for the other counties suggests a similar pattern. Probably this was occasioned by the issue of Grey's warrants for the arrest of those who had not contributed; in Norfolk the committee endeavored to encourage previous non-subscribers to 'freely and willinglie lend' by stressing the unpleasant alternatives (N.R.O., Aylsham Mss., 198 unfol., warrant of 28 April 1643. See also Suckling, *The History of Suffolk*, vol. II, p. 51).

57. Add. 22619 f. 68.

58. In Essex the warrants for the rating of the sum were issued in February 1643 (*C.J.*, II, p. 968; Morant 48 f. 81), but arrears were still being collected in the summer of 1643 (Egerton 2651 ff. 160, 167; Stowe 189 f. 12). For Suffolk, see E. 113 Box 1, part 2, the answer of William Brownrigg; for Norfolk, N.R.O., Aylsham Mss., 193 unfol., the Hanworth account; 198 unfol., warrant of 17 April.

59. Fisher, *For the knights of Suffolke*, pp. 26–9; E. 113 Box 1, part 2, the answers (separate documents) of Christopher Smith and Nicholas Bacon; Egerton 2648 f. 26.

60. Nalson XI no. 222; Tanner 62 f. 65; *C.J.*, III, p. 36; Egerton 2646 f. 243; 2647 f. 100; *L.J.*, v, pp. 636, 657; Hu. R.O., D/DM 28 1/57; P.R.O., 30/15/3 nos. 517, 525. See also Firth, 'Raising of the Ironsides', pp. 43–5.

61. S.P. 28/45 f. 77; Egerton 2646 f. 188; 2651 f. 138; Tanner 62 f. 35; Harleian 162 f. 392; 164 ff. 348v–349.

62. *C.J.*, II, p. 968; Harleian 164 ff. 249v, 357v; Egerton 2646 f. 202. See also *C.J.*, III, pp. 62, 65.

63. This clause is included in a draft of the Ordinance (H. of L.M.P., 29 April 1643). See also Egerton 2646 f. 238; *C.J.*, III, p. 102.

64. Nalson III no. 16; Add. 22619 f. 68; Harleian 165 ff. 118v–119.

65. Harleian 164 f. 357v. For the similar opposition of the Earl of Northumberland to the Associations, see *L.J.*, VI, p. 135.

66. Nalson XI no. 249; *C.J.*, III, p. 101; Harleian 162 f. 392; Clive Holmes, 'The affair of Colonel Long: relations between Parliament, the Lord General and the county of Essex in 1643', *T.E.A.S.*, 3rd series, vol. 2, part 3 (1970), pp. 210–15.

67. Robert Devereux, Earl of Essex, *A letter from his Excellencie* (1643), *passim*; *C.J.*, III, p. 129; Egerton 2643 f. 7; 2646 ff. 261, 263, 281, 283, 299; 2647 f. 86; Morant 41 ff. 221–5; 46 f. 297; Stowe 189 f. 10.

68. The Norfolk and Suffolk committees did not complete the rating of their counties for the weekly assessment for the Lord General's army until two months after the passage of the Ordinance (Suckling, *History of Suffolk*, vol. II, p. 49; G.Y.C., 19/7 f. 12; N.R.O., Aylsham Mss., 198 unfol., warrants of 10 and 17 April; 199 unfol., Hanworth rate of 17 April). For delays in the other counties of the Association, see *Firth and Rait*, I, pp. 139–41; Nalson III no. 17; Tanner 62 f. 35.

69. For Harwich, see Egerton 2646 ff. 193, 313: for Norwich, *C.J.*, II, p. 869; III, p. 134; Add. 22619 ff. 18–21, 25, 31, 69, 78, 82–6; Add. 34315 f. 14: for Hadleigh and Braintree, *C.J.*, II, p. 896; Fisher, *For the knights of Suffolke*, p. 7; E.R.O., D/P 264/8/3 f. 143.

70. Add. 22619 f. 97.

71. *L.J.*, VI, p. 11; Add. 15903 f. 30.

72. *Speciall Passages*, no. 36, p. 294; *The Knyvett Letters*, p. 112; Nalson XI no. 222.

73. Add. 15903 f. 30; *Abbott*, I, pp. 235–6; Morant 46 f. 296; Add. 22619 f. 80; Melton Constable Mss., letters of 22 May and 17 June from Sir Edward Astley to his wife.

74. Everitt, *Suffolk*, pp. 51–5, 57; Egerton 2651 ff. 140v–141; Add. 22620 f. 1.

75. Add. 15903 f. 28. See also Egerton 2646 f. 267.

76. H. of L.M.P., 29 April 1643, draft Ordinance for the Association; Nalson III no. 16; Add. 22619 f. 67; Harleian 165 ff. 118v–119.

77. Egerton 2646 ff. 219, 232.

78. *Ibid.*, f. 267; Morant 46 f. 27. See also Egerton 2647 f. 66.

79. See, for example, Add. 22619 f. 67 (b); Morant 46 f. 161.

80. E.S.R.O., HD 36/2781 no. 28. For a similar complaint of the Earl of Essex in May, see Add. 22619 f. 67 (a); Morant 46 f. 27.

81. Egerton 2646 ff. 209, 269; 2647 ff. 38, 45, 253; Add. 22619 ff. 86, 97.

82. P.R.O., 30/15/3 no. 522. For the Committee's endeavors to get money from the counties, see Egerton 2646 f. 267; Add. 15903 f. 28. For the sums collected, see Tanner 62 ff. 70, 348–53; P.R.O., 30/15/3 no. 522.

83. Egerton 2716 ff. 227, 247; Add. 15903 f. 24; Add. 22619 ff. 73, 77, 82, 84, 86; Add. 22620 ff. 10–11.

84. *L.J.*, vi, pp. 86, 104, 124, 134, 135; *C.J.*, iii, p. 172; *Mercurius Aulicus*, no. 34, p. 465.

85. Egerton 2646 f. 212; 2647 f. 64; Add. 22619 f. 68; Tanner 62 f. 181. From 23 July until the end of the month the only commissioner from a county other than Cambridgeshire was Gervaise Fullwood of Huntingdon (Egerton 2647 ff. 51, 64, 66, 93; S.P. 28/222 unfol., warrants of 27 and 29 July).

86. Add. 15903 f. 30.

87. *Abbott*, i, p. 236.

Chapter 5

1. This account of the reputation of the Lord General and of Parliamentary politics following his letter of 9 July is based upon Hexter, *Reign of King Pym*, pp. 103–52.

2. Harleian 164 f. 243.

3. Hexter, *Reign of King Pym*, p. 119; Pearl, *London*, pp. 269–73.

4. *C.J.*, iii, pp. 180, 190, 194; *Firth and Rait*, i, pp. 202–14, 223–41, 241–2.

5. *C.J.*, iii, p. 191; John Adair, *Roundhead General* (1969), pp. 102–5.

6. *The Parliament Scout*, no. 4, p. 28. See also no. 5, p. 33. For the politica alignment of this newspaper, see Pearl, *London*, p. 272.

7. *C.J.*, iii, pp. 177, 179; Egerton 2647 ff. 40, 51; Add. 22619 f. 92; Harleian 165 f. 129v; *The Parliament Scout*, no. 5, p. 35. For a fuller account of the capture of Gainsborough and the subsequent events, see Ian Beckwith, *Gainsborough in the Great Civil War* (Gainsborough, 1969), pp. 11–16.

8. *A true relation of Colonell Cromwels proceedings* (1643), *passim*; Egerton 2647 f. 61; Melton Constable Mss., letter from Sir Edward Astley to his wife of 29 July 1643.

9. *Abbott*, i, pp. 240–53; Tanner 62 ff. 205, 208, 232; Harleian 165 f. 148v; S.P. 28/239 ff. 159–63; H. of L.M.P., 19 June 1646, the petition of Captain Kingerbie; *The Kingdomes Weekly Intelligencer*, no. 29, pp. 222–3; *Certaine Informations*, no. 30, p. 231; *Mercurius Aulicus*, no. 33, p. 447; *The Parliament Scout*, no. 6, p. 47; no. 7, p. 54; no. 8, p. 61; no. 9, p. 69.

10. Egerton 2647 ff. 51, 93, 110; *Abbott*, i, pp. 251–2.

11. Egerton 2643 f. 19; 2647 ff. 41, 72, 82, 89, 125; Tanner 62 ff. 215, 230, 237.

12. *Mercurius Civicus*, no. 11, p. 83; *Abbott*, i, pp. 249–53.

13. See *The Parliament Scout*, no. 3, p. 18. This idea had been canvassed in November 1642 when the M.P. Walter Long, backed by a city petition, had proposed the raising of a 'running army' to be commanded by Skippon (*L.J.*, v, p. 446; *England's Memorable Accidents*, 7–14 November, p. 73; *ibid.*, 14–21 November, p. 84).

14. *C.J.*, iii, pp. 171, 172, 177; Harleian 165 f. 127v; Add. 31116 f. 61. The Essex horse were to link up with those raised in London, Westminster and Middlesex at a rendezvous at Tothill Fields; those of Hertfordshire were to rendezvous at Bedford with the cavalry from Buckinghamshire, Bedford and Northampton; the horse of the remaining counties of the Association were to rendezvous at Cambridge.

15. *C.J.*, iii, pp. 175, 179, 180; Tanner 62 f. 188; Egerton 2647 ff. 44, 59, 68.

16. Stowe 833 f. 5; Egerton 2647 f. 80; Morant 46 f. 15; 47 f. 371.

17. *C.J.*, iii, pp. 188, 193–4; Harleian 165 ff. 131v–132; Add. 22619 f. 93; Add. 31116 ff. 67v–68; *Firth and Rait*, i, pp. 242–5.

18. *C.J.*, III, pp. 198, 199, 200; Add. 18778 f. 14v; Add. 22619 f. 97; Harleian 165 f. 148v.

19. *L.J.*, v, p. 145; *C.J.*, III, p. 179; *Mercurius Aulicus*, no. 30, p. 404.

20. *The Kingdomes Weekly Intelligencer*, no. 27, pp. 209–10 suggested that this force would serve with Waller, but on 29 July the Commons rejected this idea (Harleian 165 f. 131v).

21. *Firth and Rait*, I, pp. 248–9; *C.J.*, III, p. 205.

22. *Ibid.*, p. 206; Tanner 63 f. 130; Egerton 2643 f. 23; 2651 f. 57; *Mercurius Aulicus*, no. 30, p. 404.

23. *The Kingdomes Weekly Intelligencer*, no. 71, p. 572. There is a good account of the siege in Ketton-Cremer, *Norfolk in the Civil War*, pp. 206–15.

24. *The Parliament Scout*, no. 13, p. 100; *The Weekly Account*, no. 6, p. 3; Tanner 62 f. 318; S.P. 28/139, the account of John Weaver, f. 6v; N.R.O., Aylsham Mss., 198 unfol., warrant of 28 September.

25. Egerton 2647 f. 241; Ketton-Cremer, *Norfolk in the Civil War*, pp. 209–11. Calculating from S.P. 28/11 f. 241 it appears that Manchester had only 22 infantry companies at Lynn during the siege, and that most of these were well under strength.

26. Egerton 2647 f. 138; S.P. 29/12/14.

27. H. of L.M.P., 23 September 1643, Manchester to the speaker of the House of Lords; Egerton 2647 f. 283.

28. *Ibid.*, ff. 223, 286; Tanner 62 f. 299; Harleian 165 f. 169v; S.P. 28/41 f. 143; Abbott, I, pp. 261–2; *A briefe and true relation of the siege and surrendering of Kings Lyn* (1643), *passim*; *The Parliament Scout*, no. 12, pp. 92–3; *Certaine Informations*, no. 38, p. 291; *A Perfect Diurnall of Some Passages in Parliament*, no. 9, pp. 67–8; Francis Maseres (ed.), *Select Tracts relating to the Civil Wars in England* (1815), vol. 2, p. 433; B. N. Reckitt, *Charles I and Hull* (1952), p. 96.

29. The best contemporary account of this campaign is *A true relation of the fight betweene the Right Honourable the Earl of Manchester's forces* (1643), *passim*; see also William Widdrington, *A true and exact relation* (1643), *passim*; *L.J.*, VI, p. 255; *H.M.C.*, Hastings, vol. II (1930), pp. 104, 105, 107; Bell (ed.), *Fairfax correspondence*, vol. 1, pp. 62–5. A good modern account is provided by A. H. Burne and Peter Young, *The Great Civil War* (1959), pp. 112–15.

30. Reckitt, *Hull*, pp. 97–8; John Vicars, *Gods arke overtopping the worlds waves* (1646), pp. 55–7; *The True Informer*, no. 6, p. 43; *A Perfect Diurnall of Some Passages in Parliament*, no. 15, p. 115.

31. *Rushworth*, part III, vol. 2, pp. 305–6. Bolingbroke castle fell in early November; Gainsborough surrendered in mid-December (*A Perfect Diurnall of Some Passages in Parliament*, no. 16, p. 127; no. 17, p. 134; *The Parliament Scout*, no. 21, p. 180).

32. *Ibid.*, no. 19, pp. 165, 168; no. 24, p. 208; no. 30, p. 253; *Mercurius Civicus*, no. 25, p. 194; no. 28, p. 222; *Mercurius Aulicus*, no. 2, p. 799; *The Weekly Post*, no. 9, p. 62; *Occurences*, no. 2, no pagination; *A Continuation of certain Speciall and Remarkable Passages*, no. 3, pp. 4–5.

33. Widdrington, *True and exact relation*, no pagination; *A Perfect Diurnall of Some Passages in Parliament*, no. 16, p. 123; *Remarkable Passages*, no. 1, no pagination; *The Parliament Scout*, no. 19, p. 168.

34. See pp. 103–4.

35. *Baillie*, II, p. 112.

36. See the Earl's letters in Egerton 2647 ff. 229, 241; H. of L.M.P., 23 September; *L.J.*, VI, pp. 255–6. See also Egerton 2647 f. 235.

37. *Ibid.*, f. 199; Morant 47 f. 59; *Certaine Informations*, no. 31, p. 240; *A Perfect Diurnall of the Passages in Parliament*, no. 7, p. 51. Impressment will be discussed in detail in the following chapter, pp. 164–8.

38. *The Parliament Scout*, no. 19, p. 165; no. 22, p. 192; no. 23, p. 200; no. 24, p. 206; *Mercurius Civicus*, no. 24, p. 89; no. 30, p. 338; *Certaine Informations*, no. 42, p. 330; *The Kingdomes Weekly Intelligencer*, no. 37, p. 284; *Good and true news from Bedford* (1643), *passim*.

39. The Essex committee were empowered to levy £13,500 upon the county for the raising of those troops originally designed to serve in Waller's army: Huntingdonshire was allowed to use the Earl of Essex's weekly assessment for frontier defence, and its sequestration revenues for the payment of Cromwell's regiment (*Firth and Rait*, I, pp. 245–6; *L.J.*, VI, p. 135; *C.J.*, III, p. 136).

40. *Abbott*, I, p. 256; Egerton 2643 f. 15; 2647 ff. 74, 181, 216; Add. 22619 f. 109.

41. Add. 18778 ff. 30v, 31v; Harleian 165 f. 167; *Firth and Rait*, I, p. 273. The Suffolk committee began to levy money upon the Ordinance almost immediately after its passage (E.S.R.O., HD 53/2786 f. 3). Essex was probably excluded from this legislation because of the sums granted to that county alone in the Ordinance of 12 August (see note 39 above).

42. *Abbott*, I, p. 259.

43. A move which had been discussed when the order for raising 10,000 men had passed the Commons on 10 August (Add. 18778 f. 13v).

44. *Ibid.*, ff. 59, 63; *C.J.*, III, pp. 260, 269; *Firth and Rait*, I, pp. 309–10.

45. See p. 80.

46. Egerton 2647 f. 296. See also *ibid.*, ff. 283, 286; *Abbott*, I, pp. 264–5. Rich's account demonstrates the truth of his complaint and also that his payments from his own resources were substantial (S.P. 28/26 f. 109; 30 f. 754). For another complaint by a Captain in October, see Nalson III no. 45.

47. Add. 22619 f. 137; Add. 18779 f. 24v; N.R.O., Norwich Mss., loose papers in case 13 shelf B. There is a copy in Tanner 115 f. 42.

48. S.P. 28/267 ff. 52–6, 92–102; 26 f. 109; 42 ff. 644–6. See also S.P. 28/36 ff. 300–6.

49. Tanner 115 f. 42.

50. The accusations and counter-charges generated by this affair took up a great deal of the time of the central Committee of Accounts. The most material evidence is S.P. 28/257 unfol., 'Articles against Sir John Norwich, and his Answers'; 28/230 unfol., the surcharge on Norwich's account; 28/259 unfol., letters of 21 and 26 February 1651/2 from the committee of Hertfordshire to the central committee of Accounts; 28/260 unfol., further articles against Norwich; 28/254 unfol., letter book of the Hertford committee of accounts, ff. 80–5. The case also led to the publication of a pamphlet in 1652 – William Bagwell, *A full discovery of a foul concealment*.

51. Egerton 2647 ff. 249, 273, 349; 2648 f. 31; Tanner 62 f. 350v.

52. Egerton 2647 ff. 197, 229. See also *ibid.*, ff. 209, 214, 221, 223, 241; Egerton 2643 f. 26.

53. The Cambridge Committee had the greatest difficulty in getting Essex to equip its levies in the correct uniform; eventually they bought the coats themselves, hoping (vainly) that the county would refund their outlay (Egerton 2647 ff. 209, 223, 258, 296).

54. Manchester never paid more than 10/– for a coat, 15/– for a musket, 6/6d for a sword, 5/6d for a pike or 36/– for a pair of pistols in 1644, and often obtained

these items for lower amounts (see warrants scattered in S.P. 28, especially 28/17 f. 333; 20 ff. 162–3). In April 1643 the Norfolk committee were paying 20/– for a musket, 7/– for a sword and 45/– for a pair of pistols (Tanner 66 ff. 3–5); in October the Essex committee were paying 5/9d–6/– for a pike and 12/– each for coats (Egerton 2647 ff. 223, 260, 267, 271). However, it should be noted that the Norfolk committee purchased nearly half their supplies from William Cory, a London merchant with contacts in the Dutch armaments industry (S.P. 28/262 unfol., warrant of 13 December 1642). Regretably his bills are not itemized; bulk purchase economies might have been effected here.

55. Egerton 2647 ff. 281, 321; S.P. 28/12 f. 216.

56. Nalson III no. 86; Tanner 62 f. 469. See also *Firth* and *Rait*, I, p. 297; *Abbott*, I, pp. 258–9, 264–5.

57. Nalson III no. 24; *C.J.*, III, p. 232; Add. 22619 f. 111. See also Nalson III no. 34.

58. S.P. 28/128, the receipt book of Sir Thomas Martyn, f. 1v; S.P. 28/222 unfol., warrant of 18 August; Egerton 2647 f. 158.

59. *Ibid.*, ff. 181, 209, 216, 222, 231, 283; 2651 f. 168; Add. 22619 f. 109; Nalson III no. 46.

60. Add. 22619 f. 137.

61. See Appendix 4 for a complete tabulation of the figures.

62. The Association's charge and the Norfolk committee's reply are in Tanner 62 ff. 348–53: the local committee also produced its accounts to substantiate its case; these are Tanner 62 ff. 325–6, 445; 66 ff. 1–10. See also Add. 22619 f. 139.

63. *Firth and Rait*, I, p. 243.

64. Egerton 2647 ff. 181, 222; Add. 22619 f. 109. The surviving warrants and letters from this period (which are not numerous) *suggest* that attendance was erratic: for instance on 13 October the Committee consisted of 3 Cambridgeshire men, 2 from Huntingdon and 1 from Hertfordshire (Egerton 2647 f. 321).

65. Nalson III no. 46. See also *C.J.*, III, pp. 274, 278.

66. *Ibid.*, pp. 279, 281; Nalson III no. 52; Egerton 2647 f. 341; 2648 f. 42; *Certaine Informations*, no. 40, p. 314; no. 41, p. 318; *A Perfect Diurnall of Some Passages in Parliament*, no. 14, p. 109; *The True Informer*, no. 5 p. 40; *The Parliament Scout*, no. 18, pp. 155, 158; no. 19, p. 163.

67. Egerton 2647 ff. 337, 339, 344, 346, 348.

68. Egerton 2646 f. 273. For the slow mobilization in Essex, Suffolk and Hertford, see Egerton 2647 ff. 341, 356, 358, 361; E.S.R.O., HD 53/2786 f. 5; S.P. 28/243 unfol., warrant of 23 October. In the eastern part of Suffolk the mobilization of the militia was probably even slower – see the warrant quoted in Suckling, *History of Suffolk*, vol. II, p. 50.

69. Egerton 2647 f. 359.

70. Egerton 2647 ff. 181–2, 186, 211; Tanner 62 ff. 299, 309; Harleian 165 f. 256; Add. 18779 ff. 34v–35; Add. 31116 ff. 103–103v; *The Parliament Scout*, no. 22, p. 192; no. 27, p. 228.

71. See my article, 'Colonel King and Lincolnshire Politics, 1642–1646', *Historical Journal*, vol. XVI (1973), pp. 452–7.

72. *C.S.P. Ven.*, 1643–7, p. 42. For the secrecy surrounding the visit, see *The Kingdomes Weekly Post*, no. 1, p. 5.

73. *C.J.*, III, pp. 310, 313; Harleian 165 f. 210v; Add. 18779 ff. 5v–6. No copy of this draft Ordinance survives except in Yonge's rough notes.

74. *C.J.*, III, pp. 338, 341, 344, 356; Harleian 165 ff. 240–241v, 245.

75. *Firth and Rait*, I, pp. 368–71; Holmes, 'Colonel King', pp. 457–8; Holmes, *Scandalous Ministers*, pp. 9–24.

76. See, in particular, *The Parliament Scout*, no. 18, p. 161; no. 21, p. 180; no. 22, p. 192. But any issue of the *Scout* from no. 18 through no. 27 demonstrates Dillingham's determination to keep the Earl in the public eye. Other editors praised Manchester's army (e.g., *Mercurius Civicus*, no. 30, p. 338) but not so consistently as did Dillingham. For the 'pensioner' charge, see *Mercurius Aulicus*, no. 23, p. 1009.

77. Everitt, *Suffolk*, pp. 45–6; Holmes, 'Colonel King', pp. 456–7.

78. Tanner 62 f. 473; *C.J.*, III, pp. 349, 350, 474; Harleian 165 f. 256; Add. 18779 ff. 34v–35; Add. 31116 ff. 103–103v; *The Parliament Scout*, no. 27, p. 228.

79. *Ibid.*, no. 30, p. 253; Add. 18779 ff. 49v–50; *C.J.*, III, pp. 354, 370; Holmes, 'Colonel King', p. 458.

80. The major Ordinance passed the Commons without a division, and the Lords without even being committeed (Harleian 165 f. 280). However, the Cambridge Committee's plea for legislation enabling them to re-organize the local militia was not immediately gratified: an Ordinance to that effect was finally passed in June (*Firth and Rait*, I, pp. 462–6).

81. *C.J.*, III, p. 318; Add. 18779 ff. 13–13v; Add. 31116 f. 95; *L.J.*, VI, pp. 505–6. See *Firth and Rait*, I, pp. 398–405.

82. *Ibid.*, pp. 333–9, 413–18; Adair, *Roundhead General*, p. 134.

83. *Baillie*, II, pp. 118–19.

84. *Ibid.*, II, p. 112: Haselrig told D'Ewes 'that hee did not know whether it weere better that the Lord Generall had an army or not, for they would obey no bodie' (Harleian 166 f. 36).

85. *C.J.*, III, pp. 326, 330, 333, 337, 339, 340, 342, 357, 360–1, 364, 367, 368, 370–1, 378, 384, 385, 408, 410, 415, 419, 421, 424, 427, 433, 439; Add. 18779 ff. 17v, 18, 21–2, 23–23v, 45, 48v, 55v, 58, 68–68v, 72, 73, 77–77v, 80; Add. 31116 ff. 108, 117v, 123–123v; Harleian 165 ff. 231–233v, 237v, 242–3, 265–265v, 275, 284, 288; 166 ff. 18, 26–7, 35, 36v; *L.J.*, VI, pp. 395–6; *C.S.P. Ven.*, 1643–7, p. 88.

86. Harleian 165 ff. 266–266v; 166 ff. 29, 31v–32v; Add. 31116 ff. 123–123v, 124v; *C.J.*, III, pp. 423, 427, 429; Tanner 62 ff. 490, 619.

87. Waller, *Vindication*, pp. 16–17. See also Adair, *Roundhead General*, pp. 106–7: Waller's vote for peace in August 1643 could not have endeared him to the 'fiery spirits' (*ibid.*, pp. 102–3).

88. *Baillie*, II, pp. 118–19, 135–6; Harleian 165 ff. 216v, 243.

89. Harleian 166 f. 36. Parliament had been bombarded with petitions from Hertfordshire concerning the exactions of Essex's unpaid force (Nalson XXII no. 70; Tanner 62 f. 578; *L.J.*, VI, pp. 440–1; *C.J.*, III, p. 404; Harleian 165 f. 16), and Skippon admitted that for want of pay discipline had broken down (Add. 31116 f. 119). The bills for damages presented to the local committee by the villages around St Albans bear out the petitions (Add. 33574 f. 11; Add. 40630 f. 133; S.P. 28/11 f. 160; 12 f. 186; many unfoliated bills in S.P. 28/230–1).

90. As is argued by Professor Lotte Glow: see her articles, 'Pym and Parliament: the Methods of Moderation', *Journal of Modern History*, vol. 36 (1964), pp. 374, 386–90; 'Political Affiliations in the House of Commons after Pym's death', *Bulletin of the Institute of Historical Research*, vol. 38 (1965), pp. 48–70.

91. Valerie Pearl, 'Oliver St. John and the "middle group" in the Long Parliament; August 1643–May 1644', *E.H.R.*, vol. 81 (1966), pp. 490–519.

92. *Ibid* , p. 508; Harleian 165 ff. 266–266v.

93. On 16 March the Commons accepted the two controversial amendments in which the phrase 'under . . . the Earl of Essex, Lord General', qualified the description of Sir William Waller as Major-General of the South-Eastern Association, but placed a proviso in the Ordinance that in the absence of Essex, Waller should exercise the full powers of the commander in chief (*C.J.*, III, p. 429).

94. Harleian 166 f. 36. See also ff. 10, 11v, 12v.

95. Harleian 165 ff. 233–233v. For Vane's attempts to gain financial provision for the Scots, see *Mercurius Aulicus*, no. 52, p. 738: Yonge confirms the existence of a party of west country M.P.s who supported Waller's command.

96. Harleian 165 f. 213v; 166 ff. 16v–17; Add. 31116 ff. 115v, 118–118v; *C.J.*, III, pp. 405, 412.

97. Add. 18779 ff. 30–30v; Harleian 165 ff. 253v–254. Two separate Treasuries existed (Add. 18779 f. 21v) and the Militia Committee ordered its troops to join Waller or to return to the City without reference to his strategic needs (Adair, *Roundhead General*, p. 150).

98. *The Parliament Scout*, no. 19, p. 168; no. 22, p. 192; *Mercurius Civicus*, no. 30, p. 338.

99. See pp. 176–7.

100. *Abbott*, I, pp. 258–9; Harleian 165 f. 240; Add. 18779 f. 22.

101. Harleian 165 f. 280.

102. Egerton 2647 ff. 285, 288, 292, 350, 352; S.P. 28/238 unfol., letter of 5 December 1643 from Sir Thomas Barrington to Edward Birkhead.

103. Egerton 2647 f. 201; Tanner 62 f. 285; Nalson III no. 32. See also *C.J.*, III, pp. 260, 271; Nalson III nos. 36, 44; Holmes, 'Colonel Long', p. 214.

104. *Mercurius Aulicus*, no. 47, p. 664; also see p. 105.

105. Add. 18779 ff. 49v–50.

106. *Mercurius Aulicus*, no. 47, p. 664; *Baillie*, II, pp. 103–4, 112.

107. Waller, *Vindication*, p. 17.

Chapter 6

1. I have discussed this point with several of the Deputy-Keepers at the P.R.O., and I feel that this was the system used rather than that any of the Committee, or the Earl and Harlackenden, signed blank warrants which were subsequently filled up. The most telling evidence for my view is in S.P. 28/223 unfol., 'Mr Leman's vouchers' bundle, where one warrant has Manchester's and the Commissary's signatures appended on a separate sheet of paper for want of space on the original. See also S.P. 28/24 ff. 141, 515; 253 A, unfol., Day Book of the Central Committee of Accounts 1651–8, p. 234; 259 unfol., the account of Thomas Russell.

2. For example, S.P. 28/17 f. 380; 18 f. 172; 24 ff. 515, 576; 223 unfol., 'Mr Leman's vouchers'. For a fuller account of the individual Treasurers, see pp. 127–30.

3. S.P. 28/22 ff. 380, 388, 389.

4. There are numerous warrants of this type scattered in the series S.P. 28, particularly in vols. 20–6; see, for example, S.P. 28/26 ff. 264, 265.

5. This was the case when Manchester moved for the renewal of his assessment Ordinance in May 1644 (Add. 18779 f. 95v) and during the summer debates on the Posture of Defense (*The Parliament Scout*, no. 54, p. 436).

6. *C.J.*, III, pp. 626, 648, 699; *A Perfect Diurnall of Some Passages in Parliament*, no. 63, p. 498; no. 68, p. 541; *The Weekly Account*, no. 67, sig. Uuu 2v.

7. P.R.O., 30/15/3 nos. 523–4.

8. See pp. 215–17.

9. Harleian 166 ff. 13v–14, 42, 45v, 129; *C.J.*, III, p. 350.

10. S.P. 28/23 f. 217; 24 f. 446; 25 f. 484; 26 f. 458. In September and October 1644 other members of the Committee were in London, probably involved in the attempt to gain control of the excise revenue (S.P. 28/18 f. 320; 20 f. 130). For further biographical information on Cooke, see p. 126.

11. S.P. 28/19 f. 294; 26 f. 365; 27 f. 163.

12. That the Cambridge Committee was in very regular correspondence with the committees of the constituent counties appears from the bills of James Blackley, the 'postmaster' of the Association (S.P. 28/18 f. 143; 24 ff. 195, 234, 418, 495; 25 f. 333; 26 f. 135).

13. N.R.O., L'Estrange Mss., P. 20 ff. 34v, 35; C.U.L., Cholmondeley (Houghton), Pell Papers, Correspondence no. 71c; S.P. 28/24 ff. 580, 627; 128 unfol., the Association Treasury book, ff. 11v, 13; Morant 46 f. 17; E.S.R.O., HD 36/2781 nos. 41, 43; Add. 22619 f. 53; S.P. 24/35 Boreham *v* Peacock; B.L., Ms. J. Walker C 1, f. 26.

14. Holmes, *Scandalous Ministers*, pp. 14–18; Tanner 61 f. 293; H. of L.M.P., 18 August 1647, the petition of Henry Henman and other Fellows of St John's College; H. of L.M.P., 4 December 1647, charges against Cawdrey and Hutton; S.P. 24/42 Griffen *v* Apethorpe; 50 Goodwin *v* Spurlinge; 58 Kimpton *v* Spurlinge. See also 50 Goose *v* Morley.

15. Everitt, *Suffolk*, p. 70. See also the order transcribed by Everitt (*ibid.*) determining the means to be used within the counties for the maintenance of maimed soldiers; Tanner 98 f. 78; Add. 22619 f. 188.

16. Everitt, *Suffolk*, pp. 68–9. See also King's Lynn, Assembly Book VIII, ff. 147, 150, 150v, 152.

17. The developing formalization of the Committee can be seen in the appointment of new subordinate officials – the doorkeeper, clerks and messengers (see S.P. 28/19 ff. 254, 397; 21 f. 21; 24 ff. 437B, 441B) and in the establishment of a weekly lecture at Trinity College, given by clergymen from parishes in the Cambridge area.

18. Tanner 62 ff. 348–53, 473; *C.J.*, III, pp. 349–50; Add. 22619 f. 137. A clause empowering Manchester to appoint the Committee, so legally terminating the powers of the local committees, was included in the 'Scandalous Ministers' Ordinance of 22 January.

19. Add. 22619 f. 63. S.P. 28/223 unfol., Manchester's warrant of 2 March.

20. Information concerning the membership of the Committee comes from two sources. (*a*) The warrants for the payment of members' stipends, which are scattered throughout the series S.P. 28, particularly in vols. 18–20, 23–8, and boxes 123 and 223. (*b*) Warrants signed by the Committee on a given day, which are scattered in even more random fashion in S.P. 28. From these it appears that between March 1644 and April 1645 29 persons attended the Committee; 7 were members of the caucus, and 7 attended only once. The other 15 were men who replaced the members of the caucus during their absences from Cambridge, and those who attended after the effective dismemberment of the Association in February 1645.

21. Alan Simpson, *The Wealth of the Gentry* (Cambridge, 1961), p. 98; *Massachusetts Historical Society: Collections*, 5th series, vol. 1 (1871), p. 13; Add. 15520 ff. 21–2; S.P. 16/73/9; Add. 25334 f. 87.

22. S.P. 28/19 f. 453; 24 f. 399.

23. Pearl, 'St John', p. 491, note 3. See N. Bacon, *An ordinance presented to the honourable House of Commons* (1646), *passim*; W. A. Shaw, *A history of the English Church during the Civil Wars and under the Commonwealth, 1640–1660* (1900), vol. 2, p. 17; Clement Walker, *The compleat history of independency* (1661), part 1, p. 169.

24. Nathaniel implicitly attacked the Rump, and Francis was quite explicit (J. T. Rutt (ed.), *The diary of Thomas Burton* (1828), vol. 3, pp. 122–3; vol. 4, p. 173). See also David Underdown, *Pride's Purge* (Oxford, 1971), pp. 232, 289, 345, 367.

25. Rutt (ed.), *Burton's diary*, vol. 3, pp. 122, 357; vol. 4, p. 173; N. Bacon, *The Annalls of Ipswich* (ed. W. H. Richardson, Ipswich, 1884); *A historicall discourse of the uniformity* (1647); *The continuation of An historicall discourse* (1651). The *D.N.B.* article is good on Nathaniel's career during the Protectorate.

26. There is a short biography in B. W. Quintrell, 'The divisional committee for southern Essex during the civil wars, and its part in local administration' (unpub. M.A. thesis, Manchester 1962), p. 180.

27. *Massachusetts Historical Society: Collections*, 5th series, vol. 1 (1871), p. 13. The Puritan minister John Rogers dedicated his *The Doctrine of Faith* (1629) to Colonel Mildmay's mother, the mother of the Bacon brothers, and the wife of Brampton Gurdon the elder, describing them as 'all of one minde in the Lord'.

28. Braybrooke (ed.), *Bramston's Diary*, pp. 123–4; Egerton 2647 f. 136; J. R. Jones, *The First Whigs* (1961), pp. 97–8, 118, 210.

29. Add. 19123 f. 252; P.C.C. 30 Nabbs; *C.S.P.D.*, 1639, pp. 366, 434.

30. This account of Walcott's background is based upon the wills of his immediate family and close relatives (L.A.C., Consistory, 1630 f. 406; 1634 (II) f. 189; 1645–6 f. 446; 1671 f. 668): *C.S.P.D.*, 1654, p. 395.

31. *C.J.*, II, p. 448; P.C.C. 91 Essex; P.C.C. 84 Fairfax; *L.J.*, IX, p. 363.

32. Based on Hu. R.O., Godmanchester borough records, boxes 25 and 26; Hu. R.O., Register Book 20 ff. 206–7; 21 ff. 186–9; Hu. R. O., Original wills bundle for 1638, no. 111; P.C.C. 30 Penn; E. 134 15 Charles II, Michaelmas 29; R. Fox, *The History of Godmanchester* (1831), pp. 160, 163–4.

33. *Massachusetts Historical Society: Collections*, 5th series, vol. 1, p. 85; Ryves, *Mercurius Rusticus*, p. 143; J. J. Muskett, *Suffolk Manorial Families* (Exeter, 1900–10), vol. 1, p. 80; E.R.O., T/P 195/12; *H.M.C.*, 14th Report, Appendix IX (1895), p. 280.

Chapter 7

1. *Firth and Rait*, I, p. 369.

2. Newton, *Colonising Activities*, pp. 77–8. Gawsell's epitaph in the chancel at Watlington church emphasizes his skill in improving his estate, while the bursar's account book 1634–61 of Gonville and Caius College suggests that he was Warwick's agent in Norfolk.

3. *Notes and Queries*, 12th series, no. 4 (1918), p. 22.

4. Firth's article in *D.N.B.* is excellent on Weaver's later political career. But see also Walker, *Independency*, part 1, pp. 95, 108; *L.J.*, x, p. 24; Rutt (ed.), *Burton's Diary*, vol. 2, pp. 377, 429; vol. 3, p. 142; T. Birch (ed.), *A collection of the state papers of John Thurloe* (1742), vol. 5, pp. 299–300; C. H. Firth (ed.), *The Memoirs of Edmund Ludlow* (Oxford, 1894), vol. 1, pp. 319, 401.

5. W. Munk, *Rolls of the Royal College of Physicians* (1878), vol. I, p. 231; P.R.O., 30/15/3 no. 505; Maseres, *Select tracts*, vol. 2, pp. 361, 384; Macray (ed.), *Clarendon's History*, book 10, para. 135; John Lilburne, *Jonahs cry out of the whales belly* (1647), p. 8; Worcester College, Oxford – Clarke Ms. 114 f. 21.

6. E.R.O., T/P 195/11; Egerton 2647 ff. 258, 296; Alan Macfarlane, *Family Life of Ralph Josselin* (Cambridge, 1970), pp. 221–2.

7. See Everitt, *Change in the Provinces*, p. 45.

8. S.P. 28/12 ff. 265, 267; 13 ff. 57–9, 209, 218; 152 part I, the account book of John Weaver, ff. 35–41.

9. S.P. 28/23 f. 149; 24 ff. 85–8, 96, 227, 569; 223 unfol., 'Mr Leman's vouchers' bundle – bills for Whalley and Patterson's quarters, and the Crowland bill.

10. S.P. 28/25 ff. 379–80; 139 ff. 43–8; 234 unfol., 'the account of Dr Stane'; 259 unfol., 'an abstract of the account of Dr Stane'. In October and November 1644 Stane received a further £587-10-0d from the sequestrators of Essex and Hertfordshire, but this was not in his previous capacity as an independent treasurer; it was by special order from Manchester, approved by Gawsell and Leman, to enable him to buy arms in London (S.P. 28/18 ff. 138, 165, 227, 301).

11. Gawsell and Leman accounted for £9689-4-3d (S.P. 28/144 no. 3) but this does not appear to include the £587-10-0d received by Stane in the autumn. I have found no account of sequestration money received between 1 January and the end of March 1645, and so have estimated the sum using the very full Norfolk account (Add. 5508 ff. 36–62); in the first three months of 1645, John Cory, the local treasurer, received a sum equalling 20% of his receipts in 1644.

12. The running expenses of the local committees, the stipends of the commissioners for scandalous ministers, the maintenance of a lecturer at Huntingdon (Add. 5494 ff. 147–8; Add. 5508 ff. 62, 135; S.P. 28/26 f. 310).

13. Walton cut down wood at Castle Rising and Kenninghall on the pretense that he would use it for the fortification of Lynn, but was accused of selling it (Add. 40630 ff. 142, 161; H. of L.M.P., 15 June and 2 August 1644, petitions from William March; 3 July 1644, the affidavit of William Ellet). Walton also seized large sums from the local sequestration agents for the maintenance of his garrison: this led to a prolonged dispute between the Norfolk treasurer and the Treasurers for Sequestrations in London, who claimed that the money appropriated by Walton should be deducted from the third part of the sequestration revenue to be paid to Manchester (Add. 5508 ff. 14, 15, 28, 30, 31).

14. S.P. 19/22 f. 305 (a complaint against members of the Huntingdon committee); Add. 5494 f. 144; *Mercurius Aulicus*, no. 40, pp. 1183–4 (against the Hertfordshire committee); E. 134 16 Charles II, Michaelmas no. 22; S.P. 28/255 unfol., the information of Edmund Scotten against James Whinnel; B.L., Ms. J. Walker C. 1, f. 26 (against a number of the Cambridgeshire committee).

15. S.P. 28/152 parts 12 and 14; 353 unfol., 'reporte upon the accompt of Robert Hynde'. See also the particularly well-documented charges against certain Hertfordshire agents: S.P. 20/1 ff. 190v, 194v, 198–198v, 365v–366; S.P. 28/209B unfol., loose accounts of various agents annotated by the local committee of accounts; 231 unfol., certificate of the frauds of William Seaward; 254 unfol., letter book of the Hertfordshire committee of accounts, ff. 35, 38, 48–9; 255 unfol., exceptions to the account of Thomas Nicholls. For Norfolk, see Tanner 62 f. 526.

16. Egerton 2647 f. 269: also see p. 80.

17. S.P. 28/11 f. 124; 12 f. 338; 14 ff. 159–60; 18 ff. 137, 397; 22 f. 323; 28 ff. 189–91; 64 ff. 647, 668; 139 unfol., the account of John Weaver, f. 6v: 152 unfol.,

the account of sales of sheep and other goods; N.R.O., Aylsham Mss. 198 unfol., warrant of 28 September 1643.

18. Tanner 133 f. 166.

19. S.P. 28/257 unfol., account of John Jubbs.

20. The leading commissioners and their areas of activity were Hippesley (Lindsey); Osbourne (Stamford area); Wright (Cambridge and Huntingdon); John Cole (Norfolk); Jeremy Cole (Suffolk); Cotton (north-west Essex); Webster (south Essex); Turpin (Hertfordshire and some adjacent Essex villages). This is based on Weaver's Treasury Book (S.P. 28/139 unfol.), certain of his papers in S.P. 28/255 unfol., and the surviving accounts of his agents (S.P. 28/155 unfol., Turpin's account; 197 part II, ff. 122–31; 234 unfol., Wright's account). For the assistant commissioners, see also S.P. 19/94 ff. 273–274v; S.P. 28/19 f. 398; 64 f. 647.

21. E.S.R.O., EE 1/01/1 f. 92. Although the commissioners in northern Hertfordshire appear to have been permanently based on Royston where they received money from the adjacent hundreds (S.P. 28/13 ff. 65–6; 197 part 2, f. 89; 155 unfol., parish account of Sandon; 209B, parish account of Benington; 231 unfol., parish accounts of Gt Hormead, Radwell, Thundridge).

22. S.P. 28/64 f. 647; 230 unfol., the account of William Turpin; 243 unfol., warrant of 10 March 1645 to Captain West; E. 134 14 Charles II, Easter no. 34; E.R.O., T/B 211/2 no. 19; Croft parish documents, the warrant of William Hill of 23 July 1644; Everitt, *Suffolk*, p. 67.

23. This is calculated from Weaver's account books (in S.P. 28/139 unfol., and 152 part 1); all sums raised from other sources have been excluded from the total. Weaver uses three distinct systems of accounting – and arrives at three separate totals for his receipts! – but all are in the vicinity of £73,000.

24. S.P. 28/152 part 5 ff. 78–82. On the Isle only 8 of 23 parishes were re-rated, producing the sum of £41-10-0d (calculated from the parish accounts (S.P. 28/152 parts 5 and 6)). Huntingdonshire produced about £360, a third of which went to pay the charges of the commissioners (S.P. 28/234 unfol., the account of Thomas Wright).

25. See Appendix 5.

26. At Layston (S.P. 28/197 part I, f. 189) the reviewers assessed 12 persons who had paid nothing on either the propositions, or the first collection of the Fifth and Twentieth part, at sums ranging from 5/- to 20/-; at Kellshall (S.P. 28/230 unfol.) 11 who had not previously been assessed were charged sums ranging from 8/- to 10/-.

27. Everitt, *Suffolk*, p. 67. In March 1644 Parliament ratified the limit set by the Ordinance (see *C.J.*, III, p. 438; *Firth and Rait*, I, p. 156), but it is clear that the Earl's commissioners continued to neglect this in favor of Manchester's figure (Croft parish documents, warrant of William Hill of 23 July 1644).

28. P.R.O. 30/15/3 no. 523. For the sums collected in the autumn, see S.P. 28/152 part 1, the account of John Weaver, ff. 19–21: from existing warrants it appears that, although he accounted for it, Weaver handled little or none of the Lincolnshire money; his local agent paid it directly to the county committee or to munitions merchants on receipt of warrants from the Earl (S.P. 28/26 ff. 391, 394, 406–8, 410, 417, 419, 431–4, 439, 445–6).

29. For an account of the development of the Parliamentary monthly assessment, see Pennington and Roots, *Committee at Stafford*, pp. xxix–xxxiii.

30. Tanner 133 f. 166.

31. See S.P. 28/12 f. 278; 24 f. 563; 25 f. 367 for the activities of Samuel Smythe; S.P. 28/25 ff. 392–7, 401, 413 for Samuel Leigh.

32. S.P. 28/27 f. 416. John Coulson, appointed auditor for Norfolk, where, in 1643, it had been suspected that money was not being collected or was being misappropriated (*C.J.*, III, p. 216), was particularly active (Add. 15903 f. 46; Add. 22619 ff. 56, 182, 193–5).

33. S.P. 28/25 f. 44; 27 f. 389; E.S.R.O., HD 36/2781 no. 41; Morant 46 f. 17.

34. Dennis Hollister, agent for Essex, was probably the Independent grocer of Bristol who was later to become a Quaker (G. F. Nuttall, *Visible Saints: the Congregational Way, 1640–1660* (Oxford, 1957), pp. 124–5).

35. E. 113, box 1, part 2, the answers of William Browning and Richard Harvey; S.P. 24/36 Browning *v* Potter; 59 Lake *v* Mann; 80 Thrower *v* Turner; Tanner 62 f. 624.

36. S.P. 28/144 no. 3; 152 part 19; Tanner 62 f. 469; Add. 18779 f. 83v. As Lincolnshire was still subject to Royalist incursions and forced to raise contributions for both parties, a substantial proportion of the Assessment due was never collected (*The Parliament Scout*, no. 84, p. 761; Add. 5508 f. 9; L.A.C., Cragg 3/69; P.R.O., 30/15/3 no. 574; Grantham Town Records – Hall Book 1, ff. 114, 116, 118v).

37. This appears in the fact that when the Lincolnshire committee paid Fleetwood's regiment, serving in the Grantham area, they were repaid in cash by the Cambridge Committee (*C.J.*, IV, p. 61; S.P. 28/20 f. 267; 21 ff. 32–6; 26 ff. 38–41).

38. S.P. 28/14 f. 183; 243 unfol., warrants for payment for supplies for the Suffolk committee. The Norfolk and Suffolk regiments involved in the Newark debacle were marched back to their counties of origin to be recruited, and were then paid by the local Treasurers (S.P. 28/24 ff. 518–19; 26 ff. 316–21, 672). In April 1644 the Huntingdonshire committee mustered and paid Manchester's own regiment which was quartered in the county prior to its march north (S.P. 18/9/12; S.P. 28/25 ff. 277B–278).

39. In Norfolk 22.7% of the first Four Months Assessment was not returned to Cambridge, but paid to the troops or creditors by John Cory, the local Treasurer; for the second and third Assessments the figures are 5.5% and 5.6% respectively (S.P. 28/26 ff. 312–21). However, troops raised or in garrison locally were paid by the county committees throughout the year: Norfolk paid the troops which it had levied to invest Crowland after it had fallen to the Royalists for the third time (S.P. 28/26 ff. 314–15); the garrisons of Abingdon, Bedford and Lothingland were paid by, respectively, the committees of Essex and Hertford (*C.J.*, IV, p. 1; S.P. 28/22 ff. 353, 358), Cambridgeshire (S.P. 28/24 ff. 141–2) and Suffolk (*ibid.*, f. 74).

40. S.P. 28/22 f. 383; 24 ff. 641–3; 129 unfol., the 'Quarters book of Wm. Turpin'; 155 unfol., the Hertfordshire quarters' account; 196 unfol., parchment book of Hertfordshire acquittances; 234 unfol., bundle of acquittances for Huntingdonshire. In 1645–6 outstanding bills for free quarter were paid from the arrears of taxes due to Manchester (S.P. 28/33 f. 279; 34 ff. 161–2).

41. Harleian 365 ff. 52–172 (in particular ff. 157, 167, 172).

42. Harleian 165 f. 167; Tanner 62 f. 514. For other jeremiads by D'Ewes on the financial ruin that he anticipated would result from high taxation, see Harleian 164 ff. 287v, 346.

43. For Aldeburgh, E.S.R.O., EE 1/01/1 ff. 88, 94; for Lynn, C.U.L., Cholmondeley (Houghton), Pell Papers, Correspondence nos. 78–80. See also Sir John Meldrum's attempt in 1645 to get the East Anglian ports to subsidize his projected assault on Scarborough castle, claiming that this would re-open their trade with the north (E.S.R.O., HD 36/2672 nos. 23, 25, 69, 70, 77).

44. C.U.L., Cholmondeley (Houghton), Pell Papers, Correspondence no. 73;

Add. 27396 ff. 144v–145. Worst hit were those gentlemen with estates in Royalist-held or contested areas, whose income was severely hit by their inability to collect their rents (Egerton 2647 f. 371; C.U.L., Cholmondeley (Houghton), Pell Papers, Correspondence nos. 59, 99, 152).

45. Harleian 387 f. 47.

46. The three Ordinances for the Four Months' Assessment instructed the tenant of a lease-hold estate held at a rack-rent to pay the assessment on the value of the land, and then deduct the sum from the rent payable to the landlord. From the few surviving estate accounts which state both the rent of the property, and the tax paid and consequently deducted from the rent by the tenant, it is possible to calculate the sum paid in taxation on rented property as a percentage of expected rent:

Estate	Nature of property	Date	% of rent as tax
Bury free school	2 Suffolk farms; urban property in Bury and London	1643–5	35.3
Essex committee sequestered estates	Farms and urban property near Chelmsford	1644	21.1
Caius College	2 Norfolk rectories	Mich. 1643– Mich. 1645	15.6
Hare family	Norfolk manor	Lady day 1643– Lady day 1645	26.3
Herts. committee sequestered estates	4 estates in Hundred of Broadwater	Mich. 1643– Mich. 1645	29.5

Sources: W.S.R.O., E 5/9 no. 203; E.R.O., Q/SBa 8; Caius College, Cambridge, Bursar's office – the Stokys account book; N.R.O., Hare Ms. 5215; S.P. 28/209B unfol., sequestrators' accounts.

47. Ketton-Cremer, *Norfolk in the Civil War*, pp. 190–1; S.P. 23/176 ff. 503, 517, 519; B.L., Ms. J. Walker C. 6 f. 48; S.P. 23/95 f. 989; S.P. 24/65 Mott *v* Russell; Egerton 2647 f. 99; E.R.O., Q/SR 322 no. 78; 324 nos. 24, 61. A few laymen refused to pay on conscientious grounds (N.R.O., L'Estrange Mss., P 20 f. 38).

48. B.L., Clarendon 31 ff. 29–31; Wenlock, *To Charles the II*, p. 25.

49. Add. 5494 ff. 147–8; S.P. 28/222 unfol., warrants for the payment of William Sedgwick and Paul Glisson, lecturers at Ely; *C.J.*, III, p. 199; *Mercurius Aulicus*, no. 29, pp. 1087–8; S.P. 28/223 unfol., 'Mr Leman's vouchers' – bill for 2000 copies of the tract.

50. For a fuller account, see my introduction to *Scandalous Ministers*, pp. 9–24.

51. There are numerous examples in surviving records of the local committees: for northern Essex, see Add. 5829; for Cambridgeshire, Add. 15672; for Norfolk, B.L., Ms. J. Walker C. 6 ff. 44–9; for Suffolk, Holmes, *Scandalous Ministers*, *passim*.

52. Everitt, *Suffolk*, p. 46. For examples of very influential anti-Parliamentarian clergymen, see Add. 15672 ff. 11, 21.

53. Stowe 833 f. 12; S.P. 24/83 Walker *v* Herring; Egerton 2647 ff. 207–8; Add. 37491 ff. 6–6v; Stowe 189 f. 12; Stowe 842 f. 1.

54. Egerton 2647 ff. 218, 276, 281; Stowe 164 f. 4; S.P. 24/84 Whitfield *v* Reynolds; Tanner 98 f. 72. For Hatcher's operations in Essex, see Egerton 2648

ff. 31, 38; Kent R.O., U 269/0274; Sackville Mss., unfol., warrant of the Essex committee of 20 July 1644; letter (27 July) Love to Earl of Middlesex; letters (28 July, 14 October) Earl of Middlesex to Essex committee. For other incidents of troops collecting assessments, see Egerton 2647 f. 247; S.P. 24/46 Emberson *v* Sedcoale. The Isle of Ely figures are calculated from S.P. 28/152 part 19.

55. Egerton 2648 f. 31. See also Egerton 2647 ff. 99, 164.

56. See *C.J.*, III, p. 370; Nalson III no. 153 for Hertfordshire: the towns of Colchester (Morant 36 f. 35; Colchester Assembly Book 1626–46, ff. 245v, 263v; *ibid.*, 1646–56, f. 50v), Ipswich (Everitt, *Suffolk*, pp. 68–9; E.S.R.O., HD 36/2672 no. 71) and King's Lynn (C.U.L., Cholmondeley (Houghton), Pell Papers, Correspondence nos. 78–80; *C.S.P.D.*, 1644–5, p. 226; King's Lynn Assembly Book VIII, ff. 147, 147v, 150v, 152) were all involved in such disputes.

57. For the history of this dispute in 1643, see p. 87. In 1644 the chief bone of contention was the assessment for the advance of the Scots (Add. 15903 ff. 32, 40; Add. 22619 ff. 43, 161, 173, 179, 200, 202, 207–12, 226; Add. 22620 f. 22), but there was still some tension over the proportions for Manchester's taxes (Add. 22619 ff. 58, 153–7). For the quarrel over the question of the audit of the City's accounts, see Add. 22620 f. 16; Tanner 133 f. 167. For the conflict between the two authorities over the status of Thorpe, see Add. 19398 f. 167; Add. 23006 f. 43.

58. Kent R.O., U 269/0274; Sackville Mss., unfol., petition (c. 1644) to the Committee of Essex; Add. 39222 f. 5.

59. E.S.R.O., HD 36/2672 no. 29; *L.J.*, IV, p. 597; H.R.O., Miscellaneous IX no. 70552.

60. E.R.O., D/DMs O 32/1, 3–6, 17–18; Add. 37491 ff. 79, 80v.

61. *Ibid.*, ff. 26v, 28v, 29v–30, 39. For Radley's case, see also S.P. 19/94 f. 271.

62. C.U.L., Cholmondeley (Houghton), Pell Papers, Correspondence, no. 92; Add. 33572 ff. 296, 306; Add. 37491 ff. 5v, 7–7v, 12–12v; H. of L.M.P., 16 May 1643, the petition of Alexander Read.

63. Add. 37491 ff. 7v, 12, 34, 104v. See also E.S.R.O., HD 53/2786 f. 3.

64. S.P. 28/152 part 1, the account of John Weaver, ff. 6–9, 32–4. The money received from Norfolk before January 1644 was disbursed in a variety of ways: large sums were employed to meet the expenses of the siege of Lynn, some was paid to certain staff officers and troops whose maintenance was not the responsibility of any particular county, and about £2000 was used to buy arms (*ibid.*, ff. 22–30).

65. *Ibid.*, ff. 35–41; S.P. 28/12 ff. 265, 267; 13 ff. 57–9, 209, 218. From August 1644 the Treasurers of the Monthly Assessment not only paid all new bills for munitions (S.P. 28/17 ff. 331, 366; 19 ff. 257, 290–1; 20 ff. 162–3), but undertook the final settlement of those bills which had already been partially paid by Weaver (S.P. 28/24 f. 416; 25 ff. 516, 522, 540).

66. P.R.O., 30/15/3 no. 528; S.P. 28/22 f. 281; S.P. 28/260 unfol., letter of 2 April 1655; *The Parliament Scout*, no. 78, p. 625; no. 80, p. 638.

67. Some soldiers made £100 apiece at the sack of the bail of Lincoln following the successful assault (*The Parliament Scout*, no. 47, p. 391). For plunder after Marston Moor, see *Ash and Goode*, no. 5, p. 8.

68. £1200 was taxed on the City of Lincoln after its surrender (S.P. 28/24 f. 390); each trooper received a week's pay for the cavalry's outstanding service at Marston Moor (S.P. 28/17 f. 186; 267 ff. 52–6); and £500 was given to Crawford's brigade after the fall of Sheffield castle (Bell (ed.), *Fairfax correspondence*, vol. 1, pp. 113–14).

69. See pp. 152–7.

70. For an account of the available sources, see Appendix 6.

71. *Firth and Rait*, I, pp. 369–70. For such certificates, signed by the Committee of the Eastern Association, see S.P. 28/267 ff. 60–3; Stowe 184 f. 189.

72. Colonel Pickering had received 87% of the half pay due to him in September 1644, and was fully paid up to 31 December only seven weeks later (S.P. 28/26 f. 293). Cromwell was equally well paid, but Quarter-Master-General Vermuyden's account was substantially in arrear (S.P. 28/17 f. 218; 21 ff. 102–3; 26 ff. 282–4).

73. S.P. 28/19 f. 338; 22 ff. 338–9.

74. Good examples are S.P. 28/17 ff. 180, 219; 24 ff. 162, 535, 593; 25 ff. 133, 139, 140; 26 ff. 17, 166, 168, 244, 267, 268, 344; 28 f. 194.

75. Debentures for 23 troops survive, many in a very poor condition; presumably the missing documents have not escaped the damp (S.P. 28/13 ff. 61, 220–1; 14 ff. 145, 161–2; 22 f. 13; 24 ff. 177, 355, 357; 25 ff. 212, 305, 435–48, 462; 28 f. 198).

76. S.P. 28/259 unfol., the account of Edward Dendy; 198 unfol., the account of Samuel Smythe.

77. S.P. 28/25 ff. 385–7, 439. In fact the latter had received free quarter in Huntingdonshire, and accordingly they were paid 1/2d a man a day; the other 1/4d was retained by the Treasurers to pay their bills for provender and accommodation on receipt of the parish accounts (S.P. 28/24 f. 355; 267 ff. 52–6).

78. Although in some cases the sum was not paid off until July (S.P. 28/25 f. 448). On some debentures there is no indication that the sum was ever finally cleared; but as one such debenture is that of Major Alford's troop (S.P. 28/14 f. 145), and his personal account shows that he did receive final payment in June (S.P. 28/267 ff. 52–6), I think it may be assumed that all these debentures were fully paid.

79. S.P. 28/17 ff. 382–95; 22 ff. 345–50. The series contains no debentures for troops in the regiments of Cromwell or Fleetwood, or for four of the dragoon companies, which, being engaged in the siege of Banbury castle (*Quarrel*, p. 30), were never mustered. Warrants were issued for the brigade to be paid £11,536-7-0d, which was estimated to be about six weeks' pay (S.P. 28/18 ff. 217, 256).

80. S.P. 28/22 ff. 326–7: it appears that the week's pay given all the troopers for their service at Marston Moor was not deducted from the men's regular pay (S.P. 28/17 f. 186).

81. S.P. 16/539/229; S.P. 28/22 ff. 338–9; John Lilburne, *Innocency and truth justified* (1645), pp. 69–70.

82. S.P. 28/26 ff. 8–101; 27 ff. 68, 91–171; 266 f. 42; 267 ff. 52–6.

83. Theoretically it should be possible to add the sums accounted as paid to, or for, an individual captain in the Treasury Books, and, by dividing the total by the average weekly pay of the troop, calculate the number of weeks' pay effectively disbursed for the troop by the Treasury. However, many Captains received money both for their own troop and for other troops operating with them, and in the Treasury Books the officer receiving the sum, not the ultimate recipient, is accountable. Nor can this method be applied to the regiments of horse as these were extremely fluid in their composition – individual troops shuttled from regiment to regiment, and new troops were embodied in the course of the year. The calculation for Alford's toop alone can be presented with confidence because the Major's personal account (S.P. 28/267 ff. 52–6) can be correlated with the Treasury's records.

84. This section, which omits discussion of the two garrison regiments (Walton's and Ayloffe's) for which few records survive, is based on Gawsell's debentures and warrants (S.P. 28/15 ff. 255–89; 16 ff. 137–65; 17 ff. 183–207; 25 ff. 1–114, 252–4, 487–97; 26 ff. 459–69, 483–6, 524–96, 602–88, 700–852), and upon the personal accounts of five foot Captains – those of Holmes (S.P. 28/42 ff. 637–51), Barnes (S.P. 28/266 ff. 134–40), Johnson (S.P. 28/267 ff. 114–23), Axtell (*ibid.*, ff. 258–68), and Silverwood (*ibid.*, ff. 290–300).

85. The three regiments involved in the Newark debacle had been paid up to mid-February while investing the town in March (S.P. 28/25 ff. 392–7, 401, 413); in April they returned to their counties of origin to be recruited, and were paid up to 25 March by the local committees (S.P. 28/26 ff. 316–21, 672; 36 ff. 300–6). Manchester's regiment was paid by the Committee of the Association until April, when it received two weeks pay from the committee of Huntingdonshire to enable it to advance into the north (S.P. 28/25 ff. 277B–278; 234 unfol., letter of 12 April 1644 from Gawsell and Leman to Gervaise Fullwood).

86. *Ash and Goode*, no. 3, p. 1. Captains' accounts survive only for Captains in the regiments of Manchester and Pickering, both of which received debentures for four weeks and were paid off in two installments; it appears most probable from Gawsell's summary totals that the Captains in regiments whose debentures were for seven or eight weeks were also paid off in two installments.

87. His regiment garrisoned Lincoln while the rest of the army advanced on York. It was much better paid than the other regiments, being fully paid up to 12 August in mid-September by the issue of four debentures upon musters; in the absence of Captains' accounts the dates of the latter cannot be ascertained.

88. *Quarrel*, p. 1; P.R.O., 30/15/3 no. 538. Although Hobart's regiment was not mustered and paid until 7 August at Torksey (S.P. 28/26 ff. 527, 535; 171 unfol., the account of Richard Harvey).

89. S.P. 28/26 ff. 483, 823, 854. Manchester's regiment was mustered three weeks earlier.

90. P.R.O., 30/15/3 no. 546; S.P. 28/19 f. 402; 24 ff. 255–6; 26 f. 5; 260 unfol., letter of 2 April 1655 from Gawsell to the central Committee of Accounts. In some companies private individuals, whether soldiers or civilians is not known, acted as money-lenders to the common soldiers (S.P. 28/27 f. 216).

91. See pp. 168–9.

92. S.P. 28/17 f. 378; 19 ff. 321, 331; 24 ff. 638, 647; 26 ff. 5, 59, 60, 482, 527 535, 606, 801, 804, 823, 854; 27 f. 142.

93. Manchester's regiment and that of Crawford received eight weeks' pay, the other regiments, six weeks' (S.P. 28/26 ff. 295/7, 307/9, 341/5; 27 ff. 262/3, 290–315).

94. S.P. 28/266 ff. 134–40. Palgrave's regiment may have received less than the others as it had been better paid in 1644.

95. Lilburne, *Innocency and truth*, pp. 69–70; Harleian 166 f. 179; S.P. 16/506/57; P.R.O., 30/15/3 nos. 543, 545; *Abbott*, I, p. 292.

96. P.R.O., 30/15/3 no. 566; *C.J.*, IV, p. 28; Bulstrode Whitelock, *Memorials of the English Affairs* (1682), p. 120; *C.S.P.D.*, 1644–5, pp. 318, 349, 354; S.P. 28/127 ff. 226–32. See also the Buckinghamshire parish accounts in S.P. 28/148–51.

97. Lilburne, *Innocency and truth*, pp. 25, 70; *Ash and Goode*, no. 5, p. 7; no. 6, p. 16; no. 7, pp. 2, 6, 7, 8.

98. For example: *Buckinghamshire* – S.P. 28/149 unfol., account of Taplow; 150 f. 573; 151 unfol., accounts of Gt Chesham, Hughenden, Little Missenden, Whitchurch; 221 unfol., account of Gt Missenden. *Hertfordshire* – S.P. 28/154 unfol., account of Standon; 230 unfol., account of Clothall. *Northants* – S.P.

28/171 unfol., account of Werrington; 172 unfol., accounts of Barnwell All Saints, Dodford, Nassington and Thrapston; 173 unfol., the account of Oundle. *Warwickshire* – S.P. 28/182 unfol., the account of Brinklow.

99. S.P. 24/37 Bushell *v* Colson; S.P. 28/203 unfol., the account of William Turpin; S.P. 28/23 ff. 13, 39, 87; 25 f. 319; 26 f. 396; Add. 31116 f. 193; *Luke Letter Book*, p. 412. See also P.R.O., 30/15/3 no. 566; *C.J.*, IV, p. 28.

100. S.P. 28/266 ff. 31–2. See also *Firth and Rait*, I, p. 370; S.P. 28/27 f. 247.

101. *Firth and Rait*, I, pp. 215–19, 245–6. For local organization in Essex, see the warrants of the county Treasurer, Birkhead, in S.P. 28/9 ff. 312, 314, 385; 227 unfol., warrants; also his accounts, in S.P. 28/153 unfol.; 259 unfol.; and his correspondence – Egerton 2647 ff. 80, 114, 123, 140, 144, 166; Stowe 189 f. 15. For Hertfordshire see S.P. 28/10 f. 46; 11 f. 99; 130 part 2, f. 15; 154 unfol., the account of Thomas Peacock, the account of the Hundreds of Odsey and Edwinstree; 209B unfol., the account of Ickleford. The documentation is far less complete for Norfolk and Suffolk, but the system employed appears to have been similar (E.S.R.O., HD 53/2786 f. 2; C.U.L., Buxton Mss., box 97, C. 77; N.R.O., Aylsham Mss. 198 unfol., warrant of 17 August 1643; E. 113 box 1, part 2, the answer of Thomas Kett).

102. Stowe 189 f. 12; S.P. 28/227 unfol., letters to Birkhead of 5 September and 9 December 1644; Egerton 2647 ff. 100, 106.

103. Calculated from Weaver's disbursements (S.P. 28/152 part 1, the account of John Weaver) and S.P. 28/197 part 2, ff. 45–7.

104. S.P. 28/22 f. 208; 24 ff. 83, 178, 276–8; 26 f. 548; 152 part 1, the account of John Weaver, ff. 6–9. In April Russell supervised the raising of horse in Norfolk and Suffolk for Cromwell's regiment (S.P. 28/24 ff. 518–19, 563; 198 unfol., the account of Samuel Smythe; 243 unfol., warrants of the Suffolk committee); in September he worked with the Hertfordshire authorities (S.P. 28/231 unfol., warrants of the committee. See also S.P. 28/18 f. 215; 25 f. 377B; 230 unfol., committee warrants).

105. S.P. 23/126 f. 569; S.P. 28/20 ff. 158, 219; 21 ff. 66, 160; 22 ff. 208–9, 214–16; 23 ff. 3, 160; P.R.O., 30/15/3 no. 528.

106. S.P. 28/18 f. 215; 20 f. 218; 23 ff. 26, 35, 59, 61; 24 ff. 205, 319. Some of these purchases were of horses captured from the enemy by infantrymen.

107. Captain Jenkins took a horse from an Eltisley man, leaving two sick horses in exchange, and agreeing to pay 30/- should one of them die (S.P. 28/223 unfol., warrant of 22 March 1643/4).

108. S.P. 28/173 unfol., account of Bozeat parish. See also, in the same box, the accounts of Barnwell All Saints, Clapton and Werrington, and S.P. 28/22 f. 76; 151 unfol., accounts of Gt Hampden and Winslow; 172 unfol., account of Thingdon; 231 unfol., account of Thundridge.

109. S.P. 28/26 f. 272. See also P.R.O., 30/15/3 no. 572.

110. S.P. 28/24 f. 9; 25 f. 365. See also 17 ff. 383, 397.

111. S.P. 28/24 f. 319; 26 f. 345; 152 part 1, the account of John Weaver, f. 15. Although there was an agent employed for the purchase of saddles and harness by the Cambridge Committee (S.P. 28/23 ff. 12, 14; 24 ff. 298, 324), individual Captains frequently made their own arrangements for their supply (S.P. 28/20 f. 281; 23 f. 59; 24 f. 230; 253B unfol., the depositions book 1645–7, f. 31v).

112. The governor of the fort at Bedford and Colonel Norwich, who spent some time operating independently of the field army (*Quarrel*, p. 21), both bought arms themselves and returned the bills to the Treasury (S.P. 28/22 f. 312; 27 ff. 49–49v).

113. Although one load of match was captured, presumably by a Royalist

privateer (*Quarrel*, p. 10), the journey to the north by sea was far more secure than that by road, given that southern Lincolnshire was still subject to the incursions of the cavaliers from Belvoir and Newark. In June they seized travellers on the road between Sleaford and Swineshead (N.R.O., Quarter Sessions, box 35, the deposition of John Titshall) and in the next month captured one of Manchester's officials near Stamford (S.P. 24/66 North *v* Fawcett). In terms of cost, the usual charge for cartage was 1/– a load-mile; a keel-boat of 40 tons burden made the return journey from Lynn to Cambridge for £4 (S.P. 28/24 f. 27).

114. S.P. 28/17 ff. 158–9, 333; 20 ff. 162–3; 21 f. 49; 22 f. 221; 24 ff. 27, 226, 232–3, 333, 439A; 25 ff. 420, 557; 26 f. 371v; 139 ff. 285–305; 223 unfol., 'Mr Leman's vouchers', warrant of 16 May 1644; P.R.O., 30/15/3 no. 542; *Mercurius Anglicus*, no. 2, p. 13.

115. S.P. 28/13 f. 196; 24 ff. 215, 224; 25 f. 520; 26 f. 311; P.R.O., 30/15/3 nos. 523, 529.

116. Although one receipt for powder and pistols survives, Wormell never details his bills so it is impossible to discover exactly what he was buying (S.P. 28/14 f. 183; 24 f. 416; 25 ff. 516, 522, 540; 27 f. 389).

117. Samuel Moody's transactions ended in April 1644 (S.P. 28/24 f. 191); the last shipment was of powder and pistols valued at £700 by Thomas Toll, a Lynn merchant and the town's M.P. (S.P. 28/17 f. 366; 22 f. 221). Part of the cost of continental munitions was met by the purchase of 600 firkins of Suffolk butter with money raised on the weekly assessment, which was then exported to Holland, so avoiding the export of specie and the costs of exchange (E. 113 box 1, part 2, the answer of Anthony Barry).

118. For example, the French pistols purchased proved to be too long for English holsters (P.R.O., 30/15/3 no. 542).

119. S.P. 28/22 f. 210; 24 ff. 240, 242, 291; 44 f. 66; 152 part 1, the account of John Weaver, ff. 6, 32.

120. The Lieutenant-General of the Ordnance made small purchases from local tradesmen while the army was on the march (S.P. 28/24 f. 250; 26 f. 442).

121. Deals with other London merchants are recorded in S.P. 16/539/221; S.P. 28/20 f. 166; 23 f. 67; 25 f. 178. Barker's bills are S.P. 28/17 ff. 331, 333; 20 ff. 162–3; 24 ff. 243–4; 26 f. 371v. Barker's purchases, valued at about £7000 between January and October 1644, included 3080 muskets, 5400 swords, 550 'harquebuser' armors, and 480 cases of pistols, besides powder and shot for the artillery.

122. Calculated from S.P. 28/197 part 2, ff. 45–7, and from Weaver's accounts in S.P. 28/139 unfol., and 152 part 1, unfol.

123. *Quarrel*, p. 10; W.O. 55/460, warrant of 31 August 1644; *C.S.P.D.*, 1644–5, p. 73.

124. S.P. 28/18 f. 234; 19 f. 257; 21 ff. 281, 284; 25 f. 345; 26 f. 136; 128 unfol., the Association Treasury Book, ff. 9v, 10.

125. Although soldiers captured by the enemy were re-equipped at the expense of the Association (S.P. 28/24 f. 519; 26 ff. 316–21).

126. S.P. 24/50 Gooch *v* the Sheriffs of London; S.P. 28/14 f. 168; 23 ff. 347–9; 24 f. 647; 65 f. 655; 223 unfol., 'Mr Leman's vouchers' – letter from Captain Harbottle to Buckley a Cambridge tailor for breeches for his troop.

127. S.P. 28/24 ff. 437A, 533; 43 f. 968. And see, for example, S.P. 28/128 unfol., the Association Treasury Book, ff. 42, 48, for sums for hats and boots put to account.

128. S.P. 28/19 f. 271; 25 f. 24; 26 ff. 289, 291–2; P.R.O., 30/15/3 no. 545.

129. S.P. 28/22 ff. 187, 294; 25 ff. 127, 136, 143–4, 162; P.R.O., 30/15/3 no. 528. See also the sums deducted from the pay of Russell's regiment at the Henley muster for boots (S.P. 28/27 ff. 290–9).

130. S.P. 28/18 f. 234; 25 f. 182; 26 f. 299; *C.S.P.D.*, 1644–5, p. 193.

131. S.P. 28/17 f. 152; 21 f. 113; 149 unfol., the Taplow parish account.

132. Foot soldiers were to be charged 6d a day, n.c.o.s 8d; a trooper was charged 1/– a day, plus the cost of provender eaten by his horse.

133. S.P. 28/22 f. 314; 26 f. 396; 152 part 1, the account of John Weaver, f. 17; 149 unfol., the Taplow parish account. See also S.P. 28/25 ff. 330–1; 172 unfol., the Eye parish account; 173 unfol., the Oundle parish account; the Fotheringhay parish account.

134. S.P. 28/151 unfol., the Chipping Wycombe parish account; 154 unfol., the Redbourn parish account; 172 unfol., the Eye parish account; L.A.C., South Kyme 12, account of Richard Taylor and John Bullye.

135. S.P. 24/62 Males *v* Watts; S.P. 28/172 unfol., the parish account of Easton Willibrooke; 173 unfol., the Oundle parish account; L.A.C., Frampton vestry book 1597–1683, *sub* 27 October 1643.

136. Thomas Edwards, *The third part of Gangraena* (1646), pp. 17–18; H.R.O., D/P 12 9/1 E 2. See also *Luke Letter Book*, pp. 133, 134; L.A.C., South Kyme 12, the account of Richard Taylor and John Bullye.

137. *Luke Letter Book*, pp. 79, 97, 117, 118, 126, 127, 136, 138, 142, 413–15, 419, 429.

138. For examples, see S.P. 28/23 ff. 149, 151, 168, 221; 24 ff. 85–8, 96; 253B unfol., the Depositions book, f. 50v.

139. S.P. 28/22 f. 383; 24 f. 88; 150 f. 247B; 154 unfol., the Redbourn parish account; 171 unfol., the Collingtree parish account.

140. S.P. 28/223 unfol., 'Mr Leman's vouchers' – letter from Lieutenant-Colonel Clifton to the Treasurers. However, Montagu's regiment at Newport Pagnell did not pay their bills (*Luke Letter Book*, pp. 61, 65, 100, 101, 147).

141. Although they might pay some of their charges (S.P. 28/24 f. 158; 28 f. 196).

142. There are many examples in the series S.P. 28, particularly in box 223; see also S.P. 28/23 ff. 168–75.

143. S.P. 28/13 f. 220; 14 f. 145; 24 f. 345. See *Firth and Rait*, I, p. 370.

144. See, for example, S.P. 28/128 unfol., the Association Treasury Book, ff. 60, 72, 84, 86.

145. S.P. 28/22 f. 383; 129 unfol., the quarters' account of William Turpin; 196 unfol., Turner's acquittance book; 155 unfol., the Hertford quarters' account.

146. In Lincolnshire the settlement of the bills for the billeting of the Association's regiments against the arrears of Manchester's assessments was still being sorted out in 1649 (L.A.C., Cragg 3/69; Brace 17/1 p. 30). The garrison of Lynn's bills were still being settled in 1647 (E. 134 15 Charles II, Michaelmas 38).

147. S.P. 28/19 f. 295; 27 f. 266; 223 unfol., 'Mr Leman's vouchers' – the Croyden bill.

148. *Ash and Goode*, no. 3, p. 1; S.P. 16/539/339; S.P. 28/22 f. 191; 25 f. 186; 26 f. 5; 27 f. 341; 151 unfol., Little Horwood parish account; 173 unfol., Byfield and Glinton parish accounts.

149. The inhabitants of Bedfordshire, for which county no parish accounts survive, were probably equally unlikely to receive payment (S.P. 24/55 Holcroft *v* Bachelor).

150. S.P. 28/18 ff. 144, 207; 24 ff. 112, 115–21, 131–2, 528, 559–60, 594; 27 f. 117. Next winter Captain Moody's troop, quartered at Stamford, was drawing from the adjacent villages in Northamptonshire (S.P. 28/171 unfol., parish account of Blatherwycke; 172 unfol., parish accounts of Easton Willibrooke, Harringworth and Maxey; 173 unfol., parish account of Oundle); Major-General Crawford's regiment at Aylesbury was drawing from the surrounding area of Buckinghamshire (S.P. 28/127 ff. 226–32).

151. S.P. 28/42 ff. 268–70, 272–9, 292–3, 312–15; 151 unfol., accounts of the parishes of Addington, Adstock, Drayton and Slapton; 171 unfol., accounts of Grafton Regis, Hartwell and Horton; 221 unfol., parish account of Mentmore; John Lilburne, *The iust mans iustification* (1646), pp. 19–20; S.P. 24/57 James *v* Pridgeon.

152. S.P. 28/22 ff. 160–74; 25 ff. 268–73, 291–304; 26 f. 275; 27 ff. 187–8.

153. He kept his post on the formation of the New Model Army (S.P. 28/30 f. 128).

154. Based on the Northamptonshire parish accounts in the boxes S.P. 28/171–3; particularly informative are those of Barnwell All Saints, Barnwell St Andrew, Wood Newton (in box 171) and Fotheringhay (in box 173): Croft parish documents, warrant of 23 May 1644.

155. S.P. 28/17 ff. 152, 158–9; 20 f. 165; 22 f. 297; 25 ff. 130, 175; E. 403/2608 pp. 148–9, 167–9, 226–7.

156. S.P. 28/22 ff. 285, 298–9; 25 ff. 151–2, 157–8, 160–2, 183, 315; *Quarrel*, p. 90; S.P. 16/503/56 xxiv; *C.S.P.D.*, 1644–5, pp. 39, 76, 95–6, 123, 127.

157. For this system in operation, see Lilburne, *The iust mans iustification*, pp. 19–20.

158. S.P. 28/22 ff. 160–74, 180–91, 194, 282; 23 ff. 6, 42; 25 f. 318; 26 f. 275; 27 ff. 187–8; *C.S.P.D.*, 1644, p. 125.

159. S.P. 28/171 unfol., parish accounts of Barnwell All Saints, Wood Newton; 173 unfol., parish account of Fotheringhay: S.P. 28/127 ff. 226–32.

160. W.H., *A relation of the good successe of the Parliaments forces* (Cambridge, 1644), no pagination; *Ash and Goode*, no. 5, p. 7; Harleian 7001 f. 170; *Quarrel*, pp. 1, 6.

161. *Ibid.*, p. 68; S.P. 16/503/56 xxiv; Simeon Ashe, *A true relation, of the most chiefe occurences* (1644), pp. 6, 9; *The Parliament Scout*, no. 75, p. 597; *C.S.P.D.*, 1644–5, pp. 64, 125; P.R.O., 30/15/3 no. 557.

162. Lilburne, *Innocency and truth*, pp. 25, 69–70. See also John Lilburne, *The copy of a letter from . . . to a friend* (1645), pp. 11–12.

163. *C.S.P.D.*, 1644, p. 328; *C.J.*, iii, pp. 572, 720; *L.J.*, vi, p. 636; *Quarrel*, pp. 3–5.

164. S.P. 28/18 ff. 137, 165; 20 f. 223; 144 no. 3; *Mercurius Aulicus*, no. 40, pp. 1183–4.

165. That Cromwell was supicious of the Treasurers is apparent from his letter to Walton in the late summer (*Abbott*, i, p. 292). For Lilburne's more vocal accusations of chicanery, see the sources cited in note 162 above.

166. *Firth and Rait*, i, p. 518; S.P. 28/22 f. 366; *C.J.*, iii, p. 720; iv, pp. 47, 56, 63; *L.J.*, vii, p. 179; Add. 19398 f. 170.

167. S.P. 28/18 f. 294; 24 f. 23; 26 f. 118.

168. P.R.O. 30/15/3 nos. 523, 548; S.P. 28/260 unfol., letter of 2 April 1655 from Gawsell to the central Committee of Accounts.

169. P.R.O. 30/15/3 nos. 523–4; *C.J.*, iii, pp. 626, 648, 655, 699; Harleian 166

f. 129; *The Weekly Account*, no. 67, sig. Uuu 2v; *A Perfect Diurnall of Some Passages in Parliament*, no. 63, p. 498.

170. P.R.O., 30/15/3 no. 574. The *H.M.C.* editor's dating of this document ('1645?' – *H.M.C.*, 8th Report, part II, p. 62) is a poor guess, for the petition was obviously drawn up before the Commons began their discussion of the New Model Ordinance. Professor Everitt (*Suffolk*, p. 80, note 2) thinks February 1644 the 'unquestionable' date. But this seems extremely unlikely, for the Association had then just been voted their new powers and fiscal provision. The signatures suggest the autumn of 1644, and it is probable that the document is either the petition presented by the Committee of the Association on 8 October (*C.J.*, III, p. 655) or that of 19 November (*ibid.*, p. 699); either date would make sense of the reference to 'five months sollicitinge'. However, the Remonstrance bears little resemblance to D'Ewes's précis of 8 October petition (Harleian 166 f. 129), so I prefer the November date.

171. P.R.O., 30/15/3 no. 574; Harleian 166 f. 129.

172. Egerton 2651 ff. 163–4; *The Parliament Scout*, no. 36, p. 302. For detailed figures and analysis, see Appendix 7.

173. These figures are calculated from S.P. 28/152 part 1, the account of John Weaver, ff. 6–9, 12–17, 32–4, 43–8, and from S.P. 28/197 part 2, ff. 45–7. The figures are monthly averages of money *disbursed* on munitions and the administration in 1644; since some arms bills were outstanding, and the Committee and its agents were not fully paid, the actual monthly cost of these items would have been larger.

174. S.P. 28/26 ff. 312–13, 335.

Chapter 8

1. Walton's (Lynn); Rainborow's (Lincolnshire); Ayloffe's (Newport Pagnell, then Abingdon); Sparrow's (Abingdon).

2. See Appendix 8(C) Captain Harvey's is the only full muster roll (i.e. one that contains the name of each soldier present at the muster) that has survived for the Association's army.

3. See Appendix 7.

4. Most companies acquired a clerk and a gentleman-at-arms, both paid at the same rate as a sergeant, and 2 or 3 lanspassadoes, each paid 10d a day. The first two ranks were certainly necessitated by the complex system of finance and the rapid turnover of men in the infantry companies. The utility of the lanspassadoes is more doubtful: no such rank is found in the New Model (for their supposed function, see Richard Elton, *The compleat body of the art military* (1659), pp. 178–9).

5. The Cambridge Committee met some of the charges when it was embodied but otherwise it was not a drain on the central Treasury (S.P. 28/128 unfol., the Association Treasury Book, f. 137).

6. C. V. Wedgwood, *The King's War* (1966), p. 308; *Mercurius Civicus*, no. 57, pp. 550–1; no. 59, p. 566; no. 60, p. 579; *C.S.P.D.*, 1644, pp. 266–7, 275, 281–2, 300–1, 324–6; Harleian 166 f. 80; *Firth and Rait*, I, pp. 272–5

7. *Quarrel*, pp. 6, 7, 8, 12; *C.S.P.D.*, 1644, pp. 383, 395, 407; *C.J.*, III, pp. 582, 589; *L.J.*, VI, pp. 663, 677.

8. S.P. 28/18 f. 402; 26 ff. 683, 688; H.R.O., Miscellaneous IX nos. 70539–41; *C.S.P.D.*, 1644, pp. 429–30, 436–7.

9. *Ibid.*, pp. 395, 480. The regiment remained at Abingdon until 1645 (Samuel Harsnett, *A full relation of the defeate given* (1645), *passim*).

10. *C.S.P.D.*, 1644–5, pp. 84, 127, 139, 233; *C.J.*, IV, p. 1. The Committee of Both Kingdom's plan must have been doubly bitter to Manchester as in October he had proposed to incorporate Sparrow's men into his regiments, dismissing their officers, but this had been vetoed by the Committee (*C.S.P.D.*, 1644–5, p. 13).

11. S.P. 28/26 ff. 730, 740, 757, 763, 770, 774.

12. Egerton 2647 f. 220.

13. Most of these were promoted n.c.o. on entering Manchester's army, and their joining the latter may have been because of the opportunities for preferment for experienced soldiers (see E. 121 2/9 no. 46 part 2, pp. 6, 40, 41; 2/10 no. 49, p. 30).

14. E.R.O., Q/SBa 2/82 f. 18; N.R.O., Norwich Court Book 1634–46, f. 420; S.P. 28/223 unfol., warrant of 15 May 1644. A strange exception to the rule that few men joined the Association's infantry regiments as volunteers is the company of Captain Playford; his men were raised at Norwich from volunteers (N.R.O., Norwich Court Book 1634–46, ff. 421–428v; Add. 22619 f. 224) but in June 1644 they were directed to join Rainborow's regiment of foot (S.P. 28/266 ff. 300–17). They may have been intended for cavalry service originally.

15. S.P. 28/15 ff. 267, 282; 26 f. 123 (215 Royalist soldiers joined Manchester after the fall of Lincoln in 1644); *Mercurius Aulicus*, no. 37, pp. 1157–8; no. 40, pp. 1183–4; *Luke Letter Book*, p. 80; S.P. 28/171 unfol., the parish account of Clapton.

16. *Quarrel*, p. 13. See also *C.S.P.D.*, 1644–5, p. 258.

17. *Ibid.*, 1644, p. 518; 1644–5, pp. 4, 197, 258; *Quarrel*, pp. 3, 6–7, 8, 12; Everitt, *Suffolk*, p. 81; Add. 22619 f. 206; Egerton 2647 f. 235; Stowe 189 ff. 16, 22, 26.

18. *Ibid.*, ff. 16, 22, 34, 35; Egerton 2647 ff. 199, 304, 314; 2651 f. 130; Morant 47 ff. 115, 158; 48 f. 115; Add. 37491 f. 3; N.R.O., L'Estrange Mss., P 20 f. 34; E.S.R.O., HD 53/2786 f. 1.

19. Morant 47 f. 158; Add. 27491 f. 19v; Stowe 842 f. 5; N.R.O., Norwich Court Book 1634–46, ff. 409v, 412; S.P. 28/243 unfol., warrant of 15 September 1644; S.P. 24/65 Morton *v* Foyson; *Mercurius Aulicus*, no. 41, pp. 474–5; no. 13, pp. 964–5; *Mercurius Britanicus*, no. 31, p. 242.

20. Stowe 189 ff. 16, 34, 35: despite these precautions, in August 1644 Captain Silverlock of the Essex militia took four impressed soldiers into his trained-band and the constables had to find replacements (Add. 37491 ff. 18, 23).

21. Add. 37491 ff. 19–20; Egerton 2647 ff. 148, 165; 2648 f. 49.

22. Abuse: E.R.O., Q/SBa 2/55, the examination of John Moorhouse. Refusal to assist: E.R.O., Q/SR 323 no. 48; Egerton 2651 f. 152; S.P. 28/152 part 20 f. 2. Threats: Egerton 2651 f. 176; S.P. 24/65 Morton *v* Foyson; 66 City of Norwich *v* Cory; 71 Roe *v* Love. Violence: Add. 37491 f. 18; Holmes, *Scandalous Ministers*, p. 61. Witchcraft: C.U.L., Diocese of Ely records E 12, Assize file for 1647, the information of Richard Denton.

23. Morant 42 f. 81; Add. 37491 ff. 6v, 18, 24v; Egerton 2651 f. 152; Stowe 189 ff. 25, 26. £2 or £3 was usually levied for each man short, but a particularly recalcitrant constable might be fined as much as £10.

24. Add. 37491 ff. 8, 19–19v; E.R.O., Q/SBa 2/58, examination of John Downes; S.P. 28/227 unfol., 'a memorial of such particulars . . . necessary'; S.P. 24/52 Harwood *v* Stirling; Add. 15672 f. 25.

25. E.R.O., Ass. 35/85/T no. 4; Stowe 189 ff. 26, 35; Add. 37491 ff. 19, 20v; N.R.O., Norwich Court Book 1634–46, ff. 403–4, 420.

26. Stowe 189 f. 16. For the dependents of an impressed man becoming a charge on the parish, see N.R.O., Stockton town book 1625–1712, f. 12; Overseers of the poor book of Gissing, *sub* 1644–5; N.R.O., L'Estrange Mss., P 20 f. 34.

27. Holmes, *Scandalous Ministers*, p. 61; N.R.O., Norwich Court Book 1634–46, f. 420; E.R.O., Q/SBa 2/91, petition of William Yorke; Q/SR 251/14; 273/31 and 84; 320/85. Other criminal elements impressed by the constables were Balls of Swaffham (W. B. Rix, *The Pride of Swaffham* (King's Lynn, n.d.), p. 38), Smith of Gissing (Gissing overseers of the poor book, *sub* 1642, 1644) and Camps of Cheshunt (W. LeHardy (ed.), *Hertford County Records* (Hertford, 1905–28), vol. v, pp. 235, 418).

28. E.R.O., Q/SR 324/56. See also H.R.O., Q/SR 6/257; W.S.R.O., Acc. 2113/7/2/3 pp. 141, 148.

29. Add. 37491 ff. 18v–20; N.R.O., Norwich Court Book 1634–46, ff. 409v, 412; *The Parliament Scout*, no. 57, p. 559 (mispagination for 459); Stowe 189 f. 16.

30. C. G. Cruikshank, *Elizabeth's Army* (1966), pp. 26–30.

31. Stowe 189 f. 22; E.R.O., Q/SBa 2/78, the petition of John Cramner; L.A.C., Archdeaconry wills, vol. 1643–4, no. 339; S.P. 28/152 part 20 f. 25v. But the Romford committee were always prepared to enforce the provisions of the Ordinance (*Firth and Rait*, I, p. 242) against impressing persons rated at £5 in goods or £3 in land in the subsidy book (Add. 37491 f. 18v).

32. N.R.O., Norwich Court Book 1634–46, ff. 400v, 403v–404, 418–20.

33. See N.R.O., Stockton Town Book 1625–1712, ff. 29v, 30, 33; E.S.R.O., HD 53/2786 f. 9; W.S.R.O., Tem. 123 ff. 43–8 for the purchase of shoes and clothing by the constables.

34. Egerton 2646 f. 223; 2647 ff. 197, 214, 223, 229; H.R.O., Miscellaneous IX nos. 70539, 70541.

35. Stowe 833 f. 6; E.R.O., Ass. 35/85/T no. 4; N.R.O., Stockton town book 1625–1712, ff. 30, 33. See also S.P. 28/154 unfol., Redbourn parish account; E.R.O., D/P 232/8/1; E.S.R.O., FB 130/I 2/10–12.

36. Egerton 2646 f. 251; 2647 ff. 199, 279; Morant 47 f. 59.

37. Egerton 2647 ff. 146, 190. In fact the failure of the Essex committee to arm their troops was as much a question of their poverty and the deficiencies of their supply system, as a matter of policy, see pp. 99–100.

38. Egerton 2647 ff. 229, 256. See also ff. 214, 241.

39. The troops raised in Essex and Hertfordshire upon the Ordinance of 12 July 1644 are an exception to this generalization, being embodied into complete companies. It is interesting to find the Hertfordshire committee refusing to issue ammunition to its conscripts and guarding them from the county with troops of horse (H.R.O., Miscellaneous IX 70539–41; S.P. 28/156 unfol., the account of the tax raised upon the Ordinance of 12 July 1644).

40. S.P. 28/22 f. 317; 25 ff. 147, 148, 350; 128 unfol., the Association Treasury Book, f. 25v; 227 unfol., warrant of 12 April 1644.

41. Add. 22619 f. 219. See also *The Parliament Scout*, no. 67, p. 535; no. 68, p. 546.

42. *Ibid.*, no. 16, p. 144; S.P. 28/24 ff. 103, 105, 341.

43. *A true relation of the late fight* (1644), p. 7; *Ash and Goode*, no. 1, p. 6; no. 5, p. 8; Ashe, *True relation*, pp. 3–4; S.P. 28/27 ff. 59, 142, 159; Peter Wenham, *The Great and Close Siege of York* (Kineton, 1970), pp. 57–66.

44. *Mercurius Aulicus*, no. 42, pp. 1206–8; *A briefe relation of the siege at Newark* (1644), p. 8. Harleian 166 f. 78v.

45. Calculated from the accounts of those Captains who made returns of sums lent to soldiers who had subsequently deserted (S.P. 28/26 ff. 5, 527, 606, 647, 801, 804). See also *Ash and Goode*, no. 1, p. 8.

46. Add. 22619 f. 137; Morant 42 f. 81; 44 f. 113; Add. 37491 ff. 8v, 63v; E.R.O., Q/SBa 6/1 f. 3; 6/2 f. 5; Stowe 189 f. 29; *The Parliament Scout*, no. 67, p. 535. There is a good series of warrants, backed by a variety of threats, to the constables of Croft ordering them to turn in any deserters who made their way back to the village (Croft parish documents, warrants of 8 June, 23 June, 22 September 1644; 19 March 1645).

47. S.P. 28/25 f. 1; 26 ff. 5, 527; *Quarrel*, p. 1; *Mercurius Aulicus*, no. 37, pp. 1157–8. See also Harleian 7001 f. 170; Hu. R.O., D/DM 32/5. In the month after 25 August 25 of Captain Harvey's foot were sent to the hospital camp at Horncastle (S.P. 28/171 unfol., the account of Captain Harvey).

48. *The Parliament Scout*, no. 66, p. 528; S.P. 28/21 ff. 324, 328; 27 ff. 290–9.

49. S.P. 28/17 f. 415; 18 f. 140; W.H., *A relation*, no pagination; *Ash and Goode*, no. 5, p. 7; *Quarrel*, p. 1.

50. *C.S.P.D.*, 1644–5, p. 139.

51. See p. 99. But some dragoons were raised in other counties – see N.R.O., quarter-sessions papers, box 35, the examination of William Snoring.

52. Egerton 2647 f. 166.

53. S.P. 28/26 f. 335; 27 f. 86. This was the case in the Royalist army (see Roy, 'Royalist Army', p. 126; C. H. Firth, *Cromwell's Army* (1902), pp. 123–4).

54. S.P. 28/13 f. 61; 265 ff. 546–58. See also S.P. 28/25 ff. 212, 305.

55. S.P. 28/18 f. 256; 27 ff. 101–3, 129, 144.

56. Lilburne, *Innocency and truth*, p. 25. See also P.R.O., 30/15/3 no. 545; S.P. 16/503/56 iv.

57. *Abbott*, i, pp. 248, 256, 261–2; Add. 22619 f. 9; S.P. 28/24 ff. 485–6. See Firth, 'Raising of the Ironsides', pp. 31–4.

58. See pp. 93–5.

59. Manchester received two Middlesex troops (S.P. 28/152 part 1, the account of John Weaver, f. 28); in March 1644 Colonel Norwich supervised the raising of a troop in Buckinghamshire (S.P. 28/133 part 2, f. 282v).

60. Tanner 62 f. 301; Add. 18778 ff. 27v, 42v; Harleian 165 ff. 178v, 190; *C.J.*, iii, pp. 238, 239; *L.J.*, vi, p. 315.

61. Although the county of Essex, when moving the Commons for power to impress men, envisaged the conscription of men to serve as troopers – a further comment on the difficulty of raising cavalry in August 1643 (Tanner 62 f. 225).

62. E. 121 3/4 L ff. 5–6.

63. E.S.R.O., HD 53/2786 f. 2; Egerton 2647 f. 251.

64. In March 1644 Colchester was still 12 men short of the 50 it was supposed to raise (Stowe 189 f. 5).

65. Egerton 2647 f. 239; *Abbott*, i, pp. 256, 258–9, 262.

66. See Appendix 9.

67. There are no cavalry muster rolls which would clarify this point, but see Egerton 2647 f. 363.

68. S.P. 28/238 unfol., the certificate of Ralph Hooker. See also the documents relating to the recruiting of the troops of Cromwell, Whalley and Disborough in March 1644 (S.P. 28/13 f. 221; 24 ff. 177, 357).

69. S.P. 28/21 f. 250; E. 121 3/4 Bb, *passim*; 3/6 (manor of East Dereham), *passim*. Five of Grove's troopers claim arrears of £22-5-6d, and twenty-one of them claim £19-1-0d. I calculate that a man serving in Cromwell's regiment from 1 February 1644 to mid-April 1645 would be 262 days' pay in arrear (£32-15-0d); one-third of this sum was deducted for free quarter, leaving £21-16-8d.

70. See the statement of arrears with dates of service given in E. 315/5, *passim*.

71. N.R.O., Norwich Court Book 1634–46, f. 439. See also (f. 421) the City's ruling that those with a large number of children and no means to maintain them should be forbidden to volunteer. For a trooper plundering, see S.P. 24/37 Bushell *v* Colson. Desertion to the enemy was not unknown (S.P. 28/266 ff. 31–2).

72. *Abbott*, I, p. 248. The piecemeal volunteers *may* have been of a higher social status than the levies of August 1643. Of 17 men Captain Dingley received from Colchester in the summer, only 2 could write their names (Morant 46 f. 289). In February 1645 21 of the 41 troopers who gave acquittances to Treasurer Leman signed their names (S.P. 28/26 ff. 115–33).

73. Whitelock, *Memorials*, p. 68; Kingston, *East Anglia*, p. 360; *Gardiner*, I, p. 48.

74. E. 121 3/4 L, f. 10; 3/6 (manor of East Dereham), f. 2; 5/5 no. 43, f. 2v; 5/7 no. 62, f. 6. Captain Horseman, who had served with Lord Grey of Groby, also brought some troopers with him (E. 121 1/6 no. 12, part 2, pp. 2, 5, 10, 14; no. 117, p. 24; 3/4 Bb, ff. 4–4v, 7).

75. Based on a survey of the relevant documents in the class E. 121. The arrears certificates of Cromwell's regiment are E. 121 3/4 L, f. 10; 5/5 no. 34, part 2, p. 2; 5/6 no. 14, part 2, pp. 23–58; no. 94, p. 1. See also S.P. 24/34 Bell *v* Harding; 52 Harlow *v* Lilley.

76. A number of Fiennes's men from the garrison of Bristol, and some of Lord Willoughby's troopers joined the army of the Association (S.P. 28/145 ff. 242–60; E. 121 2/3 no. 31, p. 2; 2/11 no. 19, part 2, pp. 1–5; 4/5 no. 94, p. 3; 5/7 no. 38, pp. 10, 22; no. 90, p. 4; E. 315/5 pp. 45–6).

77. The commanders of less well-financed armies protested frequently, but unavailingly, against this development (Firth, *Cromwell's Army*, pp. 23–5).

78. See Add. 31116 f. 117; R. Kirle, *A coppy of a letter writ from* (1643), *passim*.

79. *Baillie*, II, p. 235. See also p. 229. For a London sectary who joined the army of the Association to serve under a 'preaching' officer whose opinions he admired, see Lawrence Clarkson, *The lost sheep found* (1660), p. 10.

80 *Quarrel*, p. 72.

81. *Alas, pore Parliament, how art thou betrai'd?* (1644), no pagination.

82. The troopers are recognized as having served in 1644 from S.P. 28/26 f. 168; E. 121 5/7 no. 14, part 2, p. 32. The wills are P.C.C. 146 Ruthen; P.C.C. 472 Pell; C.U.L., Archdeaconry of Ely wills, book 10, f. 315v.

83. *Mercurius Aulicus*, no. 35, pp. 1139–40. See S.P. 24/80 Tirrell *v* Harvey for the social status of one of the Earl's gentlemen of horse.

84. Worcester College, Oxford, Clarke Ms. 41 f. 114; S.P. 28/56 f. 496; S.P. 24/34 Bell *v* Harding; 52 Harlow *v* Lilly; 62 Maltus *v* Haynes. See Firth, *Cromwell's Army*, pp. 275–6.

85. See C. B. MacPherson, *The political theory of possessive individualism* (Oxford, 1962), pp. 112–15, 121, 132.

86. A. S. P. Woodhouse, *Puritanism and Liberty* (1950), pp. 69–70. See also pp. 56, 67, 71, 74–5, 452. In his article 'Gentlemen Levellers?', *Past and Present*, no. 49 (1970), pp. 120–1, Professor Aylmer suggests that Sexby may have been an apprentice.

87. S.P. 24/67 Ormes v Guggles; E.R.O., Q/SR 366/80; Q/SO 1 f. 29; S.P. 28/26 f. 168; C.U.L., Archdeaconry of Ely wills, book 10 f. 315v; Holmes, *Scandalous Ministers*, p. 31 note 2; E. 315/5 pp. 53–4; W.S.R.O., Archdeaconry will, 424 Colman; Tanner 62 f. 225.

88. S.P. 24/84 West v Trinity College; S.P. 28/28 ff. 477, 502; 58 f. 357; Everitt, *Suffolk*, p. 72.

89. C. S. Terry (ed.), *Papers relating to the Army of the Solemn League and Covenant 1643–1647* (Edinburgh, 1917), p. 117; *A journall, or, a true and exact relation of each dayes passage* (1644), p. 2. See also *The Parliament Scout*, no. 66, p. 530; S.P. 16/503/56 xv. Manchester seems to have had few gunners on his payroll (S.P. 28/29 f. 352; 264 f. 146), while a study of the issue book of the Ordnance office (W.O. 55/460 *passim*; Add. 34315 ff. 24–25v, 48v, 69v) shows that relatively few pieces of ordnance were given to the Earl.

90. S.P. 28/29 f. 468; Firth, *Cromwell's Army*, pp. 85–8, 173–4; S.P. 28/255 unfol., 'reasons why the London committee of accounts do not concur in the establishment for artillery'.

91. S.P. 28/12 ff. 200, 204; 24 ff. 25, 62; 25 ff. 138, 229, 231, 246, 279, 312–15.

92. S.P. 24/35 Bowman v Birch; John Lilburne, *The reasons for Lieu. Col. Lilbournes sending his letter to* (1645), no pagination.

93. S.P. 16/503/6; 16/539/227: there are many claims for the billeting of sick soldiers in the series S.P. 28. See, for example, 19 ff. 243, 313; 23 ff. 109, 133–4, 166; 27 ff. 212, 266; 29 f. 342. During the winter of 1643–4 Peterhouse and Pembroke Colleges were apparently used as hospitals, but the experiment does not seem to have been repeated.

94. S.P. 28/18 f. 140; 19 f. 333; 21 ff. 54, 240–1; 23 ff. 158, 457; 24 f. 158.

95. S.P. 28/17 ff. 162–75, 182; 20 f. 236; 27 f. 52; 143 unfol., Suffolk Treasury Book, ff. 52v–72. For parish payments for sick soldiers, see W.S.R.O., Acc. 2113/12 p. 145; N.R.O., Aylsham Mss., 193 unfol., parish account of Hanworth; N.R.O., Stockton Town Book 1625–1712, ff. 32, 33. The Committee of Suffolk noted that sick soldiers returning to their villages 'usually meet with ill entertainment . . . to there greate discoragment' (Everitt, *Suffolk*, p. 69).

96. S.P. 28/243 unfol., warrants of 2, 14, 18 and 25 October 1644.

97. S.P. 28/19 f. 243; 25 f. 137; 26 ff. 5, 527; 171 unfol., the account of Captain Harvey. The Horncastle register records the burials of 20 soldiers in 1644, 10 in August and 9 in September (J. C. Hudson (ed.), *The second register book . . . of St Mary, Horncastle* (Horncastle, 1896).

98. S.P. 28/17 f. 415; 18 f. 297; 23 ff. 49, 51; 25 ff. 1–114, 149, 150, 154, 161.

99. *Luke Letter Book*, p. 476; S.P. 24/85 Willoughby v Patrick; G. F. Warner (ed.), *The Nicholas Papers*, vol. 1 (1886), pp. 227, 303.

100. S.P. 28/23 f. 8; Bell (ed.), *Fairfax correspondence*, vol. 1, p. 111; *Luke Letter Book*, pp. 29, 68–9, 357–8, 373.

101. S.P. 28/13 f. 211; 21 f. 269; 23 f. 117; 24 ff. 260–1, 371; 25 ff. 274–5, 451, 499.

102. *Abbott*, i, pp. 256, 261–2. For Margery's social status, see Holmes, *Scandalous Ministers*, p. 30, note 1.

103. It appears that most of the counties employed some professional officers: Lieutenant-Colonel Fenwick and Major Grey, 'twoe able and experienced soldyers' (Egerton 2646 f. 259), were recommended to the Essex committee for posts by Lord Grey of Warke; the Earl of Essex backed Captain Nelson for the command he was given by the Suffolk committee (Everitt, *Suffolk*, pp. 38–9). Captains Parker and Devereux Guybon, and the Dutch officer, Bartholemew

Vermuyden, were professionals employed by the Norfolk committee (Tanner 66 ff. 1–10). But some outsiders and men of low social status who did not have military experience were commissioned: Robert Huntingdon from Oxfordshire by the Norfolk committee (E. 121 1/6 no. 71, p. 2); William Poe, an Irish land-owner ruined by the rebellion, by Suffolk (H. of L.M.P., 1647 (March), the petition of William Poe); Agricola Waylett, the son of an Essex husbandman, commanded one of the county foot companies (E.R.O., will 116 BW 6). These cases suggest that there was some truth to Cromwell's remark that 'men of honour and birth' were reluctant to serve as officers (*Abbott*, I, p. 262).

104. Colonels: Sir Miles Hobart K.B. and Sir John Palgrave Bt.; Lieutenant-Colonels: Sir Isaac Astley and Robert Wilton Esq.; Majors: James Calthorp Esq. and Sir Thomas Hoogan; Captains: Pell and Nathaniel Palgrave (cadets); Harvey, Warner, Beckham (parochial gentry); Toll, Gurlyn, Sherwood, Ashwell (King's Lynn and Norwich). Source: Tanner 66 ff. 1–10. No similar document survives for any of the other counties, and it is not possible to duplicate this analysis (itself incomplete, as some captains are not mentioned in the list) for the Suffolk or Essex regiments.

105. Sparrow was from Gestingthorp (E.R.O., T/P 195/12). His regiment was raised in accordance with the Ordinance of 12 July 1644, which empowered the local committee to nominate the officers.

106. S.P. 28/24 f. 496; E.R.O., Q/SR 308/112; S.P. 28/145 ff. 420–9; E. 121 4/1 no. 53, p. 1; P.C.C. 10 Cann; P.C.C. 118 Bence; *V.C.H., Worcestershire* vol. 4 (1924), p. 343; J. Savage (ed.), *A History of New England from 1630–1649 by John Winthrop* (Boston, Mass., 1853), vol. 2, p. 300.

107. *V.C.H., Worcestershire*, vol. 4 (1924), p. 100; *C.S.P.D.*, 1659–60, p. 221; H. of L.M.P., 27 July 1648, the petition of Edward Dendy; *D.N.B.*, *sub* Thomlin-son; P.C.C. 196 Bowyer; J. Hunter, *South Yorkshire* (1828), vol. 1, pp. 298–9; P.C.C. 24 Twisse; E. 121 4/2 no. 40 part 1, p. 1; E. 121 5/7 no. 14 part 1, p. 1.

108. Keeler, *Long Parliament*, pp. 276–7. Edward's father, Sir Sidney, knight of the shire for Huntingdonshire, was disabled from sitting in the Commons in December 1642 for refusing to take the oath to support the Earl of Essex against the King (Harleian 164 ff. 177v–178v; Add. 31116 f. 13; B.L., Carte 74 f. 155; *C.J.*, II, p. 874).

109. Writing after the cessation in Ireland in 1643 Sidney expressed his dislike of the idea of taking a commission in England, but noted that military service was 'the only way of living well' for those in his predicament – younger sons 'that have not estates' (Sir J. T. Gilbert, *History of the Irish Confederation* (Dublin, 1882), vol. 2, p. xlix).

110. Sir Sidney Montagu was Master of Requests, Sir Miles Fleetwood was Receiver of the Court of Wards (Keeler, *Long Parliament*, pp. 178–9, 276–7). For Hammond and Rainborow, see *D.N.B.*, *sub* Hammond, Dr John; Rain-borow, Thomas; Rainborow, William.

111. For Walton, see Keeler, *Long Parliament*, p. 379; for Sparrow, E.R.O., T/P 195/12; for Ayloffe, S.P. 18/154/11; P.C.C. 66 Ruthen.

112. P.C.C. 95 Rivers; *D.N.B.*, *sub* Hewson.

113. The Frenchman was Colonel Mazères (see p. 286, note 118); there is a list of Scottish officers in S.P. 28/145 ff. 420–9; the three men with Irish experience were Ayloffe, Sparrow and Sidney (S.P. 28/5 f. 204; *D.N.B.*, *sub* Sidney): for the New England contingent, see Savage, *Winthrop's History*, vol. 2, p. 300.

114. For previous service with Essex, see note 116. Previous service with Waller – E. 121 5/6 no. 51, ff. 2–2v; S.P. 28/252A, part 1, the Certificate Book, f. 82v; S.P. 28/265 ff. 405–14. With Fairfax – E. 121 5/7 no. 109, p. 10; *D.N.B.*,

sub Rainborow, Thomas. With Lord Willoughby – E. 121 3/3 Cz, f. 40v; 3/4. C1, ff. 1, 2v; S.P. 28/265 ff. 546–58. With Fiennes in the garrison of Bristol – E 121 2/5 no. 57, pp. 16–17; S.P. 28/34 f. 329; 42 f. 637; 265 f. 114.

115. Those from Fiennes's brigade, and some who had served with Willoughby.

116. Lieutenant-General Hammond, Colonels Walton and Fleetwood and Major Harrison had previously been Captains of Horse with Essex (S.P. 28/2A f. 141; 7 ff. 285, 305; 10 f. 173). Lieutenant-Colonels Gryme, Hewson and Lilburne, and Major Cooke had been infantry Captains (S.P. 28/5 f. 356; 252A, part 1, the Certificate Book, f. 71; 253A, Certificate Book B, no. 186; *D.N.B.*, *sub* Lilburne, John). Captains Axtell and Dingley had previously been Lieutenants (E. 121 2/1 no. 18, p. 14; S.P. 28/7 f. 33); Husbands and LeHunt had been cornets (E. 121 2/11 no. 19, part 2, p. 12; C. H. Firth and G. Davies, *Regimental History of Cromwell's Army* (Oxford, 1940), p. 664); Armiger, Dendy, Langrish, Moody, Rich and Thomlinson had been members of Essex's life-guard (S.P. 28/120 nos. 6, 8).

117. *The Scottish Dove*, no. 21, p. 162; *Occurences of Certain Speciall and remarkable Passages in Parliament* (23 February–1 March), sig. A 4. The officer cashiered was Captain Zachary Walker of Cromwell's regiment; that his troop was disbanded appears from the small sums owed its troopers for arrears of pay (Harleian 427 ff. 121v–122v).

118. *The Parliament Scout*, no. 44, no pagination (error for 370). The *Scout* quotes the story from a sermon by Hugh Peter who spoke of a 'great French commander'. This must be Mazères. The latter was appointed a Colonel of the Essex Horse raised in July 1643, and to Pym's Council of War (S.P. 28/129 unfol., Birkhead's account; *C.J.*, III, p. 191). In January 1644 he was still serving, but was not paid after April (S.P. 28/23 f. 184; 24 f. 571; 25 f. 476A). He was not killed as in May 1645 the Commons voted that he should be paid a proportion of his arrears to enable him to return to France (*C.J.*, IV, p. 143: see also p. 701).

119. At least two officers left commands in Essex's army and rode as Reformadoes in Cromwell's regiment before receiving commissions to posts in the army of the Association no better than those they had held with the Lord General: promotion was hardly the lure in these cases (E. 121 2/1 no. 18, p. 4; E. 121 5/7 no. 14, part 2, pp. 48–50).

120. For press reports on Manchester's choice of 'godly' officers in the autumn of 1643, see pp. 108, 113. Similar panegyrics were written in the first months of 1644 – see, for example, *The Weekly Account*, no. 36, sig. A 2v.

121. Add. 18779 f. 58.

122. S. R. Gardiner (ed.), *A letter from the Earl of Manchester to the House of Lords*, in *The Camden Miscellany*, vol. VIII, pp. 2–3; *Abbott*, I, pp. 277–8; John Lilburne, *The legall fundamentall liberties of the people of England revived* (1649), p. 23.

123. The morale and discipline of the Earl of Essex's army was adversely affected by what may be described as the 'European mercenary' attitude of some of his subordinates. Commissary-General Behre allowed his troops to plunder Buckinghamshire 'more like devills then men' (S.P. 28/151 unfol., parish account of Chipping Wycombe); for the falsification of musters and accounts, see S.P. 16/503/62; S.P. 28/42 ff. 840, 873–4; Colonel John Hurry is the classic example of treachery, but other officers under Essex's command were equally culpable.

124. See pp. 197–204.

125. *The Parliament Scout*, no. 77, pp. 613–14.

Chapter 9

1. See pp. 132–3.

2. It is not easy to piece together a coherent account of the debate from the diarists, but it appears that Mildmay and Barrington favored some action against the Earl's agents.

3. *C.J.*, III, pp. 415, 438; Add. 18779 ff. 71, 83v; Add. 31116 ff. 127–127v; Harleian 166 ff. 38v, 45v. See also *ibid.*, f. 51.

4. *Ibid.*, f. 74v; *C.J.*, III, p. 533. Gurdon, Barrington, Masham and Mildmay supported Manchester's agents in the House.

5. *C.J.*, III, pp. 469, 471, 472; *L.J.*, VI, pp. 528, 529, 531, 534; *Baillie*, II, p. 178. For the Lords' objections to the Committee on the grounds that it undermined Essex's authority, see *L.J.*, VI, pp. 421, 424, 425; Add. 31116 f. 116v; Pearl, 'St John', p. 511.

6. *C.J.*, III, pp. 473, 474, 475, 479, 480; *L.J.*, VI, pp. 535–7.

7. *Gardiner*, I, pp. 403–4; *L.J.*, VI, pp. 543, 551; *C.J.*, III, pp. 489, 491.

8. Harleian 166 ff. 53v–54v, 55v; Add. 18779 f. 100.

9. See Holmes, 'Colonel King', pp. 460–2; Harleian 166 ff. 76v, 80; *Mercurius Aulicus*, no. 27, pp. 1068–9.

10. A good example is provided during the debate on the Lords' rejection of the second assessment Ordinance; the middle group M.P.s Glynne and Rouse, and other 'discreete men', endeavored to restrain the radicals who sought to provoke a show-down with the Lords (Harleian 166 f. 54v).

11. *Ibid.*, ff. 13v–14, 42; Add. 18779 ff. 83v, 85; Add. 31116 f. 128v; *C.J.*, III, p. 443.

12. *Ibid.*, p. 474. The Venetian ambassador recognized that this was little more than a debating point (*C.S.P. Ven.*, 1643–7, p. 102).

13. Add. 22619 f. 56.

14. Tanner 133 f. 166; Tanner 62 ff. 426–7. See pp. 131–2 for the local organization of the review commissioners.

15. Harleian 166 f. 74v.

16. E. 134, 14 Charles II, Easter no. 34; S.P. 28/259 unfol., 20 October 1651, Peter Fisher to the central Committee of Accounts; E.S.R.O., EE 1/01/1 ff. 88, 89, 92, 92v.

17. Lilburne, *The iust mans iustification*, p. 20. See also Holmes, 'Colonel King', pp. 464–5.

18. *Abbott*, I, p. 291; S.P. 28/255 unfol., 17 August 1644, Ireton to the central Committee of Accounts; E. 113, box 1, part 2, the answer of James Whinnel.

19. *L.J.*, V, pp. 319–20; VI, p. 196; G.Y.C., 18/7 ff. 40, 41, 42, 42v; 19/7 ff. 2, 3, 4, 7, 8, 20, 21v, 22v, 28v, 29v, 30–31v, 42; Tanner 115 f. 98.

20. G.Y.C., 19/7 ff. 36, 38v, 39; *C.S.P.D.*, 1644, pp. 119, 144; E.S.R.O., EE 1/01/1 f. 90; EE 1/P6/6; S.P. 28/24 f. 74.

21. *C.J.*, IV, pp. 55, 87; *C.S.P.D.*, 1644–5, pp. 317, 338; John Ufflet, *The Kingdomes key* (1646), *passim*.

22. For Fleetwood as a patron of the sectaries, see *Quarrel*, p. 72; Stowe 786 f. 48. One of his captains was the extremist Paul Hobson (*D.N.B.*); Clarkson and Boggis were both to become Ranters (Clarkson, *Lost Sheep*, p. 10; Thomas Edwards, *The second part of Gangraena* (1646), pp. 161–2).

23. For further discussion, see p. 214.

24. Egerton 2647 ff. 229, 239, 241, 279.

25. Tanner 133 f. 186; 286 f. 1.

26. *Firth and Rait*, I, p. 369.

27. Nalson III no. 122 (my italics). It appears that the Earl had received similar complaints from the other counties of the Association (*Quarrel*, pp. 11–12). Baillie noted the reluctance of the county authorities to allow the army to serve 'out of their own bounds' (*Baillie*, II, p. 133).

28. The best documented of these attempts is that made by the Essex committee from November 1643 to March 1644. See *C.J.*, III, p. 326; Nalson III no. 103; Add. 18779 f. 18v; Egerton 2648 f. 3; Morant 47 f. 117; 48 f. 129; Sackville Mss. (unfol.), letters from the committee to the Earl of Middlesex of 15 December 1643, 3 January 1644. See also Add. 22619 f. 159 (Norfolk); E.S.R.O., FB 130/I 1/10 (Suffolk).

29. In Suffolk the following county gentlemen, though appointed to the committee, do not appear to have served – Sir Edmund Bacon, Sir Robert Brooke, Sir Edward Duke; in Norfolk – Sir Edward Barkham, Sir Richard Berney. These names were obtained by comparing the committee lists in *Firth and Rait*, I, with the working lists of the committees: E.S.R.O., EE 1/01/1 f. 87 (Suffolk); N.R.O., Aylsham Mss., bundle 12 unfol. (Norfolk).

30. Harleian 165 ff. 190–1; *C.J.*, III, p. 238; Tanner 321 f. 8. Another local M.P., Sir John Potts, was as unenthusiastic as Holland or Gawdy (*The Knyvett Letters*, pp. 116–17; S.P. 20/1 f. 69): the committee's 'neglects or delayes' had already been criticized both locally and in the House (Add. 22619 f. 113; Tanner 62 f. 273).

31. S.P. 20/1 ff. 67–8; S.P. 28/255 unfol., letters of 26 September 1644 (Utber and Parmenter to the central Accounts Committee), 28 October 1644 (Bedle to the same).

32. *Ibid.*, letters of ? July, 18 July, 26 September, 3 and 28 October from Nathaniel Bedle to the central Committee of Accounts; Add. 5508 ff. 16, 18, 20–3, 25–6; *C.J.*, III, pp. 39–41; *The Knyvett Letters*, pp. 39–41.

33. S.P. 23/126/569. Five of the chief agents were John Taylor, a yeoman, and John Wright, a collar maker, both of Cottenham (E. 134, 16 Charles II, Michaelmas no. 22), Luke Voyce, a draper, and Jonas Dunch, a baker, of Ely (Add. 5494 f. 63; S.P. 28/207 f. 554), and James Whinnel, a Wisbech merchant (Whinnel, *Matters of great concernment*, p. 40).

34. *Ibid.*, pp. 4–7; Add. 5494 ff. 33, 35; S.P. 20/1 ff. 77, 90, 96, 105v, 160v, 169, 175v, 190; S.P. 28/208 unfol., the account of James Whinnel *et al.*; H. of L.M.P., 11 June 1660, the petition of Richard St George; Edmund Scotten, *To the Right Honourable the Lords and Commons . . . the humble petition and remonstrance of* (1644), *passim*.

35. Harleian 165 ff. 155v, 180. The M.P. Sir William Litton also used his influence to protect those liable to sequestration (Add. 40630 f. 123; *C.J.*, III, p. 355; S.P. 28/209B unfol., the account of Edward Heath and Edward Chandler).

36. *Firth and Rait*, I, pp. 289–91, 356–8. See also *Certaine Informations*, no. 36, p. 289; *The True Informer*, no. 2, p. 12; Add. 18779 ff. 30v, 31v, 32.

37. Add. 31116 ff. 100, 131v; Harleian 166 ff. 49, 101; *Mercurius Aulicus*, no. 31, p. 1104; H.R.O., Q/SR 6 no. 262; S.P. 16/502/56; *C.J.*, III, pp. 564, 571, 572. Only 6 of the old county committee of 27 were appointed to the new Militia committee, which by December 1643 consisted of 64 men.

38. Macray (ed.), *Clarendon's History*, book 6, para. 40. See also Sir Philip Warwick's comment on Manchester's personality (*Memoires of the Reign of King Charles I* (1702), p. 246).

39. Egerton 2647 f. 319; Everitt, *Suffolk*, pp. 67–8; G.Y.C., 19/7 f. 29v; Tanner 64 f. 91.

40. Sir John Cotton and other Cambridgeshire gentlemen (Add. 5494 f. 33; S.P. 28/207 ff. 538–9), Lady Capell (Add. 40630 f. 128), Bishop Hall (Joseph Hall, *Hard Measure* (1702), pp. 12–13), Sir John Sedley (Tanner 69 f. 133), John Stuteville (Harleian 378 f. 3), Thomas Knyvett (S.P. 18/128/5), Sir Hamond L'Estrange (P.R.O., 30/15/3 no. 540), and William Waldegrave (Harleian 165 f. 281) all received assistance from the Earl.

41. Tanner 62 f. 423. See also Tanner 61 f. 14; 62 ff. 431, 471, 489, 543; Ketton-Cremer, *Norfolk in the Civil War*, pp. 195–7.

42. S.P. 20/1 ff. 129v–130; Add. 5494 f. 33; *The Knyvett Letters*, pp. 136–7.

43. *L.J.*, VI, p. 503; *C.J.*, III, p. 451; Harleian 166 ff. 46, 56. In December 1644 Manchester was again in trouble with the Commons for protecting malignants (*C.J.*, III, pp. 622, 728; *Perfect Passages of Each Dayes Proceedings in Parliament*, no. 10, p. 76).

Chapter 10

1. See *Ash and Goode*, no. 7, pp. 4–8; *A journall, passim*; *The London Post*, no. 4, p. 6; *The Weekly Account*, no. 49, p. 237; *The Parliament Scout*, no. 59, pp. 473, 476; no. 64, pp. 512–13.

2. *Quarrel*, pp. 19–47; *C.J.*, III, pp. 621, 638, 658.

3. *Quarrel*, pp. 78–95. In addition to Cromwell's narrative, a number of the depositions of officers who served with the Earl between the fall of York and the battle of Newbury also comment on Manchester's performance (S.P. 16/503/56 IV–XXV): the following narrative is based on these accounts, and on the records of the Committee of Both Kingdoms.

4. For example, Manchester had refused to sanction any attack on Tickhill castle and had violently abused the officer responsible for securing its surrender (S.P. 16/503/56 IV; Lilburne, *Innocency and truth*, pp. 22–5).

5. S.P. 16/503/56 VII, XI, XV, XXI; *Quarrel*, p. 28. The Earl was present at the Committee of Both Kingdoms on 12, 14 and 19 September.

6. *C.S.P.D.*, 1644, p. 545; 1644–5, pp. 1–2, 5, 12–13, 28–9, 41, 46; S.P. 16/503/56 XIX, XX; *Quarrel*, p. 41.

7. S.P. 16/503/56 XI, XII, XIV, XV, XVIII.

8. *Ibid.* XIX. See also *ibid.* XIV, XX, XXI, XXIV.

9. Lilburne, *The legall fundamentall liberties*, p. 23; John Lilburne, *Ionahs cry out of the whales belly* (1647), p. 12; *Quarrel*, p. 79.

10. S.P. 16/503/56 XIV, XXV.

11. Gilbert Burnet, *History of his own time* (1724), vol. 1, p. 98; *Ash and Goode*, no. 3, p. 1; no. 5, p. 7; S.P. 28/25 f. 181; Hu. R.O., D/DM 32/5; *A journall*, p. 2; S.P. 28/23 ff. 4, 28, 68; 26 f. 412. See also *ibid.*, ff. 390, 396.

12. *Ash and Goode*, no. 3, p. 6.

13. *Quarrel*, p. 79.

14. S.P. 16/503/56 XII. The second part of this statement was subsequently erased from the deposition, but it scarcely makes sense without it. See also Ireton's statement (*ibid.* XXII).

15. In February 1644 the Earl was one of the peers who secured the passage of the so-called 'omnipotent Ordinance' for the Committee of Both Kingdoms in the upper House (Harleian 166 f. 64v).

16. Watson informed the investigating committee of the Earl's objections to the severity of the peace proposals offered by Parliament to the King (S.P. 16/503/56 xiv).

17. Ashe, *True relation*, p. 11; S.P. 16/503/56 xi, xii.

18. *The Parliament Scout*, no. 53, pp. 426–87 (*sic* – mispaginated).

19. *Quarrel*, pp. 59–70, 71–7. The latter is ascribed to 'an opponent of Cromwell' but I conclude that the anonymous author was William Dodson, in that his career alone corresponds to the biographical information which can be deduced from the statement.

20. Holmes, 'Colonel King', pp. 462–6; *Quarrel*, pp. 60–2; S.P. 28/49 ff. 47–8; S.P. 16/506/53, 56, 57. Crawford's suggestion that the men of Armiger's troop were purged can be verified from the records of the Treasurers of the Association (S.P. 28/18 f. 188; 26 f. 273).

21. *Baillie*, ii, pp. 500–1: the nature of these charges against other officers of Crawford's faction can be deduced from Cromwell's letter of 5 September to Walton ('Because some of us are enemies to rapine and other wickedness, we are said to be factious') and in Lilburne's later remarks about the favor which Manchester showed to 'plunderers, false musterers, lewd and deboyst persons' (*Abbott*, i, p. 292; Lilburne, *The copy of a letter*, p. 11).

22. *Baillie*, ii, pp. 229–30; Lilburne, *Innocency and truth*, p. 24. For Crawford's error during the siege, see Wenham, *Siege of York*, pp. 57–63.

23. *Abbott*, i, pp. 261–2, 277–8; Gardiner (ed.), *Manchester's letter*, p. 2. Manchester's comment on Cromwell's influence in the selection of officers is borne out by Lilburne's experience: see his *Innocency and truth*, pp. 41–2; *The iust mans iustification*, p. 5.

24. See Holmes, 'Colonel King', p. 462; *Quarrel*, p. 76.

25. For Fleetwood and Harrison as adherents of Independency, see *Quarrel*, p. 72; for Bethel, see Richard Baxter, *Reliquiae Baxterianae* (1696), pp. 53–4; for Neville, see Edwards, *The third part*, p. 253.

26. Captain Peter Bellon: the discipline of his troop was very poor and it was disbanded (S.P. 28/14 f. 168; 24 f. 433A; 223 unfol., 'Mr Leman's vouchers' – the petition of Samuel Gibson).

27. Thomas Johnson of Aldeburgh, whose troop had misbehaved in the autumn of 1643 (*Abbott*, i, pp. 261–2), was appointed by Manchester to a captaincy of a dragoon company for service in Suffolk in May 1644 (E.S.R.O., EE 1/01/1 f. 108), so it would seem unlikely that he was purged from the army. The case of Captain Sparrow is more complex: although he left Manchester's service in May 1644, he later became Captain of a troop raised in Essex by the Ordinance of 12 July 1644 for service in the garrison of Abingdon (S.P. 28/144 no. 2 f. 25). Does this imply that he was reluctant to leave the service in May?

28. S.P. 28/25 ff. 212, 305. For the February project, see *The Parliament Scout*, no. 36, p. 302.

29. The two officers retained were Captain Mercer, of whose religious and political opinions nothing is known, and Isaac Ewers, the future regicide (see *D.N.B.*).

30. S.P. 28/16 f. 128; William Prynne, *A fresh discovery of some prodigous new wandering-blasing-stars & firebrands* (1645), sig. A 1v–A 2; Edwards, *The second part*, p. 17.

31. Egerton 2647 f. 212. A further element of uncertainty is introduced in this case by the fact that Holcroft was a cadet of a family identified with Independency (Nuttall, *Visible Saints*, pp. 28–9; William Winstanley, *The loyall martyrology* (1665), p. 154).

32. For lists of Scottish officers in the army of the Association, see S.P. 28/35 ff. 367–8; 145 ff. 420–9. A number of the Englishmen appointed to commands in the same period – e.g. Colonel Sidney, Captains Grove and Dendy – cannot be identified as Independents.

33. A number of officers left other generals and rode as Reformadoes in the army of the Association before getting a commission: some of these men can be identified as Independents. See S.P. 28/16 f. 128 (Beaumont); E. 121 2/1 no. 18, p. 4 (Axtell); E. 121 5/7 no. 14 part 2, pp. 48–50 (Covell). Also see p. 171.

34. Gardiner (ed.), *Manchester's letter*, p. 2.

35. Edwards, *The third part*, pp. 17–18.

36. *Quarrel*, pp. 73, 75; William Prynne, *The lyar confounded* (1645), p. 4.

37. Holmes, 'Colonel King', p. 463; *Quarrel*, p. 59; *Abbott*, I, p. 277. It appears from Warner's will (P.C.C. 95 Rivers) that he was a member of Henry Burton's Independent congregation in London.

38. *Baillie*, II, p. 229.

39. *Ibid.*, II, p. 185; *The Parliament Scout*, no. 53, p. 426. Some corroboration is provided in *Mercurius Britanicus*, no. 41, p. 323, and in David Buchanan, *Truth its manifest or a short and true relation* (1645), p. 34. But I have not been able to identify the emissary, and the whole affair is shrouded in mystery.

40. *Quarrel*, p. 60.

41. My suggestion that Vane discussed the possibility of toleration whilst at York is derived from hints provided by David Buchanan (*Truth its manifest*, p. 34; *An explanation of some truths* (1646), pp. 11–12). But the significance of Vane's mission is still debatable. Dr Lawrence Kaplan has disposed of the 'Deposition' theory satisfactorily ('The "Plot" to Depose Charles I in 1644', *Bulletin of the Institute of Historical Research*, vol. 44 (1971), pp. 216–23), but I cannot agree with his argument that Vane's mission was purely military: Vane had no military experience, and contemporaries certainly felt that there must be something behind a man of such political eminence undertaking the journey (*C.S.P. Ven.*, 1643–7, p. 110). Violet Rowe, in her biography, *Sir Henry Vane the Younger* (1970), pp. 52–5, examines the question, but arrives at no positive conclusion concerning the significance of the mission.

42. *C.S.P.D.*, 1644, p. 358; H. W. Meikle (ed.), *The correspondence of the Scots Commissioners in London* (Edinburgh, 1917), p. 34; Beinecke Library, Yale University: Osborn Collection, box 41, no. 12.

43. Gardiner (ed.), *Manchester's letter*, p. 2.

44. *Baillie*, II, pp. 203, 208, 211, 218; *C.J.*, III, p. 626. For an example of Independent propaganda, see Leon Watson, *A more exact relation of the late battell neer Yorke* (1644), *passim*.

45. *Abbott*, I, p. 287. R. S. Paul (*The Lord Protector* (1955), p. 81) also concludes that Marston Moor was as 'decisive for Cromwell personally as it was for the war generally'.

46. Gardiner (ed.), *Manchester's letter*, p. 1; *Baillie*, II, pp. 229–30, 234–5; P.R.O., 30/15/3 no. 543; *The Parliament Scout*, no. 68, p. 546; *Quarrel*, p. 61; P.R.O., 30/15/3 no. 563; Harleian 166 f. 144; *Luke Letter Book*, p. 83; S.P. 16/506/50, 53, 57.

47. Ashe, *True relation*, p. 10. After the showdown at Lincoln Manchester was less favorably disposed towards Cromwell, but he did not, as many historians assume, immediately align with Crawford and the Prebyterians. His position as arbitrator between the two hostile factions was noted in a petition of January 1645 signed by 40 of his officers suggesting his retention in command,

or 'it would else breed a greate confusion amongst them by reason of the difference betweene Presbiterians and Independents' (Add. 31116 f. 185v).

48. S.P. 16/503/56 xi, xii.

49. *C.J.*, iii, pp. 621, 638, 658: also see pp. 158–61.

50. *C.J.*, iii, pp. 699, 703.

51. *Baillie*, ii, p. 240; *Luke Letter Book*, p. 368; *The Parliament Scout*, no. 71, p. 571.

52. *The Parliament Scout*, no. 73, p. 583. See also *The Scottish Dove*, no. 56, p. 436; *Perfect Passages of Each Dayes Proceedings in Parliament*, no. 4, p. 32; *Mercurius Civicus*, no. 77, pp. 713–14; *The Kingdomes Weekly Intelligencer*, no. 82, pp. 659–60; *The True Informer*, no. 54, p. 403; *The Weekly Account*, no. 63, sig. Rrr 3v, 4v.

53. Denzil Holles *Memoirs* (1699), pp. 27–8; *C.J.*, iii, p. 696; Add. 31116 f. 174; *Rushworth*, part iii, vol. 2, p. 731.

54. Ashe, *True relation*, p. 1. *The Parliament Scout*, no. 73, pp. 583–4, 585, 588, wrote of letters which had arrived stating that Haselrig, Waller, Skippon, Balfour and Cromwell had favored fighting. Similar letters probably explain the exculpation of individuals in other journals – *The Kingdomes Weekly Intelligencer*, no. 82, p. 660 (Middleton and Cromwell); *The Scottish Dove*, no. 58, p. 452 (Cromwell, Waller, Middleton); *Perfect Passages of Each Dayes Proceedings in Parliament*, no. 4, p. 32 (Waller). See also Add. 25465 f. 21v; *Mercurius Civicus*, no. 79, p. 731.

55. *Quarrel*, pp. 85–90. Waller's statement to the Commons does not survive, but in his subsequent deposition he too stressed these incidents (S.P. 16/503/56 xx).

56. The letter does not survive, but its general tenor may be deduced from Skippon's reply (*Rushworth*, part iii, vol. 2, pp. 730–1).

57. *The Parliament Scout*, no. 75, p. 583; Add. 25465 f. 24; *C.S.P. Ven.*, 1643–7, p. 159. (The Venetian ambassador used this phrase in referring to Essex's support of the attack upon Manchester in December; it seems more appropriate to me when applied to the Lord General's attitude before Cromwell's attack on the Earl.)

58. *C.J.*, iii, pp. 699, 704.

59. Harleian 166 ff. 113, 123v–124; *Baillie*, ii, p. 235. The attitude of the middle group appears from Nathaniel Fiennes's account of the deliberations of the sub-committee appointed to investigate culpability for the loss of the west. He writes that 'some friends of the General's' who subsequently supported the Self-Denying Ordinance, probably St John and Pierrepoint, suppressed evidence which presented Essex's behavior in a poor light (*Vindiciae Veritatis* (1654), pp. 51–2).

60. Holles, *Memoirs*, p. 20: for the Scots' suspicions of the peace-party, see *Baillie*, ii, pp. 112, 118–19, 135, 187. The best study of Anglo-Scottish relations in 1644 is provided by Lawrence Kaplan, 'The Scots and English Civil War politics' (unpublished Ph.D. thesis, Washington University, 1966), chaps. 2–4.

61. *Baillie*, ii, pp. 156, 181, 201, 203, 208–11, 218; Meikle (ed.), *Correspondence of the Scots Commissioners*, pp. 18–19; Holles, *Memoirs*, pp. 16–18; Buchanan, *Truth its manifest*, p. 36.

62. *C.J.*, iii, p. 626; *Baillie*, ii, pp. 209, 211, 230, 231, 235.

63. *Ibid.*, ii, pp. 231–2, 235; Meikle (ed.), *Correspondence of the Scots Commissioners*, pp. 43–4; Add. 5460 ff. 349–52, 364v–365.

64. Holles, *Memoirs*, pp. 20–1. For other comment on the rapport which

developed between the Scots and the pro-peace elements in Parliament in the autumn and winter of 1644–5, see *Mercurius Aulicus*, no. 9, pp. 1390–2; Buchanan, *Truth its manifest*, pp. 57, 59; Fiennes, *Vindiciae Veritatis*, pp. 73–4, 97.

65. *L.J.*, VIII, pp. 73, 76. A version of the Earl's answer is printed in *Rushworth*, part III, vol. 2, pp. 733–6: the original document is now divided between two repositories; the first section, badly torn, is in Hu. R.O., D/DM 32/5; the second part is P.R.O., 30/15/3 no. 557.

66. Gardiner (ed.), *Manchester's letter*, p. 2.

67. Whitelock, *Memorials*, pp. 111–12. (I follow Hexter's suggested dating of the meeting ('The rise of the Independent party' (unpub. Ph.D. thesis, Harvard 1936), Appendix A) in preference to that of *Gardiner*, II, p. 25 note 2.)

68. *Baillie*, II, pp. 244–5, 246.

69. *The Parliament Scout*, no. 75, pp. 601–2. See also no. 76, p. 606; no. 79, pp. 635–6; no. 83, pp. 664–5; *Mercurius Britanicus*, no. 60, p. 474.

70. Add. 31116 f. 175v; Harleian 166 f. 166; *C.S.P. Ven.*, 1643–7, p. 157.

71. See Wedgwood, *King's War*, pp. 365–7. I prefer Miss Wedgwood's argument that the Ordinance was a carefully considered political design, probably engineered by Vane, to Gardiner's notion of Cromwell's 'happy inspiration'.

72. *The Parliament Scout*, no. 77, pp. 616–17; *The Scottish Dove*, no. 60, p. 470; no. 61, pp. 477–8; *The Kingdomes Weekly Intelligencer*, no. 84, pp. 676–7; no. 85, pp. 681–2; *Mercurius Britanicus*, no. 61, p. 482. See also *Baillie*, II, p. 247.

73. See Cromwell's speech (*Rushworth*, part IV, vol. 1, p. 4). Violet Rowe (*Sir Henry Vane*, pp. 55–7) gives a good account of the background to these charges.

74. *C.J.*, III, p. 718. Valerie Pearl has detailed the political affiliations of the last four men in her article 'The "Royal Independents" in the English Civil War', *T.R.H.S.*, 5th series, vol. 18 (1968), pp. 69–96.

75. Add. 31116 f. 180; *C.J.*, III, p. 726.

76. This analysis is based on two sources. Macray (ed.), *Clarendon's History*, book 8, paras. 260–1, provides an account which has been regarded with suspicion because he included Whitelock, who, according to his own account, spoke against the Ordinance (Whitelock, *Memorials*, pp. 113, 115), as one of the M.P.s who switched sides. But Fiennes (*Vindiciae Veritatis*, pp. 51–3) confirms the basic outline provided by Clarendon.

77. Add. 31116 f. 185v; *C.J.*, IV, p. 17; S.P. 16/506/20, 58.

78. The Commons showed little enthusiasm to hear the report of Lisle's committee (*C.J.*, IV, pp. 2, 25, 27, 47; Add. 31116 ff. 187v, 192v) or the Earl's counter-accusation against Cromwell (*C.J.*, IV, pp. 2, 4, 7, 8, 18, 23, 25).

79. Thomas Carte [ed.], *A collection of original letters and papers* (1739), vol. 1, p. 78.

80. *Quarrel*, pp. 10–11, 31, 33, 36; *C.S.P.D.*, 1644–5, p. 139; S.P. 16/503/56 XIV, XVII, XVIII, XXIV, XXV; P.R.O., 30/15/3 no. 557.

81. *Quarrel*, p. 31; *Luke Letter Book*, p. 339; *The Parliament Scout*, no. 68, p. 542; *Mercurius Aulicus*, no. 40, pp. 1189–90; *Mercurius Civicus*, no. 70, pp. 658–9; *The Scottish Dove*, no. 50, p. 390; C.U.L., Cholmondeley (Houghton), Pell Papers, Correspondence, nos. 72, 75, 85. For the capture and subsequent siege of Crowland see Kingston, *East Anglia*, pp. 177–81.

82. *The Parliament Scout*, no. 72, pp. 574, 576; *Luke Letter Book*, pp. 370–1, 391, 398, 408; *The Kingdomes Weekly Intelligencer*, no. 82, p. 661; *The Scottish Dove*, no. 64, p. 502; *The True Informer*, no. 61, p. 463.

83. *The Parliament Scout*, no. 43, pp. 360, 362, 364. Regretably the Committee of Both Kingdoms' 'In' letter-book has not survived for the March–April period, so Manchester's reaction to the order to move to Aylesbury when the Royalists were at the gates of Boston cannot be ascertained. The Committee's letters to the Earl, however, do not suggest that he was opposing the policy (*C.S.P.D.*, 1644, pp. 101, 116–17, 120, 122–3, 127, 128). I have found no evidence to justify the Venetian ambassador's suggestion that Manchester's northern march was deliberately slow 'from reluctance to go far from the Associated Counties' (*C.S.P. Ven.*, 1643–7, p. 110).

84. *The Parliament Scout*, no. 50, p. 403; *A Perfect Diurnal of Some Passages in Parliament*, no. 54, p. 430; *C.S.P.D.*, 1644, p. 217; S.P. 24/66 North *v* Fawcett; N.R.O., Quarter Sessions 35, the examination of John Titshall; Margaret Toynbee and Peter Young, *Cropredy Bridge 1644* (Kineton, 1970), pp. 61–9.

85. *Quarrel*, pp. 33, 36. See also *The Countrey Messenger*, no. 2, p. 7; *C.S.P. Ven.*, 1643–7, pp. 153, 157.

86. *C.S.P.D.*, 1644–5, p. 139. For one such letter from the committee of Norfolk, see Everitt, *Suffolk*, pp. 81–2.

87. N.R.O., L'Estrange Mss., P 20 f. 37; Harleian 166 ff. 128v–129; *C.J.*, III, p. 655.

88. In September the Norfolk committee's petition prayed for a 'blessed peace'; without it, 'we feare it is impossible for the Kingdome to long subsist under the extreame burthen of this warre' (N.R.O., L'Estrange Mss., P 20 f. 37).

89. See pp. 188–9.

90. The Norfolk committee expected a sympathetic response when, in a letter to the Earl, they denounced 'some few factious sectaries favouringe independencie' (P.R.O., 30/15/3 no. 552).

91. On 7 November the Suffolk committee pressed the Committee of Both Kingdoms for a 'speedy . . . setling of the church government' (University of Chicago: Bacon Mss., no. 4552). Three days later petitions from both Norfolk and Suffolk were presented to the Commons to the same effect and also demanding universal subscription to the Covenant (*C.J.*, III, p. 692; Add. 31116 f. 173): in January petitions were circulated throughout East Anglia calling for the suppression of the sects; apparently Parliament viewed them with disfavor, and only one, that from the ministers of Suffolk, was presented to the Commons (*Mercurius Civicus*, no. 86, p. 786; *C.J.*, IV, p. 27).

92. Clauses to the same effect as the Norfolk petition of 10 November (which was ready for presentation at least a week earlier – Add. 22619 f. 230) had originally been included as part of 8 October petition against the westward march of the Association's army (N.R.O., L'Estrange Mss., P 20 f. 37; G.Y.C., 19/7 f. 49). The initial juxtaposition of these two quite disparate demands suggests that the religious requests, as well as that to keep the Association's forces for local defense, sprang from the county committee's awareness of the divisions in the army.

93. *The Parliament Scout*, no. 70, p. 558.

94. *Ibid.*, no. 83, p. 665; Everitt, *Suffolk*, pp. 82, 83.

95. P.R.O., 30/15/3 no. 553; S.P. 16/503/56 XVII (Gawsell); *ibid.* XII (Weaver). An account of the backstage politicking prior to Cromwell's launching his attack on Manchester by John Lilburne (*Ionahs cry*, pp. 7–10) suggests that Stane was expected to give evidence against the Earl, but finally refused to do so.

96. On 24 January 1645 Mildmay wrote, with reference to the political struggle, that the Cambridge Committee 'is good at this time' (Everitt, *Suffolk*, p. 83). In this period it would appear from the signatures on warrants that

Clench, Puller and Walcott were not at Cambridge. The last two had Independent contacts and neither they, nor the Independent John Brewster, attended the conference. But obviously a 'party' breakdown of the Committee can only be tentative given the very limited evidence.

97. *C.S.P.D.*, 1644–5, p. 22; *The Parliament Scout*, no. 73, pp. 589–90; *The Countrey Messenger*, no. 2, p. 7. I have found no evidence that the Cambridge Committee openly persuaded the local committees to voice their protests, but a superb example of 'indirect' encouragement is provided by the wording of their letter to the constituent counties of 14 September advising them to raise forces for local defense. The letter begins by emphasizing the 'extreame push of affayres that the Associated Countyes are put to by the emptying their forces into the west', insists that the safety of the Association depends upon the immediate efforts of the county committees, and concludes grimly 'matters will be brought very soon to such an adventure as to be prepared for the worst will be no fere' (C.U.L., Cholmondeley (Houghton), Pell Papers, Correspondence no. 71c; N.R.O., L'Estrange Mss., P 20 f. 34v). The language of this letter contrasts markedly with the Committee's straightforward appeal for assistance in June, when the King's advance to Buckingham presented a most dangerous threat to the Association (*ibid.*, f. 35). It is no wonder that the local committees bombarded the Earl with pleas for his return to their defense when the Cambridge Committee employed such alarmist rhetoric.

98. Everitt, *Suffolk*, pp. 82–3; S.P. 16/506/20, the deposition of Captain Harvey. Immediately after Cromwell's attack upon Manchester at least two of the local committees summoned general county meetings: Norfolk's to 'agitate busines of great weight and concernment' (C.U.L., Cholmondeley (Houghton), Pell Papers, Correspondence no. 89), that in Suffolk 'to consulte of greate matters of consequence for the safety of this countye and other partes of the kingdome' (E.S.R.O., HD 36/2672 no. 73). I suspect that the Cambridge Committee suggested these meetings; they certainly organized the Bury conference (S.P. 28/36 ff. 13, 529).

99. This account of the conference is derived from that prepared for Manchester and which survives in his papers (P.R.O., 30/15/3 no. 565); it has been published by Professor Everitt (*Suffolk*, pp. 84–9).

100. That old chestnut, the proportion that the City of Norwich should bear of any general charge upon the county of Norfolk, came up again (Add. 22619 ff. 153, 155, 157).

101. *C.S.P.D.*, 1644–5, p. 284; *L.J.*, VII, pp. 177–8, 180; *C.J.*, IV, pp. 42, 44, 47.

102. On 11 March 1645 the Committee of Both Kingdoms received a further petition and list of demands from the Association (*C.S.P.D.*, 1644–5, p. 341): nothing is known of the organization of this petition, although some of its specific demands can be deduced from the later responses of the Commons (*C.J.*, IV, p. 102; Nalson XIV no. 53). On 25 March a conference at Bury (attended by 14 men from Suffolk, 3 each from Norfolk and Essex, 2 from Cambridge and 1 from Huntingdon: Hertfordshire and Lincoln were not represented) complained of the neglect of their 'humble desires'. It is questionable whether they were referring solely to the requests presented on 11 March, or to the earlier 'letter with instructions' also (Tanner 60 f. 7).

103. *C.J.*, IV, pp. 99, 102; Harleian 252 f. 33.

104. Everitt, *Suffolk*, p. 34.

105. P.R.O., 30/15/3 no. 557.

106. Everitt, *Suffolk*, p. 34.

Chapter 11

1. *C.S.P.D.*, 1644–5, p. 380; *C.J.*, IV, pp. 99, 102, 149–50; Nalson XIV no. 53. The Ordinance of 12 August 1645 for the defense of the Isle of Ely nominated those who should sit on the Cambridge Committee (*Firth and Rait*, I, pp. 744–5).

2. *Ibid.*; *Rushworth*, part IV, vol. 1, p. 38; *Abbott*, I, p. 353; Nalson IV nos. 28, 57; N.R.O., L'Estrange Mss., box NP, order of the Committee of the Association of 16 July 1645; H.R.O., Miscellaneous IX no. 70547; E.S.R.O., HD 36/2672 no. 74; HD 36/2781 no. 50.

3. Add. 19398 ff. 172, 216. In July 1645 500 horse were raised in the Association under Major LeHunt, and in August a further 500 horse and 250 dragoons under Major Gibbs; 800 horse under Major Haynes, seconded from the local auxiliaries, were also used against Newark. Parliament proposed that the pay of these forces would be met ultimately from central sources, but the counties had to raise the money temporarily. See Nalson IV no. 138.

4. See *C.J.*, IV, pp. 99, 102, 115, 134, 147, 171, 196; *C.S.P.D.*, 1644–5, pp. 234, 237, 244, 281; *Firth and Rait*, I, pp. 762–6; *H.M.C.*, 8th Report (1881), Appendix, part 1, pp. 9–10; Add. 19398 ff. 174, 224; Add. 21427 f. 3; Add. 22620 f. 42; Stowe 164 ff. 3v, 11.

5. In April 1645 the Commons had voted to bring in an Ordinance 'settling and establishing' the Committee (*C.J.*, IV, p. 102) but no such legislation had been forthcoming: the powers of the Committee were, in consequence, indefinite.

6. Nalson V no. 22; Nalson IV no. 57; E.S.R.O., HD 36/2672 no. 82; Tanner 57 f. 269.

7. Add. 22620 f. 13. The date upon which the Committee's session was finally terminated is uncertain; the last meeting which I have found recorded was in January (Add. 19398 f. 172) but it clearly survived beyond this date. For the administrative functions of the Westminster Committee in 1646, see Stowe 164 ff. 14, 15v, 22; S.P. 16/514/56; Tanner 58 f. 335; *C.J.*, IV, p. 535; *L.J.*, VIII, p. 351; IX, p. 34; *H.M.C.*, 8th Report (1881), Appendix, part 1, pp. 10–11. Letters from the Norwich M.P.s to their constituents from June to October 1646 (Add. 22620 ff. 58, 60, 64, 65, 66, 76, 78, 82, 84, 91, 92) provide an interesting insight into the workings of the Committee, as does a letter to the town of Ipswich from their recorder, Nathaniel Bacon (E.S.R.O., HD 36/2672 no. 27).

8. In August 1646 the Westminster Committee agreed not to move the artillery which was the property of the Association from Cambridge castle, which was being dismantled, to London 'less by a powerful hand it should be disposed elsewhere'; the guns were to be kept in East Anglia (E.S.R.O., HD 36/2672 no. 27).

9. Parliament added a number of east midland counties to the area under their jurisdiction (Add. 19399 f. 51) while Lincolnshire became the responsibility of the Northern Committee.

10. Nothing is known of the second conference other than its date – November 1646 (H.R.O., Miscellaneous IX no. 70553).

11. Add. 22620 ff. 13, 18.

12. For the unpopularity of the excise agents in Lincolnshire, see Holmes, 'Colonel King', pp. 477–8; in Norwich, see Add. 19399 f. 26; Add. 22620 ff. 45, 56; Tanner 59 ff. 623, 649; in Suffolk, see *L.J.*, IX, p. 18.

13. This clause, extended into a demand for an immediate political as well as a religious settlement, a protest against the involvement of the army in politics and a call for its immediate disbandment, became the theme of a number of petitions from the eastern counties from 1646–8, some organized by the local committees (Essex: *L.J.*, IX, pp. 71–2; *C.J.*, V, pp. 110, 301–2 (this was organized

by the committee): Tanner 58 f. 50; *Rushworth*, part IV, vol. 1, pp. 448–50; *A new found stratagem* (1647), pp. 1–4: B.L., Clarendon 31 f. 56; *L.J.*, X, pp. 243–4; S. R. Gardiner (ed.), *The Hamilton Papers* (1880), pp. 171, 189. Norfolk: C.U.L., Cholmondeley (Houghton), Pell Papers, 9/67. Suffolk: *L.J.*, IX, p. 18). The last and most vigorously worded of these petitions, which was published in May 1648 although it was never presented to Parliament, purported to come from the inhabitants of the Eastern Association as a whole: however, there is no evidence of official involvement in its organization ((Nathaniel Ward), *To the high and honourable Parliament of England . . . the humble petitions, serious suggestions* (1648), *passim*).

14. E.R.O., D/DQs 18 ff. 49, 50v; Tanner 57 ff. 222, 224; H. of L.M.P., 22 August 1648, John Eldred to Sir Henry Mildmay; *The Moderate Intelligencer*, no. 179, p. 1493.

Bibliography

I. MANUSCRIPTS CITED

A. National depositories

1. *The Public Record Office*
(a) Exchequer (E.)

E. 113   bills presented by the Attorney-General in the reign of Charles II against defaulting accountants of the civil war period and the answers of the latter

E. 121   certificates of the sale of Crown lands: these include statements of the arrears of certain regiments to be set against the sums to be raised by the sale

E. 134   depositions taken by Commission for cases in the Court of Exchequer

E. 315/5   certificates of arrears of civil war soldiers

E. 403/2608   Commonwealth Privy Seals

(b) War Office (W.O.)

W.O. 55/460   issue book of the Office of Ordnance at the Tower

(c) Privy Council Office (P.C.)

P.C. 2   registers of the Privy Council

(d) Prerogative Court of Canterbury (P.C.C.)

previously deposited at Somerset House
wills proved in this Court from 1620 to 1680 have been used in this study; citation is in the usual form, the distinguishing name of the volume being preceded by the foliation of the will in question, e.g., P.C.C. 95 Rivers

(e) State Papers Office (S.P.)

S.P. 16   State Papers: Charles I

S.P. 18   State Papers: Interregnum

S.P. 29   State Papers: Charles II

(*n.b.* reference to documents from the above three classes is by volume and piece number.)

S.P. 19   records of the Parliamentary Committee for the Advance of Money

S.P. 20   records of the Parliamentary Committee for the Sequestration of Delinquents' estates

S.P. 23   records of the Parliamentary Committee for Compounding

(*n.b.* reference to documents from the above three classes is by volume and foliation.)

S.P. 24   records of the Parliamentary Committee for Indemnity

(*n.b.* reference to documents in this class is by box number and then by case; the latter are arranged in alphabetical order by the name of the plaintiff in each box, e.g., S.P. 24/25 Dodsworth *v* Hardmett.)

S.P. 28   records of the Parliamentary Committee for taking the Accounts of the Kingdom (otherwise known as the Commonwealth Exchequer Papers)

(*n.b.* some of the documents in this class are arranged in foliated volumes, but the majority are kept loose in boxes; for documents in this second category, I have referred to the contemporary description where one is appended; otherwise reference is by a summary description of the document cited.)

(f) Miscellaneous

P.R.O. 30/15   Montagu family papers deposited by the Duke of Manchester (*n.b.* these papers have recently been removed from the P.R.O., and the collection has been sold piecemeal and so dispersed; for a calendar of the collection, see *H.M.C.*, Eighth Report Appendix 2 (1881))

2. *The British Museum*
(a) Additional Manuscript collection
<table>
<tr><td>5460</td><td>the correspondence of Sabran and Brienne</td></tr>
<tr><td>5494, 5505, 5508</td><td>papers relating to sequestration in the Associated counties</td></tr>
<tr><td>5828</td><td>papers relating to the history of Suffolk</td></tr>
<tr><td>5829</td><td>the minute book of the committee for scandalous ministers in Essex</td></tr>
<tr><td>15084</td><td>the letter-book of the Deputy-Lieutenants for Suffolk</td></tr>
<tr><td>15520</td><td>Candler's notes on the history of Suffolk</td></tr>
<tr><td>15672</td><td>the minute book of the committee for scandalous ministers in Cambridgeshire</td></tr>
<tr><td>15903</td><td>letters and papers relating to the history of Norfolk</td></tr>
<tr><td>18777–9</td><td>the Parliamentary diary of Walter Yonge</td></tr>
<tr><td>19123</td><td>genealogical collections for Suffolk</td></tr>
<tr><td>19398–9</td><td>letters and papers relating to the history of Norwich</td></tr>
<tr><td>21427</td><td>papers of Captain Adam Baynes</td></tr>
<tr><td>22619–20</td><td>letters and papers relating to the history of Norwich</td></tr>
<tr><td>23006</td><td>letters and papers relating to the history of Norfolk</td></tr>
<tr><td>25334</td><td>collections for the history of Ipswich</td></tr>
<tr><td>25465</td><td>anonymous citizen of London's journal of public occurences, 1644–6</td></tr>
<tr><td>27396</td><td>Gawdy family correspondence</td></tr>
<tr><td>28930</td><td>Ellis family correspondence</td></tr>
<tr><td>31116</td><td>the Parliamentary diary of Laurence Whittaker</td></tr>
<tr><td>33572–4</td><td>Hale family correspondence</td></tr>
<tr><td>34253</td><td>letters addressed to the Speaker of the House of Lords</td></tr>
<tr><td>34315</td><td>register book of the Ordnance office, 1643–4</td></tr>
<tr><td>37491</td><td>the minute book of the Parliamentary committee for southern Essex</td></tr>
<tr><td>39222</td><td>Wodehouse family papers</td></tr>
<tr><td>40630</td><td>Capel family correspondence</td></tr>
</table>

(b) Egerton manuscript collection
<table>
<tr><td>2716–7, 2722</td><td>Gawdy family correspondence and papers</td></tr>
<tr><td>2643–51</td><td>Barrington family correspondence and papers</td></tr>
</table>

(c) Harleian manuscript collection
<table>
<tr><td>97, 160</td><td>miscellaneous papers of Sir Symonds D'Ewes</td></tr>
<tr><td>162–6</td><td>the Parliamentary diary of Sir Symonds D'Ewes</td></tr>
<tr><td>252</td><td>Rushworth's diary of Fairfax's proceedings in 1645</td></tr>
<tr><td>286, 383–8</td><td>correspondence of Sir Symonds D'Ewes</td></tr>
<tr><td>365</td><td>Sir Symonds D'Ewes's papers concerning ship money in Suffolk</td></tr>
<tr><td>427</td><td>statement of the arrears of Colonel Whalley's regiment</td></tr>
<tr><td>454</td><td>the diary of Sir Humphrey Mildmay</td></tr>
<tr><td>6244</td><td>orders of the standing committee for Essex</td></tr>
<tr><td>7001</td><td>correspondence of the Earl of Manchester</td></tr>
</table>

(d) Stowe manuscript collection
<table>
<tr><td>164</td><td>minute book of the Parliamentary committee for Essex</td></tr>
<tr><td>184</td><td>official papers of the Earl of Warwick</td></tr>
<tr><td>189, 833, 842</td><td>letters and papers concerning Colchester</td></tr>
<tr><td>807</td><td>collections for the history of Cambridgeshire</td></tr>
</table>

3. *The Bodleian Library, Oxford*
(a) Carte manuscripts
<table>
<tr><td>74</td><td>journal of Colonel Montagu's regiment</td></tr>
</table>
(b) Clarendon manuscripts
<table>
<tr><td>31</td><td>Clarendon's correspondence with Royalist agents</td></tr>
</table>
(c) Firth manuscripts
<table>
<tr><td>c. 4</td><td>Essex Lieutenancy book</td></tr>
</table>
(d) 'Nalson' manuscripts
<table>
<tr><td>II–V, XI–XIV, XXII</td><td>collections of papers and correspondence of the Speaker of the House of Commons, complementary to much of the material in the Tanner collection</td></tr>
</table>
(*n.b.* this collection, originally in the possession of the Duke of Portland at Welbeck

Abbey, has been deposited in the Bodleian, where its reference numbers are Ms. Dep. C. 152–76. I have chosen to use the 'Nalson' reference, as it facilitates reference to the Calendar of the collection in *H.M.C.* Portland I (1891).)

(e) Tanner manuscripts

57–69	miscellaneous letters and papers consisting of the official correspondence of Speaker Lenthall, the correspondence of Bishop Wren with his diocesan officials, and the letters and papers of several East Anglian gentlemen, notably Sir John Holland and Sir John Potts
98, 115, 286	correspondence and papers of the Hobart family
114	contains some papers relating to the formation of the Association
133	papers relating to the Diocese of Norwich
284	includes some returns for the Association in four Suffolk villages
321	the speeches of Sir John Holland

(f) J. Walker manuscripts

c. 1, c. 6	papers relating to ministers sequestered in the eastern counties; the latter contains an abstract of the minute book of the Norfolk committee for scandalous ministers.

4. *The Cambridge University Library*

(a) Buxton manuscripts
Boxes 96, 97, and that marked 'correspondence I' letters and papers of John Buxton of Tibbenham

(b) Cholmondeley (Houghton) manuscripts
Pell papers, boxes 9/67 and that marked 'correspondence' letters and papers of Sir Valentine Pell of Dersingham

(c) Patrick manuscripts

33	the autobiography of Arthur Wilson, steward to the Earl of Warwick

(d) Ely diocesan records

E. 12	Assize files

(e) Archdeaconry of Ely
Wills proved in this jurisdiction have been used; these were formerly deposited in the Cambridge University Registry

5. *House of Lords' Record Office*

(a) Main papers collection
Petitions and some letters addressed to the House of Lords in the period 1640–8, 1660
(*n.b.* The main papers are arranged chronologically; in my references I have given the date of the document, followed by a short description, e.g., H. of L.M.P. 2 May 1642, the affidavit of John Peacock.)

B. Manuscripts in local record offices

Note: wills proved in the local ecclesiastical courts exercising testamentary jurisdiction and now deposited in the County Record Offices in East Anglia have been cited in the study. However, to avoid a plethora of references, no specific reference numbers will be given in this bibliography for such wills.

1. *Bury St Edmunds and West Suffolk Record Office*

Acc. 2113	Bardwell parish records
E. 5/9 no. 203	Bury free school accounts
Tem. 123	documents relating to the parish of Wattisfield

2. *Essex Record Office*

Ass.	calendar of cases at the county Assizes
D/ABA	act book of the Bishop of London's Commissary
D/B 3	records of the borough of Maldon
D/DMs	letters and papers of the Mildmay family of Marks in Romford
D/DQs 18	diary of John Clopton of Little Wratton, 1648–51

D/P 232	Braintree parish records
D/P 264	Great Easton parish records
Q/SBa 2	petitions and affidavits to Quarter-Sessions
Q/SBa 6	parish fiscal accounts presented to the Quarter-Sessions in 1644
Q/SBa 8	sequestration accounts for Chelmsford, Rochford, and Dengie Hundreds
Q/SO	order books of the Quarter-Sessions
Q/SR	Sessions Rolls
T/P 195	Holman's collections for the history of Essex
T/P 211	microfilm of the family papers of the Bramstons of Skreens

3. *Hertfordshire Record Office*

D/P 12	Baldock parish records
Miscellaneous IX 46351	papers relating to the sequestration of Edward Jude, minister of Hunsdon
Miscellaneous IX 70539–53	papers and correspondence of Alban Coxe
Q/SR	Sessions Rolls

4. *Huntingdonshire Record Office*

Godmanchester borough records, 25–6	seventeenth-century Court Books of the borough
D/DM	letters, papers, and accounts of the Montagu family, Earls of Manchester

5. *Ipswich and East Suffolk Record Office*

EE 1	Aldeburgh borough records
FB 19	Mickfield parish records
FB 130	Gislingham parish records
HD 36/2672, 2781	collections of letters sent to the corporation of Ipswich
HD 53/2786	Hawkedon parish records

6. *Kent Record Office*

U. 269	Cranfield papers

7. *Lincolnshire Archives Committee*

Brace 17/1	Gainsborough Court Leet
Cragg 3/69	letter of the county committee concerning payment of free-quarter bills
Holywell H. 93	papers relating to the military career of Thomas Hatcher
Parochial Addlethorpe Frampton South Kyme	accounts and papers of parish officers

8. *Norwich and Norfolk Record Office*

Aylsham, boxes 12, 193, 198	official correspondence and papers of Robert Doughty of Hanworth, collector for the Hundred of North Erpingham
Bradfer-Lawrence V(10)	miscellaneous papers relating to the civil war
Hare 5215	accounts of the Hare family estates
L'Estrange, boxes P 20, NP	letters and papers of Sir Hamon Le Strange of Hunstanton and of the Calthorp family
VIS/6	visitation of the diocese in 1633
Quarter-Sessions, boxes 33–7	depositions and petitions to the Quarter-Sessions
Norwich City Records	
Court Book 1634–46	
Assembly Book 1613–42	
Assembly Book 1642–68	
Corporation of Great Yarmouth	
18/7	the second book of entries
19/6	the Assembly Book 1625–42

| 19/7 | the Assembly Book 1642–62 |
| 36/7 | papers concerning the dispute with Lowestoft |

Microfilm of the Stockton Town Book, 1625–1712

9. *Northamptonshire Record Office*
Finch-Hatton   Sir William Dugdale's lists of the Commissioners of Array
    Ms. 133

C. Manuscripts held by libraries, corporate bodies, or in private hands

1. *The Corporation of Colchester*
Assembly Book 1626–46

2. *The Corporation of Grantham*
Hall Book 1

3. *The Corporation of King's Lynn*
Common Council Book 8

4. *The Joseph E. Regenstein Library, University of Chicago*
Bacon: letters and family papers of the Bacons of Redgrave

5. *The Beinecke Library, Yale University*
Osbourne collection, box 41: letters of the Scots commissioners to Parliament

6. *Library of the Essex Archaeological Society, Colchester*
Morant Mss., 36–48: letters sent to the borough of Colchester during the civil war
period (a microfilm of this most valuable collection is now available in the Essex
Record Office, reference T/A 391/1–10.)

7. *Library of Worcester College, Oxford*
Clarke Mss., 41, 114: military accounts and petitions

8. *Cromwell Museum, Huntingdon*
letters from Elizabeth Cromwell to John Welbore

9. *The Bursary, Gonville and Caius College, Cambridge*
the Stokys account book
Bursar's accounts 1634–61

10 *Cranfield papers in the possession of Lord Sackville*
correspondence between the Earl of Middlesex and the Essex county committee
concerning assessments, 1643–4

11. *Astley letters in the possession of the Dowager Lady Hastings of Melton Constable*
letters from Lieutenant-Colonel Sir Edward Astley to his wife, May–July 1643

12. *Papers in the possession of the Rector of Croft*
an extraordinarily complete series of warrants and precepts to the village officers
and the accounts of the latter (a typescript calendar is available at the Lincolnshire Archives Committee office)

13. *Papers in the possession of the Rector of Gissing*
constables' warrants and accounts and the book of the overseers of the poor for
Gissing

II. PRINTED SOURCES

Note: (i) unless otherwise stated, all books were published in London.
(ii) titles of books published before 1700 are cited in the form given in *Short-
Title Catalogue of English Books 1475–1640*, ed. A. W. Pollard and G. R.
Redgrave (1926), or in *Short-Title Catalogue of Books Printed in England
... 1641–1700*, 3 vols., ed. Donald Wing (New York, 1945–51).

A. Contemporary books and tracts

Ashe, Simeon, *A true relation, of the most chiefe occurences* (1644)
Bacon, Nathaniel, *The continuation of An historicall discourse* (1651)

An historicall discourse of the uniformity (1647)
An ordinance presented to the honorable House of Commons (1646)
Bagwell, William, *A full discovery of a foul concealment* (1652)
Baxter, Richard, *Reliquiae Baxterianae* (1696)
Bowles, Edward, *Plaine English: or, a discourse* (1643)
Bridge, William, *A sermon preached unto the voluntiers* (1642/3)
(Brookhaven, John) *A letter sent to Mr Speaker, from the commissioners in the county of Essex* (1642)
(Buchanan, David) *An explanation of some truths* (1646)
Truth its manifest, or a short and true relation (1645)
Burnet, Gilbert, *History of his own time* (1724)
Burroughes, Jeremiah, *A vindication of Mr Burroughes against Mr Edwards* (1646)
(Butler, Samuel) *A letter from Mercurius Civicus to Mercurius Rusticus* (Oxford, 1643)
Calamy, Edmund, *A patterne for all* (1658)
(Chestlin, —) *Persecutio undecima. The churches eleventh persecution* (1648)
Clarke, Samuel, *The Lives of Sundry Eminent Persons in this later age* (1683)
Clarkson, Lawrence, *The lost sheep found* (1660)
E., R., *A perfect diurnal of the proceedings in Hartfordshire* (1642)
Edwards, Thomas, *The second part of Gangraena* (1646)
The third part of Gangraena (1646)
Elton, Richard, *The compleat body of the art military* (1659)
Essex, Robert Devereux, 3rd earl of, *A letter from his Excellencie* (1643)
Farre, Henry, *A speech spoken* (1642)
(Fiennes, Nathaniel) *Vindiciae Veritatis, or an answer* (1654)
Fisher, Peter, *For the right worshipful the knights . . . of Suffolke* (1648)
Grimston, Harbottle, *Mr Grimstone, his speech in Parliament on Wednesday the 19th of January* (1642)
H., W., *A relation of the good successe of the Parliaments forces* (Cambridge, 1644)
Hall, Joseph, *Hard measure* (1702)
Harsnet, Samuel, *A full relation of the defeate given* (1645)
Heylyn, Peter, *Cyprianus Anglicus: or the history of . . . Laud* (1669)
Holles, Denzil, *Memoirs of* (1699)
(Jordan, Thomas) *London's ioyful gratulation* (1642)
Kirle, R., *A coppy of a letter writ from* (1643)
Lilburne, John, *The copy of a letter from . . . to a friend* (1645)
Innocency and truth justified (1645/6)
Ionahs cry out of the whales belly (1647)
The iust mans iustification (1646)
The legall fundamentall liberties of the people of England revived (1649)
The reasons of Lieu. Col. Lilbournes sending his letter (1645)
M., P., *True intelligence from Lincolne-shire* (1642)
Mather, Cotton, *Magnalia Christi Americana* (1702)
(Povey, Thomas) *The moderator expecting sudden peace* (1642/3)
Prynne, William, *A fresh discovery of some prodigious new wandering-blasing-stars & firebrands* (1645)
The lyar confounded (1645)
Newes from Ipswich: discovering practices of domineering lordly prelates (Edinburgh, 1636)
Pym, John, *A speech delivered at a conference . . . January XXV, MDCXLI* (1641/2)
Rogers, John, *The doctrine of faith* (1629)
(Ryves, Bruno) *Mercurius Rusticus: or, the countries complaint* (1685)
Scotten, Edmund, *To the Right Honourable the Lords and Commons . . . the humble petition and remonstrance of* (1644)
Symmons, Edward, *A loyall subjects beliefe* (Oxford, 1643)
Scripture vindicated (Oxford, 1644/5)
Ufflet, John, *The kingdomes key* (1646)
Vicars, John, *Gods arke overtopping the worlds waves* (1646)
Jehovah-Jireh (1644)
Walker, Clement, *The compleat history of independency* (1661)
Ward, Nathaniel, *To the high and honorable Parliament of England . . . the humble petitions, serious suggestions* (1648)
Warwick, Philip, *Memoires of the Reign of King Charles I* (1702)

Warwick, Robert Rich, earl of, *A most worthy speech* (1642)
(Watson, Leon) *A more exact relation of the late battell neer Yorke* (1644)
Wenlock, John, *To the most illustrious, high and mighty Majesty of Charles the II* (1662)
Whinnel, James, *Matters of great concernment* (1646)
Whitelock, Bulstrode, *Memorials of the English Affairs* (1682)
Widdrington, William, *A true and exact relation* (1643)
Winstanley, William, *The loyall martyrology* (1665)

Anonymous tracts
  Alas, pore Parliament, how art thou betrai'd? (1644)
  A briefe and true relation of the siege and surrendering of Kings Lyn (1643)
  A briefe relation of the siege at Newark (1644)
  The clothiers petition to His Majestie (1642)
  Considerations upon the present state of the affairs of this kingdome (1642)
  Divers remarkeable passages of Gods good providence (1643)
  The English intelligencer; shewing (1642)
  The Essex watchmen's watchword (1649)
  Exceeding true and happy newes from the Castle of Windsor (1642)
  An extract of severall letters which came (1642)
  The foure petitions of Huntington shire (1642)
  A glorious and happy victory obtained by the volluntiers of Buckingham (1642)
  Good and true news from Bedford (1643)
  The grand plunderer (1643)
  The humble petition of many thousands of the inhabitants of Norwich (1642)
  The humble petition of the bailifes . . . of Ipswich (1641)
  The humble petition of the inhabitants of the County of Essex (Oxford, 1642)
  A iournall, or, a true and exact relation of each dayes passage (1644)
  Joyfull newes from the Isle of Ely (1642)
  A message sent to the Parliament from the members (1642)
  The miseries of war (1643)
  A new found stratagem (1647)
  A relation of a fight in the county of Lincolne (Oxford, 1643)
  Remarkable passages from Nottingham (1642)
  The remonstrance and petition of the county of Huntingdon (1641/2)
  A remonstrance and protestation of the gentry and commonalty of . . . Buckingham (1642)
  Three petitions: the one, of the inhabitants of . . . Colchester (1642)
  A true and exact relation of the present estate of the city of Norwich (1642)
  A true relation of a great victory obtained . . . by Lord Willoughby (1643)
  A true relation of a wonderfull and strange passage (1642)
  A true relation of Colonell Cromwels proceedings (1643)
  A true relation of the army set out by the county of Essex (1642)
  A true relation of the fight betweene the Right Honourable the Earl of Manchester's forces (1643)
  A true relation of the late fight (1644)
  Two petitions the one to the Kings most excellent Majesty. The humble petition of the Grand-Jury . . . Southampton (1642)
  The valiant resolution of the seamen (1642)

B. Newsbooks

Note: (i) where possible, reference is made in the footnotes to the issue and number of the newsbook cited, then to the relevant page. Where issues and pages are unnumbered, which is frequently the case with journals printed in 1642 and early 1643, I have given, in addition to the title of the newsbook, the dates covered by the information contained within it.

(ii) I have standardized the spelling of newsbook titles, using as a guide the list given by Joseph Frank, *The Beginnings of the English Newspaper* (Cambridge, Mass., 1961), pp. 363–70.

The following newsbooks have been used in this study:
  Certaine Informations
  A Collection of Speciall Passages and Certaine Informations
  A Continuation of Certain Speciall and Remarkable Passages (ed. Cook and Wood)

A Continuation of certain Speciall and Remarkable Passages (ed. Coles)
The Countrey Messenger
England's Memorable Accidents
An Exact and True Diurnal
The Kingdomes Weekly Intelligencer
The Kingdomes Weekly Post
The London Post
Mercurius Anglicus
Mercurius Aulicus
Mercurius Britanicus
Mercurius Civicus
The Moderate Intelligencer
Occurences
Occurences of Certain Speciall and remarkable Passages in Parliament
The Parliament Scout
A Perfect Diurnall
A Perfect Diurnall of some Passages in Parliament
A Perfect Diurnall of the Passages in Parliament
Perfect Passages of Each Dayes Proceedings in Parliament
Remarkable Passages
Remarkable Passages, or a perfect Diurnall
The Scottish Dove
Some Speciall Passages
Speciall Passages
Speciall Passages and Certain Informations
A True and Perfect Diurnal
The True Informer
Wednesday's Mercury
The Weekly Account
The Weekly Post

The Earl of Manchester's chaplains, Simeon Ash and William Goode, wrote a series of seven newsletters from the army covering the period from 20 April to 16 August 1644, which were published in London. These were numbered from 1 to 7, but the titles vary from one issue to another:

no. 1	*A particular relation of the severall removes, services and successes of the . . . Earl of Manchester's army*
no. 2	*A continuation of true intelligence from . . . the Earl of Manchester's army*
no. 3	*A particular relation of the most remarkable occurences from the united forces in the north*
no. 4 and no. 5	*A continuation of true intelligence from the English and Scottish forces in the north*
no. 6	*A continuation of true intelligence from the armies in the north.*
no. 7	*A continuation of true intelligence from . . . the Earle of Manchester.*

In footnote citations, reference is made to *Ash and Goode*, followed by the number of the issue, then the page reference.

C. Modern editions of contemporary memoirs, correspondence, etc.

1. *Official Publications*

Acts and Ordinances of the Interregnum 1642–1660, 3 vols. (eds. C. H. Firth and R. S. Rait), 1911

Acts of the Privy Council of England 1600–1631, 16 vols. (eds. J. R. Dasent and others), 1906–64

Calendar of the Committee for Compounding 1643–1660, 5 vols. (ed. by M. A. E. Green), 1889

Calendar of State Papers, Domestic Series 1625–1665, 43 vols. (eds. J. Bruce, M. A. E. Green, W. D. Hamilton), 1858–97

Calendar of State Papers and Manuscripts relating to English Affairs existing in the Archives of Venice, 1623–64, 17 vols. (ed. A. B. Hinds), 1912–32

The Journals of the House of Commons 1640–1666, vols. II–VIII of series, 1803

The Journals of the House of Lords 1628–1666, vols. IV–XI of series, n.d.

Royal Commission on Historical Manuscripts: Reports
  Fourth Report, Appendix I (1874), Denbigh Mss.
  Eighth Report, Appendix I (1881), Marlborough Mss.
  Eighth Report, Appendix II (1881), Manchester Mss.
  Tenth Report, Appendix VI (1887), Braye Mss.
  Fourteenth Report, Appendix IX (1895), Round Mss.
  Hasting, vol. II (1930)
  Portland, vol. I (1891)
  Salisbury (Cecil), vol. XXII (1971)

2. *Other publications*

Abbott, W. C. (ed.), *The Writings and Speeches of Oliver Cromwell*, 4 vols. (Cambridge, Mass., 1937–47)

(Anon.) (ed.), *Vindication of the character and conduct of Sir William Waller . . . written by himself* (1793)

Bell, Robert (ed.), *Memorials of the Civil War, comprising the correspondence of the Fairfax family*, 2 vols. (1849)

Birch, Thomas (ed.), *A collection of the State Papers of John Thurloe*, 7 vols. (1742)

Braybrooke, Richard Griffen, baron (ed.), *The autobiography of Sir John Bramston* (1845)

Carte, Thomas (ed.), *A collection of original letters and papers* (1739)

Cooper, C. H. (ed.), *Annalls of Cambridge*, 4 vols. (Cambridge, 1842–52)

Firth, C. H. (ed.), *The Memoirs of Edmund Ludlow*, 2 vols. (Oxford, 1894)
  The Memoirs of the Life of Colonel Hutchinson . . . by his widow Lucy (1906)

Gardiner, S. R. (ed.), *The Camden Miscellany, vol. VIII: a letter from the Earl of Manchester to the House of Lords* (1883)
  The Hamilton papers (1880)

Green, M. A. E. (ed.), *The diary of John Rous* (1856)

Halliwell, J. O. (ed.), *The autobiography and correspondence of Sir Simonds D'Ewes, Bart.*, 2 vols. (1845)

Hervey, Francis, Lord (ed.), *Suffolk in the XVIIth Century: the Breviary of Suffolk by Robert Reyce (1618)* (1902)

Hockliffe, E. (ed.), *The diary of the Rev. Ralph Josselin 1616–1680* (1908)

Holmes, Clive (ed.), *The Suffolk Committees for Scandalous Ministers 1644–1646* (Ipswich, 1970)

Hudson, J. C. (ed.), *The second register book . . . of St Mary, Horncastle* (Horncastle, 1896)

Jewson, C. B. (ed.), *Transcript of three registers of passengers from Great Yarmouth to Holland and New England 1637–1639* (Norwich, 1954)

Laing, David (ed.), *The letters and journals of Robert Baillie*, 3 vols. (Edinburgh, 1841–2)

LeHardy, W. (ed.), *Hertford County Records*, 5 vols. (Hertford, 1902–28)

Macray, W. D. (ed.), *Clarendon's History of the Rebellion and Civil Wars in England*, 6 vols. (Oxford, 1888)

Maseres, Francis (ed.), *Select tracts relating to the Civil Wars in England*, 2 vols. (1815)

Masson, David and Bruce, John (eds.), *The Quarrel between the Earl of Manchester and Oliver Cromwell* (1875)

Meikle, H. W. (ed.), *The correspondence of the Scots commissioners in London* (Edinburgh, 1917)

Morris, Christopher (ed.), *The journeys of Celia Fiennes* (1949)

Munk, William (ed.), *The roll of the Royal College of Physicians of London*, 4 vols. (1878)

Notestein, Wallace (ed.), *The journal of Sir Symonds D'Ewes* (New Haven, 1923)

Philip, I. G. (ed.), *The journal of Sir Samuel Luke* (Banbury, 1950)

Redstone, V. B. (ed.), *The ship money returns for the county of Suffolk 1639–1640* (Ipswich, 1904)

Richarson, W. H. (ed.), *The Annalls of Ipswich by Nathaniel Bacon* (Ipswich, 1884)

Robinson, G. W. and others (eds.), *The Winthrop Papers*, 5 vols. (Boston, Mass., 1929–47)

Rushworth, John (ed.), *Historical Collections*, 7 vols. (1682–1701)

Rutt, J. T. (ed.), *The diary of Thomas Burton, Esq.*, 3 vols. (1828)

Bibliography 307

Savage, James (ed.), *The history of New England from 1630 to 1649 ... by John Winthrop* (Boston, Mass., 1853)
Schofield, Bertram (ed.), *The Knyvett letters 1620–1644* (1949)
Scott, William and Bliss, James (eds.), *The works of the most reverend father in God, William Laud*, 7 vols. (Oxford, 1847–60)
Terry, C. S. (ed.), *Papers relating to the army of the Solemn League and Covenant, 1643–1647* (Edinburgh, 1917)
Tibbutt, H. G. (ed.), *The letter books of Sir Samuel Luke 1644–1645* (Bedford, 1963)
Warner, G. F. (ed.), *The Nicholas papers*, 4 vols. (1886–1920)
Williams, R. F. (ed.), *The court and times of Charles I* (1848)
Winthrop, R. C. and others (eds.), *The Winthrop Papers*, volume III in *Massachusetts Historical Society: Collections*, 5th series, vol. 1 (1871)

D. Secondary works cited

1. *Visitations; manorial and topographical histories*
Blomfield, Francis (completed by Parkin, Charles), *An essay towards a topographical history of the county of Norfolk*, 11 vols. (1805–10)
Campling, A. (ed.), *East Anglian Pedigrees*, 2 vols. (1939, 1945)
Campling, A. and Clarke, A. W. H. (eds.), *The Visitation of Norfolk 1664*, 2 vols. (1933–4)
Chauncy, Henry, *The historical antiquities of Hertfordshire*, 2 vols. (Bishop's Stortford, 1826)
Clay, J. W. (ed.), *The Visitation of Cambridge* (1897)
Copinger, W. A., *The Manors of Suffolk*, 7 vols. (Manchester, 1908–11)
Ellis, Henry (ed.), *The Visitation of the County of Huntingdon ... A.D. MDCXIII* (1849)
Metcalfe, W. C. (ed.), *The Visitations of Essex*, 2 vols. (1878–9)
  The Visitations of Hertfordshire (1886)
  The Visitations of Suffolk, 1561, 1577, 1612 (Exeter, 1882)
Morant, Philip, *The history and antiquities ... of Essex*, 2 vols. (Colchester, 1768)
Muskett, J. J., *Suffolk Manorial Families*, 3 vols. (Exeter, 1900–10)
Rylands, W. H. (ed.), *The Visitation of Suffolk 1664–1668* (1910)
Swinden, Henry, *The history and antiquities of Great Yarmouth* (Norwich, 1772)

2. *Official publications*
The Dictionary of National Biography (eds. Leslie Stephen and Sidney Lee), 21 vols. (Oxford, 1921)
The Victoria County Histories
  Cambridgeshire, vol. II (1948, ed. L. F. Salzman), vol. IV (1953, ed. R. B. Pugh)
  Essex, vols. IV, V (1956, 1966, ed. W. R. Powell)
  Hertfordshire, vols. I–IV (1902–14, ed. William Page)
  Huntingdonshire, vols. I–III (1926–36, eds. William Page and Granville Proby)
  Worcestershire, vol. IV (1924, ed. J. W. Willis-Bund)

3. *Books*
Adair, John, *Roundhead General* (1969)
Ashley, Maurice, *The Greatness of Oliver Cromwell* (1957)
Aylmer, G. E., *The King's Servants* (1961)
Beckwith, Ian, *Gainsborough in the Great Civil War* (Gainsborough, 1969)
Bowden, P. J., *The Wool Trade in Tudor and Stuart England* (1962)
Burne, A. H. and Young, Peter, *The Great Civil War* (1959)
Carlyle, Thomas, *Critical and Miscellaneous Essays*, vol. VII (1869)
Cliffe, J. T., *The Yorkshire Gentry* (1969)
Coates, C., *The History and Antiquities of Reading* (Reading, 1802)
Cruikshank, C. G., *Elizabeth's Army* (1966)
Darby, H. C., *The Draining of the Fens* (Cambridge, 1940)
Everitt, Alan, *Change in the Provinces: the Seventeenth Century* (Leicester, 1969)
  The Community of Kent and the Great Rebellion (Leicester, 1966)
  The Local Community and the Great Rebellion (1969)
  Suffolk and the Great Rebellion (Ipswich, 1961)
Firth, C. H., *Cromwell's Army* (1902)

Firth, C. H. and Davies, Godfrey, *Regimental History of Cromwell's Army* (Oxford, 1940)

Fox, R., *The History of Godmanchester* (1831)

Gardiner, S. R., *The History of the Great Civil War 1642–1649*, 3 vols. (1886)

Gilbert, J. T., *History of the Irish Confederation* (Dublin, 1882)

Godwin, G. N., *The Civil War in Hampshire 1642–1645* (Southampton, 1904)

Hexter, J. H., *The Reign of King Pym* (Cambridge, Mass., 1941)

Hill, Christopher, *The Century of Revolution* (1961)

Hill, J. W. F., *Tudor and Stuart Lincoln* (Cambridge, 1956)

Hunter, J., *South Yorkshire* (1828)

Jones, J. R., *The First Whigs* (1961)

Keeler, M. F., *The Long Parliament* (Philadelphia, 1954)

Ketton-Cremer, R. W., *Norfolk in the Civil War* (1969)

Kingston, Alfred, *East Anglia and the Great Civil War* (1897)

Macfarlane, Alan, *Family Life of Ralph Josselin* (Cambridge, 1970)

Macpherson, C. B., *The Political Theory of Possessive Individualism* (Oxford, 1962)

Newton, A. P., *The Colonising Activities of the English Puritans* (New Haven, 1914)

Nuttall, G. F., *Visible Saints: the Congregational Way 1640–1660* (Oxford, 1957)

Paul, Robert S., *The Lord Protector* (1955)

Pearl, Valerie, *London and the Outbreak of the Puritan Revolution* (Oxford, 1961)

Pennington, D. H. and Roots, Ivan, *The Committee at Stafford 1643–1645* (Manchester, 1957)

Reckitt, B. N., *Charles I and Hull* (1952)

Rix, W. B., *The Pride of Swaffham* (King's Lynn, n.d.)

Rowe, Violet, *Sir Henry Vane the Younger* (1970)

Shaw, W. A., *A History of the English Church during the Civil Wars and under the Commonwealth, 1640–1660*, 2 vols. (1900)

Simpson, Alan, *The Wealth of the Gentry* (Cambridge, 1961)

Smith, Harold, *The Ecclesiastical History of Essex under the Long Parliament and Commonwealth* (Colchester, n.d.)

Stearns, Raymond P., *Congregationalism in the Dutch Netherlands* (Chicago, 1940)

The Strenuous Puritan (Urbana, 1954)

Stone, Lawrence, *The Causes of the English Revolution, 1529–1642* (1972)

Suckling, Alfred, *The History and Antiquities of the County of Suffolk* (1848)

Supple, B. F., *Commercial Crisis and Change in England, 1600–1642* (Cambridge, 1964)

Thirsk, Joan (ed.), *The Agrarian History of England and Wales, vol. IV (1500–1640)* (Cambridge, 1967)

Toynbee, Margaret and Young, Peter, *Cropredy Bridge: 1644* (Kineton, 1970)

Underdown, David, *Pride's Purge* (Oxford, 1971)

Varley, F. J., *Cambridge during the Civil War* (Cambridge, 1935)

Wedgwood, C. V., *The King's War* (1966)

Wenham, Peter, *The Great and Close Siege of York* (Kineton, 1970

Wood, A. C., *Nottinghamshire in the Civil War* (Oxford, 1937)

Woodhouse, A. S. P., *Puritanism and Liberty* (1950)

Zagorin, Perez, *The Court and the Country* (1969)

4. Articles

Aylmer, G. E., 'Gentlemen Levellers?', *Past and Present*, no. 49 (1970)

Clifton, Robin, 'Popular fear of Catholics in England, 1640–1660', *Past and Present*, no. 52 (1971)

Davies, Godfrey, 'The army of the Eastern Association', *E.H.R.*, vol. 46 (1931)

'The Parliamentary army under the Earl of Essex', *E.H.R.*, vol. 49 (1934)

Firth, C. H., 'The raising of the Ironsides', *T.R.H.S.*, new series, vol. XIII (1899)

Fisher, F. J., 'The development of the London food market 1540–1640', *Economic History Review*, 1st series, vol. V (1934–5)

Glow, Lotte, 'The Committee-men in the Long Parliament, August 1642–December 1643', *Historical Journal*, vol. 8 (1965)

'Political affiliations in the House of Commons after Pym's death', *Bulletin of the Institute of Historical Research*, vol. 38 (1965)

'Pym and Parliament: the methods of moderation', *Journal of Modern History*, vol. 36 (1964)

Gordon, M. D., 'The collection of ship-money in the reign of Charles I', *T.R.H.S.'* 3rd series vol. 4 (1910)

Hill, Christopher, 'The many-headed monster', in *From the Renaissance to the Counter-Reformation*, (ed.) C. H. Carter, (1966)

Holmes, Clive, 'The affair of Colonel Long: relations between Parliament, the Lord General and the county of Essex in 1643', *T.E.A.S.*, 3rd series, vol. 2 (1970)
    'Colonel King and Lincolnshire politics, 1642–1646', *Historical Journal*, vol. 16 (1973)

Jewson, C. B., 'The English Church at Rotterdam and its Norfolk Connections', *Norfolk Archaeology*, vol. 30 (1952–4)

Kaplan, Lawrence, 'The "Plot" to Depose Charles I in 1644', *Bulletin of the Institute of Historical Research*, vol. 44 (1971)

Laslett, Peter, 'The gentry of Kent in 1640', *Cambridge Historical Journal*, vol. IX (1947–9)

Pearl, Valerie, 'Oliver St John and the "middle group" in the Long Parliament; August 1643–May 1644', *E.H.R.*, vol. 81 (1966)
    'The "Royal Independents" in the English Civil War', *T.R.H.S.*, 5th series, vol. 18 (1968)

Pennington, D. H., 'County and Country: Staffordshire in Civil War politics, 1640–1644', *North Staffordshire Journal of Field Studies*, vol. 6 (1966)

Rowe, Violet, 'Robert, second Earl of Warwick and the payment of ship money in Essex', *T.E.A.S.*, 3rd series, vol. 1 (1964–5)

Stone, Lawrence, 'The electoral influence of the second Earl of Salisbury 1614–1668', *E.H.R.*, vol. 71 (1956)

Welby, A. C. E., 'Belton fight', *Lincolnshire notes and queries*, vol. XIII (1915)

5. Unpublished theses

Boorman, D. W., 'The administrative and disciplinary problems of the church on the eve of the civil war in the light of the extant records of the dioceses of Norwich and Ely under Bishop Wren' (Oxford B.Litt. thesis, 1959)

Hexter, J. H., 'The rise of the Independent party' (Harvard Ph.D. thesis, 1936)

Kaplan, Lawrence, 'The Scots and English Civil War politics, 1643–1645' (Washington University Ph.D. thesis, 1966)

Manning, B. S., 'Neutrals and neutralism in the English Civil War' (Oxford D.Phil. thesis, 1957)

Quintrell, B. W., 'The divisional committee for southern Essex during the Civil Wars, and its part in local administration' (Manchester M.A. thesis, 1962)
    'The government of the county of Essex 1603–1642' (London Ph.D. thesis, 1965)

Roy, Ian, 'The Royalist army in the first civil war' (Oxford D.Phil. thesis, 1963)

Shipps, K. W., 'Lay patronage of East Anglian Puritan clerics in pre-Revolutionary England' (Yale Ph.D. thesis, 1971)

Williams, N. J., 'The maritime trade of the East Anglian Ports, 1550–1590' (Oxford D.Phil. thesis, 1952)

Index

Abingdon (Berks.), 146, 150, 163
Agostini, Geronimo, Venetian ambassador, 106, 203, 207, 210
Aldeburgh (Suffolk), 23, 187
Alford, Major John, 98, 145, 155, 240
Ames, Dr William, 124
Anabaptists, *see* Sectaries
Ancaster Heath (Lincs.), battle of, 72
Andrewes, Captain Henry, 83
Armiger, Captain Clement, 199
Arminianism (*see also* Clergy; Laud, William; Wren, Matthew), 9, 18, 19, 28
Army: Parliamentary (*see also* Eastern Association; New Model Army; and under the names of individual commanders), 55, 59, 69, 77, 81–2, 156, 186, 206, 207; Royal (*see also* Newark; and under the names of individual commanders), 33, 36, 37, 39, 50, 56, 59, 62, 63, 65, 66, 69, 73, 74, 82, 83, 85, 86, 89, 90, 93, 106, 121, 137, 157, 160, 163, 164, 186, 191, 195, 196, 197, 198, 204, 206, 207, 213, 214, 220, 221; prisoners of war from, 159, 175, 197
Ash, Simeon, 197–8, 206, 215
Associations (*see also* Eastern Association), 110, 224; ideals of, late 1642, 62–4, 226; of the midland counties, 1, 2, 63, 64; of the south-eastern counties, 2, 12, 109, 112, 224–5, 226, 228; of Warwickshire, Staffordshire and Shropshire, 1–2, 12, 228; of the northern counties (Royalist), 62
Astley, Lieutenant-Colonel Sir Edward, 75
Audley, Sir Thomas, 36
Axholme, isle of (Lincs.), 168, 174
Aylesbury (Bucks.), 70, 146, 148, 213
Ayloffe, Colonel Thomas, 176, 236
Ayloffe, Sir Benjamin, 46–7, 67

Bacon family, 123–5, 126
Bacon, Francis, 123–5, 126
Bacon, Nathaniel, 123–5, 126

Baillie, Robert, 96, 114, 172, 203, 208–9
Baldock (Herts.), 153
Barbor, Gabriel, 125
Barker, Edward, 151
Barking (Essex), 125, 165
Barnardiston family, 29
Barnardiston, Sir Nathaniel, M.P., 22–3, 50–2
Barnes, Captain Francis, 146
Barrington family, 29
Barrington, Lady Judith, 103–4
Barrington, Sir Thomas, M.P.; and 1640 election, 21–2; in Parliament, 29, 160, 185; and government of Essex in the civil war, 38, 47, 70, 79, 104, 139, 190
Bateman, Mrs Thomas, 165
Beaumont, Captain Richard, 201, 202
Beccles (Suffolk), 22, 127
Becontree, hundred of (Essex), 140
Bedford, 103, 105, 150
Bedfordshire, 29, 72, 148
Bedwall, Edward, 23
Beerechurch (Essex), 36
Belvoir Castle (Leics.), 91, 213
Bence, Alexander, M.P., 50
Bendish, Sir Thomas, 46
Berkeley, Sir John, 128
Bertie, Robert, Earl of Lindsey, 56
Bethell, Captain Christopher, 176, 201
Béza, Theodore, 124
Bishops, petitions against their sitting in the Lords, 25–8, 44–5
Bishop's Stortford (Herts.), 19
Bishops' War, The, 8, 22, 167
Boggis, John, 189
Bolingbroke Castle (Lincs.), 95–6
Boston (Lincs.), 92, 94, 95, 98, 125, 151, 200, 213; governor of, 105, 108, 188 (*see also* King, Colonel Edward)
Boteler, Sir John, 53
Botterell, William, 150–1, 155
Bourne (Lincs.), 92
Bozeat (N'hants.), 150
Braintree (Essex), 8, 84
Brentford (M'sex.), 37